Constitutional Law in France

Constitutional Law in France

Marie-Luce Paris
Julie Foulon
Hugo-Bernard Pouillaude
Julien Sterck

This book was originally published as a monograph in the International Encyclopaedia of Laws/Constitutional Law.

Founding Editor: Roger Blanpain
General Editor: Frank Hendrickx
Volume Editors: André Alen & David Haljan

Wolters Kluwer

Published by:
Kluwer Law International B.V.
PO Box 316
2400 AH Alphen aan den Rijn
The Netherlands
E-mail: international-sales@wolterskluwer.com
Website: lrus.wolterskluwer.com

Sold and distributed in North, Central and South America by:
Wolters Kluwer Legal & Regulatory U.S.
7201 McKinney Circle
Frederick, MD 21704
United States of America
Email: customer.service@wolterskluwer.com

Sold and distributed in all other countries by:
Air Business Subscriptions
Rockwood House
Haywards Heath
West Sussex
RH16 3DH
United Kingdom
Email: international-customerservice@wolterskluwer.com

Printed on acid-free paper

ISBN 978-94-035-0734-7

e-Book: ISBN 978-94-035-0735-4
web-PDF: ISBN 978-94-035-0740-8

Printed in the United Kingdom.

The Authors

Dr Marie-Luce Paris is Assistant Professor in Law at UCD Sutherland School of Law, University College Dublin (Dublin, Ireland). She is a graduate of the University of Paris II Panthéon-Assas (*Magistère de Juriste d'Affaires*, 1996) and the Ecole D'Avocats Du Barreau De La Cour D'Appel De Paris (Barrister-at-Law/*CAPA*, 1997). She was awarded a PhD (Laws) for her work on The Implementation of the European Convention on Human Rights (ECHR) by the United Kingdom (Paris II, 2006). Before she joined UCD in 2000, she worked as a trainee barrister in law firms. Her primary research areas are in comparative constitutional law and European human rights law, as well as legal education. She has published nationally and internationally in these areas. She is the co-editor, with Professor Bell from Cambridge University, of Rights-Based Constitutional Review: Constitutional Courts in a Changing Landscape (Edward Elgar 2016). She is currently the Academic Director of two French Law programmes in UCD, namely the BCL Law with French Law and the dual degree BCL/*Maîtrise*.

Marie-Luce Paris contributed in General Introduction, Part II, Selected Further Readings, Selected Bibliography, Text of the Constitution, Tables, Index, and general editing work.

Co-Authors

Julie Foulon is a PhD candidate in Environmental Law and Governance at UCD Sutherland School of Law, University College Dublin (Dublin, Ireland). She works within the team of the European Research Council-funded project 'Effective Nature Laws (2015–2020)'. She graduated in 2014 with a master's degree in International and European Environmental Law at CERIC Institute (Aix-en-Provence, France). She is also a graduate from the College of Europe, Bruges, Belgium (LLM in Environmental Law, 2015). Her thesis focused on the GMO's regulatory framework in the European Union (EU) and the analysis of its compatibility with the internal market and the World Trade Organization (WTO). She is a teaching assistant in the BCL Programme of the UCD School of Law.

Julie Foulon contributed in parts of the General Introduction and parts of Part II.

Dr Hugo-Bernard Pouillaude is a practising Barrister-at-Law (*Avocat*) with Houdart & Associés (Paris) where he specialized in public economic law, public property and public contract law. He is also Associate Professor in Public Law at the University of Paris-Est Créteil. He was awarded a PhD (Laws) for his work on The Liability of Public Authorities (Paris II, 2011). His primary research areas are in administrative liability, health law and, more broadly, French administrative law. He has published nationally and internationally in these areas and co-authored a reference monograph on Public Property (Editions du Moniteur, 2015). He lectures in public property law, health law and liability law.

Hugo-Bernard Pouillaude contributed in Part III, Part IV Chapters 1, 4 & 5.

Dr Julien Sterck graduated from the University of Montesquieu Bordeaux IV and from the University of Kent. He holds a DEA in Theory and Philosophy of Law from the University of Paris X Nanterre and a PhD in Law from University College Dublin and the University of Montesquieu Bordeaux IV. He held lectureships in Trinity College Dublin, University College Dublin and the University of Essex. He now holds the position of Legal Secretary at the Court of Justice of the European Union (CJEU). His main research interests lie in the areas of European and comparative constitutional law as well as of legal theory, with a particular focus on the notion of national and constitutional identity. He has published a number of articles in international peer-reviewed journals on these areas.

Julien Sterck contributed in Part I, Part IV Chapters 2 & 3, Part V.

The Authors

Table of Contents

The Authors 3

List of Abbreviations 21

Acknowledgements 23

General Introduction 25

§1. An Outline of French Constitutional History 25
I. From Constitutional Revolutions to the Emergence of the Parliamentary Regime (1789–1875) 26
II. The Third Republic (1875–1940) 28
A. The Institutions of the Third Republic 30
B. The Practice of the Regime 31
III. The Fourth Republic (1946–1958) 32
A. The Institutions of the Fourth Republic 33
B. The Practice of the Regime 34
IV. The Fifth Republic (1958 to Present) 35
A. Adoption of the Constitution 35
B. Evolution of the Constitution 36

§2. Characteristics of the French State 37
I. The Indivisibility of the Republic 37
A. A Unitary State 37
B. A Decentralized Organization 38
II. Secularism 38
III. A Democratic and Social Republic 38
A. Democracy and the Rule of Law 38
B. A Social Republic 41
IV. The Political Regime 41
A. A Parliamentary Republic 41
B. A Semi-Presidential Regime 42
1. The Pre-eminence of the President of the Republic 42
2. The Periods of Cohabitation 43

§3. State Territory 44
I. A Complex Territorial Organization 44

II. Powers of Local Authorities 45

§4. POPULATION AND DEMOGRAPHICS 45

Selected Further Reading 46

Part I. Sources of Constitutional Law 49

Chapter 1. Treaties 50

§1. THE TREATY-MAKING POWER 50

§2. THE POSITION OF INTERNATIONAL TREATIES IN THE DOMESTIC NORMATIVE HIERARCHY 50
I. The Supra-Legislative and Infra-Constitutional Position of International Treaties 51
II. The Subordination of International Treaties to the Constitution 52
A. The General Subordination of International Treaties to the Constitution 52
B. The Special Constitutional Position of EU Law 53

Chapter 2. The Constitution 55

§1. THE CHARACTERISTICS OF CONSTITUTIONAL NORMS 55
I. The Supremacy of the Constitution 55
II. The Extent of the Constitution: The Block of Constitutionality 56
A. The Content of the Block of Constitutionality 56
B. The Conciliation Between Constitutional Norms 59

§2. AMENDING THE CONSTITUTION 60
I. The Amendment Procedure 60
A. Amending the Constitution under Article 89 of the Constitution 60
1. Limits to the Amending Power 60
2. The Procedure of Constitutional Amendment 60
B. The Use of Article 11 to Amend the Constitution 61
II. The Issue of Supra-Constitutionality 62

§3. THE SUPREMACY OF THE CONSTITUTION 63

Chapter 3. Laws and Legislation 64

§1. TYPES OF LEGISLATION 64
I. Organic Laws 64
II. Ordinary Laws 65
A. The Area of Legislation 65

1. Definition of the Area of the Legislative Power 65
2. Review of the Area of the Legislative Power 66
3. Review of the Normativity of Ordinary Laws 68

B. The Different Categories of Legislative Norms 68
1. Ordinances under Article 38 of the Constitution 68
2. Referendum Laws under Article 11 of the Constitution 69
3. Legislative Norms in Application of Article 16 of the Constitution 70

§2. THE POSITION OF LEGISLATION IN THE NORMATIVE HIERARCHY 71

Chapter 4. Case Law 72

Chapter 5. Customary Law, Unwritten Law, General Principles of Law 73

§1. CUSTOMARY AND UNWRITTEN LAW 73

§2. GENERAL PRINCIPLES OF LAW 74
I. The Nature of General Principles of Law 74
II. The Position of General Principles of Law in the Normative Hierarchy 75

Chapter 6. Administrative Regulations and Orders 77

§1. THE NATURE OF ADMINISTRATIVE REGULATIONS AND ORDERS 77
I. The Definition of Administrative Regulations and Orders 77
II. The Diversity of Administrative Regulations and Orders 77
A. The General Regulatory Power 77
B. The Specialized Regulatory Powers 78
C. Administrative Circulars 79

§2. THE POSITION OF ADMINISTRATIVE REGULATIONS AND ORDERS IN THE NORMATIVE HIERARCHY 79
I. The Hierarchical Position of Administrative Regulations and Orders in Relation to Other Legal Norms 79
II. The Internal Hierarchy of Administrative Regulations and Orders 80

Chapter 7. Codification, Interpretation and Publication 81

§1. CODIFICATION 81

§2. INTERPRETATION 81

§3. PUBLICATION 82

Selected Further Reading 83

Part II. Form of Government 85

Chapter 1. General 86

§1. Introduction 86

§2. Political Parties, Lobbies and Interest Groups 87
I. Definition and Historical Context 87
II. Current Political Parties in France 93

Chapter 2. Head of State 95

§1. Election and Mandate 95
I. Election of the President of the Republic 95
A. The 1962 Electoral Reform 95
B. Electoral Rules 96
1. Eligibility Rules 96
2. The Electoral Campaign 97
3. The Election 98
II. Mandate of the President of the Republic 98
A. The Presidential Term 98
B. Interruption of the Presidential Term 99

§2. Legal Status 99
I. Political Unaccountability 99
II. Temporary Inviolability 100

§3. Presidential Function and Office 101
I. The Dignity of the Presidential Function 101
II. The President's Office 101
III. Presidents of the Fifth Republic 101

Chapter 3. The Legislature 102

§1. The Organ of State 102
I. Members of the National Assembly 103
II. Members of the Senate 105

§2. Legal Status 106
I. Mandate of the MPs 106
II. Incompatibilities, Immunities and Privileges 106

§3. Powers 110

I. Legislative Function 110
A. Article 34 of the Constitution on the Law 110
1. Definition of the Law 111
2. Control of the Area of the Law 111
B. The Law-Making Process 112
1. Ordinary Procedure 112
2. Extraordinary Procedures 115
II. Supervision of and Control over the Executive 116
A. The Right to Hold the Government Accountable 117
B. The Right to Request Information from the Executive 118
C. Other Forms of Control 119

§4. The Workings of Parliament 120
I. Structures and Working Bodies of Parliament 120
A. The President of the Houses of Parliament 120
B. The Bureau of the Houses of Parliament 121
C. The Conference of the Presidents 121
D. Parliamentary Committees 121
E. Political Groups 122
II. Parliamentary Sessions 122
A. Ordinary Sessions 123
B. Extraordinary Sessions 123
C. Other Types of Sessions 123
III. Parliamentary Agenda 123
IV. Parliamentary Vote 123

Chapter 4. The Executive 125

§1. The Organ of State 125
I. The Traditional Way of Forming a Government 125
II. Composition and Organization of the Government 126
A. Collegial and Hierarchical Structure 126
B. Organization 127

§2. Legal Status 127
I. Obligations and Incompatibilities 127
II. Criminal Liability of Members of Government 128

§3. Powers 129
I. Division of Powers Between the President of the Republic and the Government 129
A. Discretionary Powers of the President of the Republic 130
B. Shared Powers 133
II. Regulatory Powers 134
A. Autonomous Regulatory Power 135
B. Regulatory Powers Necessary for the Implementation of Laws 135

C. Regulatory Powers of Ministers 135
III. Powers relating to National Defence and Foreign Affairs 136
A. National Defence 136
B. Foreign Affairs 137
C. Treaty-Making Powers 137
IV. Powers regarding Parliament 137
V. Powers regarding the Judiciary 137
VI. Other Powers 138

§4. The Council of Ministers 138

§5. Miscellaneous 139
I. Nomination Powers 139
II. Powers in Times of Crisis 139

Chapter 5. The Judiciary 140

§1. Organization of the Judiciary 140
I. General Introduction 140
A. French Dual Judicial Organization: Distinguishing Between the Ordinary and the Administrative Courts 142
B. Subdivisions within the Courts of Ordinary Jurisdiction 143
1. The Courts of Ordinary Jurisdiction 143
2. The Court of Cassation 149
C. Subdivisions within the Courts of Administrative Jurisdiction 150
1. The Courts of Administrative Jurisdiction 150
2. The Council of State 151
D. Other Courts 152
1. The Court of Auditors 152
2. The High Court 155
3. The Court of Justice of the Republic 155
II. Constitutional and Legal Status of Members of the Judiciary 157
A. The Independence of the Judiciary 157
1. The Superior Council of the Judiciary 158
2. The Independence of Administrative Judges 159
B. Limited Interference by the Executive with the Functions of the Judiciary 159
1. The President of the Republic and the Judiciary 159
2. The Public Prosecutor's Office 160
III. Judicial Proceedings 160
A. Civil Proceedings 160
B. Criminal Proceedings 161
C. Administrative Proceedings 161
IV. State Liability for the Torts of Judges or of Members of the Public Prosecutor's Office 162

§2. Judicial Review 163

I. Judicial Review in French Constitutional Law 163
A. The Meaning of Judicial Review 163
B. Judicial Review of Legislation in French Constitutional History 164
1. The Principle of the 'Inviolability of the Law' 164
2. The Principle Undermined 165
II. The Constitutional Council 165
A. Jurisdiction 166
1. The Substance of the Review 166
2. Proceedings Before the Constitutional Council 167
B. Composition 169
C. Organization and Operation 169
D. Critical Assessment 170

Chapter 6. Independent Advisory Bodies at the Legislative and Executive Levels 171

§1. The Council of State 171
I. General 171
II. Powers 171

§2. The Economic, Social and Environmental Council 172
I. General 172
II. Role and Working Methods 173

§3. The Defender of Rights 174
I. General 174
II. Powers and Independence 175

Selected Further Reading 176

Part III. The State and Its Subdivisions 179

Chapter 1. The Structure of the State, a Decentralized Unitary State 180

§1. Unity and Indivisibility of the Republic 180
I. Principles 180
II. Unity of Action of the State 181
A. The Legislative and Constitutional Monopoly 181
B. External Relations 182
III. The Integrity of the Territory 183

§2. The Process of Decentralization 184
I. The 1982 Legislation 184
II. The 2003 Constitutional Amendment 185

III. Latest Reforms 187

Chapter 2. The Different Local Authorities in the Republic 189

§1. Ordinary Local Authorities 189
I. Data on Municipalities 189
II. Data on Departments 189
III. Data on Regions 190
IV. Observations on Inter-Municipality and the Metropolitan Cities 190

§2. Local Authorities with Special Status 192
I. Corsica 192
II. Overseas Departments and Regions, Overseas Territories, and New Caledonia 194
A. Overseas Departments and Regions 194
1. Guadeloupe, Réunion and Mayotte 195
2. French Guiana and Martinique 195
B. Overseas Territories 196
C. New Caledonia 198

Chapter 3. Decentralized Local Authorities 200

§1. The Principle of Free Administration of Local Authorities 200
I. A Constitutional Principle 200
II. The Elections of Local Authorities 202
A. Local Elections in the Municipality 202
1. The Elections of the Municipal Council, Mayor and Deputies 202
2. The Functions of the Municipal Council, Mayor and Deputies 203
B. Local Elections in the Department 204
1. The Elections of the Departmental Council, President and Standing Committee 204
2. The Functions of the Departmental Council, President, Standing Committee and Vice-Presidents 205
C. Local Elections in the Region 205
1. The Elections of the Regional Council and of the President of the Regional Council 205
2. The Functions of the Regional Council and of its President 206
D. Incompatibilities and Ineligibility 206
III. The Decision-Making Autonomy 207
A. The General Jurisdiction Clause and Conferred Powers 207
1. The General Jurisdiction Clause 208
2. Conferred Powers 208
B. Public Property and the Local Civil Service 209
C. Budgetary Autonomy 210

1. Local Taxes 210
2. The 'Determining Share' of the Budget of Local Authorities and Transfers of Powers 211
3. Equalization 212

§2. The Principle of Non-guardianship of One Local Authority over Another 213

§3. State Supervision 214
I. State Supervision over Local Authorities 214
A. Dissolution of the Municipal Council, Suspension and Revocation of the Mayor or Deputies 214
B. State Supervision over the Budget 215
II. Judicial Review of Acts of Local Authorities 215

Selected Further Reading 216

Part IV. Citizenship and the Administration of Justice 219

Chapter 1. French Citizenship 220

§1. Introduction 220

§2. Obtaining French Nationality 221
I. The Attribution of French Nationality 221
II. The Acquisition of French Nationality 222
A. Acquisition by Marriage 223
B. Acquisition by a Child Born to Foreign Parents 223
C. Naturalization 224

§3. The Effects Attached to French Nationality 226
I. The Principle of Equality 226
II. Personal Effects 226
III. Political Rights and Civic Duties 227

§4. Loss of French Nationality 227
I. The Voluntary Loss of French Nationality 228
A. Renunciation of French Citizenship 228
1. Renunciation by a Child Whose One Parent only is French 228
2. Renunciation by the Spouse of a Foreign National 228
B. Loss of French Nationality by Government Authorization 228
II. The Imposed Loss of French Nationality 229
A. Loss of French Nationality Imposed by a Decision of the Government 229

1. Loss of Nationality Based on Articles 23-7 and 23-8 of the Civil Code 229
2. Deprivation of Nationality 230
3. Revocation of a Naturalization Certificate 231
B. Other Cases of Loss of French Nationality 231

Chapter 2. Fundamental Rights and Liberties 232

§1. General 232
I. Sources of Fundamental Rights and Liberties 232
A. International and European Sources 232
B. Domestic Sources 233
II. Implementation of Fundamental Rights and Liberties 234
A. Authorities in Charge of the Implementation of Fundamental Rights and Liberties 234
1. Legislative Implementation 234
2. Administrative Implementation 235
B. Regimes of Implementation of Fundamental Rights and Liberties 236
C. Limitations to Fundamental Rights and Liberties 236
III. The Protection of Fundamental Rights and Liberties 238
A. The Protection of Fundamental Rights and Liberties at Domestic Level 238
1. Nonjudicial Protection of Fundamental Rights 238
2. Judicial Protection of Fundamental Rights 239
B. The Protection of Fundamental Rights and Liberties at International Level 241

§2. Civil and Political Rights 242
I. Physical Freedoms 242
A. The Right to Life, Integrity and Human Dignity 242
1. Human Dignity 242
2. The Right to Life and Physical Integrity 243
3. Medical Issues Related to the Right to Life 243
B. The Right to Individual Safety 245
1. Principles of Criminal Law and the Right to Individual Safety 245
2. Procedural Guarantees of the Right to Safety 247
C. The Right to Privacy 249
1. The Right to Respect for Private Life 250
2. The Right to Personal Autonomy 253
II. Intellectual Freedoms 255
A. Freedom of Opinion and Expression 255
1. Constitutional Basis and Scope of Freedom of Opinion and Expression 255
2. Protection of Freedom of Expression 256
B. Freedom of Religion and Freedom of Education 258

1. Freedom of Religion 258
2. Freedom of Education 261
C. Collective Freedoms 262
1. Freedom of Association 263
2. Freedom of Assembly, Right to Protest and Right to Address Petitions 263

§3. Economic, Social and Cultural Rights 264
I. The Constitutional Status of Economic, Social and Cultural Rights 265
II. The Implementation of Economic, Social and Cultural Rights 266
A. The Right to Property 266
B. Employment Rights 266
C. The Right to Asylum 267
D. Rights to Family Life, Health and Housing 268

Chapter 3. Constitutional Problems of Minorities 270

§1. The Principle of Equality 270
I. The Constitutional Principle 270
II. The Absence of Recognition of Group Rights 271

§2. Minorities and the French Approach to Equality 272
I. Equality and the Protection of Minorities 272
A. The Protection Against Discrimination 272
B. Substantive Equality Through the Recognition of Differences 272
II. Equality and the Limited Recognition of Social Differences 274
A. Gender Equality 274
B. The Constitutional Development of Differentiation 275

Chapter 4. Judicial Control of Administrative Action 278

§1. Introduction 278

§2. The Independence of the Administrative Judge 279
I. Constitutionally Guaranteed Independence 279
II. Constitutionally Guaranteed Jurisdiction 280

§3. Judicial Review 281
I. Appeal for Excessive Use of Power 281
A. Constitutional Value of the Right to Appeal on Ground of Excessive Use of Power 282
B. Scope of the Right to Appeal on Ground of Excessive Use of Power 282
1. Fair Trial 282
2. Annulment of an Administrative Act 283
3. Injunction and Penalty 283

II. Interlocutory Proceedings 284
III. Administrative Responsibility 284

Chapter 5. Rights and Status of Foreigners 286

§1. Introduction 286

§2. Entry into French Territory 286

§3. Stay in French Territory 288
I. The Residence Permit 288
A. The Temporary Residence Permit 288
B. The Residence Permit 289
II. The Protection of Private and Family Life 290
III. The Application of the Principle of Equality 291

§4. Asylum 292
I. Constitutional Protection 292
II. Subsidiary Protection 293

§5. Deportation and Expulsion 294

Selected Further Reading 295

Part V. Specific Issues 297

Chapter 1. War, Treaty and Foreign Affairs Powers 298

§1. War and National Defence 298

§2. Treaties and Foreign Affairs 299
I. Diplomatic Representation and Representation in Supranational Organizations 299
II. The Treaty-Making Power 300
A. The Negotiation of Treaties 300
B. The Ratification of Treaties 300
C. Parliamentary Powers in Relation to EU Law 301

Chapter 2. Taxing and Spending Powers 303

§1. The Constitutional Specificities of Financial Legislation 303
I. Finance Laws 303
II. Social Security Financing Laws 304

§2. Constitutional Principles relating to Budget and Taxation 305
I. Constitutional Principles Relating to Budget 305

A. The Principle of Annuality 305
B. The Principle of Specialty 305
C. The Principle of Unity 306
D. The Principle of Universality 306
E. The Principle of Sincerity 307
II. Constitutional Principles of Taxation 307
A. The Principle of Legality 307
B. The Principle of Equality 307
C. The Principle of Annuality 308
D. The Principle of Necessity 308

Chapter 3. Emergency Powers 309

§1. Presidential Extraordinary Powers under Article 16 of the Constitution 309
I. The Enforcement of Article 16 of the Constitution 309
A. The Conditions of Enforcement of Article 16 309
B. Scrutiny of the Enforcement of Article 16 309
II. The Nature of the Presidential Powers under Article 16 of the Constitution 310

§2. The State of Siege 311

§3. The State of Emergency 311

Chapter 4. The Constitutional Relationship Between Church and State 313

Selected Further Reading 313

Selected Bibliography 315

Table of Legislation 317

Table of Case Law 325

Index 335

List of Abbreviations

AJDA	Actualité juridique de droit administratif
CC	Decision of the Constitutional Council
CE	Decision of the Council of State
CJEU	Court of Justice of the European Union
D.	Recueil Dalloz
DC	*Décision de Conformité*: type of decision of the Constitutional Council about constitutional review of ordinary laws, organic laws, treaties and rules of procedure of Houses of Parliament
ECHR	European Convention on Human Rights
ECtHR	European Court of Human Rights
EEA	European Economic Area
EP	European Parliament
EU	European Union
EU law	European Union law
ICLQ	International and Comparative Law Quarterly
JO	Journal Officiel de la République Française
MEP (MEPs)	Member(s) of the European Parliament
MP (MPs)	Member(s) of Parliament
OJ	Official Journal of the European Union
RDP	Revue du droit public et de la science politique en France et à l'étranger
Rec.	Recueil des décisions du Conseil constitutionnel
Rec. Lebon	Recueil Lebon (Council of State)
RFAP	Revue française de l'administration publique
RFDA	Revue française de droit administratif
RFDC	Revue française de droit constitutionnel
RIDC	Revue internationale de droit comparé
TC	Decision of the Disputes Court
TEU	Treaty on European Union

List of Abbreviations

TFEU	Treaty on the Functioning of the European Union
The 1789 Declaration	Declaration of the Rights of Man and of the Citizen of 26 August 1789
The 1946 Constitution	The Constitution of the Fourth Republic of 27 October 1946
The Constitution	The Constitution of the Fifth Republic of 4 October 1958
UN	United Nations

Acknowledgements

Marie-Luce Paris would like to acknowledge the generous support of the UCD College of Social Sciences and Law (Research Fund) for research and translation work. Part of the bibliographical research work was done by Juliette Fauvarque who is a graduate of the UCD BCL/*Maîtrise* dual degree. Translation work for Part III and Part IV (Chapters 1, 4, and 5) was done by Emma Keane. Emma graduated with a BCL European from UCD and is currently an Advisory Counsel at the Office of the Attorney General in Ireland.

General Introduction

1. This Part provides a vignette of French constitutional history as well as some significant features of the current regime, including information on the State and its territory, as well as up-to-date data on population and demographics.

§1. An Outline of French Constitutional History

2. In order to understand the present, one must be aware of past events. Each political regime stems from a reaction to previous regimes. The current French constitutional and political regime is no exception as it is made up of a complex sum of reactions – positive and negative – to a long line of constitutional experiments. In that respect, it is generally agreed that the landmark starting point is the Revolution of 1789. Although there was an organized polity under the old regime (*Ancien Régime*), with a kind of customary constitution as embedded in the fundamental laws of the Kingdom, there was no constitution in the modern sense – that is understood as a set of rules and principles regulating the relationships between government and those being governed. The Revolution of 1789 represents this significant break from previous political tenets. While representing a significant trauma in the French society at the time, it really marked a fresh start towards the institutional and constitutional principles as we know them today, which include the separation of powers, the principle of a bill of rights, the primacy of the constitution, the principle of sovereignty and the right of suffrage.

3. Legal historians and constitutionalists have various views on how to divide up the different stages of French constitutional history. This is so because France has experimented with an unusually high number of constitutional texts, especially in the first century after the revolutionary period.[1] The aftermath of the revolutionary period marked the start of a search for a consensual and efficient regime which

1. There is no agreement as to how many constitutions France has actually experienced so far. Fourteen constitutions seem to be the number with three constitutions under the revolutionary period, three under the Consulate and the Empire, two charters and the so-called Hundred Days Constitution of 1815, plus the Constitutions of 1848, 1852, 1875 and, eventually, the Constitutions of 1946 and 1958. However, this number comprises a couple of constitutions which were never applied (Constitution of 1793) or for only a very short period of time (Constitution of 1815). Besides, it does not take into account the periods without any constitutional text in force such as the revolutionary government of 1793–1794, the provisional governments of 1848 and 1870 and, despite having been annulled in law, the Vichy regime of 1940.

could not be found until a number of constitutional issues had been agreed upon. These issues revolved mainly around the right of suffrage, the form – monarchical, imperial or republican – of the political regime and the relationships between the Executive and the Legislative. It is generally agreed that French constitutional history can be divided into four main identifiable periods: the first period (1789–1875) deals with the aftermath of the revolutionary period with a succession of constitutional attempts aimed at establishing a definitive regime; the second period concerns the rather long period of the Third Republic (1875–1940) which saw the installation of the parliamentary regime, albeit with many defects including that of governmental instability; the third period represents, by contrast, the short period of the Fourth Republic (1946–1958) with a mitigated attempt to rationalize the rules of the parliamentary regime, while the fourth period deals with the second longest-running political regime in France, namely the Fifth Republic from 1958.[2]

I. From Constitutional Revolutions to the Emergence of the Parliamentary Regime (1789–1875)

4. Year 1789 opens the way to a revolutionary period which saw the most significant transformations in the political and institutional order of France. Overall, the century following the 1789 Revolution is marked by three traits: (1) the acceptance or rejection by the successive political regimes of the principles posed in 1789; (2) the fact that the English and American systems of government were a constant source of inspiration for the drafters of the various constitutional texts; and (3) the numerous attempts to restore the monarchy which postponed the installation of the republican regime until the last quarter of the nineteenth century.

5. The break with the absolute monarchy is complete with the *coup d'état* of the third state on 17 June 1789. The National Constituent Assembly convened on the occasion issued two foundational acts, namely (1) the 1789 Declaration and (2) the Constitution of 3 September 1791. The 1789 Declaration is inspired by the ideas of the Enlightenment and English and American experiences of bills of rights. As such, it encapsulates the ideas of liberalism and individualism of the so-called *bourgeoisie éclairée*. It is universal in character in that it proclaims the existence of natural and fundamental rights applicable to all men and citizens at all time and in the whole society. Today, the 1789 Declaration, as an integral part of the Preamble to the Constitution, is positive law and, as such, is used as a norm of reference in the judicial review of constitutionality of laws. The Constitution of 3 September 1791 was inspired by the US Constitution of 1787 and consecrated a presidential regime with a strict separation of powers and the principle of national sovereignty. It endowed the King, in charge of the Executive, with a suspensive legislative veto that could last up to six years.

---

2. *See*, for example, Pierre Bodineau and Michel Verpeaux, *Histoire constitutionnelle de la France* (Que Sais-Je? PUF 2000) 5–7, on the artificial character of these divisions.

6. A new period of turmoil ensued following the abolition of the monarchy on 20 September 1792 and the death sentence of Louis XVI on 21 January 1793. Two other constitutions followed suit in this period. The Constitution of 24 June 1793 (Year I of the First Republic), although never applied, contained interesting features such as the principle of popular sovereignty and the introduction, for the first time in French constitutional history, of direct universal suffrage. The revolutionary government and the Terror episode under the dictatorship of Robespierre were the immediate unfortunate events after the establishment of the First Republic. The Constitution of 22 August 1795 (Year III of the First Republic) was drafted by the survivors of the Terror and, as such, was strongly marked by a fear of the return to a dictatorial regime, hence its emphasis on an absolute separation of powers. It also introduced the notion of bicameralism. However, unable to collaborate, the institutions were consistently fighting each other. This regime ended with the *coup d'état* of Napoléon Bonaparte on 9 November 1799 (18 Brumaire of Year VIII).

7. The period between 1799 and 1848 is characterized by a dictatorship of the Executive, with two distinct periods: (1) the first one (1799–1814) with the Consulate and the First Empire under the reign of Napoléon Bonaparte and (2) the second one (1814–1848) with the return of the monarchy to power. The Constitution of 13 December 1799 (22 Frimaire Year VIII) is tailor-made to the needs of Napoléon Bonaparte who established the Consulate based on the dictatorship of the Executive. It was characterized by the prominent role of the First Consul and the neutralization of the legislative power which was deprived of the power of legislative initiative. Progressively, the Consulate evolved towards a fully fledged authoritarian regime with the establishment of the Consulate for life (Constitution of 2 August 1802) and of the First Empire (Constitution of 18 May 1804). Overall, the Napoleonic regime featured the traits of a dictatorship, internally, with increased powers of the police and suppression of a number of freedoms, as well as externally, with conquest wars. The military defeat of Napoléon at Waterloo in 1815 definitely swept away the regime, despite his efforts to root and legitimize it (i.e., the interlude of the so-called Hundred Days or *Cent jours* with the additional law to the constitutions of the Empire of 22 April 1815). Despite this swift turn around, the Consulate and the First Empire left a significant legacy to subsequent regimes in terms of institutional and legal instruments, many of which are still in existence today (e.g., the Council of State, the Civil Code).

8. The return to the monarchy in 1814 was possible due to the support of a number of European allies, namely in Austria, England, Prussia and Russia. The *Restauration* started off when Louis XVIII (grandson of Louis XV, House of Bourbon) granted a constitutional Charter to his people (Charter of 4 June 1814). The 1814 Charter maintained a number of principles from the Revolution, as regards the protection of individual freedoms in particular, and also laid down the foundations of the parliamentary regime. The King, who had been in exile in Great Britain, took inspiration from the English system with, for instance, the establishment of a bicameral Parliament (House of Peers and House of deputies) and an embryo of parliamentary control with the introduction, for the first time, of the right of dissolution. However, the major defect of the 1814 Charter was the lack of government political accountability to the Houses of Parliament. The revolutionary days of 1830 ensued provoked by the much less apt, politically, successor of Louis XVIII, namely his brother Charles X.

9. The July Monarchy started with the ascent of Louis Philippe the First (House of Orléans) to power. The Charter of 1830 represented a compromise between the monarch and Parliament which afforded more powers to the latter, notably via the right of legislative initiative. The eighteen years of reign of Louis Philippe allowed the parliamentary system to take root. However, the increasing intrusion of the monarch in public affairs, especially after 1840, prevented its normal development. In the troubled context of economic and social upheaval throughout Europe at the time, a revolt burst in 1848. After the fall of Louis Philippe, a temporary government proclaimed the (Second) Republic on 24 February 1848. The government decided to elect, by universal suffrage, a Constituent Assembly which produced, during an insurrectional climate, the Constitution of 4 November 1848. The drafters of the 1848 Constitution took inspiration, among others, from the US Constitution of 1787. It enshrined the principle of direct universal suffrage and a strict separation of powers. However, this last feature was responsible for the downfall of the 1848 Constitution, the public powers being unable to resolve their conflicts in the absence of a right of dissolution of Parliament and government liability before it. In the meantime, the Prince-President Louis-Napoléon Bonaparte (nephew of Napoléon Bonaparte), having failed to revise the ban imposed on the President of the Republic to be re-elected immediately, decided to obtain by force what he could not obtain by constitutional means. His *coup d'état* of 2 December 1851 allowed him to draft the Constitution of 14 January 1852. Despite its republican character and adherence to the main 1789 principles, the 1852 Constitution re-established the institutions of the Empire under the reign of Napoléon III. The regime later evolved towards a more parliamentary one. However, the Second Empire ended with the defeat against Prussia at Sedan on 1–2 September 1870.

II. The Third Republic (1875–1940)

10. The Third Republic was sandwiched between two (defeat) wars. It represents, however, the longest (sixty-five years) regime in French constitutional history despite the significant perils that marked this period, the trauma of the First World War in particular.[3] The landmark events marking the start and the end of the Third Republic are the following ones. After the capitulation of Napoléon III on 4 September 1870, a peace treaty (Treaty of Frankfurt) was concluded on 10 May 1871 which ended the Franco-Prussian war. Internally, unrest ensued because of the Paris Commune (*Commune de Paris*) which was a radical socialist and revolutionary government that ruled Paris during several months in 1871 as a direct result of

3. Approximately 6 million dead per day during the four years of war. Proportionally, in terms of soldiers killed in combat, France was the most affected countries with 1.45 million deaths and disappearances, as well as 1.9 million injured soldiers which represented around 30% of the active male population at the time.

the decomposition of the Second Empire and the pressing influence of socialist movements at the time. Order was progressively restored and a string of temporary constitutional laws, representing a much needed compromise between the monarchists and the republicans after a period of deep trouble, were adopted. These constitutional laws led to the more definitive set of constitutional laws of 1875 which established the Third Republic.

11. The first temporary constitutional law (*Constitution Rivet)*, adopted on 31 August 1871, assigned the official title of 'President of the Republic' to the head of the Executive. His functions consisted of the right to promulgate laws and ensure their implementation. The President of the Republic had the right to appoint his ministers whose role was to assist him. One particular feature of the constitutional law resided in the political accountability of the President of the Republic and the ministers towards the Assembly of elected representatives of the citizens with the practice of the countersignature (i.e., all acts by the President would be countersigned by the relevant minister since the President was irresponsible politically). The *Constitution Rivet* was partially amended by a second temporary constitutional law (*Constitution de Broglie*), adopted on 13 March 1973. It mainly aimed at limiting the intervention of the then President of the Republic (Adolph Tiers) at the Assembly. The third temporary constitutional law called the *Loi du Septennat*, adopted on 20 November 1873, established a compromise between the two monarchic dynasties, namely (1) the *Orléanists* and (2) the *Legitimists*. The compromise consisted of giving to the Count of Chambord, the Legitimist pretender, the throne as the future Henry V. As he did not have any descendants, the heir to the throne would have come from the *Legitimist* dynasty. However, his steady refusal of the tricolour flag, which reflected his desire to re-establish an absolute monarchy, aborted the compromise. Parliament eventually decided to establish a provisional regency of seven years for the sole benefit of Marshal Patrice de MacMahon, Duke of Magenta. MacMahon was conferred the executive power intuitu personae until the coming of a King. Nonetheless, from a personal seven-year term of office, the constitutional law of 25 February 1875 established an impersonal seven-year term. The National Assembly eventually adopted – by a very narrow majority of 353 votes in favour, against 352 – the so-called Wallon amendment on 30 January 1875 whereby the President of the Republic was to be elected at an absolute majority of the votes cast by both the Senate and the House of Deputies convened in a National Assembly. The significance of the Wallon amendment cannot be underestimated since it changed the nature of the regime and officially (re-)established the Republic.[4]

12. Following on the preceding laws, another set of constitutional laws was adopted, namely the constitutional laws of 24 February 1875, of 25 February 1875 and of 16 July 1875, which formed the basis of the Third Republic Constitution. As a result of a compromise between the Republicans and the moderate Monarchists,

4. Symbolically, that was one of the first constitutional provisions to be abrogated by the Vichy laws in July 1940.

these laws were short, without any mention of fundamental principles, just aimed at laying down the rules organizing the functioning of the public powers.

13. In terms of the end of the Third Republic, the German invasion of 1940 resulted in the resignation of the President of the Council (Paul Reynaud) who was replaced by Marshal Pétain. Pétain signed the armistice on 22 June 1940 and started a regime of collaboration with the occupying forces.[5] The constitutional law of 10 July 1940 endowed Pétain and his Government, based in the town of Vichy, with the full powers to draft a new constitution which would primarily guarantee the values of 'work, family and homeland' (*travail, famille, patrie*).[6] The Vichy Government abrogated all pre-existing constitutional texts, substituted the French (metropolitan) State to the Republic and negated all protection of individual rights and freedoms. Concomitantly, the Government of Free France (*Gouvernement de la France libre*) was being installed at the initiative of General De Gaulle who launched his appeal on 18 June 1940 to continue the fight against the occupier and invite any resistant to join the Free French Forces (*Forces françaises libres*). During the victorious Campaign of France (1944–1945), the provisional Government of the French Republic reinstalled, by the Ordinance of 9 August 1944, the republican legality and declared null and void all acts taken under the Vichy Government.

A. *The Institutions of the Third Republic*

14. Under the Third Republic, the public powers were organized in a parliamentary regime. A two-headed Executive, a bicameral Parliament and classical mechanisms of this type of regime were thus put in place. The Executive consisted of the President of the Republic and the ministers. The former was granted important powers (i.e., appointment of the ministers, right of legislative initiative and right of dissolution of the House of Deputies with the approbation of the Senate), although these were only formal due to the two basic principles of the parliamentary regime, namely the ministerial countersignature and the political irresponsibility of the President of the Republic. The Cabinet government was a collegial body whose members were solidarily responsible before the Houses of Parliament of the decisions taken by the government. The customary institution of the President of the Council (of ministers) had (yet) no textual basis at the time, although the practice increasingly gave prominence to the role. The Legislative consisted of the two Houses of Parliament with equal powers (*bicaméralisme parfait*). The perfect bicameralism meant that both Houses were granted a fully fledged legislative power which comprised the right of legislative initiative and the fact that laws had to be voted in identical terms by both Houses. Both Houses had also the power, under different conditions, to commit the responsibility of the government – save for finance

5. By 1942, the totality of the French territory was occupied by the Germans.
6. Constitutionally, the 1940 constitutional law was invalid since it did not respect the normal procedure for constitutional amendments; the government, instead of the National Assembly, proceeded to amend the constitutional texts, including infringing one of the fundamental tenets of the French regime, namely its republican nature.

and budgetary bills which had to be tabled and voted upon by the House of Deputies in the first place. The House of Deputies comprised 500 to 600 members elected for a four-year term by universal direct suffrage in a two-round first-past-the-post system. The three hundred members of the Senate were elected by indirect universal suffrage for a nine-year renewable term (with seventy-five of them, irremovable, elected by the National Assembly). The Upper House of Parliament represented a rather conservative assembly from the countryside and small towns, although still defending the republican values of the regime. The relationships between the Executive and the Legislative were supposed to be balanced based on the two reciprocal means of pressure of the parliamentary regime, namely the principle of political responsibility of the government before both Houses of Parliament, on the one hand, and the right of dissolution of the House of Deputies, after consultation of the Senate, in the hands of the President of the Republic, on the other.

B. The Practice of the Regime

15. The regime of the Third Republic, although long in duration, was unsuccessful in many respects. A political crisis in 1877 discredited the right of dissolution for a long time. Generally, the dysfunctional parliamentary mechanism resulted in a chronic governmental instability which precipitated its downfall.

16. On 16 May 1877, the then President of the Republic (Marshal Patrice de MacMahon) accused his President of the Council (Jules Simon) of undue concessions in favour of the Republicans. After the legislative election of 1876, Simon enjoyed a strong support of the House of Deputies, composed in majority of Republicans. Refusing to appoint a President of the Council from the ranks of the Republicans, MacMahon appointed Albert de Broglie, a monarchist, to take up the position of President of the Council. Facing a strong opposition from the deputies, MacMahon then dissolved the Lower House on 25 June 1876, with the approbation of the Senate. However, the Republicans prevailed again during the following legislative election of 1877, as well as during the senatorial election of December 1877. As a consequence, MacMahon resigned on 30 January 1879 and was replaced by Jules Grévy. The 1877 crisis revealed the confrontation of two conceptions of the parliamentary regime: on the one hand, a dualist conception whereby the government is responsible before both the House of Deputies *and* the President of the Republic, as advocated by MacMahon, and on the other, a monist conception whereby the government is responsible only before the House of Deputies, as advocated by the Republicans. The consequences of the 1877 crisis contributed to clarify a number of ambiguities on the nature of the regime: first, a definitive installation of a monist type of parliamentary regime as well as of the republican form of government;[7] second, a disregard of the right of dissolution which was from then on perceived as

7. There were very few constitutional amendments during the Third Republic; one of them was introduced with the Law of 14 Aug. 1884 according to which, among other changes on the secularization of the institutions, the republican form of government could not be subject of an amendment.

dangerous for the Legislative. The unfortunate perverse effect was a progressive submission of the Executive to Parliament in a so-called *régime d'assemblée*.

17. The Third Republic experienced one hundred and seven governments between 1875 and 1940, of which eight were dissolved by the Senate. The chronic governmental instability was due to the combination of several factors: (1) The fact that the procedure to engage the responsibility of the government before Parliament was not regulated; (2) the fact that the government could be held responsible before both Houses of Parliament therefore increasing the chances of such an occurrence (also, the absence of incompatibility between ministerial and parliamentary mandates played a role in the instability, parliamentarians trying to dissolve the government to become minister); (3) the non-use, since the 1877 crisis, of the right of dissolution hereby depriving the government of a key means of pressure leading de facto to the dependence of the Executive vis-à-vis the Legislative; (4) the existence of multipartism which caused difficulty in terms of forming strong majorities since successive governments were in fact based on fragile alliances and coalitions between political parties. Despite the adoption of a number of measures in order to mitigate such defects (e.g., the adoption of decree laws which allowed the government to intervene in the legislative area), the regime of the Third Republic could not be cured and ended in a context of growing anti-parliamentarism and rise of the extremist political parties, the far right in particular.

III. The Fourth Republic (1946–1958)

18. The Fourth Republic was established after the Second World War. Despite a few attempts towards its rationalization, the regime failed to function properly and efficiently. In many respects, it appeared to mark a return to the regime of the previous Republic. The landmark events marking the start and the end of the Fourth Republic are the following ones. On 3 June 1944, the French Committee of National Liberation became the first temporary government of the French Republic. As an extension of the Government of Algiers, it was neither in conformity with the legality of the Third Republic, nor that of Vichy, but derived its legitimacy from the Resistance movement. The temporary government gave the French people the following alternative: either to re-establish the regime of the Third Republic or to vote for a national constituent assembly that would be granted the – limited or unlimited – power to draft a new constitution. The French people favoured the latter in the referendum of 21 October 1945.[8] A second temporary government was established in accordance with the constitutional law of 2 November 1945. Also adopted by referendum, it granted limited powers to the national constituent assembly (i.e., the imperative to draft a project of constitution within seven months and to submit it to a referendum) and provided for the interim organization of public authorities.

8. The referendum allowed French women to exercise their right to vote for the first time in history, right which had been granted by the Ordinance of 21 Apr. 1944.

19. A first constitutional draft was rejected on 5 May 1946 for political (i.e., fear of a constitution inspired by communist ideas) and institutional (i.e., distrust of the planned assembly regime based on a single legislative assembly) reasons. In the end, the divergences between De Gaulle, who advocated a strong executive power,[9] and the Socialists and Communists in government proved irreconcilable which steered De Gaulle to resign. After the election of a new constituent assembly, the French people approved – albeit with almost a third of abstention – a toned-down constitution which came into force on 27 October 1946.

20. In terms of the end of the Fourth Republic, the degradation of the regime was due to two factors: (1) government instability and (2) the recourse, despite its prohibition under the 1946 Constitution, to delegated legislation. Government instability had itself various causes, including the difficulty to obtain a solid majority in Parliament due to the disintegration, a few years after the war, of the three-party system, the tendency to partisanship instead of efficient solidarity within government, as well as the mode of suffrage which included some proportional representation. Also, delegated legislation proved problematic because of its large use, first, by means of framework laws when Parliament determines the limits of the action of government, and second, by recourse to decree laws in case the government would overstep the legislative framework.

A. The Institutions of the Fourth Republic

21. The Fourth Republic revolved around the legislative assembly, where the position of President of the Republic was not predominant. The Executive was composed of the President of the Republic and the President of the Council of Ministers. The President of the Republic was, like under the Third Republic, elected for seven years (re-eligible only once) by indirect universal suffrage by Parliament. Endowed with only formal powers, he no longer had the power of legislative initiative nor the right of dissolution of Parliament. As being politically irresponsible, his acts were all countersigned by the President of the Council or by the ministers. However, the power to appoint the President of the Council allowed him to enjoy a certain amount of strategic power. The President of the Council, whose appointment by the President of the Republic had to be approved by the National Assembly, was the real holder of the executive power. As the head of government, he had the power to appoint (and dismiss) his ministers, under the procedure of the so-called *double investiture* whereby the President of the Council was approved by the National Assembly, in the first place, and together with his whole government, in the second place. The Legislative consisted of the National Assembly, which succeeded the House of Deputies, and the Council of the Republic, which succeeded the Senate, with unequal powers (*bicaméralisme imparfait*). Members of the National Assembly were elected by direct universal suffrage for a period of seven years, although the choice of the electoral mode (i.e., proportional representation within the department) prevented the establishment of stable majorities, especially

9. *See* below the Bayeux Speech of 16 Jun. 1946.

from the mid-1950s when the Communist Party turned against the regime. The National Assembly was endowed with full legislative powers (i.e., right of legislative initiative and unlimited area of the law) and the mission to control the action of the government. The Council of the Republic, like the Senate before, represented conservative trends of the countryside and small towns. Its political powers were greatly diminished since the last word belongs to the National Assembly in terms of law-making; also, the government was no longer responsible before the Senate. The Senate was no longer able to control the action of the Executive.

B. The Practice of the Regime

22. The Fourth Republic had attempted to rationalize the parliamentary regime inherited from the previous Republic. Despite this, its practice was not that satisfactory with a persistence of governmental instability (i.e., twenty-four different governments over its short twelve years of existence). The parliamentary mechanisms concerned by the rationalization provided for in the 1946 Constitution were the motion of censure, the vote of confidence and the right of dissolution. New conditions were put in place in order to make it more difficult to engage the responsibility of the government. The motion of censure had to be voted upon one day after it was tabled (to allow the government to gather support and to allow deputies to think their decision through), at an absolute majority of the votes cast. No motion of censure was ever adopted under these conditions The vote of confidence, aimed at obtaining the support or confidence of the National Assembly regarding the general policy or a specific text, was submitted to the same strict conditions as the motion of censure. As far as the dissolution was concerned, the objective was to make it more difficult to resort to it; it was decided by the President of the Republic at the request of the President of the Council who could not resort to it within eighteen months of a general election.[10] The only constitutional amendment of the 1946 Constitution was made by Law of 7 December 1954 in order to rationalize the *double investiture* procedure, with two changes. First, the approval of the appointment of the President of the Council and his government was made in one go before the National Assembly hereby making the installation of the government quicker. Second, the approval by the Assembly had to be voted by a relative majority of the votes cast, meaning that abstention would play in favour of the government.

23. Overall, the regime was characterized by a banalization of the political responsibility of the government and a right of dissolution of the National Assembly which was made difficult to use. Indeed, the rules regulating the political responsibility of the government were diverted by the members of the National Assembly who deliberately chose to express their distrust of governments by voting at an absolute majority of the votes cast, or by a simple majority vote – the so-called practice of calibrated vote (*vote calibré*). According to this practice, the deputies would agree, after consultation of the political groups, to vote the just amount of votes to

10. The right of dissolution was used again in 1955 only – with a gap of nearly a century since 1877 – by René Coty, at the request of Edgar Faure, for tactical reasons.

put the government in minority. Without a strong majority to implement its programme, while at the same time being unable to dissolve the Assembly, the government was forced to resign. On the twenty-four governments of the Fourth Republic, only five were dismissed by constitutional rules, and the others were dismissed by the practice of 'calibrated vote'.

IV. The Fifth Republic (1958 to Present)

24. The Fifth Republic is the political system currently in force in France. It is based on the Constitution adopted on 4 October 1958 (hereafter the Constitution). The Constitution established a parliamentary regime, despite a quick shift towards a form of presidential regime which has rendered it 'hybrid' or 'mixed' over the course of its sixty years of existence.

A. Adoption of the Constitution

25. The Constitution was born out of a specific historical context linked to the instability of the previous Republics and the immediate events of the Algerian War. The collapse of the Fourth Republic and, concomitantly, the return of De Gaulle to power led to the adoption of a new constitutional text. The Algerian troubles degenerated with the crisis of 13 May 1958 when a number of civilians and military, in favour of maintaining Algerian in the French Republic, triggered an uprising. The confused situation overseas and the absence of reaction from the central power led the then President of the Republic (René Coty) to call De Gaulle to solve the crisis. Entrusted with full powers under the constitutional law of 3 June 1958, De Gaulle was given the mission to draft a new text – by total derogation to the normal amendment procedure under the 1946 Constitution. To this end, he accepted the conditions posed by the Member(s) of Parliament (MPs), namely to respect a number of formal commitments (i.e., to submit the revised constitutional text to a consultative committee composed of two-thirds of MPs, to consult the Council of State and to submit the approved text to referendum) and substantial commitments (i.e., to guarantee the right of universal suffrage, source of sovereignty; to respect the separation between the executive and legislative powers; to respect the principle of responsibility of the government before Parliament; to guarantee the independence of the judiciary; and to provide for the organization of new relationships with the overseas associated peoples).

26. The sources of inspiration of the Constitution are diverse stemming not only from its main instigator, De Gaulle, but also from other key figures. In his Bayeux Speech of 16 June 1946, De Gaulle had given the outline of what he regarded as the constitution that was needed for France at the time. In reaction to the absolutism of Parliament and the general weaknesses of the previous regimes, the necessity was to strengthen the role of the executive power around a President of the Republic who would act as the 'arbiter' between public powers, as a kind of outsider able to represent the continuity of the regime detached from political manoeuvring. Other contributions were of a more technical nature such as the one by Michel Debré, a close ally of De Gaulle, in terms of refining the organization of parliamentary work under the direction of the government and the delimitation of the areas of the legislative power and that of the regulatory power; former Presidents of the Council (notably, Guy Mollet and Pierre Pfimlin), who later became ministers under De Gaulle's presidency, contributed, among other areas, to the reform of the mechanism of government responsibility and the delegated legislation.

27. The Constitution was approved by referendum on 28 September 1958 at a vast majority (79.25%) with a low abstention (only 15.6%), a few notable dissenting voices (among them, Pierre Mendès France and François Mitterrand), and a rejection by the people of Guinea who then obtained their independence. It came into force on 4 October, and De Gaulle became the first elected President of the Fifth Republic.

B. Evolution of the Constitution

28. The Constitution is composed of provisions organizing the institutions, describing their missions, attributions and their relations with one another. Its preamble refers to two fundamental texts, namely (1) the 1789 Declaration and (2) the Preamble to the 1946 Constitution. The 2004 Charter for the Environment was subsequently added to this ensemble by a 2005 constitutional amendment.[11] These three texts are a good representation of the recognition of the different phases in right protection, from the traditional civil and political rights, to post-war social rights and, more recently, collective environmental rights. The Constitution and its preamble form a so-called block of constitutionality (*bloc de constitutionnalité*) which is the basis for judicial constitutional review exercised by the Constitutional Council.[12]

29. The main contribution of the Constitution lies in the rationalization of the parliamentary regime, meaning the organization of balanced relationships between the public powers. The Constitution established a regime which is parliamentary in essence, despite a quick shift towards a form of presidential regime as resulting from the election of the President of the Republic by universal direct suffrage from 1962, the use of the referendum by the President and, more generally, the mark left by De Gaulle. The Constitution has had many critics over the years – for example, Francois Mitterrand who was, however, satisfied with the Constitution when he became President. The Constitution has passed the test of time as the institutions have been flexible enough, for example, to allow periods of cohabitation on three occasions (*See* below). However, given some deeper dysfunctional traits such as, for instance, the unusual prominence given to the Head of State and the articulation of his role with that of the Prime Minister, the question of the adoption of a Sixth Republic arguably remains open.

11. Constitutional Law No 2005-205 of 1 Mar. 2005 on the Charter for the Environment.
12. *See* below Part II Form of Government, Chapter 5. The Judiciary, §2. Judicial Review.

§2. CHARACTERISTICS OF THE FRENCH STATE

30. The Constitution defines, in its First Article, the essential characteristics of the French State: 'France is an indivisible, secular, democratic and social Republic.' The particular functioning of the political regime – as, in essence, a parliamentary Republic albeit functioning as a semi-presidential regime – is also an interesting fundamental trait.

I. The Indivisibility of the Republic

31. By stating that the French Republic is indivisible, the Constitution affirms the unitary character of the State. The 2003 constitutional amendment qualified this unitary form of the State by allowing for the decentralized organization of the Republic.[13]

A. A Unitary State

32. The principle of indivisibility of the Republic is of constitutional value. It has a twofold dimension. First, it is attached to the notion of French people which, accordingly, cannot be subdivided into communities whether locally based or ethnicity-based; in other words, the French people are 'a unit incapable of any subdivision by law'.[14] Moreover, the principle of indivisibility of the Republic is opposed to the recognition of collective rights to a group defined by a community of origin, culture, language or belief as decided in relation to the European Charter for Regional or Minority Languages.[15] Second, the indivisibility of the Republic is attached to the territory which, accordingly, cannot be divided. Local authorities cannot be granted normative powers attributed to the legislature by the Constitution, save under the specific limits authorized by decentralization and territorial administration. The unity of the legislative power over the territory of the Republic, and the powers attributed to Parliament and the government, must be preserved.[16] Moreover, even if 'the law can lay down the conditions for the autonomy of the administration of local authorities; it is subject to preserving the prerogatives of the

13. *See* below Part III The State and its Subdivisions.
14. CC Decision No 91-290 DC of 9 May 1991, *Loi portant statut de la collectivité territoriale de Corse*, *Rec.* 50, pt 11*. The mention of Corsica in the Constitution as is proposed in the constitutional amendment, currently (June 2018) under discussion in Parliament, is likely to be a bone of contention in this regard.
15. CC Decision No 99-412 DC of 15 Jun. 1999, *Charte européenne des langues régionales ou minoritaires*, *Rec.* 71*.
16. CC Decision No 91-290 DC of 9 May 1991, *Loi portant statut de la collectivité territoriale de Corse*, *Rec.* 50, pt 15*.

central State'.[17] The Constitutional Council specified that these prerogatives cannot be restricted or deprived of effect, even temporarily.[18]

B. A Decentralized Organization

33. Indivisibility and decentralization are not incompatible. The French State has had a long tradition of deconcentration and decentralization of its territory. Continuing the process of devolution and empowerment of local authorities initiated in 1982, a major reform occurred with the 2003 constitutional amendment which refers to the decentralized nature of the Republic in the following terms: 'France is an indivisible, secular, democratic and social Republic. [The Republic] shall ensure equality of all citizens under the law without discrimination based on origin, race or religion. [The Republic] respects all beliefs. *Its organization is decentralized* (emphasis added).' However, the constitutionalization of decentralization has not questioned the unity of the Republic. Decentralization cannot cross the frontier which separates it from federalism.

II. Secularism

34. *See* below Part V. Specific Issues, Chapter 4. The Constitutional Relationship between Church and State.

III. A Democratic and Social Republic

35. Any political regime is built around a number of values and the Fifth Republic is no exception. Its democratic and social character refers to a number of traditional republican values that the Republic took over and which revolve around the social republican order, on the one hand, and the affirmation and protection of fundamental rights, on the other hand.

A. Democracy and the Rule of Law

36. The Fifth Republic is based on the rule of law. This refers to core specific principles of the republican order, namely the recognition of the right to universal suffrage – with the express recognition of political parties and groups which contribute to its expression thereto – the respect for public freedoms and fundamental rights, the principle of national sovereignty and 'government of the people, by the people, and for the people' (Article 2 Constitution). The power of the State proceeds from the Nation that is from the body of French citizens. The concepts of both

17. CC Decision No 82-137 DC of 25 Feb. 1982, n°82-137, *Loi relative aux droits et libertés des communes, des départements et des régions*, *Rec.* 38, pt 4.
18. *Ibid.*

Nation and citizenship are *acquis* from the 1789 Revolution, irremediably linking citizenship to nationality. A French citizen is entitled to civic rights, the right to vote and stand for election in particular. Nationality may be attributed or obtained in different ways and is regulated by law (i.e., 1993 Code of Nationality, amended a number of times). Nationality law is part of civil law and is litigated before the ordinary courts.[19] All French nationals are regarded as citizens as long as they enjoy their civil and political rights (with the particular situations concerning citizens of the European Union (EU) and those of New Caledonia). A contrario, all those people who do not possess French nationality are regarded as foreigners, who are, as a matter of principle, not entitled to vote in domestic elections (except for EU citizens residing on the French territory who are entitled to vote in EU elections and local domestic elections).

37. Also, other characteristics are worth noting as follow: the language of the Republic is French; its emblem is the tricolor flag 'blue, white and red'; its national anthem '*La Marseillaise*'; and its motto '*Liberté, Egalité, Fraternité*'. Concerning the language, French is the official language that must be used in all oral and written communication by and with the public administration. The use of a regional or local language is for private or cultural purposes only. While the use of such a language ought to be supported and even encouraged, the principles of indivisibility of the Republic and of unity of the French people bar any recognition of a special status of linguistic minorities.[20] The constitutional status of regional languages is that they simply form part of French heritage (Article 75-1 Constitution).

38. Respect for the rule of law also refers to the fundamental principle of the separation of powers which has structured the French constitutional legal order since the 1789 Declaration. Under its Article 16, 'any society in which the guarantee of rights is not guaranteed, nor the separation of powers determined, has no Constitution'. Separation of powers appears as the necessary corollary of the limitation of power and hence the protection of human rights: the mutual control exercised by the three powers towards one another preserves the individual from the threats on his fundamental rights. However, this theory has not always been strictly implemented under the successive regimes. A too strict separation led to the paralysis of the institutions during, for example, the *Directoire* period (1795–1799), or under the Second Republic (1848–1851), where the conflict between the Executive and the Legislature had each time ended in a *coup d'état*. What has been primarily favoured in that regard is a system of collaboration of the different (separated) powers, instead of their strict separation. A flexible separation of powers refers to the organization of the State where the different powers – legislative, executive and judicial – are distinct but have the opportunity to collaborate and dialogue in order to guarantee the regular functioning of public authorities. As a consequence, the executive power can intervene in the drafting of laws and the legislative power can intervene in regulatory functions. The power of the President of the Republic to dissolve the

19. *See* below Part IV. Citizenship and the Administration of Justice, Chapter 1. French Citizenship.
20. CC Decision No 99-412 DC of 15 Jun. 1999, *Charte européenne des langues régionales ou minoritaires*, *Rec.* 71, pt 10*.

National Assembly, the possibility for the legislative power to overthrow the government, the submission of public prosecutors to the hierarchical authority of the government are all manifestations of a flexible approach to the separation of powers.

39. In addition, the separation of powers had specific consequences in the French legal system. Indeed, historically, ordinary judges could not interfere with government affairs. Courts were deprived of the jurisdiction to deal with disputes concerning the administration under the Laws of 16 and 24 of August 1790 and the Decree of 16 *Fructidor* Year III (2 September 1795). Based on a distrust of judges as well as due respect for the separation of powers, it meant that the acts of the legislative power and the executive power were not susceptible to judicial review on the ground that ordinary courts did not have sufficient legitimacy to judge acts emanating from authorities proceeding from universal suffrage and acting in the name of the general interest. An aggrieved individual had to sue the administration before the administration itself, up to ministerial level (the so-called minister-judge system where the administration is judge and party at the same time). The establishment of administrative courts, namely the Council of State by the Constitution of Year VIII (1799), and the departmental prefectural councils by the Law of 28 *Pluviôse* Year VIII (17 February 1800), and the subsequent development of administrative law,[21] modified this situation by allowing acts of the administration to be challenged before a separate set of courts, namely the administrative courts. In that sense, the 'French conception of the separation of powers'[22] is today associated with a dual judicial order, namely the ordinary judicial order (*ordre judiciaire*) with the Court of Cassation (*Cour de cassation*) at its top, and the administrative judicial order (*ordre administratif*) with the Council of State (*Conseil d'Etat*) at its top.

40. The development of a constitutional court came about more recently with the establishment of the Constitutional Council (*Conseil constitutionnel*) under the Constitution. Originally, a body with limited power of review, it has developed into a constitutional court akin to that of other European jurisdictions. While the Council of State is empowered to judicially review the conformity of regulatory acts adopted by the government to the Constitution, the Constitutional Council has the power to review the conformity of laws with the Constitution, whether before they are promulgated (a priori review), or after their promulgation (a posteriori review).[23]

---

21. Notably the Law of 24 May 1872 which allowed the Council of State to become a fully fledged administrative court deciding without interference from the Executive in a so-called system of 'delegated justice' (*justice déléguée*), and the *Cadot* Case of 13 Dec. 1889 in which the Council of State abandoned the doctrine of the minister-judge.
22. CC Decision No 86-224 DC of 23 Jan. 1987, *Loi transférant à la juridiction judiciaire le contentieux des décisions du Conseil de la concurrence*, *Rec.* 8, pt 15.
23. *See* below Part II. Form of Government, Chapter 5. The Judiciary, §2. Judicial Review.

B. A Social Republic

41. The meaning of the social character of the Republic is somewhat elusive. In essence, it means that the French democratic regime is associated with a specific project of society which ensures the collective cohesion of all individuals and groups of individuals. In other words, the Republic is not fully achieved unless it adds to its democratic character a minimum of social content. This is an *acquis* from the 1789 Revolution. The National Constituent Assembly (1789–1791) proclaimed at the time that 'every man at birth is entitled to protection and help from humanity (sic)', thereby establishing a close association between the promotion of human rights and the recognition of social rights. This idea was consecrated by subsequent regimes, notably under the legislation of the Third Republic and the recognition of economic and social rights as enshrined in the Preamble to the 1946 Constitution. For some authors,[24] the realization of the social character of the Republic translates into the existence and development of a branch of law dedicated to the protection social rights (*droit social*), the development of the public service, and the constant promotion of a social policy based on solidarity. Other principles manifest the social character of the Republic such as the fraternity principle based on citizenship, the equality of opportunity provided for by the schools of the Republic, the social interventionism of the State, the pursuit of the common good, as well as the national solidarity recognized between citizens, on the one hand, and between the different parts of the territory of the Republic, on the other hand.

IV. The Political Regime

42. The regime of the Fifth Republic is atypical in that it is at root parliamentary, albeit functioning with some traits of a presidential regime.

A. A Parliamentary Republic

43. The political regime established in 1958 is parliamentary, based on the principle of the responsibility of government before Parliament, before the National Assembly in particular (Article 50 Constitution). The government has to resign in case of the adoption of a motion of censure by the National Assembly or after a negative vote on its programme or a declaration of general policy. However, in an effort to break from the assembly regime and the governmental instability that characterized the previous regimes, the Constitution aims at strictly regulating the prerogatives of Parliament for the benefit of the government, in order to preserve the latter from increase domination by the former. Another novelty is the delimitation of the area assigned to the legislature which is now limited to those matters enumerated under the Constitution (Article 34 Constitution). The area of competence

24. Michel Borgetto and Robert Lafore, *La mise en œuvre de la République sociale: Contribution à l'étude de la question démocratique en France* (La Politique éclatée PUF 2000).

of the regulatory power held by the government is thus extended to all other matters. Furthermore, the Constitution has established a constitutional review of legislation adopted by the National Assembly to review its conformity with the Constitution (Article 61 Constitution). Finally, the incompatibility between ministerial functions and the parliamentary mandate represents a strict separation between members of government and MPs. The Constitution has also increased the legitimacy of the President of the Republic by changing the regime of his election in comparison to the two previous republics; the Head of State was elected – before it was further changed in 1962 – by an electoral college composed of deputies and senators, and extended to representatives of local authorities (i.e., departments and municipalities). It reflected the wish of De Gaulle to avoid the presidential election being monopolized by political parties.

B. *A Semi-Presidential Regime*

44. The two democratic elections in France allow for the designation of the President of the Republic (presidential election), on the one hand, and for the designation of a parliamentary majority (legislative election) which role is to support the President and his government, on the other hand. From there, the practice of the regime has revealed two different types of situations, primarily caused by the difference in duration between the presidential term of office and the parliamentary mandate. A first situation arises when the President of the Republic is of the same political hue as the majority in Parliament which corresponds to the normal functioning of the regime because there is a perfect alignment between the President, the government and the majority in Parliament (*fait majoritaire parfait*); the President of the Republic thus benefits fully from the prominence of his role. The second situation comes from the fact that the two types of elections have returned a different majority each, so the alignment is broken; this *fait majoritaire imparfait* has led to the phenomenon of cohabitation whereby the President of the Republic has to appoint a Prime Minister reflecting the majority in Parliament (but not necessarily the leader of the victorious political party); this is an abnormal functioning of the regime although it is more in line with the parliamentary nature of the regime.

1. The Pre-eminence of the President of the Republic

45. Originally conceived as a parliamentary regime, the Fifth Republic has become a semi-presidential type of regime since the referendum of 28 October 1962 which established the election of the President of the Republic by direct universal suffrage. The modification of the mode of election of the President of the Republic has had a profound impact on the institutional balance. Indeed, because of a newly acquired democratic legitimacy, the Head of the State found himself at the centre of the institutional system. The President of the Republic would, from then on, really stand as the actual keystone of the political and institutional system, while the right of dissolution that he is entrusted with has had the effect of limiting the possibility for the National Assembly to question the accountability of the government. The legitimacy of the President of the Republic has, to that extent, become superior to one of the deputies as deputies are elected within limited constituencies and are divided into different political groups. The President of the Republic, meanwhile, is elected by all citizens and, as such, represents all French people regardless of their political tendencies.

46. The reinforcement of the legitimacy of the President of the Republic has also had an effect on the relationship of his government with Parliament, especially as regards the vote of confidence on the programme of the government by the National Assembly (Article 49 Constitution). Because the Prime Minister derives his authority from the President of the Republic who appoints him – except for periods of cohabitation (*See* below) – the practice has been that a number of governments have come into office without seeking the confidence of the National Assembly while others have made a declaration of general policy, without it being necessarily followed by a vote. Another related issue, which further illustrates the pre-eminence of the President of the Republic, concerns the appointment of the Prime Minister. While, in the republican tradition, the Head of Government would always come from Parliament, the pre-eminence of the President of the Republic has allowed 'external' appointments as shown with the choice of Georges Pompidou in 1962. By appointing one of his personal collaborators, who had never held a parliamentary mandate, De Gaulle signified to the National Assembly its diminished role in the appointment of the Prime Minister. Concurrently, the responsibility of the Prime Minister towards the President of the Republic has evolved in practice through the interpretation of certain constitutional provisions. The President of the Republic has repeatedly demanded the resignation of the government without the National Assembly having managed to pass a motion of censure – as was the case for the resignation of Michel Debré in April 1962, Jacques Chaban Delmas in July 1972, Pierre Mauroy in July 1984, Michel Rocard in May 1991, and Edith Cresson in April 1992. In this context, the parliamentary nature of the regime has lost its relevance with a President of the Republic appearing as the real head of the Executive albeit not responsible before Parliament. If the government is constitutionally responsible before the National Assembly, it is in fact only before the President of the Republic. The parliamentary majority is primarily intended to support the presidential policy. Before the 2000 constitutional amendment (*See* below), the legislative election was in fact an election confirming the result of the presidential election the main function of which was the election of a political majority to give the President of the Republic and his government the means to govern.

2. The Periods of Cohabitation

47. The defeat of the presidential majority in the legislative elections of 1986, 1993 and 1997 resulted in periods of so-called cohabitation. Indeed, the President of the Republic, whose party was voted in the opposition, had to appoint a Prime

Minister within the parliamentary majority.[25] Such periods marked the return to a more parliamentary functioning of the regime with the President of the Republic losing his position as leader of the Executive since the legitimacy resulting from the presidential election was somehow erased by the result from the legislative elections. In such situations, the Prime Minister was no longer responsible to the President of the Republic and could govern by relying only on the National Assembly, which thus appeared as the sole and only source of legitimacy for the government.

48. Nevertheless, the President of the Republic retains important prerogatives during a period of cohabitation as per the constitutional provisions dedicated to his powers such as, for example, the presidency of the Council of Ministers and the power of appointment of civil and military officials of the State. These significant powers of the President of the Republic in periods of cohabitation have no equivalent in a parliamentary system where the role of the Head of State is of a formal nature, generally limited to the authentication of the acts of the Head of Government. This institutional situation is a reminder of the atypical nature of the Fifth Republic, which is neither presidential nor parliamentary – hence the numerous terms attributed to the French regime from 'hybrid' to 'mixed', or 'semi-presidential'. Without changing this *état de fait*, the alignment of the presidential term of office to five years (instead of seven) with that of the parliamentary mandate with, correlatively, a coincidence of both elections, was an attempt to reduce the risk of cohabitation, as it would be unlikely that the French people vote for a completely different majority a few weeks apart.[26]

§3. State Territory

49. The territorial organization of the French Republic is rather complex as it is based on different layers of local authorities endowed with a range of various powers.[27]

I. A Complex Territorial Organization

50. The local authorities of the Republic are the municipalities, the departments, and the regions, as well as the local authorities with special status and overseas territories (Article 72 Constitution). These three levels of local government constitute both local authorities and subdivisions of the State administration, which representatives are, respectively, the mayor, the prefect and the regional prefect. As a result, the organization of deconcentrated State services is based on the same territorial divisions.

25. The three periods of cohabitation were as follows: 1986–1988: François Mitterrand (President) and Jacques Chirac (Prime Minister); 1993–1995: François Mitterrand (President) and Édouard Balladur (Prime Minister); 1997–2002: Jacques Chirac (President) and Lionel Jospin (Prime Minister).
26. Constitutional Law No 2000-964 of 2 Oct. 2000 on the term of office of the President of the Republic.
27. *See* below Part III. The State and its Subdivisions.

II. Powers of Local Authorities

51. The principle of free administration of local authorities is constitutionally guaranteed and shall be exercised 'under the conditions prescribed by law' (Article 72 paragraph three Constitution). This principle applies both to the relationships of local authorities with the State but also to those relationships between local authorities. As a result, there can be no supervision or guardianship of one local authority over another. Since the beginning of the decentralization process, Parliament has endeavoured to organize homogeneous blocks of powers, specific to each level of local authorities. Therefore, the municipalities exercise their main powers in the areas of urban planning, housing and the environment. The departments are responsible for two major areas, namely social action (i.e., childhood, disabled and elderly) and planning (i.e., rural equipment, sea and inland ports, departmental roads). The powers of the regions essentially cover economic development, planning and non-urban transport. However, many competencies such as those related to sport activities, tourism, the promotion of regional languages, or education, still happen to be shared between different levels of local authorities. For example, in the field of education, primary education is the responsibility of the municipalities, secondary education of the departments, and higher education of the regions. The 2003 constitutional amendment also established the regulatory power of local authorities, which may, under the conditions provided for by law, contribute to the exercise of local powers (Article 72 third paragraph Constitution).

§4. Population and Demographics

52. In February 2018, the population of France is 65.1 million inhabitants for a total land area of 547.56 Km^2 (i.e., 211.413 sq miles). The population density is thus 119 per Km^2.[28] The French population has increased by over 2 million between 2010 (62.8 million inhabitants) and 2018 and is forecast to reach more than 70 million by 2050. This increase is not due to immigration – the net migration being only slightly positive – but to a natural dynamic thanks to a favourable fertility rate of 1.98 children per woman of childbearing age, the highest in the EU with that of the Republic of Ireland which is, however, due to slightly decrease over the years. Yet, the demographic dynamism in France does not concern all the territory. No less than twenty departments on the French metropolitan territory, including *Ardennes, Cantal, Haute-Marne, Hautes-Pyrénées, Lozère, Nièvre, Orne*, and two overseas territories, namely *Martinique* and *Guadeloupe*, are concerned by a decrease of their inhabitants, while five others – *Manche, Moselle, Seine Maritime, Somme, Vendée* – are just able to stabilize their population. Most of these areas are located on a diagonal from the *Ardennes* to the *Massif Central*. The French population tends to increase only in certain places, in a smaller number of departments including important regional cities. Furthermore, one out of five French people lives in one of the hundred most populated cities in France. However, migrations do not concern the

28. The figures are based on the latest UN estimates (February 2018). *See* < http://www.worldometers.info/world-population/france-population/#> accessed on 11 Feb. 2018.

centre of these big cities but rather their periphery. The development of economic activities and the need to build accommodation for new workers in departments with strong demographic growth strengthens the phenomenon of 'peri-urbanization'. Overall, 80.5% of the French population is urban (i.e., 52.9 million people).

53. The median age of the population in France is 41.4 years, set to increase to 44.3 by 2050. The proportion of the population aged 65 and over has continually increased since the start of the 1990s, from 14% in 1991 to 19% in 2016. The increase accelerated from 2011 when the first generation of *baby boomers* born in 1946 turned 65 years old. In parallel with this increase, the proportion of those under 25 years of age has been declining for the last quarter of the century, from 35% in 1991 to 30% in 2016. In terms of economic activity, the last survey puts the labour force at an estimate of 28.7 million people aged 15 and over in metropolitan France, with 25.8 million of employed people and 2.9 million of unemployed people, that is a rate of 9.7% of unemployed.[29] The employment rate is thus rather low in France as compared to other European countries with, however, a higher employment rate for women than the European average.

Selected Further Reading

On French Constitutional History

Pierre Bodineau and Michel Verpeaux, *Histoire constitutionnelle de la France* (PUF 2000).
Sophie Boyron, *The Constitution of France: A Contextual Analysis* (Hart 2013).
René Cassin, 'Un coup d'Etat. La soi-disant constitution de Vichy', *La France libre*, Vol. 1, Nos 2 &3, December 1940/January 1941, 162 & 252.
Jacques Chapsal, *La vie politique en France de 1940 à 1958* (PUF 1996).
Jean-Jacques Chevallier et alii, *Histoire de la Ve République (1958–2015)* (15th ed., Dalloz 2015).
Gérard Conac, Xavier Prétot and Gérard Teboul (eds), *Le préambule de la Constitution de 1946* (Dalloz 2001).
Gérard Conac, Marc Debene and Gérard Teboul (eds), *La Déclaration des droits de l'Homme et du citoyen de 1789* (Economica 1993).
Maurice Deslandres, *Histoire constitutionnelle de la France depuis 1789* (Armand Colin 1933–1937, 3 Volumes).
La Documentation Française, Volume I *Des origines de la loi constitutionnelle du 3 juin 1958 à l'avant-projet du 29 juillet 1958*, 1987; Volume II *Le Comité consultatif constitutionnel: De l'avant-projet du 29 juillet 1958 au projet du 21 août 1958*, 1988; Volume III *Du Conseil d'Etat au référendum: 20 août – 28 septembre 1958*, 1991; Volume IV *Commentaires sur la Constitution (1958–1959)*, 2001.

29. Tables of the French Economy 2017, Institut National de la Statistique et des Etudes Economiques (INSEE).

Selected Further Reading

Alain Laquièze, *Les origines du régime parlementaire en France (1814–1848)* (PUF 2002).
Michel Troper, *La séparation des pouvoirs et l'histoire constitutionnelle française* (LGDJ 2014).
Michel Troper and Lucien Jaume (eds), *1789 et l'invention de la Constitution* (Bruylant LGDJ 1994).
Serge Velley, *Histoire constitutionnelle française de 1789 à nos jours* (3rd ed., Ellipses 2009).
Pierre Villard and Louis-Augustin Barrière, *Histoire des institutions publiques de la France de 1789 à nos jours* (10th ed., Dalloz 2013).

ON THE CHARACTERISTICS OF THE FRENCH STATE

Michel Borgetto and Robert Lafore, *La mise en œuvre de la République sociale: Contribution à l'étude de la question démocratique en France* (PUF 2000).
René Chapus, *Dualité de juridictions et unité de l'ordre juridique*, RFDA, 1990, 739.
Eoin Daly, 'The indivisibility of the French Republic as political theory and constitutional doctrine', 11 European Constitutional Law Review 458 (2015).
Eoin Daly, 'Reframing the Reframing the Universalist Republic. Legal Pluralism in the French Periphery', 24(4) Social & Legal Studies (2015).
Maurice Duverger, *Le système politique français* (PUF 1996).
Alain Laquièze, 'Le modèle du régime présidentiel sous la Ve République', Droits, 2006, 45.
Jean Massot, *Alternance et cohabitation sous la Cinquième République* (La Documentation française 1997).
Bertrand Mathieu and Michel Verpeaux (eds), *La République en droit français* (Economica 1999).
Philippe Raynaud, *L'esprit de la Ve République* (Perrin 2017).
Dominique Schnapper, *De la démocratie en France: République, nation, laïcité* (Odile Jacob 2017).
Bernard Stirn, *Quelques réflexions sur le dualisme juridictionnel*, 3 Justices: Revue générale de droit processuel 41 (Janv.-Juin 1996).
Christophe Vimbert, *La tradition républicaine en droit public français* (LGDJ 1992).
Patrick Weil and Nicolas Truong, *Le sens de la République* (Grasset 2015).
Patrick Weil (ed.), *Politiques de la laïcité au Xxème siècle* (PUF 2007).

ON THE STATE TERRITORY

See below Selected Further Reading under Part III. The State and its Subdivisions.

ON POPULATION AND DEMOGRAPHICS

Virginie de Luca Barrusse, *La population de la France* (La Découverte 2016).

Selected Further Reading

Part I. Sources of Constitutional Law

54. This Part is concerned with the different norms that are constitutive of the French legal order. It also considers the mechanisms that structure the domestic hierarchy of norms.

Chapter 1. Treaties

55. The Executive, and notably the President of the Republic, have a central role in the treaty-making power. In French law, international treaties have an infra-constitutional and supra-legislative position in the hierarchy of norms.

§1. The Treaty-Making Power

56. The importance of the President of the Republic among the institutions of the Fifth Republic finds a specific expression in the fields of diplomacy and foreign policy.[30] The President of the Republic 'shall be the guarantor of national independence, of the integrity of the territory, and of due respect for treaties'. (Article 5 Constitution). As a result, the President is vested with the treaty-making power. The President is competent to negotiate and ratify international treaties (Article 52 Constitution), though such ratification requires the countersignature of the Prime Minister (Article 19 Constitution). Under the provision thereof, the President of the Republic must be informed of any negotiations relating to an international agreement that does not require ratification. Some international treaties can only be ratified on the basis of a law. The list provided for in Article 53 of the Constitution includes '[p]eace treaties, trade agreements, treaties or agreements relating to international organizations, those which commit the finances of the State, those which modify provisions of a legislative nature, those which relate to the status of persons, and those which involve the transfer, exchange or acquisition of territory'. The laws enabling the ratification can either be enacted by Parliament or put to a referendum when, according to Article 11 of the Constitution, the treaty, 'albeit not repugnant to the Constitution, would impact on the functioning of the institutions'.

§2. The Position of International Treaties in the Domestic Normative Hierarchy

57. The French legal system adheres to the monist theory as regards the relationship between domestic and international law. Domestic and international laws are regarded as being part of the same legal system. Therefore, international treaties do not need to be transposed into the domestic legal order through a national instrument in order to be enforceable therein. However, conceiving domestic and international law as part of the same legal order does not predetermine the position of international law in the normative hierarchy. From a French legal perspective, international law is superior to domestic law, and thus also to infra-legislative norms, but has to yield to the ultimate supremacy of the Constitution. Within this general framework, the development of European integration has justified a special status to be granted to European Union law (EU law).

30. *See also* below Part V. Specific Issues, Chapter 1. War, Treaty and Foreign Affairs Powers, §2. Treaties and Foreign Affairs, II. The Treaty-Making Power.

I. The Supra-Legislative and Infra-Constitutional Position of International Treaties

58. In the first place, international law has a supra-legislative status. The principle of superiority of international law over domestic law has not been without difficulties. Originally, French courts were considering that international treaties had, in the hierarchy of norms, the same position as the laws necessary for their ratification. Normative conflicts were thus resolved according to the principle *lex posterior derogat legi priori*. International treaties would prevail over previous laws but would be overridden by subsequent conflicting ones. The Fifth Republic changed this normative relationship. Under Article 55 of the Constitution, '[t]reaties or agreements which have been duly ratified or approved shall, upon publication, prevail over laws, subject, with respect to each agreement or treaty, to its application by the other party'. However, this principle was not immediately applied by domestic courts, which still relied on their traditional case law. The compliance with the principle contained in Article 55 resulted from a decision of the Constitutional Council. In a 1975 Decision on The Voluntary Interruption of Pregnancy Act,[31] the Council requested to draw the normative consequences from Article 55. In a later decision, the Council also gave constitutional value to the principle *pacta sunt servanda* on the basis of the fourteenth paragraph of the Preamble to the 1946 Constitution which declares that '[t]he French Republic, faithful to its traditions, shall respect the rules of public international law'.[32] In the above-mentioned 1975 Decision, the Constitutional Council stated, however, that it lacked competence to review the conformity of laws with international treaties. It argued that, on the one hand, its review under Article 61 of the Constitution had an unconditional and final character – as is clear from Article 62 which prohibits the promulgation or implementation of any provision declared unconstitutional – while, on the other hand, the superiority of international treaties was relative and contingent, being restricted to the ambit of the treaty and subject to reciprocity, which itself depends on the behaviour of the signatory state or states and on the time at which it is to be assessed. This position of the Council as regards international law has been consistent since.[33]

59. Judicial review of legislation in France is thus divided between the Constitutional Council and ordinary courts. The former exercises a review of constitutionality whereby the conformity of laws with the Constitution is assessed. The latter are entrusted with the review of conventionality which consists of enforcing the superiority of international treaties over domestic laws. The two judicial orders – namely, the ordinary legal order and the administrative legal order – reacted differently to the 1975 Decision of the Council at the time. The ordinary courts (i.e., of the *ordre judiciaire*) followed the constitutional case law right away when the Court

31. CC Decision No 74-54 DC of 15 Jan. 1975, *Loi relative à l'interruption volontaire de grossesse*, *Rec.* 19*.
32. CC Decision No 92-308 DC of 9 Apr. 1992, *Traité sur l'Union européenne*, *Rec.* 55, pt 11*.
33. CC Decision No 2010-605 DC of 12 May 2010, *Loi relative à la concurrence et à la régulation du secteur des jeux d'argent et de hasard en ligne*, *Rec.* 78*.

of Cassation accepted to exercise its review of conventionality in the 1975 *Cafés Jacques Vabre* Case.[34] By contrast, the administrative courts (i.e., of the *ordre administratif*) recognized the prevalence of international treaties over domestic laws under Article 55 of the Constitution only after a late-coming decision by the Council of State in the 1989 *Nicolo* Case.[35] Article 55 of the Constitution has been narrowly interpreted. The superiority of international law is limited to treaties and has not been extended to international customary law.[36] Nonetheless, this superiority also concerns norms derived from international treaties, and applies to secondary law of the EU in particular.

II. The Subordination of International Treaties to the Constitution

60. The Constitution is the supreme norm of the French legal order, the superiority of which international law has to respect. Within the general framework of the relationship between domestic and international law, the deepening of the process of European integration has led the Constitutional Council to grant EU law a special position in the domestic legal order.

A. The General Subordination of International Treaties to the Constitution

61. International treaties remain at an infra-constitutional level in French law. Courts have interpreted Article 55 of the Constitution literally and inferred that the primacy of international law over domestic law does not apply to constitutional norms. The Constitution is thus the supreme norm in the domestic legal order. This constitutional interpretation has been endorsed by both the Council of State[37] and the Court of Cassation.[38] The Constitutional Council has confirmed the supremacy of the Constitution 'at the summit of the domestic legal order' in a string of more recent decisions.[39]

62. The protection of the supremacy of the Constitution is preventive. Article 54 of the Constitution enables the President of the Republic, the Prime Minister, the President of each House of Parliament, or sixty deputies or sixty senators to refer an international treaty to the Constitutional Council prior to its ratification in order to review its compatibility with the Constitution. The Council reviews whether the

---

34. C. cass., Ch. mixte, 24 May 1975, *Administration des Douanes c. Sociétés 'Cafés Jacques Vabre'*, *Bull. Ch. mixte* 1975, No 4.
35. CE, Ass., 20 Oct. 1989, *Nicolo*, *Rec. Lebon* 190.
36. CE, Ass., 6 Jun. 1997, *Aquarone*, *Rec. Lebon* 206.
37. CE, Ass., 30 Oct. 1998, *Sarran, Levacher et autres*, *Rec. Lebon* 368; CE, 3 Dec. 2001, *SNIP (Syndicat national de l'industrie pharmaceutique)*, *Rec. Lebon* 624.
38. C. cass., Ass. plén., 2 Jun. 2000, *Fraisse*, *Bull. Ass. plén.* 2000, No 4.
39. CC Decision No 2004-505 DC of 19 Nov. 2004, *Traité établissant une Constitution pour l'Europe*, *Rec.* 173*; CC Decision No 2007-560 DC of 20 Dec. 2007, *Traité de Lisbonne modifiant le traité sur l'Union européenne et le traité instituant la Communauté européenne*, *Rec.* 459*; CC Decision No 2009-595 DC of 3 Dec. 2009, *Loi organique relative à l'application de l'article 61-1 de la Constitution*, *Rec.* 206*.

provisions of the treaty are repugnant to constitutional provisions if they 'call into question constitutionally guaranteed rights and freedoms',[40] or if they 'adversely affect the fundamental conditions of the exercising of national sovereignty'.[41] The latter criterion applies, notably as regards EU treaties, in case of transfers of competences in matters which are inherent to the exercise of sovereignty or due to modifications of the decision-making process in competences already transferred. If an international treaty is indeed repugnant to the Constitution, it cannot be ratified without previous amendment to the Constitution. The Constitutional Council may also review the compatibility of a treaty with the Constitution via its review of the law authorizing its ratification under Article 61 of the Constitution. These mechanisms aim at preventing normative conflicts between international treaties and the Constitution, thus guaranteeing the supremacy of the Constitution in the French legal order. However, the effectiveness of the supremacy of the Constitution over international treaties has a number of limits. Once ratified, and even though they may not have been referred beforehand to the Constitutional Council, international treaties cannot be reviewed for their compatibility with the Constitution.[42]

B. The Special Constitutional Position of EU Law

63. The principle of the primacy of the Constitution in French law finds a specific expression in relation to EU law. In 2004, the Constitutional Council gave judicial recognition to Article 88-1 of the Constitution which, introduced in relation to the 1992 Treaty of Maastricht, states that '[t]he Republic shall participate in the European Union consisting of States which have freely chosen to exercise some of their powers in common'. The Council deduced from this provision that 'the constituent power formally acknowledged the existence of a Community legal order integrated into the domestic legal order and distinct from the international legal order'.[43] In the particular decision, the Council therefore concluded that Article I-6 of the 2004 Treaty establishing a Constitution for Europe relating to the primacy of EU law was indeed compatible with the Constitution – which the Council regarded as nonetheless still at the summit of the domestic legal order. On the basis of the same Article 88-1, the Constitutional Council also regarded the implementation of EU directives as a constitutional requirement.[44] It follows that, in reviewing the constitutionality of implementing laws, the Council has to assess their conformity with the requirement derived from Article 88-1 of the Constitution and sanction them in

40. A condition introduced by CC Decision No 2004-505 DC of 19 Nov. 2004, *Traité établissant une Constitution pour l'Europe*, *Rec.* 173, pt 7*.
41. A test that is consistent since CC Decision No 1992-308 DC of 9 Apr. 1992, *Traité sur l'Union européenne*, *Rec.* 55, pt 14*.
42. CC Decision No 70-39 DC of 19 Jun. 1970, *Traité des Communautés européennes*, *Rec.* 15.
43. CC Decision No 2004-505 DC of 19 Nov. 2004, *Traité établissant une Constitution pour l'Europe*, *Rec.* 173, pt 11*; CC Decision No 2007-560 DC of 20 Dec. 2007, *Traité de Lisbonne modifiant le traité sur l'Union européenne et le traité instituant la Communauté européenne*, *Rec.* 459, pt 7*.
44. CC Decision No 2004-496 DC of 10 Jun. 2004, *Loi pour la confiance dans l'économie numérique*, *Rec.* 101.

case they manifestly contravene the relevant EU directive.[45] At the time, this did not go without difficulties especially as regards the Council's traditional case law on the distinction between review of constitutionality and review of conventionality. The constitutional requirement as to the obligation to implement EU directives is not absolute. It finds a limit in a 'rule or principle inherent in the constitutional identity of France'[46] – which simply reflects the expression of the supremacy of the Constitution in French law.

64. However, the expression of this supremacy is relaxed in relation to EU law in several respects. First, the Constitutional Council has yet to identify the constitutional provisions participating in the constitutional identity of France and susceptible to be opposed to EU law. Rather, its case law bears witness to an unusual use of reservations, of interpretation, an interpretative method used to avoid normative incompatibility via constructive interpretation in order to construe EU law as being compatible with the Constitution.[47] Second, the constitutional identity of France is not an immutable limit to the process of European integration. It could be waived if 'the constituent power consents thereto'.[48] Third, the reference to norms participating in the constitutional identity of France as a limit to the constitutional requirement to implement an EU directive means that this European commitment may prevail over other constitutional provisions. Formally, this does not challenge the supremacy of the Constitution since it is the result of a balance between a constitutional requirement derived from Article 88-1 of the Constitution and other constitutional principles. Nonetheless, indirectly and substantively, EU rules contained in the directive may, in some instances, prevail over constitutional provisions. The position of the Council of State differs from that of the Constitutional Council in that respect.[49] While both Councils have recognized the constitutional obligation to implement EU directives on the basis of Article 88-1 of the Constitution and affirmed the ensuing specificity of constitutional review as regards regulatory instruments relating to implementation, the Council of State has refused to identify, among constitutional provisions, those that could be regarded as participating in the constitutional identity of France. For the Council of State, the implementation of an EU directive will be valid from a constitutional perspective as long as the directive thereof conforms to EU principles that, as interpreted by the Court of Justice of the European Union (CJEU), mirrors constitutional provisions.

45. CC Decision No 2006-543 DC of 30 Nov. 2006, *Loi relative au secteur de l'énergie*, *Rec.* 120*.
46. CC Decision No 2006-540 DC of 27 Jul. 2006, *Loi relative au droit d'auteur et aux droits voisins dans la société de l'information*, *Rec.* 88*.
47. CC Decision No 2004-505 DC of 19 Nov. 2004, *Traité établissant une Constitution pour l'Europe*, *Rec.* 173*, for EU primary law; CC Decision No 2006-540 DC of 27 Jul. 2006, *Loi relative au droit d'auteur et aux droits voisins dans la société de l'information*, *Rec.* 88*, for EU secondary law.
48. CC Decision No 2006-540 DC of 27 Jul. 2006, *Loi relative au droit d'auteur et aux droits voisins dans la société de l'information*, *Rec.* 88, pt 19*.
49. CE, Ass., 8 Feb. 2007, *Société Arcelor Atlantique et Lorraine et autres*, *Rec. Lebon* 56.

Chapter 2. The Constitution

65. Even though French law favours a formal definition of the Constitution, norms of constitutional value stretch beyond the text of the Constitution itself. The Constitution is rigid meaning that amending it can only intervene pursuant to a specific procedure. The Constitution also provides for various judicial mechanisms as regards the enforcement of its supremacy in the domestic legal order.

§1. The Characteristics of Constitutional Norms

66. The supremacy of the Constitution has to be understood in light of the traditionally significant role afforded to the law in the French legal order. The range of norms of constitutional value, known as the 'block of constitutionality' (*bloc de constitutionnalité),* is linked to the incremental evolution of the Constitutional Council as the organ exercising constitutional review over legislative provisions.

I. The Supremacy of the Constitution

67. French law has long been characterized by the place it affords to the law as the central norm in the legal system (the so-called *légicentrisme*). This feature finds its origin in the French conception of democratic sovereignty. According to Article 6 of the 1789 Declaration, '[t]he Law is the expression of the general will'. Therefore, the introduction of the constitutional paradigm, understood as viewing the Constitution as the expression of sovereignty which makes the validity of domestic norms dependent on the supremacy of the Constitution, has been the result of an incremental evolution. The creation of the Constitutional Council in the early days of the Fifth Republic did not originally correspond to the introduction of a full mechanism of judicial constitutional review of legislation. The initial aim was to ensure that Parliament remained within the limits of its competence and did not infringe on the normative powers granted to the government. Nonetheless, the Council gradually developed into an organ ensuring the supremacy of the Constitution over the law. The following quote from one of its decisions best embodies how the Council envisages its role under domestic constitutional law: the law 'is the expression of the general will only in accordance with the Constitution'.[50] The endorsement of a full review of constitutionality by the Constitutional Council, in contrast with its initial role as regards the division of normative competences provided for in Article 34 and Article 37 of the Constitution, is the result of its Freedom of Association Decision of 1971.[51] Assuming the role of a court entrusted with judicial review of legislation raises the question of the norms used to exercise this review, especially since the text of the Constitution contains little references to

---

50. CC Decision No 85-197 DC of 23 Aug. 1985, *Loi sur l'évolution de la Nouvelle-Calédonie*, *Rec.* 70, pt 27.
51. CC Decision No 71-44 DC of 16 Jul. 1971, *Loi complétant les dispositions des articles 5 et 7 de la loi du 1er juillet 1901 relative au contrat d'association*, *Rec.* 25*.

rights and freedoms. The norms referred to by the Constitutional Council in the fulfilment of its constitutional review role are known as being constitutive of the 'block of constitutionality' which results from the above-mentioned 1971 Decision in which the Council adopted a formal but extensive definition of the Constitution.

II. The Extent of the Constitution: The Block of Constitutionality

68. The extent of the block of constitutionality (i.e., the norms of reference used by the Constitutional Council in its task of reviewing legislation for their conformity with the Constitution) consists of all the provisions which can be connected with the text of the Constitution including its Preamble. The Constitutional Council ensures a balance between these provisions of constitutional value without, however, establishing a hierarchy between the norms within the block of constitutionality.

A. *The Content of the Block of Constitutionality*

69. The block of constitutionality includes all the Articles of the Constitution. Moreover, since the Preamble to the Constitution has been recognized as of constitutional value, the instruments referred to herein are also included in the block of constitutionality. The Preamble to the Constitution states that '[t]he French people … solemnly proclaim their attachment to the human rights and the principles of national sovereignty as defined in the 1789 Declaration, as later confirmed and complemented by the Preamble to the 1946 Constitution, as well as to the rights and duties laid down in the 2004 Charter for the Environment'. As a result, the 1789 Declaration, the Preamble to the 1946 Constitution as well as the 2004 Charter for the Environment are all part of the constitutional norms of reference used by the Constitutional Council.

70. Like the Preamble to the Constitution, the Preamble to the 1946 Constitution makes reference to other norms. These are therefore included in the block of constitutionality due to the textual connection they have with the Constitution. First, the Preamble to the 1946 Constitution makes a reference to the 1789 Declaration. Second, the Preamble to the 1946 Constitution lists a number of principles known as the 'Principles of Law Particularly Necessary to our Time' (*principes particulièrement nécessaires à notre temps*). These include social rights, notably the principle of equality between men and women (paragraph 3), the right to employment (paragraph 5), the right to strike (paragraph 7), the protection of the family (paragraph 10), as well as the protection of health, material security, rest and leisure (paragraph 11). These principles also concern a number of political principles such as the right to claim asylum (paragraph 4) or the respect for international law (paragraph 14). Furthermore, the Preamble to the 1946 Constitution mentions the 'Fundamental Principles recognized by the Laws of the Republic' (*principes fondamentaux reconnus par les lois de la République*). This category is the most controversial one since, by allowing the Constitutional Council a great discretion in their discovery, it carries the risk of judicial activism. In this category, the Council has notably developed principles such as the right to education and freedom of thought,[52] freedom of association,[53] the independence of administrative courts,[54] and academic freedom.[55] The Council has further refined the criteria used to identify these principles. First, the principle must be embodied in a text of legislative value, bearing in mind that this text must have been adopted under the Republican regime, to the exclusion of laws passed during either the monarchy or the First and Second Empires. In that context, the Council only takes into account laws that are anterior to the 1946 Constitution.[56] Second, constitutional value is not attributed to the laws as such. This only applies to a principle contained in the law. Third, the principle has to be fundamental. Even though the appreciation of this criterion involves a degree of judicial discretion, a principle can only be regarded as fundamental if it has been constantly applied over time. An exceptional period of non-application of the principle will prevent such principle from being qualified as fundamental. Even though, the 'Fundamental Principles recognized by the Laws of the Republic' have a textual link with the Constitution, this link is tenuous, in particular due to the indeterminacy of the content of this category. This may explain why the Constitutional Council has abandoned the reference to this particular category of principles in its more recent case law. The difficulties associated with the weak link between the 'Fundamental Principles recognized by the Laws of the Republic' and the text of the Constitution are particularly emphasized when the Constitutional Council has recourse to constitutional principles that are not grounded in a textual provision. In its case law, the Council has referred to different kinds of sources – namely constitutional principles, objectives of constitutional value, constitutional requirements or legitimate objectives – without necessarily establishing their textual basis, in a very similar manner as the reasoning used by the Council of State as regards the development of general principles of law. For example, the Constitutional Council developed in such manner principles such as the principle of continuity of the public service[57] or the principle of the accessibility and intelligibility of the law.[58] The ex nihilo creation of constitutional principles carries the risk of exposing the Council to the criticism of judicial activism.

71. The inclusion of a particular set of norms and principles in the block of constitutionality depends on their textual link with the Constitution. Conversely, this

---

52. CC Decision No 77-87 DC of 23 Nov. 1977, *Loi complémentaire à la loi n° 59-1557 du 31 décembre 1959 modifiée par la loi n° 71-400 du 1er juin 1971 et relative à la liberté de l'enseignement*, *Rec.* 42.
53. CC Decision No 71-44 DC of 16 Jul. 1971, *Loi complétant les dispositions des articles 5 et 7 de la loi du 1er juillet 1901 relative au contrat d'association*, *Rec.* 25*.
54. CC Decision No 80-119 DC of 22 Jul. 1980, *Loi portant validation d'actes administratifs*, *Rec.* 49.
55. CC Decision No 83-165 DC of 20 Jan. 1984, *Loi relative à l'enseignement supérieur*, *Rec.* 30; CC Decision No 2010-20/21 QPC of 6 Aug. 2010, *M. Jean et autres [Loi Université]*, *Rec.* 203.
56. CC Decision No 88-244 DC of 20 Jul. 1988, *Loi portant amnistie*, *Rec.* 119.
57. CC Decision No 79-105 DC of 25 Jul. 1979, *Loi modifiant les dispositions de la loi n° 74-696 du 7 août 1974 relatives à la continuité du service public de la radio et de la télévision en cas de cessation concertée du travail*, *Rec.* 33.
58. CC Decision No 99-421 DC of 16 Dec. 1999, *Loi portant habilitation du Gouvernement à procéder par ordonnances, à l'adoption de partie législative de certains codes*, *Rec.* 49.

formal requirement excludes from the block of constitutionality other norms that do not display the same linkage. Despite their significance, organic laws are not generally included in the block of constitutionality. When the Constitutional Council refers to them, it is not as such but due to an express reference made to them within a constitutional provision as regards their application.[59] In this instance, an ordinary law, which is repugnant to an organic law, would be equally repugnant to the Constitution itself. For the same reason, the Rules of Procedures of the Houses of Parliament are not included in the block of constitutionality.[60] The issue of international law is more ambiguous. On the basis of the strict distinction between the review of constitutionality and that of conventionality, international norms are generally excluded from the block of constitutionality. However, this state of affairs has been challenged by the development of EU law. First, in its 1992 Decision on The Treaty of Maastricht, the Constitutional Council recognized the rule *pacta sunt servanda* on the basis of the fourteenth paragraph of the Preamble to the 1946 Constitution.[61] More importantly, the Council referred to both the Treaty on European Union (TEU) and an EU directive in order to review the conformity with the Constitution of an organic law pertaining to the electoral status in France of EU citizens.[62] However, this was done only because Article 88-3 of the Constitution stated that this electoral status had to be granted in accordance with EU law. The Council thus took EU law into account due to its textual link with the Constitution. The affirmation that Article 88-1 of the Constitution entails a constitutional requirement as to the implementation of EU directives generalizes this state of affairs. The Constitutional Council has ruled increasingly on the conformity of domestic laws with EU law provisions.[63] However, this has not involved the integration of EU law as such in the block of constitutionality. EU law is taken into account in the constitutional review of legislation because of a constitutional referral and in order to enforce a constitutional provision. This explains why the Council has only censured manifest disregard of EU directives by the implementing laws,[64] and that EU law has not been taken into account in cases of laws that do not aim at implementing EU directives.[65] In the

59. CC Decision No 78-95 DC of 27 Jul. 1978, *Loi complétant les dispositions de l'article 7 de la loi n° 60-791 du 2 août 1960 relative à l'enseignement et à la formation professionnelle agricole*, *Rec.* 26.
60. CC Decision No 80-117 DC of 22 Jul. 1980, *Loi sur la protection et le contrôle des matières nucléaires*, *Rec.* 42.
61. CC Decision No 92-308 DC of 9 Apr. 1992, *Traité sur l'Union européenne*, *Rec.* 55*.
62. CC Decision No 98-400 DC of 20 May 1998, *Loi organique déterminant les conditions d'application de l'article 88-3 de la Constitution relatif à l'exercice par les citoyens de l'Union européenne résidant en France, autres que les ressortissants français, du droit de vote et d'éligibilité aux élections municipales, et portant transposition de la directive 94/80/CE du 19 décembre 1994*, *Rec.* 251*.
63. CC Decision No 2006-543 DC of 30 Nov. 2006, *Loi relative au secteur de l'énergie*, *Rec.* 120*.
64. CC Decision No 2006-540 DC of 27 Jul. 2006, *Loi relative au droit d'auteur et aux droits voisins dans la société de l'information*, *Rec.* 88*.
65. CC Decision No 2006-535 DC of 30 Mar. 2006, *Loi pour l'égalité des chances*, *Rec.* 50.

same manner, the Council has excluded the constitutional requirement of implementation of EU directives from the rights and freedoms guaranteed under the Constitution which is the basis of its review in the context of the review under the priority preliminary ruling on the issue of constitutionality procedure.[66]

B. The Conciliation Between Constitutional Norms

72. By depending solely on a textual link with the Constitution, the norms contained in the block of constitutionality derive from heterogeneous legal sources. This heterogeneity is multifaceted, as being formal, chronological and ideological. For instance, the 1789 Declaration and the Preamble to the 1946 Constitution are two different legal instruments that display, respectively, a liberal and a social inclination. This begs the question of the ordering or conciliation between the different components of the block of constitutionality. The Constitutional Council has regarded any component of the block of constitutionality as having an equal status and has refused the primacy of one over the other on grounds of chronological or hierarchical considerations. The question was notably raised as regards the relationship between the 1789 Declaration and the 'Principles of Law Particularly Necessary to our Time' contained in the Preamble to the 1946 Constitution. The latter being subsequent in time could have been considered as prevailing over the former instrument. Conversely, the Preamble to the current Constitution has upheld principles defined by the 1789 Declaration, as confirmed and complemented by the Preamble to the 1946 Constitution. The principles contained in the Preamble to the 1946 Constitution would thus have been regarded as ancillary and the 1789 Declaration would have to prevail in case of conflict. However, the Council has discarded any hierarchy between the 1789 Declaration and the principles introduced by the Preamble to the 1946 Constitution and, in general, between the components of the block of constitutionality.[67]

73. Norms are included in the block of constitutionality insofar as they derive from the same formal source (i.e., the Constitution). Therefore, they have an equal and relative value. The Constitutional Council has refused to grant an absolute scope to any of these norms and rather has proceeded to ensure the conciliation between these different principles. Rights and freedoms can be assessed between themselves or in light of the public order. However, there is no predetermined method that would guide this conciliation. The outcome of the conciliation exercise between the components of the block of constitutionality has not clearly displayed, in the case law of the Council, a recurrence of certain rights and freedoms as invariably weighting more than others – a state of affairs that would have implicitly led to the creation of a hierarchy within the block of constitutionality. The Council has strived to balance the different constitutional principles in concreto by taking into consideration the specifics of the case.

66. CC Decision No 2010-605 DC of 12 May 2010, *Loi relative à la concurrence et à la régulation du secteur des jeux d'argent et de hasard en ligne*, *Rec.* 78*.
67. CC Decision No 81-132 DC of 16 Jan. 1982, *Loi de nationalisation*, *Rec.* 18.

§2. AMENDING THE CONSTITUTION

74. The Constitution is rigid. The procedure governing its amendment differs from, and is stricter than, the procedure to pass laws. In addition, French law rejects supra-constitutional rules that would go beyond the scope of the amendment procedure.

I. The Amendment Procedure

75. Constitutional amendments are normally governed by Article 89 of the Constitution, even though Article 11 has also been used for this purpose.

A. *Amending the Constitution under Article 89 of the Constitution*

76. Article 89 is the unique provision of Title XVI of the Constitution that is entitled 'Of the Revision'. It sets limits to the amending power and provides for a specific procedure for that purpose.

1. Limits to the Amending Power

77. Article 89 of the Constitution sets limits to the possibility of amending the Constitution. The first limit concerns the circumstances of the amendment process. Amendments to the Constitution cannot be 'instituted or carried out where the integrity of the national territory is impaired'. Adopted in response to the amendment of the Constitution of the Third Republic which took place in July 1940, this limit aims at making impossible the revision of the Constitution under the pressure of an invading power. In addition to this limit set under Article 89, Article 7 of the Constitution prohibits any constitutional amendments 'during the vacancy of the office of the President of the Republic or during the period elapsing between the official declaration of the permanent incapacity of the President of the Republic and the election of his successor'. Constitutional amendments are also impossible when the President of the Republic exercises the extraordinary powers provided for under Article 16 of the Constitution.[68] Article 89 also sets a substantive limit to the amending power since the republican form of the government cannot be the subject of a constitutional amendment.

2. The Procedure of Constitutional Amendment

78. The initiative of constitutional amendments belongs, on a proposal of the Prime Minister, to the President of the Republic, as well as to MPs. Amendments to

68. CC Decision No 81-132 DC of 16 Jan. 1982, *Loi de nationalisation*, *Rec.* 18.

the Constitution are carried out through a two-stage procedure. First, a bill to amend the Constitution must be voted, by a simple majority, in identical terms by both Houses of Parliament. In contrast to the legislative procedure, the last word cannot be given to the National Assembly when it comes to amending the Constitution. In this respect, the Senate has a power of veto. The second stage depends on the authority that initiates the procedure. Where a bill is introduced by an MP, the constitutional amendment must be approved by a referendum. Where a bill is introduced at the initiative of the Executive, the President of the Republic has the choice between two routes, namely the referendum route or the parliamentary route. The President can have recourse to a referendum. Alternatively, he may choose to convene Parliament in Congress (i.e., the two Houses sit together) in order to adopt the bill which must be approved by a three-fifths majority of the votes cast.

79. Since 1958, the Constitution has been amended twenty-four times.[69] Only once, in 2000, in order to amend the term of office the President of the Republic from seven to five years, the amendment procedure was carried out by a referendum. The President of the Republic has generally favoured the parliamentary route since it is regarded as a more efficient and predictable route than the recourse to popular approval.

B. The Use of Article 11 to Amend the Constitution

80. Aside from Article 89 of the Constitution, two constitutional amendments were carried out on the basis of Article 11. Article 11 allows the President of the Republic to put to a referendum any government bill which deals with, among others, 'the organization of public powers'. In 1962, Article 11 was used successfully by de Gaulle in order to introduce the election of the President of the Republic by direct universal suffrage, while, in 1969, a bill relating to the regions and the modification of the Senate failed. In both instances, the recourse to Article 11 was politically motivated. The hostility of Parliament towards these constitutional amendments made the Article 89 route risky. Relying on Article 11 appeared as a better option which would allow bypassing parliamentary opposition. However, amending the Constitution on the basis of Article 11 led to heavy criticism. It was claimed, at the time, that the use of this provision was not appropriate since it literally dealt with legislative bills only. Constitutional amendments could only be carried out via the special procedure provided for under Title XVI of the Constitution. On the contrary, proponents of the recourse to Article 11 responded that, the people being sovereign, its expression could not be subject to any specific procedure. Another argument invoked at the time was that the use of Article 11 on the occasion of the 1962 referendum had somehow created a constitutional precedent which could be relied upon on the occasion of the 1969 referendum. In conclusion, it is

69. The last major constitutional reform occurred in 2008 under Sarkozy Presidency. A government bill proposed by the Philippe Government in April 2018 about a vast constitutional reform is currently under discussion in Parliament (June 2018).

arguably possible to amend the French Constitution on the basis of Article 11, especially since the Constitutional Council refused to review referendum laws on the ground that they constitute 'the direct expression of the national sovereignty'.[70] Nonetheless, Article 11 has not been used to amend the Constitution since the failed 1969 referendum and the procedure has thus become obsolete.

II. The Issue of Supra-Constitutionality

81. The question has been raised, in the context of the process of European integration and of the constitutional amendments it has necessitated, as to whether there exist supra-constitutional rules in the French legal order. The notion of supra-constitutionality reflects the distinction between the original constituent power (i.e., the power that adopted the Constitution) and the derived constituent power (i.e., the power that is empowered to amend the Constitution). Being established under the Constitution, the derived constituent power can arguably be limited. Supra-constitutional norms are those which are beyond the ambit of the derived constituent power and correspond to constitutional principles that cannot be amended. As a result, the Constitutional Council would be competent to review bills to amend the Constitution and could censure those bills which challenge supra-constitutional rules. The proponents of the existence of supra-constitutional rules have found some support in the case law of the Constitutional Council. In a 1992 Decision, the Council ruled that the constituent power was sovereign, subject to the limits provided for by Articles 7, 16 and 89 of the Constitution.[71] Some supra-constitutional limits would thus restrain the power to amend the Constitution. This primarily concerns the republican form of the government which would exceed the mere prohibition to (re)establish a monarchy. It has been argued that the republican government also encompasses the fundamental principles that shape the distinctive features of the French constitutional order. However, the Constitutional Council has not explicitly recognized the existence of supra-constitutional principles that would limit the constituent power and bar the validity of certain amendments to the Constitution. In a 2003 Decision, the Council ruled out its competence to review constitutional amendment bills, even though the parliamentary rather than the referendum route had been chosen in that case.[72] Similarly, while the introduction of the notion of 'constitutional identity' in the case law of the Council led to the view that some constitutional provisions stand as permanent features that cannot be amended, the

70. CC Decision No 62-20 DC of 6 Nov. 1962, *Loi relative à l'élection du Président de la République au suffrage universel direct, adoptée par le référendum du 28 octobre 1962*, *Rec.* 27, pt 2; CC Decision No 92-313 DC of 23 Sep. 1992, *Loi autorisant la ratification du traité sur l'Union européenne*, *Rec.* 94, pt 2.
71. CC Decision No 92-312 of 2 Sep. 1992, *Traité sur l'Union européenne*, *Rec.* 76*.
72. CC Decision No 2003-469 DC of 26 Mar. 2003, *Révision constitutionnelle relative à l'organisation décentralisée de la République*, *Rec.* 293.

Council prevented such an interpretation by deciding that constitutional provisions inherent to the constitutional identity of France could be waived if 'the constituent power consents thereto'.[73]

§3. The Supremacy of the Constitution

82. The Constitution is 'at the summit of the domestic legal order'[74] which is guaranteed by different mechanisms. The primacy of the Constitution over international law is ensured by Article 54 of the Constitution. In case of an incompatibility between a treaty and the Constitution, a constitutional amendment would be required before ratification of the treaty. The primacy of the Constitution over the law is guaranteed through the review of constitutionality under the a priori review mechanism (Article 61 Constitution), and a posteriori review mechanism (Article 61-1 Constitution). However, the Constitutional Council has adopted a strict interpretation of its competence in that matter restricting its review to the laws adopted by Parliament and declining to review the laws adopted by referendum since these are regarded as 'the direct expression of the national sovereignty'.[75] The supremacy of the Constitution over administrative regulations, which are not passed in application of a law, is enforced by the Council of State.

---

73. CC Decision No 2006-544 DC of 14 Dec. 2006, *Loi de financement de la sécurité sociale pour 2007*, *Rec.* 129, pt 18.
74. CC Decision No 2004-505 DC of 19 Nov. 2004, *Traité établissant une Constitution pour l'Europe*, *Rec.* 173, pt 10*; CC Decision No 2007-560 DC of 20 Dec. 2007, *Traité de Lisbonne modifiant le traité sur l'Union européenne et le traité instituant la Communauté européenne*, *Rec.* 459, pt 8*; CC Decision No 2009-595 DC of 3 Dec. 2009, *Loi organique relative à l'application de l'article 61-1 de la Constitution*, *Rec.* 206, pt 14*.
75. CC Decision No 62-20 DC of 6 Nov. 1962, *Loi relative à l'élection du Président de la République au suffrage universel direct, adoptée par le référendum du 28 octobre 1962*, *Rec.* 27, pt 2; CC Decision No 92-313 DC of 23 Sep. 1992, *Loi autorisant la ratification du traité sur l'Union européenne*, *Rec.* 94, pt 2.

Chapter 3. Laws and Legislation

83. Domestic laws, while subject to the Constitution and to international law, are superior to all other domestic norms. Laws can be defined as those norms depending either on their form or on their position in the hierarchy of norms. While the latter criterion is favoured in French law, rules of legislative value also extend beyond parliamentary legislation.

§1. Types of Legislation

84. While they are also formally referred to as a form of legislation, organic laws have to be distinguished from ordinary laws.

I. Organic Laws

85. Organic laws are a specific form of legislation the purpose of which is to specify the conditions of application of certain constitutional provisions. The requirement for an organic law is explicitly mentioned in the relevant provisions of the Constitution. Organic laws are inferior to the Constitution but superior to ordinary laws.

86. Organic laws are adopted according to the parliamentary legislative procedure. However, due to their special importance, this procedure differs from that related to the adoption of ordinary laws (Article 46 Constitution). First, the period between the tabling and the first reading of the bill is generally the same as that for ordinary laws. However, in contrast with the ordinary parliamentary procedure, if the government decides to apply the accelerated procedure, a fifteen-day period is still required before the bill is discussed by the House. Second, in case of disagreement between the National Assembly and the Senate, the bill can be passed by the National Assembly on final reading. However, in contrast with the ordinary parliamentary procedure, the required majority is the absolute majority of the members of the National Assembly rather than the traditional majority of the votes cast. Furthermore, organic laws *must* be referred, before promulgation, to the Constitutional Council for review of their conformity with the Constitution. Two types of organic laws are submitted to a stricter procedure whereby they must be passed in identical terms by both Houses of Parliament. These organic laws are those related to the Senate (Article 46 Constitution), and those related to the right of EU citizens to vote and stand as a candidate in local elections (Article 88-3 Constitution). The necessary approval of the Senate as regards the latter is explained by the importance of the delegates of local councils in the composition of the electoral college of members of the Senate.

II. Ordinary Laws

87. By giving a material – as opposed to a formal – definition of legislation, the Constitution has restricted the intervention of Parliament to specific subject matters. In addition, norms having a legislative value are not limited to instruments adopted by Parliament.[76]

A. *The Area of Legislation*

88. The Constitution defines both the material limits to the scope of provisions of legislative nature and provides mechanisms for their respect. Recently, the Constitutional Council has also paid greater attention to the normativity of ordinary laws.

1. Definition of the Area of the Legislative Power

89. As defined by Article 6 of the 1789 Declaration, laws are the 'expression of the general will'. This explains the pre-eminence of legislative norms in the French legal tradition, what is described as '*légicentrisme*'. Under the previous regimes, the law had an organic and formal definition and corresponded to the legal instruments enacted by Parliament in compliance with a specific procedure. In that context, the area of the law was unlimited.

90. The Constitution of the Fifth Republic aims at rationalizing the parliamentary regime whereby various mechanisms now ensure a proper balance between the organs of the State. In this constitutional design, the definition of legislative norms received a particular attention. This issue was considered as one of the mains factors of the imbalance of the previous regimes in favour of Parliament, leading to the confusion between democratic sovereignty and parliamentary sovereignty. The drafters of the Constitution saw in the division of the normative competences between the Legislative and the Executive – and in a restrictive definition of the law – one of the solutions to ensure the stability of the new regime. Under the Fifth Republic, the definition of the law is still partially organic and formal. Article 24 of the Constitution states that 'Parliament shall vote the law.' However, this definition is also material since legislation is restricted to certain areas. According to Article 34, the law 'shall lay down the rules with respect to' a list of topics including, among others, fundamental rights and freedoms, nationality, the determination of criminal offences or the nationalization of companies, as well as 'shall lay down the fundamental principles [of]' certain areas such as the general organization of

76. *See also* below Part II. Forn of Government, Chapter 3. The Legislature, §3. Powers, I. Legislative Function, A. Article 34 of the Constitution on the Law.

national defence, education, or the protection of the environment. The constitutional amendment currently (June 2018) under discussion in Parliament proposes to include the 'necessity to fight against global warming' as part of the definition of the area of the law.

91. These limits to the ambit of ordinary legislation laid down in Article 34 of the Constitution have to be nuanced. Despite the semantic difference between 'lay down the rules with respect to' and 'lay down the fundamental principles with respect to', these expressions are regarded as synonymous. Furthermore, the list of areas given by Article 34 is not exhaustive. This provision indicates that this list may be completed by an organic law. More importantly, other constitutional provisions expand the legislative area. For instance, according to Article 35 of the Constitution, war has to be authorized by Parliament and, under Article 53, the ratification of treaties requires the enactment of a law. Similarly, Articles 72 to 74-1 require the adoption of laws as regards the organization of local authorities. Lastly, the delimitation of the legislative area has entailed the creation of an autonomous regulatory power. What was regarded as controversial back in 1958 was that the area of law would be governed by the conferral principle. By contrast, the Executive would be entrusted with a competence of principle (or general competence) as regard its regulatory power. Under Article 37 of the Constitution, '[m]atters other than those that fall within the area of the law are of a regulatory nature'. When compared with the primacy of law (and that of Parliament) which existed in previous regimes, the division established between Article 34 and Article 37 appears radical. However, even though the area of the law is expressly limited, it is still extensive and covers the most important aspects of the regulation of society. As a result, the principle remains that the legislative power is entrusted with initiating the normative process while the regulatory power is mainly concerned with the specifics of normative application.

2. Review of the Area of the Legislative Power

92. Originally, the primary role of the Constitutional Council was to review the distribution of normative competences between ordinary laws and regulations, and more particularly to prevent encroachment by Parliament beyond the limits of its competence. Different mechanisms fulfil the protection of the area of competence of the regulatory power. In addition to the general competence of the Constitutional Council to review the conformity of laws with the Constitution, two specific procedures are dedicated to this purpose. The first procedure is preventive in nature and provides for a procedure of inadmissibility which takes place during the discussion of a bill (Article 41 Constitution). During the legislative process, the government or the president of the House of Parliament concerned can argue as to the admissibility or not of a private member's bill or its amendment. In case of disagreement, the Constitutional Council shall rule on the issue within eight days. However, the Council has rarely intervened in this respect since these disagreements between the government and Houses of Parliament have tended to be exceptional. The second procedure is curative. Referred to as a procedure of 'declassification', and laid down in the second paragraph of Article 37 of the Constitution, the procedure aims at challenging the legislative nature of enacted provisions which may then be amended by decree since they have 'lost' their legislative nature. For legislative provisions enacted before 1958 (i.e., before the introduction of the division between the legislative and regulatory areas), such modification by decree is possible after consultation of the Council of State. As regards legislative instruments enacted after 1958, the Constitutional Council must decide whether these exceed the legislative area before their possible modification by decree.

93. Infringements on the area reserved to the regulatory power can also be challenged through the general review of constitutionality provided for in Article 61 of the Constitution. This procedure primarily concerns MPs since the Prime Minister usually has recourse to the dedicated mechanisms. Initially, the Constitutional Council considered that MPs could not avail of such action. Considering that the division established by Article 34 and Article 37 of the Constitution was a means to protect the government's competence, only the government could ask for its enforcement.[77] This position could be justified by the fact that the division between Articles 34 and 37 is not objective but, as an instrument of the rationalization of the parliamentary regime, is a device aimed at ensuring the collaboration between the political authorities. An infringement of the regulatory power would not be invalid if the government would agree to it. However, the connection between the government and its parliamentary majority has contributed to increasingly blur the division between Article 34 and Article 37. The discussion by Parliament of provisions beyond its area of competence is arguably detrimental to the quality of legislation. The clarity and intelligibility of legislation have recently become a concern for the Constitutional Council which has allowed parliamentary challenges relating to the infringement of Article 37 of the Constitution. However, a decision by the Council in that case would not result in the invalidity of those legislative provisions adopted beyond the limits of Article 34. Rather, these will be requalified as being of regulatory nature and therefore amendable by decree.[78] There is no specific provision protecting the legislative area from regulatory infringements. However, administrative courts and, in the last instance, the Council of State, are competent to review administrative acts on ultra vires grounds. These courts may thus sanction decrees enacted in the legislative area. In criminal matters, this function is entrusted with criminal courts and, in the last instance, with the Court of Cassation, under Article 111-5 of the Criminal Code. Challenges to the parliamentary legislative competence can also come from Parliament itself. This is the case when Parliament relinquishes the full exercise of its powers and entrusts the regulatory power with the determination of issues that pertain to its own area of competence. In this case, the Constitutional Council would exercise its review for negative incompetence of a law leaving an excessive leeway to the regulatory power due to an incomplete exercise of its legislative function by Parliament.

---

77. CC Decision No 82-143 DC of 30 Jul. 1982, *Lois sur les prix et les revenus, notamment ses articles 1, 3 et 4*, *Rec.* 57.
78. CC Decision No 2005-512 DC of 21 Apr. 2005, *Loi d'orientation et de programme pour l'avenir de l'école*, *Rec.* 72.

3. Review of the Normativity of Ordinary Laws

94. The concern for the accessibility and intelligibility of the law has recently emerged as a new objective of constitutional value in the case law of the Constitutional Council.[79] One of the aspects of this objective concerns the nature of the provisions contained in ordinary legislation. In particular, and in contrast with constitutional provisions, the Constitutional Council has considered that ordinary laws are not intended to have a declaratory function but should limit themselves to a normative purpose. Therefore, the Council will regard 'legislative neutrons' (i.e., provisions without a normative scope) as being repugnant to the Constitution.[80] If declaratory provisions of legislative nature are allowed, it is only in the framework provided for by Article 34 of the Constitution as, for example, in the case of programming laws.

B. The Different Categories of Legislative Norms

95. Legislative norms can be defined by their position in the hierarchy of norms, rather than according to the specific form in which they are enacted as a result of the legislative process. As a result, norms of legislative value encompass more than ordinary laws. These legislative norms, enacted outside the legislative process, primarily concern ordinances under Article 38 of the Constitution, referendum laws governed by Article 11 of the Constitution as the expression of popular sovereignty and, marginally, the powers exercised by the President of the Republic in exceptional circumstances under Article 16 of the Constitution.

1. Ordinances under Article 38 of the Constitution

96. The regime of ordinances under Article 38 of the Constitution allows for modifications to the normative division of competences established by Articles 34 and 37 to the benefit of the regulatory power. Accordingly, Parliament can temporarily enable the government to take measures by ordinances (i.e., to exercise its regulatory power) in areas that normally pertain to the legislative power (Article 38 Constitution). The validity of such enabling legislation requires the fulfilment of a number of conditions. First, even though the government does not need to communicate the content of the ordinances it intends to implement, their purpose must be precisely laid down.[81] Second, such regulatory power can only be granted for a limited period of time. Therefore, the enabling legislation has to specify two periods.

79. CC Decision No 99-421 DC of 16 Dec. 1999, *Loi portant habilitation du Gouvernement à procéder par ordonnances, à l'adoption de la partie législative de certains codes*, *Rec*. 49.
80. CC Decision No 2005-512 DC of 21 Apr. 2005, *Loi d'orientation et de programme pour l'avenir de l'école*, *Rec*. 72.
81. CC Decision No 76-72 DC of 12 Jan. 1977, *Loi autorisant le Gouvernement à modifier par ordonnances les circonscriptions pour l'élection des membres de la chambre des députés du territoire Français des Afars et des Issas*, *Rec*. 31.

The first one concerns the period during which the government can act by means of ordinances. Upon expiry of this period, the division between the regulatory and legislative areas is re-established according to Articles 34 and 37 of the Constitution. The second period then consists of the term at the expiration of which the government has to table the bill of ratification of the ordinances before Parliament.

97. Ordinances are issued in the Council of Ministers and, pursuant to Article 13 of the Constitution, require the signature of the President of the Republic who can refuse to sign them (i.e., discretionary power). In that case, ordinances can only be amended by means of legislative bills. As for any regulatory act, ordinances come into force upon publication. Conversely, private member's bills and amendments cannot be introduced in the area covered by the enabling law and the procedure of inadmissibility of Article 41 of the Constitution can be used in that case. Until their ratification by Parliament, ordinances are of administrative nature and can be challenged before administrative courts. Since the 2008 constitutional amendment, ratification of ordinances must be explicit. If the government does not table a bill of ratification before Parliament, or if their ratification is refused, ordinances are deemed null and void. Upon ratification, ordinances acquire legislative nature. This transformation is retroactive from the date of their signature.

2. Referendum Laws under Article 11 of the Constitution

98. The introduction of referendum laws provided for under Article 11 of the Constitution contrasts with the French republican tradition of representative democracy. According to Article 3 of the Constitution, '[n]ational sovereignty belongs to the people who shall exercise it through their representatives or by way of referendum'. Nonetheless, this can explain why Article 11 restricts referendum laws to certain areas. Article 11 was greatly amended in 1995 and its current version allows for a referendum to be held as regards 'any government's bill on the organization of public powers, or on reforms relating to the economic, social or environmental policy of the Nation and the public services which contribute thereto, or concerning the ratification of a treaty which, albeit not repugnant to the Constitution, would impact on the functioning of the institutions'. However, these areas can be broadly interpreted, in particular with regard to 'the economic, social or environmental policy of the Nation'. In applying Article 11, the President of the Republic has a discretionary power to submit to referendum a bill on a proposal from the government or on a joint proposal from both Houses of Parliament. When the President of the Republic decides on the basis of a government's proposal, the government must make a declaration before each House and this declaration is followed by a debate.

99. The 2008 constitutional amendment introduced a new, rather complex, referendum procedure that complements the traditional procedure designed in 1958. It bears witness to the difficulty to reconcile direct democracy with the representative democratic tradition. This procedure can, in the same matters as those listed under the first paragraph of Article 11, be initiated by one-fifth of the MPs supported by one-tenth of the voters enrolled on the electoral lists. However, this procedure cannot aim to repeal a law promulgated for less than one year. When these conditions are met, the referendum is not automatic and can be suspended by Parliament. It is only if the two Houses of Parliament have not considered the bill within six months that the President of the Republic shall submit it to a referendum.[82] If the private member's bill is rejected by referendum, it is not possible to introduce a new referendum bill on the same subject within a two-year period from the date of the vote.

100. The Constitutional Council has also a role vis-à-vis such referendums. Under the fourth paragraph of Article 11, the Council is given the power to review whether, prior to the holding of the referendum, the procedural and substantive conditions have been fulfilled. In addition, and similarly prior to the referendum, the Council reviews whether a private member's bill contains provisions that are repugnant to the Constitution (Article 61 Constitution). However, once the referendum has been held, the Constitutional Council will refuse to exercise its review as regards laws that have been passed by referendum as these are considered as 'the direct expression of the national sovereignty'.[83] However, despite this formulation, the expression of the people's voice through referendum is not regarded as having a special binding force. The absence of constitutional review in that case is rather due to the restrictive interpretation of its role by the Council as being circumscribed to the review of constitutionality of parliamentary legislation. Therefore, referendum laws can be modified or repealed by a law passed by Parliament. Similarly, while the Council has refused to enforce the supremacy of the Constitution upon referendum laws, such laws can nonetheless be subject to the review of conventionality.[84]

3. Legislative Norms in Application of Article 16 of the Constitution

101. In exceptional circumstances, by virtue of Article 16 of the Constitution, the President of the Republic is vested with extensive or extraordinary powers. Article 16 was only applied once in 1961.[85] Acts taken under such circumstances can be either regulatory or Legislative. The Council of State has ruled that such acts are of a legislative nature when they fall within the areas as defined under Article 34 of the Constitution, since they are beyond its review.[86] Due to the competence of

82. A period defined by Organic Law No 2013-1114 of 6 Dec. 2013 implementing Art. 11 of the Constitution.
83. CC Decision No 62-20 DC of 6 Nov. 1962, *Loi relative à l'élection du Président de la République au suffrage universel direct, adoptée par le référendum du 28 octobre 1962*, *Rec.* 27, pt 2. This position was reaffirmed in CC Decision No 92-313 DC of 23 Sep. 1992, *Loi autorisant la ratification du traité sur l'Union européenne*, *Rec.* 94.
84. CE, Ass., 30 Oct. 1998, *Sarran, Levacher et autres*, *Rec. Lebon* 368.
85. *See* below Part II Form of Government, Chapter 4. The Executive, §3. Powers, I. The Division of Powers between the President of the Republic and the Government, A. Discretionary Powers of the President of the Republic.
86. CE, 2 Mar. 1962, *Rubin de Servens*, *Rec. Lebon* 143.

the Constitutional Council being limited to constitutional review of laws enacted by Parliament, such presidential acts would thus be immune from judicial review.

§2. The Position of Legislation in the Normative Hierarchy

102. The conditions of validity of legislation being governed by the Constitution, laws have an infra-constitutional rank. Ordinary laws may be subject to constitutional review (Articles 61 and 61-1 Constitution. However, such review is mandatory as regards organic laws before they are promulgated (Article 46 Constitution), as well as regards private members' bills on a referendum (Article 11 Constitution). However, issues of judicial competence may prevent the exercise of constitutional review in respect of some legislative norms. For instance, laws passed by referendum cannot be subject to constitutional review. In application of Article 55 of the Constitution, norms of legislative value are inferior to international law. These norms may, however, be subject to a review of conventionality which is exercised by ordinary courts. With the exception of the Constitution and international law, laws are superior to other legal norms. This is notably the case as regards regulatory acts of the Executive. The superiority of laws over administrative acts participates in the principle of legality which is enforced by administrative courts.

Chapter 4. Case Law

103. In accordance with the principle of the separation of powers, which forms part of the French republican regime and civil law tradition, the role of domestic courts is conceived as *applying* rather than *creating* general legal rules. The Judiciary is described as the 'mouth of the law' (*bouche de la loi*). French case law lacks the two features that distinguish the precedent in the common law tradition. In France, judicial decisions cannot create general norms and cannot bind other jurisdictions. Article 5 of the Civil Code prohibits what are known as '*arrêts de règlement*' – in other words, courts cannot create general provisions when ruling on legal disputes. Furthermore, the binding force of res judicata is, in principle, relative. Under Article 1351 of the Civil Code, the res judicata principle only obliges in relation to the object, cause and parties to a particular dispute. The relativity of res judicata allows for limited exceptions. These exceptions primarily concern criminal proceedings and decisions of administrative courts on grounds of ultra vires. Similarly, decisions of the Constitutional Council have an erga omnes effect (Article 62 Constitution) and their authority applies to both the operative part and the reasoning part of the ruling.[87]

104. The relatively weak position of case law in French law needs to be nuanced. Article 4 of the Civil Code sanctions the denial of justice by judges who would refuse to decide on a case 'on the pretext of the silence, obscurity or deficiency of the law'. Initially based on a certain conception of codification whereby a law would be complete, clear and coherent, this principle requires courts to develop legal principles when the law is ambiguous, incomplete or antonymic, and, more generally, when a decision requires some degree of interpretation. Furthermore, the domestic judicial hierarchy commands that lower courts often follow the case law of Supreme Courts (i.e., the Court of Cassation for the ordinary judicial order, and the Council of State for the administrative judicial order). However, in comparison with the doctrine of precedent, this phenomenon results more of necessity than obligation. Even though it does not have the same importance as in the common law tradition, case law is far from being insignificant in French law. Domestic administrative law, for instance, finds its origin in case law. Case law remains an important part of this branch of law despite the development of written rules in the area. However, due to the absence of a doctrine of precedent, French case law does not afford the same binding force to established decisions. The evolution of case law has proceeded from more abrupt changes known as 'case law reversals' (*revirements de jurisprudence*) whereby courts change their interpretation on a particular legal issue, sometimes in total opposition as to their previous position.

87. CC Decision No 6-18 L of 16 Jan. 1962, *Nature juridique des dispositions de l'article 31 (alinéa 2) de la loi n°60-808 du 5 août 1960 d'orientation agricole*, *Rec.* 31.

Chapter 5. Customary Law, Unwritten Law, General Principles of Law

105. The French legal system is characterized by its textualism whereby the law is first and foremost considered as a written phenomenon. Therefore, sources of law are divided between formal (or primary) sources, which refer to written rules, and informal (or secondary) sources. The latter, being unwritten, are regarded as of lesser importance. As a result, customary law, and more generally unwritten law, has an ambiguous status in French law. Nonetheless, general principles of law have played an important role.

§1. Customary and Unwritten Law

106. The uneasy recognition of customary law in the French legal order is noticeable in the area of constitutional law. An example is the refusal by the Council of State to include international customary law in the ambit of Article 55 of the Constitution, a provision that ensures the primacy of international treaties over domestic laws.[88] This lack of formal recognition contrasts with what appears to be the practice under the regime of the Fifth Republic.

107. The Constitution introduced a rationalized form of parliamentary regime to ensure an improved balance between the branches of government. In this constitutional design, the President of the Republic is the cornerstone of the institutional set-up. This particular feature was accentuated in 1962 with the introduction of the election of the President of the Republic by direct universal suffrage. As a result, the regime is animated by two sources of legitimacy and its dynamics depend on the interaction between the presidential majority and the parliamentary majority. In periods of cohabitation (i.e., when the two majorities differ), the institutions function according to a strict interpretation of the constitutional provisions and display a traditional understanding of the parliamentary regime. However, these periods are the exception. In contrast, the coincidence between the presidential majority and the parliamentary majority has been the normal functioning of the regime in practice. In this case, the interaction between the institutions departs from the constitutional text and such practice has led to reflect the actual predominance of the President of the Republic. For instance, the government is only responsible before the National Assembly (Article 49 Constitution). Therefore, the President of the Republic can only 'terminate [the Prime Minister's] appointment on the presentation by the latter of the resignation of the government'. (Article 8 Constitution). Nonetheless, the Prime Minister is also regarded as responsible before the President of the Republic in the normal functioning of the institutions. In that sense, the regime of the Fifth Republic is a dualist parliamentary regime. Similarly, the President of the Republic exercises, to a greater or lesser extent, the powers formally attributed to the government in order to 'determine and conduct the policy of the Nation' (Article 20

88. CE, Ass., 6 Jun. 1997, *Aquarone*, *Rec. Lebon* 206.

Constitution), under the direction of the Prime Minister who directs the action of the government (Article 21 Constitution). The President of the Republic is seen as the leader of the political majority and the role of the government is to implement the political agenda. These dynamics have been accentuated by the reduction of the presidential term of office from seven to five years. The coincidence of the presidential and parliamentary terms of office makes the occurrence of cohabitation less likely. Furthermore, the shorter term justifies and legitimizes a greater political interventionism by the President of the Republic.

108. In conclusion, the constitutional practice of the regime has been playing an important role under the Fifth Republic and, to that extent, French constitutional law could be described as being partly of customary nature. For instance, in 1969, it is as a constitutional custom that the second attempt to amend the Constitution on the basis of Article 11 was justified. However, equating the practice of the regime with constitutional customs would be misleading. In particular, it is difficult to establish on which basis such constitutional customary law would gain validity in French law. Without denying its importance in the actual functioning of French constitutional law, constitutional practice remains, by definition, a de facto rather than a de jure phenomenon and could be better understood as giving rise to constitutional conventions. In particular, without being constitutional rules themselves, these reflect the impact of political dynamics on the exercise of constitutional powers. This partly explains why contraventions of these conventions lead to political consequences rather than to legal sanctions.

§2. General Principles of Law

109. General principles of law, as developed by French courts and by the Council of State in particular, play an important part in the domestic legal system. The question of their position in the hierarchy of norms is partly the result of their nature.

I. The Nature of General Principles of Law

110. General principles of law represent the main category of unwritten legal norms in French law. Their unwritten nature distinguishes them from the Fundamental Principles recognized by the Laws of the Republic that form part of the block of constitutionality and are developed by the Constitutional Council. Principles included in the latter category are discovered by the Constitutional Council in the corpus of laws which predates the 1946 Constitution. In contrast, general principles of law do not present the same textual basis. Nonetheless, the Constitutional Council has also included in the block of constitutionality constitutional principles without grounding them in the text of the Constitution.

111. General principles of law have been developed mainly in the case law of the Council of State. The reasons for their importance in administrative law are to be found in the development of this branch of law itself. Due to the lack of written rules in the area, administrative courts have favoured the discovery of unwritten legal principles in order to subject the administration to the respect of legality. General principles of law act as axioms that, while not explicit, structure the French legal order. Even though administrative courts have affirmed that they merely 'discover' general principles of law, it can be argued that their origin resides in judicial creativity. However, not all arguments developed by the administrative courts in the absence of a text can be regarded as general principles of law. In order to be included in this category, such principles must display a fundamental importance. It is often possible to find a link between general principles of law and written rules. For instance, a parallel can be drawn between the general principles of law relating to the principle of equality and the 1789 Declaration.[89] Similarly, some general principles of law consist of the translation in administrative law of rules explicitly established in other areas of law. For instance, in its 1973 *Dame Peynet* Decision, the Council of State reproduced in the administrative legal order the prohibition to dismiss public officials due to their pregnancy, a rule which was already included in the Labour Code at the time.[90] Nonetheless, despite the possibility of establishing a connection with written norms, what characterizes general principles of law is that they are binding even without text. This was stressed in the first explicit reference made by the Council of State to a general principle of law,[91] and has been reaffirmed since.[92] In that respect, the existence of one of the most important general principles of law – that review on ultra vires grounds is always open against administrative acts – has been established independently from a textual basis.[93] Even though they do not have the same importance as general principles of law in administrative law, ordinary courts have also developed unwritten rules, in private law. One of the most famous examples dates from the nineteenth century in a decision which authorized actions for unjust enrichment.[94]

II. The Position of General Principles of Law in the Normative Hierarchy

112. The question of the position of general principles of law in the normative hierarchy has long been controversial. Being imposed upon administrative acts, it could be argued that these principles have the same value as laws. The introduction of a division between the legislative and regulatory fields, with the existence of an autonomous regulatory power, has contributed to change this analysis. In directly reviewing the conformity of autonomous administrative regulations with the Constitution, administrative courts have developed a number of general principles of

89. *See*, for instance, the principle of equality before public services (CE, 9 Mar. 1951, *Sociétés des concerts du Conservatoire*, *Rec. Lebon* 151), the principle of equal access to public employment (CE, Ass., 28 May 1954, *Barel*, *Rec. Lebon* 305), or the equality of citizens before the courts (CE, Ass., 12 Oct. 1979, *Rassemblements des nouveaux avocats de France*, *Rec. Lebon* 371).
90. CE, Ass., 8 Jun. 1973, *Dame Peynet*, *Rec. Lebon* 406.
91. CE., Ass., 26 Oct. 1945, *Aramu*, *Rec. Lebon* 213.
92. CE, Sect., 26 Jun. 1959, *Syndicat général des Ingénieurs-Conseils*, *Rec. Lebon* 394.
93. CE, Ass., 17 Feb. 1950, *Ministre de l'Agriculture c. Dame Lamotte*, *Rec. Lebon* 110.
94. C. cass., Req., 15 Jun. 1982, *Patureau-Miran*, DP 1892 1, 596.

law which have arguably been regarded as being of constitutional rank. This could be supported by the frequent similarity of content between these principles and the norms developed by the Constitutional Council as part of the block of constitutionality. Nonetheless, it is now generally accepted that the status of general principles of law depends on the mission the Council of State is entrusted with. In its role of censor of administrative action, the Council of State has used general principles of law which are regarded as being superior to decrees but as inferior to laws. The difference in status between the principles used by the Council of State and those used by the Constitutional Council is thus dependent on the functions respectively carried out by these courts. In particular, the non-constitutional value of general principles of law can be inferred a contrario from the case law of the Council of State. In the *Koné* Decision, for example, the Council of State discovered a principle recognized by the laws of the Republic in the area of extradition law (i.e., the obligation to refuse an extradition when requested for political purpose).[95] The necessity of having recourse to this normative category of constitutional value, the discovery of which is normally the preserve of the Constitutional Council, is the sign that, qualified as a general principle of law, this principle would not have had a constitutional value and could not achieve the judicial outcome sought for by the Council of State.

95. CE, Ass., 3 Jul. 1996, *Koné*, *Rec. Lebon* 255.

Chapter 6. Administrative Regulations and Orders

113. Administrative regulations and orders correspond to a heterogeneous set of norms. Therefore, the question of their normative value has to be assessed in relation to other legal rules but also within their own category.

§1. The Nature of Administrative Regulations and Orders

I. The Definition of Administrative Regulations and Orders

114. Generally speaking, the regulatory power is the ability for executive and administrative authorities to unilaterally adopt legal instruments of a general and impersonal scope. The Constitution introduced a major development in this regard by creating an autonomous regulatory power insofar as, under Article 37, it is not exercised to give application to legislative instruments but intervenes in areas other than those attributed to the legislative power under Article 34 of the Constitution. In addition, the Executive also holds the traditional regulatory power necessary for the implementation of legislation. This power is attributed to the Prime Minister (Article 21 Constitution). Laws themselves can refer to implementing decrees to be adopted by the regulatory power. However, the Prime Minister is not dependent on laws requiring implementing decrees. S/he can, on his/her own initiative, take the measures that are necessary for the application of legislation. This is even an obligation and the Executive can be sanctioned for failure to do so within a reasonable time.[96]

II. The Diversity of Administrative Regulations and Orders

115. Historically speaking, the regulatory power was attributed to the President of the Republic under the Third Republic while it was attributed to the Prime Minister under the Fourth Republic. Under the Fifth Republic, the regulatory power is shared by both authorities. Besides the general regulatory power exercised by the Prime Minister and the President of the Republic, other authorities can be entrusted, in specific circumstances, with regulatory powers.

A. The General Regulatory Power

116. In principle, and subject to Article 13 of the Constitution, the general regulatory power belongs to the Prime Minister (Article 21 Constitution). Acts of the Prime Minister must be countersigned by the minister(s) in charge of their implementation (Article 22 Constitution). In conjunction with Article 37 of the Constitution, Article 21 enables the Prime Minister to take acts either in relation to the

96. CE, 28 Jul. 2000, *Association France Nature Environnement*, *Rec. Lebon* 322.

autonomous regulations or in order to implement legislation. The Prime Minister also exercises the general policing power throughout the territory as recognized in the case law of the Council of State.[97] The President of the Republic is also entrusted with the exercise of a general regulatory power (Article 13 Constitution). Acts taken by the President have to be, with some exceptions, countersigned by the Prime Minister and, where required, by the ministers concerned (Article 19 Constitution). Incidentally, when the President of the Republic acts on the basis of Article 16 of the Constitution, the acts taken in extraordinary circumstances are of a regulatory nature when they intervene in this field of competence. In contrast, ministers do not hold a regulatory power. However, there are exceptions to this principle. First, as head of their administration, ministers hold such regulatory power in relation to the organization of their respective civil service.[98] Furthermore, ministers can benefit from a delegation of powers from the Prime Minister as provided for under Article 21 of the Constitution. Lastly, ministers take part in the exercise of the regulatory power through the requirement of countersignature of certain acts. Some decrees must be deliberated within the Council of Ministers. In that case, the regulatory power is shared between the Prime Minister and the President of the Republic in accordance with Articles 13 and 21 of the Constitution. The same principle applies to ordinances. The requirement to adopt decrees in the Council of Ministers can be expressed by the Constitution (such as under Article 36 as regards the state of siege), by law or even by decree. Yet, these provisions do not provide for an exhaustive list of the circumstances under which a decree must be deliberated in the Council of Ministers. The decision to deliberate a decree in this manner depends, to a large extent, on the importance given to its subject matter.

B. The Specialized Regulatory Powers

117. Aside from the general regulatory power exercised by the Prime Minister and, in certain circumstances, by the President of the Republic, a number of public authorities are endowed with a specialized regulatory power, either *ratione materiae* or *ratione loci*. The law can attribute a specific regulatory power to independent administrative authorities. Nonetheless, this attribution is only valid if it is limited both as to the scope and content of the regulation, and if it is exercised under ministerial control.[99] In the same vein, the possibility to attribute a regulatory power to independent administrative authorities cannot amount to subordinate to their assent the exercise by the Prime Minister of his regulatory power.[100] A specialized regulatory power is also attributed to local authorities by Article 72 of the Constitution for the exercise of their powers. This is in addition to the traditional policing power exercised by mayors in their municipalities. Moreover, the competences of

---

97. CE, 8 Aug. 1919, *Labonne*, *Rec. Lebon* 737.
98. CE, Sect., 7 Feb. 1936, *Jamart*, *Rec. Lebon* 172.
99. CC Decision No 96-378 DC of 23 Jul. 1996, *Loi de réglementation des télécommunications*, *Rec.* 99.
100. CC Decision No 2006-544 DC of 14 Dec. 2006, *Loi de financement de la sécurité sociale*, *Rec.* 129.

local authorities can be temporarily extended on an experimental basis so that they can derogate, for a limited purpose and duration, to legislative or regulatory provisions of national scope (Article 72 paragraph four Constitution). However, this cannot affect 'the essential conditions for the exercise of a public freedom or of a constitutionally guaranteed right'.

C. Administrative Circulars

118. The regulatory power is exercised in the form of either decrees (*décrets*) or orders (*arrêtés*). In addition, administrative authorities, and ministers in particular, often issue circulars (*circulaires*) by which they determine or clarify the rules to be applied by their civil service. Nonetheless, these circulars do not always have a descriptive scope. They can include further criteria and add to an existing law. Initially, administrative courts used to distinguish between interpretative and regulatory circulars. The latter, which aim at establishing new legal rules that can be opposed to citizens, could be reviewed on grounds of ultra vires in particular.[101] However, distinguishing interpretative circulars from regulatory ones was not without uncertainties. Since 2002,[102] this distinction has been replaced by a difference between circulars including imperative provisions and circulars without imperative scope. The now relevant criterion is not whether the circular has a mere interpretative purpose or goes beyond interpretation but whether the content of the circular is mandatory. Interpretative circulars can thus be concerned as long as they demand the application of a certain interpretation of an existing law. In that case, circulars can be challenged before administrative courts insofar as they adversely affect citizens.

§2. The Position of Administrative Regulations and Orders in the Normative Hierarchy

119. Due to the diversity of administrative regulations and orders, the question of their position in the hierarchy of norms concerns their relation both to others legal rules and within their own category.

I. The Hierarchical Position of Administrative Regulations and Orders in Relation to Other Legal Norms

120. As part of the administrative action, the regulatory power must respect the principle of legality, a principle which is enforced by administrative courts. This principle goes beyond subjecting regulations to the superiority of laws. In addition, regulatory instruments have to respect the primacy of the Constitution. This is notably relevant as regards the autonomous regulatory power which is not exercised to

101. CE, 29 Jan. 1954, *Institution Notre Dame du Kreisker*, *Rec. Lebon* 64.
102. CE, Sect., 18 Dec. 2002, *Mme Duvignères*, *Rec. Lebon* 463.

implement a law and is therefore directly subject to the primacy of the supreme norm. Regulations are also subject to the superiority of international treaties and EU law via the review of the conventionality of national law. Lastly, regulations must conform to the general principles of law as developed by administrative courts.

II. The Internal Hierarchy of Administrative Regulations and Orders

121. Regulations have also their own internal hierarchy. The most important regulatory instruments – those enacted by the Prime Minister and the President of the Republic – are the decrees. Some decrees are known as decrees in the Council of State whose validity is dependent upon the prior opinion of the Council of State as to their quality and coherence. As for the decrees deliberated within the Council of Ministers, this requirement depends on what is provided for in the Constitution such as, for instance, under the second paragraph of Article 37, or what is provided for under a law or a decree. This procedure can also result from a decision of the government in light of the importance of the decree. Decrees that are not decrees in the Council of Ministers or decrees in the Council of State are referred to as simple decrees. Decrees in the Council of Ministers, decrees in the Council of State and simple decrees form an internal hierarchy. As such, a decree in the Council of Ministers can only be amended by another decree in the Council of Ministers,[103] unless the initial decree or a rule hierarchically superior states otherwise. The same principle applies to decrees in the Council of State, which cannot be amended by simple decrees. Administrative orders, may they be taken by ministers, prefects, mayors or other competent authorities, are inferior to decrees. In addition, ministerial orders prevail over prefectural ones, which are themselves superior to orders taken by mayors.

103. CE, Ass., 10 Sep. 1992, *Meyet*, *Rec. Lebon* 327.

Chapter 7. Codification, Interpretation and Publication

§1. Codification

122. The French legal system is strongly infused with the process of codification of which the Civil Code is the most emblematic manifestation. Yet, codification can refer to different activities. Codification can be associated with the Napoleonic era where the Civil Code was drafted in 1804, quickly followed by the Code of Civil Procedure (1806), the Commercial Code (1807), the Code of Criminal Procedure (1808), and the Criminal Code (1810). This type of codification exceeds the coherent presentation of positive law. The Napoleonic codification took place in the context of the fragmentation of the law over the French territory. The codification had thus a creative and reformative scope. It provided France with a unified, complete and coherent system of rules reflecting the evolutions of the Revolution of 1789.

123. This first wave of codification is different from contemporary codifications. What is known as 'codification of existing law' (*codification à droit constant*) consists of the compilation and consolidation of legal instruments related to the same field of activity. This latter type of codification does not have the same reformative scope. Its purpose is mainly to increase the clarity and accessibility of the law in a very similar manner as the US Restatements of the Law. In contrast with the original codes which are of a legislative nature, codification of existing law encompasses both legislative and regulatory instruments. Procedurally, the codification is effected by administrative commissions. However, as regards the legislative components of these codes, a law must be passed, as a matter of principle, by Parliament for their enactment. However, these codifications are often carried out by means of ordinances under Article 38 of the Constitution. The provision allows the government to intervene in the legislative area and was notably used in 1999 in relation to provisions in the Code of Administrative Justice, the Code of Public Health, the Education Code, the Rural Code, the Commercial Code, the Environmental Code, the Highway Code, the Monetary and Financial Code, and the Code of Social Action and Family.[104]

§2. Interpretation

124. Interpretation is central in constitutional law and its importance varies according to the theory of interpretation one adopts. In a narrow sense, interpretation is required when a provision is ambiguous; a situation that often arises in constitutional law. First, this may be the result of the generality and vagueness of the constitutional provision at issue. Second, constitutional provisions originate from different periods of time and require as, for example, for the 1789 Declaration, to be adapted to contemporary circumstances. Finally, being deprived of an absolute

104. Law No 99-1071 of 16 Dec. 1999 enabling the Government to proceed, by way of ordinances, with the enactment of the legislative part in respect of certain codes.

scope, constitutional provisions are always included in a balancing exercise whereby interpretation prevails. According to a broader understanding, the interpretative process is inherent in the application of law if one considers that the determination of norms and of constitutional norms in particular consists of the decision as to the appropriate meaning among the different potentialities included in legal texts.

125. Their action being dependent on the Constitution, constitutional organs necessarily produce and rely on the interpretation of the Constitution as developed by the Constitutional Council. However, the Council is not the only organ delivering authoritative interpretation, in particular due to its limited competence. Under Article 5 of the Constitution, the President of the Republic, as guardian of the Constitution, is also one of its authentic interpreters. This is notably the case for issues that exceed the competence of the Constitutional Council. One example is the interpretation of Article 13 of the Constitution in relation to the signature of ordinances by the President of the Republic. Furthermore, the Council is not the only judicial instance competent to interpret the Constitution, a function which can also be performed by the Supreme Courts of the ordinary judicial order and of the administrative judicial order. In particular, the Council of State interprets the Constitution when reviewing autonomous regulatory acts, the validity of which directly depends on the respect of the Constitution. The recent introduction of a mechanism of priority preliminary ruling on the issue of constitutionality has expanded the scope of constitutional interpretation in the hands of the Council of State and Court of Cassation, as well as the judicial dialogue they entertain with the Constitutional Council.

§3. Publication

126. The publication of legal instruments is governed under Article 1 of the Civil Code as amended in 2004.[105] Publication is mandatory for laws, ordinances, decrees and a number of administrative acts as determined by law or decree. Hence, the obligation of publication concerns administrative acts of a regulatory nature but it may also apply to individual administrative acts. Publication is made in the Journal Officiel de la République Française (*JO*), both on paper and electronically. By exception, some administrative acts are only published electronically.[106] As regards decentralized local authorities, the publication of their regulatory orders is generally made through means specific to them. In addition to domestic norms, international agreements also have to be published in the *JO*. As for EU law, norms are published in the Official Journal of the European Union (OJ). As provided for by Article 1 of the Civil Code, laws and administrative acts generally come into force

105. Ordinance No 2004-164 of 20 Feb. 2004 on the modalities and effects of the publication of laws and certain administrative acts.

106. Decree No 2004-617 of 29 Jun. 2004 on the modalities and effects of the electronic publication of certain administrative acts in the *JO*.

on the day after publication and, in case of emergency, on the very day of their publication. However, this principle has become the exception. Laws and administrative acts often come into force at a date they specify. Moreover, when a law requires implementing measures, its coming into force is dependent on the coming into force of these measures. Nonetheless, publication remains the necessary condition for the opposability of legal instruments to legal actors.

Selected Further Reading

Pierre Avril, *Des conventions à la révision de la Constitution*, 5 RFDC 49 (2008).

Olivier Beaud, *Les mutations de la Ve République ou comment modifier une Constitution écrite*, 4/99 Pouvoirs 19 (2001).

Jean-Claude Bécane, Michel Couderc and Jean-Louis Hérin, *La loi* (2nd ed., Dalloz 2010).

Denis de Béchillon, *Hiérarchie des normes et hiérarchie des fonctions normatives de l'Etat* (Economica 1996).

John Bell, Sophie Boyron and Simon Whittaker, *Principles of French Law* (2nd ed, Oxford University Press 1998).

Julie Benetti et alii, *Révision de la Constitution: mode d'emploi* (Dalloz 2017).

Jean-Jacques Bienvenu et alii, *La Constitution administrative de la France* (Dalloz 2012).

Jean-Pierre Camby, *La loi* (LGDJ 2015).

René Capitant, *La coutume constitutionnelle*, RDP 959 (1979).

Véronique Champeil-Desplats, *Les principes fondamentaux reconnus par les lois de la République: Principes constitutionnels et justification dans les discours juridiques* (Economica 2001).

Jean-Paul Duprat, 'Le référendum constitutionnel dans le système français dominé par une logique représentative', RIDC 553 (2006).

Louis Favoreu, *L'interprétation de l'article 55 de la Constitution*, RFDA 993 (1989).

Patrick Gaïa, *Le Conseil constitutionnel et l'insertion des engagements internationaux dans l'ordre juridique interne* (Economica 1991).

Bruno Genevois, *Les limites d'ordre juridique à l'intervention du pouvoir constituant*, RFDA 929 (1998).

Bruno Genevois, *Une catégorie de principes de valeur constitutionnelle: les principes fondamentaux reconnus par les lois de la République*, RFDA 477 (1998).

Stefan Goltzberg, *Les sources du droit* (2nd ed., PUF 2018).

Matthias Gyyomar, *Les 25 ans de la relance de la codification* (LGDJ 2017).

Arnaud Haquet, *La loi et le règlement* (LGDJ 2007).

Jean-Paul Jacqué, *Droit constitutionnel et institutions politiques* (11th ed., Mémentos Dalloz 2016).

Philippe Jestaz, *Les sources du droit* (2nd ed., Dalloz 2015).

Marie-Aimée Latournerie, *Les collectivités territoriales de la République dans la Constitution: Quel retour sur le dernier siècle pour quelles orientations?*, RDP 895 (2017).

La loi, Pouvoirs No 114 (2005/3).

Selected Further Reading

Anne-Marie Le Pourhiet, *Les ordonnances. La confusion des pouvoirs en droit public français* (LGDJ 2011).
Bertrand Mathieu, *La loi* (3rd ed., Dalloz 2010).
Bertrand Mathieu, *La part de la loi, la part du règlement*, No 114 Pouvoirs 73 (2005/3).
Marie-Luce Pâris-Dobozy, 'Still Alive? Some Observations about the Two-Hundred Years of Existence of the French Code Civil of 1804', 12 *Irish Journal of European Law* 72 (2005).
Benoît Plessix, *Droit administratif général* (2nd ed., LGDJ 2018).
Jean Rivero, *Les principes fondamentaux reconnus par les lois de la République: une nouvelle catégorie constitutionnelle?*, D. 265 (1972).
Michel Verpeaux, *La Constitution* (2nd ed., Dalloz 2016).
Michel Verpeaux (ed.), 'Révision de la Constitution: La Ve République rénovée? A propos de la loi constitutionnelle du 23 juillet 2008', JCP (2008).
Michel Verpeaux, 'Le 'référendum local' et la Constitution', 12 Cahiers de droit constitutionnel 124 (2002).
Michel Verpeaux, *La naissance du pouvoir réglementaire* 1789–1799 (PUF 1991).
Marcel Waline, 'Les rapports entre la loi et le règlement avant et après 1958', RDP 699 (1959).

Part II. Form of Government

127. This Part is concerned with the form of government of the French State. General introductory considerations are provided. After developments on the Head of State, the three branches of power, namely the Legislature, the Executive and the Judiciary are examined. Under the Fifth Republic, the President of the Republic has significant executive powers which will be examined under the corresponding heading rather than under the Head of State section.

Chapter 1. General

128. After some general considerations about the system of government in France, an overview of the development of political parties, lobbies and other interest groups will be examined.

§1. Introduction

129. The system of government in France is a parliamentary representative democracy characterized by a strong Executive. In essence a parliamentary political regime, the French Fifth Republic displays features which set it apart from other typical parliamentary systems of government such as, for example, the British or Irish ones. The aim of the drafters of the Constitution was to establish a parliamentary regime while at the same time seeking to avoid the deformations and perverse effects that had occurred under the previous Republics. Constitutional provisions as well as practice of the regime have contributed to 'hybridize' the nature of the French form of government. Often dubbed a 'mix' or 'hybrid' regime to describe its ambiguous nature, the French regime is also described as 'semi-presidential' pointing in that regard to its main unusual feature which affords strong powers to the President of the Republic.

130. Overall, the Fifth Republic represents a break from previous traditional republican regimes in that it puts an end to the absolute sovereignty of Parliament. It seeks to rationalize Parliament's powers by limiting the power of the law under Article 34 of the Constitution, by giving a more prominent control by the government on the law-making process, and by introducing a limited form of judicial reviewing of legislation. Correlatively, the primacy of the Executive is enhanced via the powers afforded to the government, most notably to the President of the Republic. The significant powers afforded to the President of the Republic, which includes the appointment of the Prime Minister, the right to dissolve Parliament, and the right to initiate a legislative referendum, are unprecedented. They can be explained by the historical and contextual circumstances of the time. These important powers enjoyed by the President of the Republic have led to a so-called presidentialization of the regime which can be explained by two further factors. First, the election, from 1962, of the President of the Republic by direct universal suffrage has given him a popular legitimacy comparable, at least in constitutional terms, to that enjoyed by the National Assembly. Second, the occurrence of the *fait majoritaire* (i.e., the conjunction of a presidential majority with a majority in the National Assembly of the same political hue) has contributed to enhance the power of the President of the Republic whose government appointed by him exercises its powers with the support of a strong parliamentary majority. The *fait majoritaire* embodies the normal functioning of the regime. However, it can be derailed by a '*cohabitation*' which occurs when the presidential majority is of a different political orientation than the majority in the National Assembly. This has happened three times so far: in 1986–1988, a cohabitation between Mitterrand (left-wing President) and Chirac (right-wing Prime Minister); in 1993–1995, a cohabitation between Mitterrand (left-wing President) and Balladur (right-wing Prime Minister); and in 1997–2002, a cohabitation between Chirac (right-wing President) and Jospin (left-wing Prime Minister). The holding of the presidential elections just a few weeks before the general elections which correspond to a rapprochement of the duration of the presidential mandate and legislature's term – a five-year term for both – has greatly contributed to reduce the risk of such discrepancy in the majorities, presidential and Legislative.[107]

§2. Political Parties, Lobbies and Interest Groups

131. The following developments define political parties as well as other forms of influencers (i.e., lobbies and interest groups) and give an overview of their emergence in France. The state of the main current political parties is also examined.

I. Definition and Historical Context

132. The development of political parties is largely the corollary of the democratization of the right of suffrage. Political parties may be described as organized groups of citizens who rally around a common ideology, defend the interest of these citizens as well as provide the financial and logistical means to the candidates representing these groups at the various elections. The ultimate goal of political parties is to conquer and exercise public power. Political parties have thus two main functions: one function is to serve as a go-between the people and the public power; another function is to direct the policy of the Nation once they are in power. Political parties are distinct from pressure groups and lobbies which only seek to influence public power by using various direct and indirect means. These pressure groups which lobby political parties have become more important and can be found in various forms such as trade unions, associations of employers, financial institutions, industrial, professional or social organizations, religious associations, and so on. These groups have often been criticized because of the more or less respectable goal they pursue or means they use. This has to be nuanced though. In terms of their goals, a distinction should be made between those groups which goal is akin to the general interest (e.g., environment, public health, underprivileged minorities) from those which private or sectoral objectives may conflict with the general interest (e.g., financial groups aiming for profit, or the tobacco industry) – the latter groups should be the object of a strict vigilance from public authorities. In terms of methods, a distinction has also to be made between those groups which take action in the open and serve transparency from those which act in the shadow – the latter often coinciding with groups defending self-serving private interests. In any case, it shows that these groups are heavily politicized in their composition and action.

107. *See* below Chapter 2. Head of State, §1. Election and Mandate, II. Mandate of the President of the Republic.

133. Political parties are of different types and the famous distinction proposed by Maurice Duverger is between 'cadre political parties' (*partis de cadre*) and mass political parties' (*partis de masse*).[108] The first type refers to elite-based parties which emerged thanks, in the first place, to the influence of their representatives at local or national level. They were regarded as the direct successors of nineteenth-century parties composed of bourgeois or *notables*. These parties were traditionally not very structured nor centralized as they were of a relatively modest size, depending on a leader in Parliament and on generous funding from sponsors to pursue concrete political actions. Parties of the second type refer to mass-based parties which emerged at the start of the last century with the socialist and then communist ideology – the Communist Party established in 1920 being the first of this type. Their development was very much linked to the development of universal suffrage when popular masses could exercise their right to vote. However, since these voters could not provide as much funding as the well-established benefactors of elite-based parties, the objective was to gain as many adherents as possible. These parties favoured dissemination of people's ideas and values. As the end objective was to transform society towards more equality for popular masses, these parties required a rigorously structured and hierarchical organization in order to channel ideas and win elections which often implied instructing voters on how to vote.

134. The above distinction has lost most of its relevance today, including in France. The political landscape has witnessed the emergence of a new generation of political parties which main aim has been to bring together adherents around common shared values rather than strictly dividing ideological party lines. This has resulted in a refocus of French political life around centrist political parties. The UNR (or *Union pour la Nouvelle République*), established in 1958 and aimed at supporting De Gaulle, is one example of this new generation of parties. The domestic political landscape has been marked by two main political parties, namely the Republicans (*Les Républicains* or LR) and the Socialist Party (*Parti Socialiste*). This quasi-bipartism is relatively recent since other political formations used to gravitate around the two main political forces: to the LR, successors of Gaullists, were also associated the centre-right party of the UDF (or *Union pour la Démocratie Française*) which has today been absorbed by the LR; the Communists (*Parti Communiste Français* or PCF) would be associated, at some stage, in government with the Socialist Party before being progressively weakened since the early 1980s. The 2017 election of President Emmanuel Macron, with the support of his own movement *En Marche!*, has further changed the political landscape. The recent emergence, in July 2016, of *En Marche!*, as a grass root movement, has certainly captured most of the political momentum which galvanized the French electorate during the last presidential elections, resulting in the weakening of the traditional left and right political parties, including its extreme representations. Since then *En Marche!* has transformed itself into the main political party in power under the name of LREM or *Les Républicains En Marche*.

108. Maurice Duverger, *Les partis politiques* (Collection Points 1981, A. Colin 1951).

135. The Constitution expressly acknowledges the existence and role of political parties. Under French constitutional law, political parties and groups 'contribute to the expression of suffrage. They shall be formed and exercise their activity freely. They shall respect the principles of national sovereignty and democracy' (Article 4 Constitution). The original provision therefore emphasized as much the freedom of establishment of political parties derived from the freedom of association recognized under French law as the limitations to such freedom should one party infringes basic constitutional principles. No political party has ever been prohibited on this ground under the Fifth Republic though. The 2008 constitutional amendment added two paragraphs to Article 4 on, respectively, the principle of gender equality – which political parties contribute to promote in public life – and the principle of pluralism – which receives its expression through the equitable participation of political parties and groups to the democratic life of the Nation. For a long time, political parties in France have enjoyed a large freedom as regards their creation under the general text of Law of 1 July 1901 on Associations (the 1901 Law). However, during the last three decades, the legislative framework has tightened up as regards the requirements for more transparency in their financial activities and sources of funding. This is due to a series of scandals about illicit and covert financing by a number of political formations in the 1980s. A set of laws was adopted aimed at, first, regulating the funding of political parties,[109] second, capping the amount of electoral expenses,[110] and third, controlling the financial situation of elected representatives. While regulations have been put in place since the late 1980s regarding the last issue, these have not prevented further scandals especially those involving conflicts of interests. Another set of laws was adopted in 2013 to establish a new High Authority for Transparency in Public Life (*Haute Autorité pour la Transparence de la Vie Publique* or HATVP) to which a number of those in elected political or administrative offices must provide a statement listing their assets at the start and end of their mandate as well as a statement of their financial

109. Law No 88-227 of 11 Mar. 1988 on the financial transparency of political life, as amended by Law No 90-55 of 15 Jan. 1990 on the limitation of election expenses and the clarification of the financing of political activities, provides for regulations concerning the public and private funding of political parties. Public funding comes directly from the State with a first fraction awarded to all political parties under certain conditions and proportional to the number of votes obtained in the legislative elections, and a second fraction limited to the political parties represented in the National Assembly and proportional to the number of elected representatives. The second type of funding is sourced from private donors which donations are strictly controlled with a prohibition, for example, of donations by foreign States.

110. Law No 62-1292 of 6 Nov. 1962 on the election of the President of the Republic by universal suffrage, as amended by Organic Law No 2012-272 of 28 Feb. 2012 on the reimbursement of campaign expenses of the presidential election. The 1962 Law, as amended, provides that candidates to the presidential election must appoint a special association or agent to manage their expenses as well as hold a financial account of them. For the 2017 presidential election, the expenses were capped at EUR 16,851,000 in the first round, and at EUR 22,509,000 in the second round. For all other elections, the requirements are quite similar as provided in the 1990 Law (*See* above) as completed by Law No 93-122 of 29 Jan. 1993 on the prevention of corruption and the transparency of economic life and public procedures.

interests.[111] The range of personnel subject to these obligations is quite wide: members of the government; MPs and Member(s) of the European Parliament (MEPs); major executives elected at local level; members of quangos (or independent administrative authorities); collaborators in ministerial departments and in the President's Office; the official employees of the government appointed in the Council of Ministers; the executives of the main State-owned companies. A new set of laws was adopted in 2016 and 2017 which overall aim is the 'moralization of public life' and includes, among other measures,[112] more regulation of the financing of political parties and election campaigns.[113] However, the submission of political parties to a special regime of financial supervision is necessarily limited by the respect due to their 'constitutionally guaranteed freedom'.[114] Although political *parties* represent only one means of contributing towards the suffrage, they have progressively acquired a central role in the most important national elections. As regards the presidential elections for example, the legislation on sponsorship (or *parrainage*), which requires a candidate to obtain a certain number of supporters, makes it difficult, almost impossible, for any given candidate to stand for election as an independent without the support – ideological, financial and logistical – of a political formation. In the words of Maurice Duverger: 'The choice of candidates to stand for the presidential elections is as important as the choice between these candidates. This is the reason why no presidential election has ever been won in a developed nation by a candidate running as an independent.'[115] The same is true for referendums. Despite aimed at bypassing partisan lines in giving the vote directly to the people, political parties very much contribute to shaping popular expression since the French legislation grants them the exclusive right to take part in the official referendum campaigns in proportion to their representativity on the national scene.[116]

136. The existence of political parliamentary *groups* has been recognized in the Constitution since the 2008 constitutional amendment. Political groups are regarded as expressing the different political ideas of parties and formations within the National Assembly and allow the deputies to form groups according to their affinities. Rules relating to the establishment and organization of these parliamentary

111. Organic Law No 2013-906 of 11 Oct. 2013, as complemented by Law No 2013-907 of 11 Oct. 2013, on transparency of public life.
112. The other measures concern the exemplary character and probity of elected officials, the prevention of conflicts of interest, and, generally, transparency of political life.
113. Organic Law No 2016-506 of 25 Apr. 2016 on the modernization of the rules applicable to the presidential election and Law No 2016-508 of 25 Apr. 2016 on the modernization of various provisions applicable to the elections; Law No 2017-286 of 6 Mar. 2017 aimed at reinforcing the accounting obligations of the political parties and the candidates; Law No 2017-1339 of 15 Sep. 2017 for trust in political life.
114. CE, Sect., 9 Jun. 2010, *Association CAP SUR L'AVENIR 13*, No 327423.
115. Maurice Duverger, *La monarchie républicaine, ou comment les démocraties se donnent des rois* (Robert Laffont 1974) 54–55.
116. CE, Ass., 1 Sep. 2000, *Larrouturou, Meyet et autres*, *Rec. Lebon* 365; CC Decision No 2000-23 REF of 23 Aug. 2000, *Larrouturou*, *Rec.* 137, and CC Decision No 2000-24 REF of 23 Aug. 2000, *Hauchemaille*, *Rec.* 134.

groups are, however, different from those of applicable to political parties. The number of seats these groups hold in Parliament will determine their level of representation within the Bureau of the National Assembly and in standing committees, as well as their allotted speaking time in public sessions. The presidents of political groups enjoy special prerogatives as regards the law-making process, in order to protect the rights of the opposition in particular. Specific rights are guaranteed for the groups in the opposition and minority groups (Article 51-1 Constitution). In order to form a group, the opposition only needs to make a formal declaration to be handed, by its president, to the president of the National Assembly. A minority group is simply declared in existence as one which has not made such declaration.

137. In addition to pressure groups and lobbies, the competition between political parties also uses the medium of broadcasting. The primary role which is played in today's society by the radio and television, and now the Internet, has given rise to issues surrounding the status and control of the media. In a pluralist regime, the principle dictates that media should impart information without any political bias and give equal and fair access to the media to all political parties. As for the broadcasting regime, it can either be based on the principle of freedom or be based on a public monopoly. The first model is used in the USA whereby any private actor may broadcast provided they have obtained a license to do so from the president of a special commission which reviews essentially a number of technical requirements. The second model is the one practiced in several countries in Western Europe, including France. Since the end of the 1980s, the trend has been towards a privatization of part of the broadcasting network with, for example, one or two televisions channels remaining under the control of the State while others enjoy different levels of licensing from public authorities rendering this system of 'controlled liberalism'[117] a bit more complex. The overall principle remains that the principle of pluralism of opinions shall be respected as well as the equal and fair access of political parties to broadcast. In France, Law of 30 September 1986 on freedom of communication (the 1986 Law)[118] established the principles of freedom and pluralism in audiovisual communication.[119] The Higher Audiovisual Council (*Conseil Supérieur de l'Audiovisuel* or CSA) is the regulatory body entrusted by law to enforce the rules to be respected by the audiovisual media in the field of pluralism which revolves around the notion of 'speaking time' during electoral periods and in a non-electoral context.[120] Outside of electoral periods, a specific system is set up to record and track the speaking and broadcasting times of politicians hereby consecrating a quantitative approach to political pluralism.[121] By law, the speaking time of politicians on television and radio services recorded by the CSA is monthly communicated to

117. Ferdinand Mélin-Soucramanien and Pierre Pactet, *Droit constitutionnel* (33rd ed, Sirey 2014) 127.

118. Law No 86-1067 of 30 Sep. 1986 on freedom of communication. *See also* CC Decision No 86-217 DC of 18 Sep. 1986, Loi relative à la libert*é de communication*, *Rec.* 141.

119. For example, political advertising is prohibited on radio and television (Art.14 of the 1986 Law).

120. This pluralism has been defined as 'internal' meaning that the balance between views and opinions has to be respected by each television channel or radio station.

121. The speaking time of the President of the Republic is not traditionally being counted as part of the speaking time of the political party to which s/he belongs. However, this must be nuanced. Since

the presidents of both Houses of Parliament and to the leaders of the political parties represented in Parliament, as well as published on the CSA's website. In that framework, the CSA checks the respect of the so-called principle of reference. This principle is based on the ternary rule of respecting a balance of intervention time between, first, those representatives of political parties in government, second, those in the majority, and third, those in the opposition. Since a 2000 reform, politicians of political parties not represented in Parliament also benefit from an equitable time in audiovisual programming and broadcasting. In electoral periods, the CSA sets the rules concerning the conditions of production, programming and broadcasting of programmes relating to election campaigns that public radio and television stations are required to produce and broadcast. It does even intervene before the opening of the official campaign to specify the conditions of respect of pluralism that may vary depending on the type of election. It addresses, for the duration of the electoral campaigns, recommendations to the radios and the televisions, as well as to the local services of the cable, in order to fix the rules concerning the access of the candidates to the audiovisual media. For each election, the CSA applies its general recommendation of 2011 on the principle of political pluralism in radio and television services during an election period,[122] as well as a particular recommendation setting the list of the audiovisual services to be controlled. The guiding principles are those of quantitative control of airtime and speaking time of the candidate and his/her supporters, and qualitative control as regard the respect of a number of ethical principles and the obligation for broadcasters to act with moderation and honesty. Also, the respect of equity between candidates is part and parcel of pluralism.[123] If the CSA finds an obvious imbalance, it can ask the channel, including by a written notification, to restore the balance between candidates, lists or political parties.

138. The print media also exerts a considerable influence on public opinion which can only be meaningful within the context of a pluralist regime which favours a healthy and unbiased competition between the different political parties. There is always the danger though that this freedom be reduced by the dependence, because of its cost, of print media towards private benefactors or publicity providers. Also, this kind of press, with the exception of larger groups which operate their own correspondents' network, is heavily dependent on news agencies which are themselves controlled either by private actors or by the government. This danger is exacerbated by the general decline of the political press to the advantage of news media. In several countries, including France, the former holds a relatively strong presence

---

2009, while the constitutional status of the Head of State imposes the non allocation of his/her spoken words to a particular political party, these can nevertheless be taken into account in the evaluation of the respect of pluralism in a non-electoral context, to the exclusion of when the President of the Republic expresses himself/herself as the Head of State.

122. Recommendation No 2011-1 of 4 Jan. 2011 on the principle of political pluralism in radio and television services during an election period (*JO* 1 Feb. 2011) as amended.

123. Again the rules regarding the presidential election are a bit different. While the principle of *equity* of airtime and speaking time prevails before the publication of the list of candidates running in the first round, the rule of *equality* takes over from the moment of that publication *See* below Chapter 2. Head of State, §1. Election and Mandate, I. Election of the President of the Republic, B. Electoral Rules, 2. The Electoral Campaign.

despite a decreasing influence on public opinion. There is also a trend towards a concentration of media outlets with a decrease in the number of major daily newspapers thus reinforcing the influence of large companies over the formation of public opinion. Under French law, the freedom of the press is protected by Law of 29 July 1881, as amended by Law of 1 August 1986 on The Reform of the Legal Regime of the Press Media[124] and Law of 4 January 2010 which guarantees The Confidentiality of Journalists' Sources.[125]

II. Current Political Parties in France

139. French political parties have traditionally been organized around a right-left wing division. The same political majority (of the right) was in power for a long period of time – twenty-three years without any interruption between 1958 and 1981 – under the Presidencies of De Gaulle, Pompidou and Giscard D'Estaing. This changed with the election of Mitterrand of the Socialist Party in 1981 which opened the way to a political *alternance*. The last four decades have been marked by the multiplication of political formations and parties, not all in power or represented in Parliament, but voicing various specific and, often local, concerns of the French people. Also, the long-enduring right-left division has been lately disturbed by the election, in May 2017, of the so-called centrist Macron to the office of President of the Republic. The current main French political parties, which represent the most representative current of ideas, are the right-wing parties, the extreme right-wing parties, the left-wing parties and the extreme left-wing parties. The developments below will present the three major political formations which, at some stage, have managed to send one of their representatives to the highest office since the start of the Fifth Republic.

140. The Republicans (*Les Républicains* or LR) are the main right-wing political party in France. LR was founded in 2002, under the former name of Union for a Popular Movement (*Union pour un Mouvement Populaire* or UMP) itself founded under the leadership of Chirac, by the merger of the two political parties *Rassemblement pour la République* (RPR, Gaullist) and the Liberal Democracy (DL, liberal). The Republicans are a conservative political party, member of the European People's Party like the German CDU and the Spanish People's Party. The Republicans are the party of the former President of the Republic Sarkozy and, since the legislative elections of June 2012, the first opposition party. It endured a severe setback after the 2017 presidential elections with the emergence of the political movement *En Marche!* and the defeat of the LR candidate Fillon, favourite candidate after the primary right-wing elections. The Socialist Party (*Parti Socialiste* or PS) is the main left-wing political party which has existed under this name since 1969. It was created by the merger of the French Section of the Workers' International (*Section Française de l'Internationale Ouvrière* or SFIO), the Union of Socialist Groups and Clubs (*Union des Groupes et Clubs Socialistes* or UGCS) and the Union of the

124. Law No 86-897 of 1 Aug. 1986 on the reform of the legal regime of the press.
125. Law No 2010-1 of 4 Jan. 2010 on the protection of journalists' sources.

Clubs for the Renewal of the Left (*Union des Clubs pour le Renouveau de la Gauche* or UCRG). The PS is a traditional social democratic political party, a member of the Party of European Socialists like most of the social democratic parties of the European continent. The Socialist Party had not held the presidency of the Republic for almost twenty years since the end of the mandate of Mitterrand in 1995, nor the post of prime minister since the fall of the government of Lionel Jospin in 2002. In 2012, the victory of Hollande in the presidential election and the arrival of Jean-Marc Ayrault as Prime Minister, have made the French Socialist Party one of the most powerful political parties in Europe. The rapidly declining popularity of the Head of State, as well as the electoral defeats that followed in the 2014 municipal elections and the severe defeat during the 2017 presidential election definitely brought it back in the shadow. Currently in demise, although still in existence, the Socialist Party does not appear as a credible force of the opposition. The last party is the current presidential party of The Republic on the March! (*La République En Marche!* or LREM). Under the current regime, the President of the Republic has usually been elected from one of the two major political parties: either coming from the Socialist Party or coming from the Republicans. These two political forces have also usually obtained a majority in the National Assembly. However, breaking from this long-standing state of affairs, the presidential election of 2017 stood out in that, for the first time under the Fifth Republic, the President of the Republic was elected from another new political formation, the so-called centrist political party of LREM created in 2016 by the then candidate Macron. LREM presented candidates to the subsequent legislative elections of June 2017 in alliance with another centrist political party called the Democratic Movement (*Mouvement Démocratique* or MoDem) led by Bayroux. Together, they won three hundred seats – a substantial majority – in the National Assembly at the expense of the Socialist Party, reduced to thirty seats, and the Republicans, reduced to one hundred and twelve seats.

Chapter 2. Head of State

141. The Executive is, pursuant to the Constitution, two-headed as it is vested in the President of the Republic, as Head of State, and the Prime Minister, as Head of Government. Appointed by the President of the Republic, the Prime Minister is, together with his/her government, directly accountable before the National Assembly. The President of the Republic, who is directly elected by the people, is responsible before it. The dualism of the Executive is not a new feature since it was already in place under the Third and Fourth Republics. However, under the Fifth Republic, the question of whether the Head of State or the Head of Government is the real head of the Executive has gained a new relevance given the particular status and range of powers enjoyed by the former. While the text of the Constitution gives a prominent place to the government and the Prime Minister, the practice of the regime has shifted this prominence to the advantage of the President of the Republic whose legitimacy is based on his/her election by direct universal suffrage making him a real 'republican monarch'.[126] This explains why the French political regime appears as one of its kind in comparison with other parliamentary systems. The authority enjoyed by the President of the Republic does not stem only from his/her election by universal suffrage but also from the extensive powers s/he is entrusted with. The Constitution has moved away from the classical model of parliamentary regime of a politically irresponsible Head of State towards a new type of parliamentary regime which grants significant powers to the President of the Republic that allow him/her to fully exercise his/her function as arbiter of public powers.

142. This Chapter briefly sets out the general rules governing the election and mandate, as well as status and accountability of the Head of State. The powers of the President of the Republic will be examined under Chapter 4. on The Executive below.

§1. Election and Mandate

143. Two major reforms changed the mandate of the Head of State: one reform concerned the mode of election, the other concerned the duration of the mandate.

I. Election of the President of the Republic

A. The 1962 Electoral Reform

144. Originally, and due to various legal reasons,[127] the President of the Republic was indirectly elected via an electoral college. This Electoral College was of the

126. *See* Maurice Duverger, *La monarchie républicaine, ou comment les démocraties se donnent des rois* (Robert Laffont 1974).

127. One of these reasons was that the President of the Republic was still, at the time, the President of the so-called 'Community' formed by the former French colonies overseas.

same type as the one electing the Senate and comprised MPs, general councillors, representatives of local councils. De Gaulle believed that the Head of State should have a more solid legitimacy basis with a view to appear as the 'strong man (sic)' in charge. This contention was not strictly self-serving. De Gaulle had also in mind the situation that his successors would face when taking office since he thought they would arguably not benefit from the same historical aura as him. Another concern for De Gaulle was to sever the connections with Parliament. The relationships between De Gaulle and Parliament had greatly deteriorated at the time. This was partly due to the appointment of Pompidou as Prime Minister. The appointment of such an outsider, who was not an MP and had never been elected to a representative mandate, was regarded as an unfortunate choice at the time. Another reason was the hostile stance of De Gaulle towards the European integration project which stirred up the tension in the relationships with loyal members of the majority party in government, namely the Popular Republic Movement (*Mouvement Républicain Populaire* or MRP), and forced some of these members to resign.

145. The constitutional amendment of 6 November 1962, approved by referendum to a large majority of 62.2% of the votes cast, established the election of the President of the Republic by direct universal suffrage on the basis of a single (i.e., voting for one candidate only) majority vote with two rounds. The 1962 amendment has had a considerable institutional and political impact on the balance of powers in French constitutional law. Institutionally speaking, the President of the Republic has, since then, appeared as the central political figure of the State and the actual Head of the Executive, bar periods of cohabitation. While the text of the Constitution emphasizes his/her role as an arbiter and protector of the institutions (Article 5 Constitution) – which necessarily implies some kind of distance from political controversies – the election by direct universal suffrage has had the effect of propelling the Head of State into the realm of day-to-day politics. Politically speaking, the presidential election has become a key moment of in the political life of the Nation bolstered by strategic electoral alliances aimed at creating a winning support for the candidate, often the one of the majority in power. This, in turn, has led to structuring the political landscape around the most powerful political parties into a 'bipolarization' of political life.

B. Electoral Rules

1. Eligibility Rules

146. In order to be eligible to stand for a presidential election, a candidate must be eighteen years of age (twenty-three years of age until 2011), without any prior conviction causing his/her ineligibility and in compliance with his/her military obligations. Given the solemnity of the post, the other significant requirement is the obligation to be sponsored (i.e., system of '*parrainages*') by five hundred elected representatives such as mayors, departmental councillors, regional councillors, and MPs. These representatives must be drawn from at least thirty different departments or overseas territories and without one-tenth being from the same department. The sponsorship system aims at avoiding the multiplication of unserious candidacies. However, it does not make them completely impossible, even concerning a candidate with no representation in Parliament. The system has even arguably been encouraging a degree of manipulation when a candidate, for example, would incite local representatives to sponsor another candidate in order to weaken a third candidate, often a serious opponent. Candidates must provide a statement listing their assets to the Constitutional Council with only the statement of the successfully elected candidate being subsequently disclosed to the public.

2. The Electoral Campaign

147. The presidential electoral campaign lasts a fortnight for each electoral round. The principle of equality of treatment from public authorities applies to all candidates, under the supervision of the National Commission in Charge of Controlling the Electoral Campaign relating to the Election of the President of the Republic (*Commission Nationale de Contrôle de la Campagne Electorale relative à l'Election du Président de la République*).[128] The same equality principle applies concerning the interventions of candidates in the audiovisual media, under the supervision of the Higher Audiovisual Council (*Conseil Supérieur de l'Audiovisuel* or CSA).[129] Some changes were introduced in this regard in 2016 aiming at modernizing the rules applicable to presidential election.[130] While still based on the principle of political pluralism, the principle of *equity* now replaces the principle of *equality* in terms of airtime and speaking time during the period which lasts from the publication of the list of candidates until the eve of the official fifteen-day campaign. It means that only the last two weeks before the election are still subject to the rule of equal airtime and speaking time in radio and television media.

148. As regards the funding of the presidential electoral campaign, each candidate is liable to provide a campaign account which must extend to accounts held in the twelve months before the vote. The Constitutional Council receives and reviews this account. In 2017, electoral expenditures were limited to EUR 16,851,000 for each of the candidates present in the first round and to EUR 22,509,000 for each of the candidates present in the second round, with the possibility of updating these limits according to the Consumer Price Index. As for other elections, donations made by a natural person to finance the campaign of one or more candidates in the

128. Article 13 of Decree No 2001-213 of 8 Mar. 2001 implementing Law No 62-1292 of 6 Nov. 1962 on the election of the President of the Republic by universal suffrage.
129. *See* above Chapter 1. General, §2. Political Parties, Lobbies and Interest Groups, I. Definitions and Historical Context.
130. Organic Law No 2016-506 of 25 Apr. 2016, as complemented by Law No 2016-508 of 25 Apr. 2016, on the modernization of the rules applicable to the presidential election. *See also* the specific recommendations adopted by the CSA for the 2017 presidential elections in its recommendation 2016-2 of 7 Sep. 2016 in relation to radio and television services in the presidential election which supplements the general rules previously laid down.

same elections may not exceed EUR 4,600. Legal persons, with the exception of political parties or groups, may not participate in the financing of a candidate's election campaign.

3. The Election

149. The presidential election takes place in two rounds. To be elected in the first round, a candidate must obtain an absolute majority of the votes cast. The second round is only between the two candidates who have obtained the highest number of votes in the first round. This is in order to ensure that the successful candidate obtains a consistent and solid majority at the end of the final round. The results of the presidential election are proclaimed by the Constitutional Council which is also in charge of judicial review relating to the same. The election can be disrupted by a number of occurrences such as the death of one of the candidates or other event preventing a candidate from participating in one of the election rounds. Constitutional provisions lay down the rules concerning such incidents, whether these occur before the deadline for declaring one's candidacy, or in between this deadline and the first round, or in between the two rounds (Article 7 Constitution).

II. Mandate of the President of the Republic

A. *The Presidential Term*

150. Originally, the President of the Republic was elected for a seven-year term, as this was the case under the previous Republics when the President of the Republic had a rather neutral role. There was a clear distinction between the 'short term' (i.e., five years) relevant to the day-to-day governmental and parliamentary running of the country, and the 'long term' (i.e., seven years) 'necessary to a certain kind of vision and reflection on the evolution of the world' which was more germane to the role of the President.[131] This changed with the Law of 2 October 2000, adopted by referendum,[132] which instituted the five-year term to coincide with the term of deputies elected in the National Assembly for the same five-year duration.[133] One of the reasons for the reform – which had long been discussed before it actually occurred – was to avoid as much as possible episodes of *cohabitation*. Such periods occur when a President of the Republic of a political majority would 'co-govern' with a Prime Minister of a different political majority in Parliament. This 'abnormal' situation is caused when different majorities result from the election of the President of the Republic, on the one hand, and the election of the Members of the National

131. Declaration by President Chirac on 14 Jul. 1997.
132. Constitutional Law No 2000-964 of 2 Oct. 2000 on the term of office of the President of the Republic. The referendum was adopted at a large majority of 73.21% albeit with a strong abstention of nearly 70%.
133. The 2008 constitutional amendment limited to two consecutive terms in office the number of terms that the President of the Republic can seek re-election for.

Assembly, on the other hand, mainly due to the discordance in time between the presidential election and the parliamentary election, but can also be due to the possibility of a dissolution of the National Assembly during the presidential term. While the former factor has been eradicated with the concomitance of the presidential and parliamentary terms, a period of cohabitation can still occur in case of a dissolution of the National Assembly, or in case of an unanticipated end of the presidential mandate (e.g., death, impeachment, resignation).

B. Interruption of the Presidential Term

151. The presidential mandate can be interrupted before the end of the five-year term in case of a vacancy caused by death, resignation or removal from office, all of these occurrences being declared by the Constitutional Council. Contrary to the situation of vacancy, other circumstances can prevent the President of the Republic from exercising his/her powers, such impediment being whether definitive or temporary. In the case of such events, the role of the Head of State is filled in by the President of the Senate acting as the interim President of the Republic. The interim President can exercise all powers normally exercised by the President of the Republic including the powers under Article 16 of the Constitution. However, s/he cannot exercise other significant powers such as deciding to hold a referendum or to dissolve the National Assembly; also, the Constitution cannot be revised during the interim presidency. Less serious than the interim is the situation of a short replacement of the President of the Republic (who can be sick, or on a visit abroad, for example) and allows the Prime Minister to deputize for the Head of State at a Council of Ministers on a given agenda. A period of interim has happened on two occasions under the current regime – once on the occasion of the resignation of De Gaulle in 1969, and the other time on the occasion of the untimely passing of Pompidou in 1974. In both cases, the interim was held by Poher, president of the French Senate at the time.

§2. Legal Status

152. The accountability of the Head of State is weak relatively to the significance of his/her powers. The President of the Republic is politically unaccountable and enjoys a temporary inviolability while in office.

I. Political Unaccountability

153. During his/her term of office, the President of the Republic's unaccountability is total, certainly as regards Parliament and also as regards the Nation. The President of the Republic stays in office until the end of his/her term which is when an unfavourable vote against a new term can be perceived as testing the President's accountability. Also, the President of the Republic is not constitutionally obliged to resign from office after a negative referendum (even though this happened when De

Gaulle left office in 1969 after losing the referendum about the regions and the Senate), or even after losing his/her majority in parliamentary elections. The principle of political unaccountability even applies after the President of the Republic has left office. The President of the Republic is not accountable for the acts accomplished in his/her quality of Head of State (Article 67 Constitution). While this is understandable under a regime where a weak Head of State is not endowed with political powers as such, this is less so under the Fifth Republic which affords significant powers to the President of the Republic. This is somehow mitigated by the possibility to remove the Head of State from office in case of serious breach of presidential duties which is manifestly incompatible with the exercise of the President's functions (Article 68 Constitution). However, it is not clear which kind of responsibility this procedure – which has never been applied so far – refers to, whether it is of a strictly political nature or of a criminal nature. The field of application of Article 68 would be, in any case, limited to the most extreme cases of treason qualified as such by MPs sitting as a High Court (*Haute Cour*) and presided over by the president of the National Assembly.[134] In terms of procedure, the High Court has one month to decide by a two-thirds vote of its members on the removal of the President of the Republic from office. The vote is personal and secret. Proxy voting is not permitted in that situation. The procedure is similar to that of the impeachment procedure of the President of the USA.

II. Temporary Inviolability

154. The President of the Republic is no ordinary citizen and, as such, should be exempt from undue pressure while in office. S/he cannot be the object of any judicial proceedings, whether criminal, civil or administrative during his/her term (Article 67 Constitution). This inviolability is temporary and ends one month after leaving office when proceedings can be brought against him/her, or be resumed, in a court of law. This temporary irresponsibility has been criticized by some who have invoked the situation, however largely theoretical, of a President committing a murder and facing no prosecution. It is likely though that, in such a case, Parliament will initiate the procedure under Article 68. There are two exceptions to the principle of irresponsibility of the President of the Republic, namely the possibility of bringing proceedings before the International Criminal Court of Justice for serious crimes such as genocide, war crimes and crimes against humanity (Article 53-2 Constitution), on the one hand, and the possibility of removal from office under the 'impeachment procedure' (Article 68 Constitution), on the other hand.

134. *See* below Chapter 5. The Judiciary, §1. Organization of the Judiciary, I. General Introduction, D. Other Courts, 2. The High Court.

§3. PRESIDENTIAL FUNCTION AND OFFICE

155. The following developments are about the dignity of the presidential function and the President's Office, and provide a list of the successive Presidents of the Fifth Republic.

I. The Dignity of the Presidential Function

156. The President of the Republic is the first public figure and, as such, is awarded the highest civil and military honours at official ceremonies. An offence to the person of the President of the Republic allows punishing any person responsible for verbal abuse against him/her unless criminal proceedings have already been brought for the same facts. The existence of this particular offence, for the exclusive benefit of the Head of State, has often been criticized as being no longer justified in a modern State. Also, under legal provisions of dubious origin (i.e., a text signed by the Prime Minister in 1985), former Heads of State benefit from significant advantages after leaving office such as an official car, rent-free accommodation and services, as well as special police protection. They also receive a salary as life member of the Constitutional Council.

II. The President's Office

157. The President of the Republic may appoint a number of advisers, such as *chargés de mission* or collaborators with specific responsibilities, who are responsible for their work to the General Secretary of the *Élysée* (i.e., location of the presidency) and the Chief of Staff in the President's Office. Military staff works in the President's Office for liaison purposes with the armed forces.

III. Presidents of the Fifth Republic

158. Below is a list of the Presidents of the Fifth Republic.
Charles De Gaulle (1959–1969)
Georges Pompidou (1969–1974)
Valéry Giscard D'Estaing (1974–1981)
François Mitterrand (1981–1995)
Jacques Chirac (1995–2007)
Nicolas Sarkozy (2007–2012)
François Hollande (2012–2017)
Emmanuel Macron (2017–present)

Chapter 3. The Legislature

159. The legislative power is exercised by a bicameral Parliament made up of the National Assembly and the Senate. While members of the former (i.e., deputies) are elected by direct universal suffrage as representatives of the French people, members of the latter (i.e., senators) are elected by indirect universal suffrage and represent the local authorities of the Republic. The bicameral Parliament is unequal in the sense that the National Assembly has more power than the Senate as is, for example, the case concerning the accountability of the government that can be challenged by only the National Assembly.

160. Under the Fifth Republic, the role of Parliament was considerably weakened in an attempt to depart from the situation under the previous Republics characterized by much governmental instability due to a too powerful legislature. This 'rationalization' of the parliamentary system has resulted in a shift of the centre of gravity of the decision-making power from the legislative power towards the executive power. Parliament now appears like a 'rubber-stamping Chamber' of the action of the government as indeed only a minority of laws is generally initiated by MPs. Most of the French legislation originates in government bills. Also, the constitution of political majorities within the National Assembly in full support of the government has meant that the power of deputies to control the action of the Executive has lost most of its relevance. Finally, Parliament is not in full control of important national choices since these are often influenced by European norms and policies. However, the 2008 constitutional amendment represents a shift in the other direction. With that reform the role of Parliament has been reassessed in many respects. In a parliamentary system based on a strong political majority, stemming from directly elected deputies as well as a directly elected Head of State, there is no reason to put so much constraint on Parliament; successive political majorities will benefit from the alignment of legitimacies (i.e., that of the President of the Republic and that of the National Assembly) to be able to govern to the fullest. The only caveat is that the Prime Minister, whose position was more prominent before 2008, now finds himself/herself more compelled to cooperate with his/her majority in Parliament. In a nutshell, the steady decline of the influence of the French Parliament over national policy has resulted in a redefinition of its role.

§1. The Organ of State

161. The French Parliament consists of deputies (i.e., members of the National Assembly) and senators (i.e., members of the Senate) who are elected according to different rules but have the same status. The electoral regime of the two Houses of Parliament is determined by law. There have been calls to constitutionalize the rules governing elections in Parliament so that these rules do not depend on the majority in power. However, the idea has not been taken up so far. Generally, the electoral regime concerning Parliament has not changed much since the start of the Fifth Republic, except from a few changes concerning the National Assembly under the first mandate of Mitterrand (1981–1988). To be eligible to stand for election in Parliament, a citizen must be over eighteen years of age as regards elections in the National Assembly, and over twenty-four years of age as regards elections in the Senate. In addition, one must enjoy all of his/her civil and political rights, as well as not have been deprived of his/her rights or being incapacitated or ineligible in law.

I. Members of the National Assembly

162. The five hundred and seventy-seven deputies of the French National Assembly[135] are elected for five years from within a department constituency. The boundaries of electoral constituencies must be reviewed at regular intervals in order to take into account demographic changes. Since the 2008 constitutional amendment, a public opinion is sought from an independent commission as regards any change in constituency boundaries and the correlative distribution of seats within the National Assembly.[136] Deputies are elected by direct universal suffrage in a two-round single majority voting system. To be elected in the first round, a candidate must obtain an absolute majority of the votes cast and represent at least 25% (i.e., one-fourth) of the registered voters. To stand for election in the second round, a candidate must have obtained at least 12.5% of the votes cast of the registered voters in the first round. The candidate who is eventually elected is the one who obtains the majority of the votes cast.

163. The financing of legislative electoral campaigns is strictly regulated and relates to management rules, fundraising rules as well as rules on expenses and rules on reimbursement thereof.[137] The year before the election and before any fundraising, the candidate must appoint a designated financial agent (i.e., natural person or association).[138] The financial agent is tasked with entering in the specially opened bank account all the funds raised during the campaign, record the candidate's

135. This figure is fixed in the Constitution since the 2008 constitutional amendment (Art. 24 para. three Constitution). In April 2018, the Philippe Government has proposed to reduce the overall number of MPs by 30%, or about one-third, as part of a larger constitutional and institutional reform.

136. The independent commission comprises one member appointed by the President of the Republic, one member appointed by the president of the National Assembly, one member appointed by the president of the Senate, a judge from the Council of State elected by his/her peers, a judge from the Court of Cassation elected by his/her peers, and one member from the national Court of Auditors elected by his/her peers. The commission is chaired by a president appointed by the President of the Republic pursuant to the procedure under Art. 13 of the Constitution. *See* Law No 2009-39 of 13 Jan. 2009 on the commission provided for under Art. 25 of the Constitution and the election of deputies.

137. Organic Law No 2011-410 of 14 Apr. 2011 on the election of deputies and senators. Senatorial elections must comply with the same kind of rules as the legislative elections governing the financing of the election campaigns regarding the appointment of a financial agent, the opening of a campaign account, the control of the accounts by the CNCCFP, and expenditure limits, albeit with a few adaptations.

138. The proxy cannot be the candidate himself/herself and, if the candidate uses an election financing association, s/he cannot be a member of the association thereof. In addition, the candidate can only have one proxy at a time and a proxy can act on behalf on one candidate only.

income (including donations and financing by political parties) and expenditure as well as generally manage all expenses. This campaign account cannot be in deficit. It is forwarded, two months after the election, to the National Commission of Campaign Accounts and Political Financing (*Commission Nationale des Comptes de Campagne et des Financements Politiques* or CNCCFP). The CNCCFP is an independent administrative authority which main role is to control campaign accounts in all – not just legislative – elections and, more broadly, to ensure the respect by political parties and candidates of their accounting and financial obligations. Rules regarding fundraising allow a candidate to raise funds from political parties but, in order to improve transparency and avoid external pressure, explicitly prohibit donations from any other legal persons such as a private company, a foreign State, trade unions or associations and charities. Natural persons may contribute to campaign fundraising by making donations, albeit capped at EUR 4,600 for the entire campaign. Campaign expenditure is limited which was, for the 2017 legislative elections, limited to EUR 38,000 (plus EUR 0.15 per inhabitant of the constituency). This limit is updated each year according to the cost-of-living index.[139] If this limit is exceeded, the campaign accounts may be subject to rejection by the CNCCFP which leads to the non-reimbursement of electoral expenses as well as, as the case may be, to the ineligibility of the candidate for the next three years. Under certain conditions, the State will reimburse electoral expenses: the candidate must have obtained at least 5% of the votes cast; these expenses must be electoral expenses (i.e., official leaflets, posters on electoral signs and bulletins); the candidate's campaign account must have been approved by the CNCCFP. The reimbursement amount is decided by the CNCCFP within the limit of 47.5% of the limit set for each constituency.

164. The electoral system of the National Assembly has resulted in stable majorities and has contributed to the bipolarization of political life. Small political formations have pushed for some degree of proportional voting in the legislative elections that would ensure a better representation of the diversity of political affiliations and hence the citizens. This is especially true as regards the 12.5% rule which has the effect of eliminating modest political parties before the second round. Several attempts have been made over the years to put forward a system combining majority voting with a dose of proportional voting. One such proposal was made in 2012 by the Commission on the Renewal and Ethics in Public Life (*Jospin Commission*)[140] which proposed that a small portion (i.e., fifty-eight out of five hundred

139. The budget legislation for 2012 (Law No 2011-1977 of 28 Dec. 2011 on finances for 2012) has frozen this limit until the balance of public finances has been restored.
140. Decree No 2012-875 of 16 Jul. 2012 on the creation of a commission for the renovation and deontology of public life. *See* Commission de rénovation et de déontologie de la vie publique, *Pour un renouveau démocratique*, November 2012, <http://www.ladocumentationfrancaise.fr/var/storage/rapports-publics/124000596.pdf> (accessed 10 Jun. 2018).

and seventy-seven) of deputies could be elected by a list voting system with proportional representation. The current Philippe Government has made a bit more ambitious proposal by recommending that 15% of deputies should be elected by proportional voting.[141]

II. Members of the Senate

165. The three hundred and forty-eight senators of the French Senate[142] are elected for six years, with partial renewal every three years. The election is by indirect universal suffrage by an electoral college consisting of elected representatives (i.e., senators, deputies, regional councillors, departmental councillors, local councillors). The voting system varies according to the number of senators to be elected in any constituency, namely a majority two-round system except in departments where at least four senators are to be elected where a proportional voting system at the highest average is used. The voting system reflects the intention of the constituent power – unchanged since the Third Republic – to feature local representation in the Upper House of Parliament. This is also the reason why the Senate has been regularly criticized since it favours an overrepresentation of small local constituencies which are traditionally more conservative, as exemplified by an almost non-interrupted domination of a right-wing majority, bar the 2011–2014 period which saw a brief left-wing majority. By reason of its indirect mode of election and its limited powers, the Senate has been the object of recurrent criticisms. The combination of an overrepresentation of rural municipalities with a lengthy mandate has shaped the Senate into a conservative House seemingly out of touch with people's concerns. The following quotes reveals how problematic has been the image carried over by the Senate in the history of the French Republic: 'A senator is a deputy who persists' (Robert de Jouvenel, journalist, 1882–1924); 'The Senate is an assembly of men with fixed ideas fortunately corrected by a high mortality rate' (Edgar Faure, politician, 1908–1988); 'A House [of Parliament] such as the Senate … is an anomaly in contemporary democracies' (Lionel Jospin, former Prime Minister from

141. On only one occasion, in 1986, was the proportional voting system actually used in the general elections. Mitterrand's decision to restore proportional representation for the first time in thirty years raised fears of a return to the parliamentary instability of the Fourth Republic. It was also a cause for political outrage since the opposition accused him of wanting to strengthen the National Front (*Front National* or FN) in order to weaken the Republican Right, which was favourite to win according to the polls. Indeed, proportional representation was the only electoral system which was considered likely to allow the election of FN deputies. This is what eventually happened since the FN was able to form a parliamentary group with thirty-five elected members. This also marked the start of the first cohabitation under the Fifth Republic with the winning right-wing coalition in the majority.

142. This figure is fixed in the Constitution since the 2008 constitutional amendment (Art. 24 para. three Constitution). In April 2018, the Philippe Government has proposed to reduce the overall number of MPs by 30%, or about one-third, as part of a larger constitutional and institutional reform.

1997 to 2002). However, and after being reformed on a number of occasions,[143] the Senate has survived until now as a political counterweight to the National Assembly.

§2. LEGAL STATUS

166. The current legal status of MPs is the result of a long evolution. Several rules have been put in place over the years to protect the independence of MPs against the Executive. The most significant development has been the regime of incompatibilities attached to the parliamentary mandate.

I. Mandate of the MPs

167. The mandate of MPs is representative and collective. The principle of national sovereignty means that their mandate cannot be imperative. MPs do not represent the electorate as such. Rather MPs represent the entire Nation and speak in its name and in its interest. MPs must provide a statement listing their assets at the start, and again at the end, of their mandate, as well as during the mandate in case of changes in their patrimonial situation. The regime of these statements is almost similar to those made by ministers except that MPs' statements are not published but only made available for consultation in the prefectures.

II. Incompatibilities, Immunities and Privileges

168. Ineligibilities may concern the individual (e.g., incapacitated individuals under guardianship) or his/her function (e.g., member of the judiciary). A number of incompatibilities also restrain the possibility to hold a parliamentary mandate. Article 23 of the Constitution provides for the incompatibility between a parliamentary mandate and a governmental post. An MP cannot be at the same time an MEP.

169. A recurrent feature of the French Parliament under the Fifth Republic is the so-called accumulation of mandates that is the possibility for MPs to hold more than one electoral mandate concurrently. This phenomenon is very unique to France where in 2012, for example, four hundred and seventy-six out of five hundred and seventy-seven deputies (82%) and two hundred and sixty-seven out of tree hundred and forty-eight senators (77%) held at least one other elective mandate, mainly at local level as a mayor, president of a Departmental Council or president of a Regional Council. The proportion of MPs holding multiple mandates is much lower

143. The first of these reforms occurred in 1969 when De Gaulle put to referendum a proposal with a view to merge the Senate with the Economic and Social Council into a purely consultative body with no veto power.

on average in the rest of Europe (20%).[144] Several limitations have been put in place to curtail this phenomenon. A set of legislative measures adopted in 2000 resulted in a number of clear and sensible limitations such as the incompatibility between the mandate of deputy and the one of senator, and between the mandate of Member of the French National Assembly and the one of MEP.[145] The principle is that these incompatibilities do not prevent the deputy or senator to stand for election for another mandate than the one s/he currently holds but it does impose on him/her the obligation to choose the mandate s/he wishes to exercise by renouncing to one of his/her mandates.[146] This new stance as regards the prohibition of holding multiple mandates has pervaded other spheres of power. For example, recent governments have de facto established an incompatibility for ministers since they have to renounce their local executive mandate once appointed. Also, a number of political parties (e.g., *Europe Ecologie-Les Verts*, Socialist Party) have adopted internal rules of incompatibilities, depending on the length of the mandate in question and on the nature of the function exercised, which they can impose on their elected members. A set of laws adopted in 2014 further tightened the framework of parliamentary incompatibilities as regards local executive mandates in particular.[147] This was part of an ongoing effort which started under the Sarkozy presidency and was pursued under the Hollande presidency to improve the working and transparency of political institutions.[148] Also, since the MP mandate becomes effectively a full-time activity, this should contribute to raise the profile of the work of Parliament. The general incompatibility between a parliamentary elective mandate and an executive local mandate was decided in March 2017. It came into force at the date of the relevant election for each type of MP that is in July 2017, as regards deputies in the National Assembly, and in October 2017, as regards senators in the Senate, and will come into force in May 2019 as regards MEPs.[149] The prohibition to cumulate mandates does not prevent MPs from holding a non-executive local mandate. Moreover, the possibility for an MP to choose the mandate s/he wishes to keep is discontinued; the new rule is that the MP retains the most recent mandate and renounces de facto

144. *See* Vie Publique, *Cumul des mandats: Une pratique restreinte à compter de 2017*, 25 Apr. 2017, <http://www.vie-publique.fr/actualite/dossier/cumul-mandats-2017/cumul-mandats-pratique-restreinte-compter-2017.html> (accessed 10 Jun. 2018).
145. Organic Law No 2000-294 of 5 Apr. 2000 on incompatibilities between electoral mandates, and Law No 2000-295 of 5 Apr. 2000 on the limitation of multiple electoral mandates and functions and their conditions of exercise.
146. In the case of MEPs and local elected representatives, they have the obligation to renounce the oldest mandate, that is the one they have been holding for the longer time.
147. Organic Law No 2014-125 of 14 Feb. 2014 prohibiting the cumulation of local executive functions with the mandate of deputy or senator, and Law No 2014-126 of 14 Feb. 2014 prohibiting the cumulation of local executive functions with the mandate of representative in the European Parliament.
148. *See* Comité de réflexion et de proposition sur la modernisation et le rééquilibrage des institutions de la Ve République, *Une Ve République plus démocratique*, October 2007, <http://www.ladocumentationfrancaise.fr/var/storage/rapports-publics//074000697.pdf> (accessed 10 Jun. 2018), and the 2012 Report (*See* above note 140).
149. The incompatibility is also between a parliamentary elective mandate and more than one of the following mandates: regional councillor, departmental councillor, member of the Assembly of Corsica, member of the Assembly of the capital city of Paris, local councillor of municipalities of more than 3,500 inhabitants.

of his/her older mandate. These recent measures have been criticized under diverse claims. The first claim has denounced the perverse effect of these incompatibilities which would arguably have the effect of cutting off MPs from their grass roots by making it more difficult for them to fully appreciate their fellow citizens' concerns. According to other claims, these incompatibilities, on the contrary, do not go far enough in prohibiting multiple mandates over time. One suggestion would be to limit to the number of mandates per MP to three consecutive elective mandates which would arguably also encourage access of a new generation of politicians to elective functions at national level. The current Philippe Government has announced this reform in its package of institutional and constitutional reforms, currently (June 2018) under discussion in Parliament, in the form of a prohibition to hold three 'consecutive, identical and full-termed' mandates, except for mayors of small municipalities (i.e., less than 9,000 inhabitants).

170. Except from the incompatibility between the mandate of MP and member of the government, the exercise of the parliamentary mandate is incompatible with the exercise of all functions of a public nature, and a number of non-elective public offices in particular (e.g., member of the Constitutional Council, member of the judiciary, civil servant except in higher education institutions),[150] as well as a number of private professional activities which could lead to conflicts of interest (e.g., chairperson or member of the Board of Directors of public companies, or private companies in receipt of public aid).[151] As regards private activities, MPs must notify the bureau of their respective House the activities they wish to retain and must drop the incompatible activity within fifteen days of being elected. In case of doubt on any incompatibility, the bureau, the MP himself/herself or the Minister for Justice may refer the issue to the Constitutional Council which will decide upon the removal from office unless the MP has already put his/her activities in order.

171. The High Authority for Transparency in Public Life (*Haute Autorité Pour la Transparence de la Vie Publique* or HATVP) is the national 'anti-corruption body'. It was established in 2013 with the objective to improve transparency of public life. It does so by, first, reviewing the statements of assets of the highest-ranking elected and appointed public officials,[152] second, preventing conflicts of interest,[153]

150. There are two exceptions concerning deputies in the National Assembly in this regard: deputies can cumulate their elective mandate with a professorial activity at university, or with the function of religious minister in the territory of Alsace-Lorraine. It is also possible for MPs to be tasked by the government with a clearly defined six-month mission without affecting their mandate.

151. MPs who are lawyers by profession cannot exercise their activity in certain cases where a conflict of interests may arise.

152. French public officials have been subject to the obligation to produce a statement of their assets since 1988. The 2013 legislation on the transparency of public life has considerably broadened the scope of public officials subject to the High Authority's auditing while also strengthening the reporting requirements (*See* Law No 2013-907 of 11 Oct. 2013 on transparency of public life). Since the entry into force of the 2013 legislation, the High Authority has received and reviewed the statements of some 15,000 public officials. Public officials, falling within the scope of the 2013 laws, must disclose a statement of assets and liabilities in which they provide information on their real estate, securities and investments, life insurance, bank accounts and loans. Statements must be submitted to the High Authority on two occasions, namely at the beginning and at the end of their

and third, counselling and training public officials on ethical principles. More broadly, the High Authority aims at promoting transparency in public life by, for example, publishing some of the statements it receives, thus giving citizens and transparency watchdogs the opportunity to share information which they may possess on breaches of probity, and providing protection for whistleblowers. This independent administrative authority may impose criminal sanctions and refer serious cases of maladministration (e.g., corruption, bribery, jobbery and influence peddling, electoral and tax frauds) to the relevant administrative or judicial authorities.[154]

172. Immunities aim at guaranteeing the independence of MPs. They establish a derogatory regime protecting MPs in the exercise of their functions against proceedings which could prevent them to properly exercise their mandate. Two categories of immunities are to be distinguished, namely unaccountability and inviolability. First, Article 26 of the Constitution provides that '[MPs] shall not be subject to any prosecution, investigation, arrest, detention or trial for the opinions or votes expressed by them while in office.' This unaccountability, which is absolute and permanent, exempts MPs from all judicial civil and criminal proceedings by reason of all acts they accomplish during their mandate (e.g., interventions, votes). For example, an MP cannot be prosecuted for defamation, although s/he must still abide by the rules of his/her House. Second, inviolability extends to acts committed outside of the parliamentary function but concerns only acts of criminal nature and is limited to the duration of the mandate. The aim is to avoid that MPs be the object of pressure or other kind of influence undermining his/her action and preventing him/her to seat in Parliament. Deputies or senators can be charged by a judicial authority but cannot be remanded in custody or be the object of any other measure involving deprivation of liberty without the authorization of the bureau of their respective House, except when caught red-handed or on the basis of a previous conviction by a final judgment. The House of Parliament has, however, the possibility to suspend the criminal measures during the parliamentary session. To ensure that MPs can work independently and without financial pressure of any kind, a generous parliamentary allowance is provided. This is also an essential factor in the democratization of the political system which allows every citizen to be able to claim to enter Parliament without relying on personal wealth or other (dubious) financial arrangements. Moreover, the necessary financial autonomy of the MPs, long symbolized by the payment of parliamentary indemnity, has been reinforced alongside the development of the means of the executive power, by various facilities and endowments in individual or collective material means. This trend reflects a growing professionalization of the parliamentary mandate. The parliamentary

---

term. Furthermore, if there is a significant change in the composition of their assets, following a sale, donation, or inheritance, for example, declarants have to notify the High Authority by filing a new statement.

153. The goal here is to supervise and review declarations of interest in order to detect situations in which public or private interests may clash with the proper exercise of a public duty.

154. *See* Law No 2016-1691 of 9 Dec. 2016 on transparency, the fight against corruption and the modernization of economic life, and Organic Law No 2016-1690 of 9 Dec. 2016 on the competence of the Defender of Rights for the guidance and protection of whistleblowers.

allowance is aligned with the average 'off-scale' remuneration of top civil servants in the State, and complemented by a duty allowance which is one-fourth of the remuneration thereof.[155] Deputies also receive a monthly fixed allowance for secretarial expenses[156] and are allowed a credit for the remuneration of their staff.[157] In case this credit is not spent entirely, the available share shall be forfeited to the budget of the National Assembly or may be transferred by the deputy to his/her political group for the staff remuneration of that group.

§3. Powers

173. Under Article 24 of the Constitution, the French Parliament is assigned two essential functions, namely to elaborate the law, on the one hand, and to control the action of the Executive, on the other.

I. Legislative Function

174. The French Parliament has the task to vote on laws of different kinds. The major novelty of the Constitution is the rationalization of Parliament work in two respects. First, the establishment of a distinction between the legislative and regulatory areas has reduced the area of competence of Parliament and, concomitantly, recognized an autonomous power for the government to enact regulations. Second, the government has been granted a number of prerogatives in the law-making process which has made it easier to push forward its bills without too much turbulence until the final vote. The 2008 constitutional amendment has not changed much this state of affairs. Parliament has (re)gained a new prominence in the control over the Executive and in the assessment of public policies in particular. However, the law-making process largely remains in the hands of the government which has still the means to overcome filibustering.

A. *Article 34 of the Constitution on the Law*

175. The Constitution adds a substantive requirement, in addition to the formal one, to determine if a norm is defined as a law (*loi*): not only a law is an Act adopted

155. *See* Ordinance No 58-1210 of 13 Dec. 1958 on the Organic Law on the allowance of MPs. As of February 2017, the monthly gross salary of deputies was EUR 7,209.74. The parliamentary allowance is taxable. It can be cumulated with another allowance attached to a local elective mandate within the limits of a certain amount (at EUR 2,799.90 per month per deputy in 2017).
156. As of February 2017, the monthly amount of this allowance has been EUR 5,840 gross.
157. This credit is calculated in principle for three employees but may, at the discretion of the MP, be paid out to a number of staff ranging from one to five. The MP has the status of employer: s/he recruits, dismisses, fixes the working conditions and the salary of her/his staff. As of February 2017, the monthly amount of the credit was EUR 9,618.

by Parliament but it is also an Act which falls under one of the areas specifically laid down in Article 34 of the Constitution.[158]

1. Definition of the Law

176. Article 34 of the Constitution provides for a substantive definition of the law by enumerating a list of areas of competence entrusted with the legislative power. The sphere of competence of Parliament is therefore clearly distinct from the sphere of competence assigned to the government through its power to adopt regulations under Article 37. While the former is the exception, the latter stands as the rule. The law determines the rules relating to such areas as civil rights and fundamental freedoms; freedom, pluralism and the independence of the media; limitations to citizens' rights and property by reason of national defence; nationality, status and capacity of legal persons, matrimonial regimes; the definition of criminal offences and the penalties applicable to them, criminal procedure, the establishment of new orders in the court system and the status of judges; tax and currency regimes. The law also determines the fundamental principles as regards matters such as the general organization of the national defence; the free administration of local authorities, powers and resources; education; the protection of the environment; property rights; employment law, trade union law and the social security regime. New areas may be added to this list by an organic law.[159]

2. Control of the Area of the Law

177. The Constitution provides for mechanisms aimed at ensuring that the proposed law is relevant to the areas defined under Article 34. There are two facets to the issue. First, the Constitutional Council controls that Parliament does respect the regulatory area and does not act ultra vires in areas which are not of its competence. The government and, since the 2008 constitutional amendment, the president of either House of Parliament, have the possibility to declare that a private members' bill, or an amendment to it, is inadmissible as outside the confines of Article 34 (Article 41 Constitution). The bill in question will be referred to the Constitutional Council for the purpose of determining its legislative or regulatory character in the event of a disagreement between the government and the president of the House concerned. The approach of the constitutional judge has been overall in favour of Parliament, ruling in several cases that the bill under discussion had a regulatory character. Before 2008, Article 41 of the Constitution was rarely invoked by the government. This was not regarded as a particularly strategic move since it deprived

158. *See also* above Part I. Sources of Law, Chapter 3. Laws and Legislation, §1. Types of Legislation.

159. The Constitution seems to distinguish between areas for which the law determines the *rules* and those for which it determines the *fundamental principles*, although the Constitutional Council has been quite accommodating in that regard. *See*, e.g., CC Decision No 59-1 FNR of 27 Nov. 1959, *Proposition de loi déposée par MM. Bajeux et Boulanger, sénateurs, tendant à la stabilisation des fermages (et à abroger le décret n° 59-175 du 7 janvier 1959 relatif au prix des baux à ferme)*, *Rec.* 71.

the government of an area of action and added to the areas of Parliament's activity. Besides, the Constitutional Council may decide to 'de-legalize' provisions of a law which had been adopted in the regulatory area in order to allow the government to amend the text in question by decree (Article 37 paragraph two of the Constitution). Similarly to Article 41, this has been seldom used. Second, the Council of State, under administrative law, may annul a regulatory act which pertains to the legislative area.

B. The Law-Making Process

178. The law-making process consists of three stages, namely the legislative initiative, the parliamentary debates and the promulgation of the law. The ordinary procedure must be distinguished from the extraordinary procedure.

1. Ordinary Procedure

179. The ordinary procedure is characterized by a number of prerogatives in the hands of the government in order to facilitate the discussion and vote on the bills it proposes before Parliament.

a. Preparatory Work

180. The Prime Minister, in the form of government bills (*projets de lois*), and MPs, in the form of private members' bills (*propositions de lois*), share the power of legislative initiative (Article 39 Constitution). Government bills must first be discussed in the Council of Ministers and submitted for an opinion to the Council of State.[160] The government may also request an opinion from the Economic, Social and Environmental Council as regards both government bills and private members' bills, and it is a mandatory requirement as regards bills bearing economic, social or environmental implications. Also, the government is constitutionally obligated to conduct an impact study before tabling bills before Parliament (Article 39 Constitution as amended). This is in order to rationalize parliamentary work by sparing Parliament of discussion about irrelevant, costly or frivolous legislative proposals.[161] Failure to conduct such impact study, or to conduct it properly, may result in the bill not being put on the agenda.

160. The opinion of the Council of State is not a mere formality but mandatory. *See* CC Decision No 2003-468 DC of 3 Apr. 2003, *Loi relative à l'élection des conseillers régionaux et des représentants au Parlement européen ainsi qu'à l'aide publique aux partis politiques*, *Rec.* 325, pt 7. The request for an opinion of the Council of State is facultative as regards private members' bills at the initiative of the president of either House of Parliament, except when the instigator of the bill is against such a request.

161. Impact studies were originally required as regards government bills in the area of the environment. This requirement was later extended to all government bills – bar finance bills, social security bills, programming bills, and bills relating to constitutional revisions–, the extension of emergency measures, and the authorization to approve or ratify an international agreement.

181. Similarly to most of parliamentary regimes, French legislation has mainly a governmental origin which is understandable in a system where the government benefits from a majority in Parliament as well as from the support of the administration which assists in the implementation of its action.[162] Besides, parliamentary initiative is limited in two ways: first, a private members' bill must deal with an area as defined under Article 34 of the Constitution; second, a private members' bill must have neutral implications in terms of public spending (Article 40 Constitution). In other words, a private members' bill will be outrightly rejected and declared inadmissible if it has the effect of increasing public spending or decreasing public income.

b. Parliamentary Debate

182. The discussion phase is a key moment in the law-making process during which the government may intervene by using different procedures provided for in the Constitution. First, a bill will be discussed within a standing committee or a specific committee in each House of Parliament. Amendments can now be tabled before a parliamentary committee, except in the case of discussion of finance bills, social security bills, and bills relating to constitutional revisions (Article 42 Constitution). This is a significant change which has contributed to an increase of parliamentary committee work allowing an in-depth debate of the technical aspects of the proposed legislation while avoiding the time constraints of plenary sessions. Then, the bill is tabled for debate before the relevant plenary House to be discussed as a whole, and then article by article.[163] A 'cooling-off' period of six weeks between the tabling of a bill and its discussion in plenary session is provided for to avoid the adoption of laws in haste.[164] Amendments to the bill are examined at this stage. The tabling of a massive number of amendments can be a problem which can equate to a practice of efficient parliamentary filibustering. Therefore, the right of amendments is strictly circumscribed. First, express constitutional provisions on inadmissibilities are powerful restrictions in this regard (Articles 40 and 41 Constitution). Second, an organic law defines the right of amendment (Article 44 Constitution as amended). A number of restrictions have been laid down in this regard such as the inadmissibility of amendments when the bill is ready to be discussed in public session.[165] Other restrictions may be put in place by the rules of procedure of the Houses of Parliament. Third, an amendment must have a link, whether direct or indirect, with the bill under discussion (Article 45 Constitution).

---

162. Less than 10% of laws voted in the France actually originates in Parliament.
163. MPs may, at this stage, trigger various procedures in order to interrupt the deliberative process. First, they may consider voting on a bill without prior discussion if need be. Also, it may declare the bill inadmissible for discussion and voting on ground of unconstitutionality. They can also request that the bill be referred back to the committee stage.
164. A four-week period is allowed between the submission of the bill from one House of Parliament to the other House and its examination thereof. These periods of reflection are not applicable as regards finance laws and laws governing Social Security financing, as well as government's bills relating to crisis measures.
165. *See* Organic Law No 2009-403 of 15 Apr. 2009 concerning the application of Arts 34-1, 39 and 44 of the Constitution.

183. The government may use different procedures in order to put an end to the debates in case these become stalled. Pursuant to the so-called blocked vote procedure (*vote bloqué*), the government may impose to vote on a bill, or part of it, under discussion hereby 'blocking' any further debate (Article 44 paragraph three of the Constitution). Only amendments which have been proposed or approved by the government will be included in the bill submitted to the vote, hereby restraining the freedom of action of MPs who have to accept the bill as it stands, or not accept it at all. This procedure aims at rallying the majority around the government by impeding deputies to deform too much a text with unrequested amendments. In other words, such procedure acts as a substitute for a motion of confidence which does not entail to hold the government accountable.[166] The '49.3' procedure is another, even more radical, procedure which allows the government to put pressure on MPs by forcing them to adopt a law without any discussion and without any vote (Article 49 paragraph three Constitution). It is part of the mechanisms whereby the government engages its responsibility before the National Assembly. The provision, as amended by the 2008 constitutional amendment, provides that: 'The Prime Minister may, after deliberation of the Council of Ministers, request a vote of confidence before the National Assembly on a finance bill or a Social Security financing bill. In such a case, the bill shall be deemed adopted unless a vote of no confidence, tabled in the following twenty-four hours, is passed pursuant to the conditions provided for in the above paragraph. The Prime Minister may, in addition, resort to the procedure thereof in relation to one government bill or one private member's bill per session.' The procedure aims at tackling filibustering attempts by the opposition. It can also be used to discipline a weak parliamentary majority when this majority has taken to dismantle the bill proposed by the government. In that context, the deputies face the tough alternative to either approve the text as it is or, by rejecting it, dismiss their government and provoke the dissolution of the National Assembly. In practice, the '49.3' procedure has been used in over eighty occurrences since 1958 with fifty motions of no confidence being tabled, albeit none passed. Prime Minister Rocard (1988–1991) holds the record of its highest number of uses at twenty-eight.[167]

184. The voting phase consists of the approval of the bill by absolute majority of the votes cast by, first, the deputies in the National Assembly, and then by the senators in the Senate – or vice versa, depending on which House the bill was examined in the first place. Since a bill must be voted on in identical terms by both Houses of Parliament, constitutional mechanisms are provided for in case of disagreement. In the first place, the bill may 'come and go' between the two Houses in order to achieve a common text – hence the so-called mechanism of the parliamentary 'shuffle' (*navette parlementaire*). In the second place, and in case of a disagreement between the two Houses of Parliament on a government bill, and after two

166. CC Decision No 59-5 DC of 15 Jan. 1960, *Résolution modifiant les articles 95 et 96 du règlement de l'Assemblée nationale*, *Rec.* 15.

167. *See* below II. Supervision and Monitoring of the Executive, A. The Right to Hold the Government Accountable.

readings by each of the Houses, except in case of accelerated procedure,[168] the Prime Minister may convene a joint parliamentary committee (Article 45 Constitution).[169] The committee, which consists of an equal number of deputies and senators, is tasked with accommodating the disagreements and coming up with a common text. In case the committee succeeds to do so, the government may submit the agreed text to both Houses for approval. However, if the text is not approved, the government may give the last word to the National Assembly which shall then vote on the last version of the bill as voted by the deputies and possibly amended by the senators. In case the government does not so proceed, the 'shuffle' procedure resumes. In the event that the joint parliamentary committee fails to come to an agreement, the government may, after a final reading by the National Assembly and the Senate, request the National Assembly to finally approve the text, hereby expressing the unequal bicameralism which gives the last word to the directly elected House of Parliament.

c. Promulgation

185. The promulgation of a voted law is the competence of the President of the Republic (Article 10 Constitution). The Head of State may, within a fifteen-day time frame between the vote of the law and its promulgation, refer the adopted law to the Constitutional Council for a priori constitutionality review. There is also the possibility of requesting a new deliberation of the law in Parliament, possibility which has been exceptionally used so far – twice since 1958 – by the President of the Republic.

2. Extraordinary Procedures

186. Organic laws deal with the organization and the functioning of public powers and are provided for by the Constitution. In principle, their adoption is pursuant to the procedure applicable to ordinary laws, with a few exceptions and peculiarities as follows. Organic Laws may be examined and voted for only a fortnight after they have been tabled before Parliament. When the National Assembly has the last word on the vote, organic laws must be adopted by absolute majority of the votes cast. Organic laws relating to the Senate must be adopted in identical terms by both Houses of Parliament which de facto grants to the Upper House a veto on the adoption of such laws. Lastly, organic laws *must* be referred to the Constitutional Council so that the Council can review their conformity with the Constitution.

187. Finance laws are adopted under the conditions prescribed by an organic law. Discussion and approval of the overall public budget must take place within a

168. Since the 2008 constitutional amendment, the Conference of the presidents of the Houses of Parliament may oppose the implementation of the accelerated procedure.
169. The right to convene a joint parliamentary committee can also be exercised jointly by the presidents of both Houses of Parliament as regards a private member's bill.

seventy-day period, forty days being reserved for debate before the National Assembly, twenty days before the Senate and ten days for the 'shuttle' procedure between the two Houses of Parliament. On the expiration of this period, the public budget enters into force by way of an ordinance. Such a short period has arguably the advantage of guaranteeing that the State budget is up and running at the beginning of each financial year, in contrast to the previous situation where the adoption of the budget could be delayed by several months. Laws relating to social security financing aim at governing the conditions for a balanced budget of the Social Security system by determining in particular expenditure objectives according to the anticipated income under the conditions laid down by an organic law. The procedure for the adoption of these laws is quite similar to the procedure described above as regards finance laws. Social Security financing laws are also tabled before the National Assembly in the first place (Article 39 Constitution). Since these two categories of laws (i.e., finance laws and Social Security financing laws) are of great significance in terms of public finance, the government enjoys a number of prerogatives in the law-making process in this regard: these laws are tabled by priority on the agenda; periods of reflection applicable for ordinary laws do not apply; and the '49.3' procedure may be applicable without any limitation. Programming laws aim at providing the framework for medium and long-term specific actions of the government in the economic and social areas as well as multiannual guidelines in the area of public finances (Article 34 Constitution as amended). These laws, which do not have normative force, are adopted pursuant to the procedure for ordinary laws, albeit with the distinct feature that the bills thereof must be submitted to the Economic, Social and Environmental Council for its opinion (Article 70 Constitution). Treaties and international agreements shall be ratified or approved by Parliament before being ratified by the President of the Republic (Article 53 Constitution). This provision specifically applies to peace treaties, trade agreements, treaties or agreements relating to international organizations, those relating to State finances, those relating to personal status, as well as those which amend legislative provisions and those which involve the ceding, exchanging or acquiring of territory. Since a treaty cannot be amended once signed, all Parliament can do is to approve or reject the treaty in question. The authorization of ratification may be put to a referendum.

II. Supervision of and Control over the Executive

188. The main innovation of the Constitution lies in the rationalization of the procedures, as described below, whereby Parliament may hold the government accountable. This was in order to remediate the governmental instability that plagued the previous Republics. While the 2008 constitutional amendment did not add any fundamental change in this regard, it certainly reasserted the general supervisory role of Parliament over the Executive. This is reflected, for instance, in the parliamentary calendar where one session out of four is dedicated in priority to the control of governmental action. The modalities of this control are varied, ranging from a sanction type of control when the National Assembly holds the government accountable, to an information type of control which includes the possibility of investigative committees, questions to members of the government and other means.

A. The Right to Hold the Government Accountable

189. The National Assembly – and only the National Assembly – may hold the government accountable for its action. The rationale for this exclusive power of the National Assembly is twofold: first, only the National Assembly is directly elected by the citizens, thereby making it the only legitimate political institution entrusted with the power to overthrow a government appointed by a President himself/herself elected by direct universal suffrage; second, the Senate cannot be the object of dissolution which is the reason why the senators cannot be entrusted with the power of holding the government accountable since it would create an undesirable discrepancy in the mutual means of pressure between the Senate and the government. If the government may request the approval of the Senate on a general policy declaration, an unfavourable vote does not entail any legal obligation for the government which is not obliged to resign (Article 49 paragraph four Constitution).

190. The National Assembly may hold the government accountable in three distinct ways (Article 49 Constitution). First, the government may engage its responsibility by putting up for a vote its programme or a general policy declaration before the National Assembly (Article 49 paragraph one Constitution). A negative vote of the majority of the votes cast will result in the resignation of the government. The practice of the so-called investiture whereby the newly installed government presents its programme to the National Assembly has been erratic so far. There has seemingly been a recent revival of the practice, albeit without any clear perk for the government since it enjoys a wide parliamentary majority most of the time. Second, the National Assembly may vote on a motion of no confidence (Article 49 paragraph two). This motion shall be initiated by at least one-tenth of the deputies and approved by the absolute majority of them, without a deputy being able to table more than three motions per parliamentary session. Deputies shall vote on the motion after a period of reflection of forty-eight hours from the time it has been tabled. In addition, only the votes cast in favour of the motion are counted towards the final ballot which must be at the absolute majority of the deputies in the National Assembly – in other words, abstentions will count against the motion and in favour of the government. The final ballot therefore gives a clear indication of whether the government faces an overly hostile majority, as opposed to a strong majority in its favour. This procedure has primarily been used by the deputies in the opposition as a means to challenge the majority in government on a general policy issue rather than a way to overthrow the government. Only one motion has been successful so far, the one that resulted in the demise of the Pompidou Government in 1962. Third, the National Assembly may pass on a motion of no confidence which has been triggered by the government's decision to resort to the '49.3' procedure. The 2008 constitutional amendment has put further restrictions on this procedure which has widely been regarded as one of the most drastic means of pressure on Parliament in the current domestic democratic regime. These restrictions are as follows. The procedure can be used as regard only one ordinary bill per parliamentary session.[170] The conditions to vote on the motion of confidence are similar to those explained above.[171] The novelty of the procedure is that the law is deemed voted and approved if no motion of no confidence is tabled in the National Assembly or if, in case such motion is tabled, it is not approved. No government has ever resigned on the basis of a successful vote of no confidence.[172]

191. The government must resign in the eventuality of a vote of no confidence in the National Assembly, or a negative vote on the government's programme or on a declaration of general policy (Article 50 Constitution). The outgoing government will deal with current business until the installation of the new one. The occurring of a ministerial crisis may prompt the President of the Republic to anticipate on a possible resignation of the government by triggering the dissolution of the National Assembly. In other words, before the threat of a government's departure materializes, it often appears preferable to ask the electorate to settle the dispute between the government and the National Assembly and vote for a 'refreshed' majority of deputies. The dissolution then appears as a means to mitigate the drastic consequences of a government's resignation.

B. The Right to Request Information from the Executive

192. The efficiency of parliamentary control is directly related to the quality of the information provided to Parliament. MPs may gather information on governmental action via a number of channels. First, with respect to the exercise of the monitoring and evaluation missions Parliament is constitutionally entrusted with (Article 24 paragraph one Constitution), committees of inquiry can be set up within each House (Article 51-2 Constitution). These committees will, under the conditions provided for by law, collect information on specific facts concerning matters such as the management of a public service (e.g., the state of prisons, the dysfunction of the justice system, the functioning of the intelligence services in the monitoring and surveillance of armed radical movements), or of a national company, or social issues (e.g., immigration, working hours, AIDS, energy). Each House can establish a committee of inquiry by adopting the proposal of one of its members

170. This limitation does not apply as regards finance laws and laws governing Social Security financing.
171. It is possible for a deputy to vote on a motion of no confidence more than three times per session in the context of the '49.3' procedure. In other words, the limitation which is applicable to the ordinary procedure on motions of no confidence does not apply in the context of this procedure.
172. The '49.3' procedure has been used on eighty-six occasions so far in relation to fifty-one texts. Fifty motions of no confidence have been tabled, albeit none of them passed. The procedure has led to the adoption of major laws. One of its most controversial uses was under the Villepin Government (2005–2007) in relation to legislation governing first employment contacts, and under the Valls Government (2014–2016) on four occasions including on the very controversial employment law (Law No 2015-990 of 6 August for growth, activity and equal economic opportunities, or *Loi Macron*). The Rocard Government (1988–1991) established the record of using the '49.3' procedure twenty-eight times.

(i.e., parliamentary resolution) thus making it possible to have two such committees from each House on the same matter. To respect the separation of powers principle, no parliamentary investigation can be conducted into facts that are subject of ongoing legal proceedings. An investigative committee includes MPs from all groups, up to thirty deputies and up to twenty-one senators, and lasts up to six months maximum. A period of one year must separate the establishment of two commissions investigating identical facts within the same House. The specificity of the committee of inquiry resides in their particular powers which include an obligation to respond to their convocations, hearings under oath, investigative powers of evidence and on location by the rapporteurs, possibility of making their hearings public (via television broadcast). Failure to comply with these obligations may give rise to criminal prosecution. The reports of the committees of inquiry are published, unless the House objects, and may be subject of a debate in the House without a vote. These reports often lead to recommendations and sometimes to the tabling of a bill. The follow up given to the work of these committees is however politically subject to the agreement of the government and its majority.

193. Second, MPs may ask written and oral questions to members of the government. While the former are widely used, the latter are less successful. Written questions may be asked to any minister, including the Prime Minister, who is then requested to answer within a month. The practice of written questions is used as a means to obtain useful and diverse information from the government on legal issues in particular. The government addresses oral questions on a weekly basis. These can be followed by a debate, although oral questions with a debate are seemingly waning. The specific procedure of the questions to the government allows MPs to prepare oral questions in advance, albeit on a short notice (i.e., two hours at the latest before the session). The time allocated to the various MPs is proportional to the political representation of the group to which they belong.[173] Third, members of the government may make formal declarations before the National Assembly. While these declarations may be followed by a debate, and possibly by a vote in case the government so requests (Article 50-1 Constitution), the government cannot, in principle, be held accountable in that context. It cannot be excluded, however, that the government threatens to resign in case of an unfavourable vote on a declaration.

C. *Other Forms of Control*

194. The 2008 constitutional amendment re-established the practice of resolutions whereby the Houses of Parliament may give an opinion on a particular topical issue.[174] The adoption of such resolutions is strictly defined by law in order to avert the excesses observed under the previous Republics. Resolutions have no legally

173. The questions to the government by deputies of the National Assembly are broadcast.

174. Resolutions were not originally provided for in the Constitution. The reason was to avert the practice of challenging the government on a bill that Parliament would have disapproved of and that could force the Executive to engage its responsibility in order to obtain a favourable vote.

binding effect. Those which are susceptible to challenge the action of the government are declared inadmissible (Article 34-1 Constitution). One such resolution was adopted, for example, by the socialist group of the National Assembly on 2 December 2014 requesting the French Government to recognize the Palestinian State. Another form of control is the monitoring of EU law (Article 88-1 to Article 88-7 Constitution) including the respect of the principle of subsidiarity in particular: 'The National Assembly or the Senate may issue a reasoned opinion as to the conformity of a draft European legislative act with the principle of subsidiarity … ' (Article 88-6 Constitution). Both Houses of Parliament have an increased role in the evaluation of public policies with, among others, the creation of specific monitoring bodies such as the Committee on Evaluation and Control of Public Policies of the National Assembly. They are assisted for this purpose by the French Court of Auditors and a range of experts.

§4. The Workings of Parliament

195. The rules governing the organization and functioning of the French Parliament are provided for in the rules of procedure adopted by each House of Parliament. The independent enactment of such rules marks the autonomy of the Houses of Parliament from the government. These rules of procedure must be referred to the Constitutional Council upon adoption for review of their conformity with the Constitution (Article 61 paragraph one Constitution). Developments below concern the structures and working bodies of Parliament, as well as the different parliamentary sessions, the determination of the parliamentary agenda and parliamentary voting procedures.

I. Structures and Working Bodies of Parliament

196. Both Houses of Parliament are organized and managed by a number of internal bodies, namely the president of the House, the Bureau of the House, and the Conference of the Presidents. The working formations of Parliament consist of parliamentary committees and political groups.

A. The President of the Houses of Parliament

197. The president of the National Assembly is elected at the legislative elections which take place every five years, unless anticipated elections are held after dissolution of the House, for example. The president of the Senate is elected every three years when one-third of the House's membership is renewed. The presidents of both Houses of Parliament belong to the political majority of the respective House and enjoy significant powers. They shall, for example, be consulted upon dissolution of the National Assembly, or in the case of the application of the extraordinary powers under Article 16 of the Constitution. The presidents of both Houses have an appointment power of three members of the Constitutional Council (Article

56 Constitution). Also, they may refer a law to the Council before its entry into force (Article 61 paragraph two Constitution). The president of the Senate will also act as the acting President of the Republic in case of vacancy of the presidency (*See* above). This happened twice in the history of the Fifth Republic, once on the occasion of De Gaulle's resignation in 1969, and the second time on the occasion of the untimely death of Pompidou in 1974. The presidents of both Houses of Parliament have an essential role in the law-making process which includes organizing parliamentary debates, acting as the equivalent of whips – albeit acting as regards all MPs and not just as regards those in the majority – by giving the floor to MPs and reminding them of the discipline of the House.

B. The Bureau of the Houses of Parliament

198. Each House of Parliament is administered by a Bureau (or Office) which is headed by the president of the respective House and consists of elected MPs, according to the representativity of their political group in the House, and civil servants. As the collegial management body of the legislature, the Bureau directs the work of MPs and can, for example, decide upon the admissibility of a private member's bill or an amendment to a private member's bill, or decide upon the arrest of an MP.

C. The Conference of the Presidents

199. The Conference of the Presidents in each House of Parliament consists of the president of the relevant House, its vice-presidents, the presidents of the standing committees, and the presidents of the parliamentary groups. The Conference of the Presidents plays a significant role in many aspects of the law-making process which include the determination of the calendar of parliamentary work and agenda of parliamentary sessions. It also ensures, for example, that the procedure for tabling of a government bill before Parliament has been lawfully respected.

D. Parliamentary Committees

200. Each House of Parliament hosts two types of committees, namely standing committees and committees of inquiry, with also the possibility to set up ad hoc committees. The role of standing committees, as small-sized parliamentary formations, is to prepare the work of the main House by examining bills before these are debated and voted on at the plenary session. Therefore, such committees play a key role in the law-making process by assisting in the elaboration of the law. Their role has been reinforced since the 2008 constitutional amendment as the House concerned will discuss and vote on government bills as amended by the standing committees and not as first tabled by the government. Another aspect of the role of standing committees is to organize hearings of experts on different topics on the model of the USA Congress committees. The number of standing committees in each House of Parliament cannot exceed eight. Each MP can be a member of only one standing committee. The appointment of MPs in these committees is proportional to the representativity of political groups. Committees of inquiry are temporary and are set up to last up to six months maximum. Their existence has been constitutionally recognized since the 2008 constitutional amendment. The conditions of their establishment are defined by the rules of procedure of each House of Parliament and rules governing their organization and operation are defined by law. Committees of inquiry allow MPs to collect information and investigate on a particular issue, such as the management of a public service or a public company or an overall societal issue. These committees have specific investigative powers. To ensure transparency, hearings before such committees and their reports are public unless decided otherwise. The recommendations contained in their reports may be translated into legislation. Ad hoc committees may be established in order to examine a specific government bill or a private member's bill at the request of the government or at the request of the House of Parliament concerned. In practice, such committees are very rarely used.

E. Political Groups

201. Political groups consist of the grouping of MPs according to their political affinity and, as such, they represent national political parties within Parliament, except for those independent members who do not belong to any group, the so-called non-registered MPs. The formation of a political group does not require any formality other than the lodging of a declaration in the relevant House of Parliament and the gathering of a minimum of fifteen members per group. Political groups play a key role in the activity of Parliament since they are involved in the appointment of members of the bureau, in the work of the committees, as well as, among others, in the determination of the agenda and allocation of speaking time. These groups determine the official political stance on important votes and expect their members to follow the party line.

II. Parliamentary Sessions

202. The determination of a parliamentary calendar is key for the working of Parliament. Article 29 paragraph one of the Constitution governs the regime of parliamentary sessions while Article 33 governs the regime of parliamentary sittings. Both Houses of Parliament sit simultaneously. As Parliament cannot sit permanently, its sessions are limited hereby providing a safe period during which the government cannot be held accountable. The rules of procedure of each House of Parliament determine the frequency and length of parliamentary sessions. Two weeks are monthly assigned to the examination of bills and items on the agenda determined by the government; one week is monthly assigned to the control of governmental action and evaluation of public policies, while one sitting day is assigned to the agenda determined by groups of the opposition and minority groups, and a minimum of one session per week is assigned to questions to the government. Ordinary sessions take place during the working civil year complemented, if need be, by extraordinary sessions over the summer.

A. Ordinary Sessions

203. Since the 1995 constitutional amendment, the ordinary legislative session starts on the first working day of October and ends on the last working day of June with a cap of one hundred and twenty-one sitting days. Extra sessions may be decided by the majority of MPs in either House of Parliament or at the request of the Prime Minister after consultation of the House concerned.

B. Extraordinary Sessions

204. The President of the Republic, at the request of the Prime Minister or of the majority of deputies in the National Assembly, may convene Parliament in extraordinary sessions.

C. Other Types of Sessions

205. Parliament is automatically convened under certain circumstances as provided for in the Constitution such as after dissolution of the National Assembly and subsequent general elections (Article 12 paragraph three Constitution), or during the application of the extraordinary powers (Article 16 Constitution).

III. Parliamentary Agenda

206. The 2008 constitutional amendment has given back to Parliament a certain control over its own agenda. Just two weeks per month are allocated in priority to government bills and other texts that the government wishes to be tabled. For the rest of the month, Parliament is free to set up its own agenda within the double constraint that, on the one hand, one week per month must be allocated to the control over the action of the government and the evaluation of public policies, and, on the other hand, one session per month must be for the use by minority groups and opposition groups. Also, at least one session per week is reserved to questions to the government.

IV. Parliamentary Vote

207. Corollary of the prohibition of the imperative mandate, the vote of deputies and senators is personal and the possibilities of delegation limited. Except for the case of votes on personal appointments (e.g., election of the president of the

National Assembly at the beginning of the legislature), all votes are public. As a general rule, the vote is by a show of hands, unless an uncertainty in the count requires a vote by distinguishing between the MPs standing as opposed to the MPs who have remained seated. Public voting is by ordinary public ballot (electronic vote) or by ballot in the gallery or in the adjoining rooms of the House. MPs have the choice between three voting positions, namely 'for', 'against', or 'abstention'.

Chapter 4. The Executive

208. The French Executive is dualist and is split between the President of the Republic, elected by direct universal suffrage, and a government appointed by the President and accountable to Parliament.

§1. The Organ of State

209. While the President of the Republic is endowed with significant powers and acts as the driving force behind government action, s/he does not possess the necessary legal and administrative means to make executive decisions to run the State nor does s/he have any power to directly intervene in the law-making process. The President of the Republic must display strong will and tenacity in order to push a reform forward. In other words, the President of the Republic cannot implement political decisions without the support of the government and that of the Prime Minister in particular, bearing in mind that the functioning of the duo President-Prime Minister much depends on their respective personality. The traditional way of forming a government will be examined before the description of the composition and organization of the government.

I. The Traditional Way of Forming a Government

210. The choice of the Prime Minister, as Head of Government, is a prerogative of the President of the Republic (Article 8 Constitution). Although the President has great freedom in his/her choice, s/he must choose someone who can effectively act as an Executive, while also enjoying the support of the National Assembly in order to be able to implement legislation. The President of the Republic appoints the members of the government on a proposal from the Prime Minister (Article 8 paragraph two Constitution). In practice, and when the presidential majority is aligned with that in Parliament, the President enjoys significant leeway to impose his/her choice of who to appoint in government. The situation is different in a period of cohabitation where the Prime Minister has a real say in the choice of government members who then must align with the majority in Parliament which is not, in that case, the one of the President of the Republic.

211. The Prime Minister presents the resignation of his/her government to the President of the Republic who then formally removes the Prime Minister from office (Article 8 paragraph one Constitution). This occurs as a result of a vote of no confidence by the National Assembly on the government's programme or on one of its general policy declarations. Although the President of the Republic may not, on his/her own initiative, remove the Prime Minister and the government from office, practice has shown that this can happen. This is the case when a member of the government, including the Prime Minister, disagrees over governmental policy and is therefore constrained to leave under the pressure of the President of the Republic. This leads to the well-known practice of Cabinet reshuffles.

II. Composition and Organization of the Government

A. Collegial and Hierarchical Structure

212. Under Article 20 paragraph one of the Constitution, '[t]he government shall determine and conduct the policy of the Nation'. The government is a collegial body which enjoys a degree of legitimacy since it is responsible before the National Assembly. Individual members of the government are not politically accountable for their actions. The resignation of the Prime Minister entails the resignation of the whole government. Another consequence of governmental solidarity is that a minister who would not approve of the political action of the government would have to resign since s/he would not be in a position to endorse the responsibility to support such action before Parliament. However, the practice of including ministers of the other side of the political hue, starting especially under the Sarkozy presidency (2007–2012), has somehow made the functioning of governmental solidarity more problematic since concerned ministers could then express their opinion which did not necessarily always coincide with the mainstream view within government.

213. The composition of the government is not laid down in the Constitution itself but rather in the decrees of appointment of the different ministers and members of the government. In recent years, successive governments have tended to diversify their different areas of competences by creating an increasing number of ministerial portfolios for reasons pertaining to an increasing intervention of the State but also by reason of pure political strategy. Apart from the Prime Minister and the Minister for Justice, the Constitution does not contain any provision about the structure of the government. Each government determines the number of its members and the remit of their attributions. Generally, the government consists of several categories of members structured on a hierarchical basis. First, the Prime Minister is the *primus inter pares* (i.e., first among equals) and has authority on the other members of government. S/he proposes their appointment to the President of the Republic, as well as their removal from office should they fail to respect governmental solidarity or act in a manner incompatible with the action of the government. The Prime Minister is also entitled to settle any disagreement which may occur between ministers, in the preparation of the budget, for example, between the Minister for Finance and other ministers. Second, the ministers of State (*ministres d'Etat*) are placed at the top of the hierarchy. They enjoy an honorary title, often because of their prominence in the political majority, and head a ministerial department. Third, 'plain' ministers have oversight of a ministerial department and sit in the Council of Ministers. Fourth, deputy ministers (*ministres délégués*) report to the Prime Minister or relevant minister in their area of competence and act on delegation from them. Similarly to ministers, deputy ministers head their ministerial department and take part in the Council of Ministers. A minister heads a particular ministerial department and, as such, has responsibility for organizing its services. Lastly, the secretaries of State report to the Prime Minister or relevant minister in their area of competence. They do not sit on the Council of Ministers except when these are concerned with items in their remit.

B. Organization

214. The government sits in different formations. The main formation is the Council of Ministers where all important decisions are made, such as the decision to commit the responsibility of the government, the adoption of government bills, or the adoption of ordinances and a number of other acts). The Cabinet Council (*Conseil de Cabinet*) brings together the ministers under the chairmanship of the Prime Minister. Its existence is not provided for under the Constitution and is in practice quite rare, except during a cohabitation where the Prime Minister regains a leadership power. The interministerial committees (*comités ministériels*) bring together ministers concerned by a particular issue which allow the Prime Minister to coordinate and decide on the action of his/her different ministers. The select ministerial councils (*conseils restreints*) are headed by the President of the Republic and group a number of members of government and senior officials concerned with a particular issue.

§2. Legal Status

215. Members of government are subject to a number of obligations and incompatibilities. Also, they may incur criminal liability according to a specific regime.

I. Obligations and Incompatibilities

216. Within the overall context of fostering more transparency in public life, members of the government must comply with a number of obligations of financial nature. Within two months of their appointment, and two months after leaving office, members of the government must submit a statement of their assets[175] and a statement of interests to the High Authority for Transparency in Public Life.[176] These statements are made public.[177] In addition, members of the government are subject, on appointment, to a tax audit and must, while in office, entrust the management of their financial interests to a third party.

217. In addition, a ministerial office is incompatible with a number of other activities and functions. First of all, in order to ensure their independence and full commitment to their function, ministers cannot exercise any other activity of public or private nature. Second, a ministerial office is incompatible with that of an MP and MEP (Article 23 Constitution). Incompatibility does not mean ineligibility

175. The statement of assets is neither an income tax return nor a wealth tax return. The statement covers all of the government member's own property, as well as property held in common for married persons under the community regime, and undivided property. The spouse's, or partner's own property, needs not be declared.
176. *See* above Chapter 1. General, §2. Political Parties, Lobbies and Interest Groups, I. Definitions and Historical Context.
177. The High Authority for Transparency in Public Life decided to publish, for the first time in a presidential election, the statement of assets of the 2017 presidential elections candidates.

though and a minister can stand for parliamentary elections. Once elected, the minister has one month to opt for his/her seat in Parliament or hold onto his ministerial position. In the latter case, s/he will be replaced, while in office, by his/her substitute in the National Assembly or the Senate. The minister will regain his/her seat in Parliament when s/he leaving the government.[178] The incompatibility between a ministerial position and a local mandate has been controversial. Those in favour of the compatibility justify the holding of multiple offices by the necessity for the minister to keep grass roots activity with his/her constituency. The cons, who militate for the prohibition of multiple mandates, invoke the necessity for the minister to fully commit to his/her office. The prohibition of holding several mandates at a time would also arguably leave the opportunity to other aspiring politicians to stand for parliamentary elections in a renewed political landscape. While there is yet any legislation in the area, the practice of recent governments on multiple mandates has been quite uneven.

II. Criminal Liability of Members of Government

218. Members of the government are criminally liable for offences committed while in office (Articles 68-1 and 68-2 Constitution). However, ordinary jurisdictions are not competent to deal with cases of ministerial responsibility. Instead, a special court, namely the Court of Justice of the Republic (*Cour de Justice de la République*),[179] will decide on these cases. The Court is made up of fifteen judges, namely twelve MPs (i.e., three deputies and three senators) and three sitting judges from the Court of Cassation. Proceedings before the Court of Justice of the Republic are brought by any individual who claim his/her rights have been infringed by a government official. A commission consisting of professional judges may decide either to dismiss the case or to refer it to the Court of Cassation for formal referral to the Court of Justice of the Republic. The possibility for the victim of governmental criminal action to bring judicial proceedings represents an improvement of the rule of law. However, the procedure has also been criticized in a number of respects. For instance, the individual parties cannot take part in the proceedings; moreover, the disjoining of cases from those of top administrators which are brought before ordinary administrative courts makes it difficult to bring them to testify. The suppression of the Court of Justice of the Republic is on the cards as announced by the Philippe Government in April 2018 as part of major constitutional and institutional reform currently (June 2018) under discussion in Parliament.

178. Article 25 of the Constitution. *See also* Organic Law No 2009-38 of 13 Jan. 2009 implementing Art. 25 of the Constitution.

179. *See* below Chapter 5. The Judiciary, §1. Organization of the Judiciary, I. General Introduction, D. Other Courts, 3. The Court of Justice of the Republic.

§3. POWERS

219. The dualism of the French Executive is reflected into the way powers are attributed to its different components, namely the President of the Republic and the government, the Prime Minister in particular. This specific division of powers is explained below before turning to the description of the other kinds of executive powers.

I. Division of Powers Between the President of the Republic and the Government

220. The role of the President of the Republic is defined under Article 5 of the Constitution according to which s/he 'shall ensure the respect of [the] Constitution', and 'under [her]/his arbitration, the normal operation of public powers as well as the continuity of the State'. Also, the President of the Republic is 'the guarantor of national independence, of the integrity of the territory, and of due respect for treaties'. Article 20 of the Constitution defines the general role of the government which 'shall determine and conduct the policy of the Nation'.

221. The main innovation of the Constitution is the attribution of specific powers that the President of the Republic exercises on his/her own, in contrast to his/her other powers which exercise is shared with the government. However, in practice, the scope of the powers of the President of the Republic depends on the configuration of the regime, that is whether the President has the support of a majority in Parliament or whether s/he 'cohabitates' with a different majority (i.e., cohabitation). In the former situation, supposedly the 'normal' functioning of the Fifth Republic, the presidential powers enjoy the maximum scope since the President of the Republic dictates the choice of the Prime Minister and then the orientation of the composition and action of the government. Indeed, when the majority in Parliament coincides with the presidential majority – which has been the case most of the time – the government has regarded itself bound to apply the political programme as championed by the President of the Republic. This has represented a departure from a strict constitutional interpretation whereby the government acts and the President of the Republic is the driving force behind such action. In the latter situation, which is a period of cohabitation and represents a distortion of the functioning of the regime, the scope of the powers of the President of the Republic must comply with the strict reading of the Constitution, notably to Article 20 since the government applies its programme with the support of the majority in Parliament. In any case, a distinction must be made between the discretionary powers granted to the President of the Republic and the powers shared with the government, with the Prime Minister in particular.

A. Discretionary Powers of the President of the Republic

222. The President of the Republic is granted a number of discretionary powers which do not require the countersignature of a member of the government for their exercise. These powers are expressly enumerated (Article 19 Constitution). They relate to the relationships between the President of the Republic and other constituted powers and authorities, namely the government, Parliament, the Constitutional Council and the people. These discretionary powers also refer to emergency powers.

223. First, as regards the government, the President of the Republic appoints the Prime Minister. This appointment is exercised freely, meaning that the Prime Minister may not belong to Parliament (e.g., Pompidou, De Villepin). However, during periods of cohabitation, the margin of manoeuvre of the President of the Republic is reduced since s/he has to choose a Prime Minister who belongs to the newly elected parliamentary majority (e.g., Chirac, Balladur, Jospin). In principle, the President of the Republic does not have the power to remove the Prime Minister from office but can only accept the resignation that is formally presented by him/her. The practice of the regime, bar periods of cohabitation,[180] has shown that the President of the Republic actually holds this power. Indeed, the Prime Minister cannot rely on the majority in Parliament to support his/her actions since the majority supports the President of the Republic in the first place.[181] Also, the President of the Republic convenes, approves the agenda for, and presides at the Council of Ministers which takes place weekly, normally every Wednesday.

224. Second, as regards Parliament, the President of the Republic has the power to dissolve the National Assembly (Article 12 Constitution).[182] Although strictly defined under the Constitution, this is a discretionary power which is only subject to the consultation of the presidents of both Houses of Parliament and the Prime Minister. The dissolution can be used at any moment – except within a year of a previous dissolution in order to prevent instability. The dissolution has the effect of provoking early general elections in the National Assembly which must be held within a twenty to forty days time frame. The power of dissolution – or rather the threat to resort to it – has been one of the essential means to ensure the stability of the regime. Dissolution may be useful to solve a serious political crisis when the President of the Republic seeks to call on the people to renew the majority within the National Assembly, as did De Gaulle on two occasions, in 1962 and in 1968. The other dissolutions which occurred under the Fifth Republic were done for slightly different reasons. In 1981 and in 1988, Mitterrand dissolved at the start of his seven-year mandate in order to get a comfortable majority in the National

180. The Prime Minister is 'irremovable' in that case since a conflict between him/her and the President of the Republic would lead to a conflict with the National Assembly, possibly ending with its dissolution.
181. The only voluntary resignation of a Prime Minister was the one presented by Chirac to Giscard D'Estaing in 1976.
182. As the non-directly elected House of Parliament, the Senate cannot be dissolved.

Assembly. The 1997 dissolution is the odd one out since it was decided by Chirac for purely electoral reasons. The then President of the Republic had announced that the dissolution was to 'give the opportunity to the French people to decide on the scope and frequency of political changes in the years to come' while it was in fact a tactical move to rekindle with a parliamentary majority which had been weakened by an internal conflict affecting right-wing leaders.[183] The electors did not understand the underlying reason and the dissolution proved to be a strategic failure since a left-wing majority returned in the National Assembly forcing Chirac into a period of cohabitation. The 1997 dissolution had also the effect of casting aside the use of the procedure itself for a long time. Pursuant to the separation of powers principle, the President of the Republic cannot sit in Parliament and may only deliver messages to the Houses (Article 18 Constitution). Since the 2008 constitutional amendment, the President of the Republic can speak before Parliament convened as the Congress (i.e., both Houses of Parliament sitting in Versailles) and the President's statement may be followed by a debate without a vote.[184]

225. Third, the President of the Republic appoints three members of the Constitutional Council as well as chooses the president of the Council. The appointment procedure is subject to approval by the parliamentary standing committees of each House of Parliament. A negative vote of three-fifths of the members of these committees against a particular nominee will prevent the appointment to be made. Also, the President of the Republic has the power to refer for review to the Constitutional Council not-yet-ratified international agreements which are allegedly incompatible with the Constitution (Article 54 Constitution), as well as laws which are allegedly unconstitutional (Article 61 Constitution).

226. Fourth, the President of the Republic may directly consult the people by way of referendum. Among the three types of national referendums, only the legislative referendum pursuant to Article 11 of the Constitution is a discretionary power of the President of the Republic.[185] The initiative of the Article 11 referendum belongs to the Prime Minister in the case of cohabitation as s/he is the formal and real initiator of the referendum.[186] However, in practice, the President of the Republic is the instigator of the referendum – which s/he has often already hinted at in public. However, the decision *to hold* a referendum is then strictly that of the President of the Republic. The initiative of a referendum may also come from Parliament (Article 11 paragraph three Constitution)[187] whereby one-fifth of MPs and one-tenth of registered voters may put forward a private member's bill calling for a referendum. The bill's conformity with the Constitution is reviewed before it being

183. The conflict was between Chirac and former Prime Minister Balladur (1993–1995) whose feud started when both ran for the 1995 presidential elections.
184. Hollande used this procedure on 16 Nov. 2015 after the Paris terrorist attacks.
185. The President of the Republic is also endowed with a referendum power concerning the accession of a new Member State to the EU (Art. 88-5 Constitution). The government bill authorizing the ratification of the accession treaty shall be put to a referendum by the Head of State.
186. No referendum on the basis of Art. 11 has been instigated during a cohabitation period so far.
187. This type of referendum was introduced by the 2008 constitutional amendment. *See also* Organic Law No 2013-1114 of 6 Dec. 2013 implementing Art. 11 of the Constitution.

put to the referendum. The bill will only be put to the referendum by the President of the Republic if it has not been examined by Parliament in the first place. In other words, the procedure only allows the expression of the voice of the people in case of parliamentary inaction, hereby rendering the whole procedure quite limited in occurrence. The object of the referendum is limited to 'the organization of public powers', 'reforms relating to the economic, social or environmental policy of the Nation and the public services which contribute thereto, or to the 'ratification of a treaty which, albeit not repugnant to the Constitution, would impact on the functioning of the institutions'.[188] The addition of the environmental dimension by the 2008 constitutional amendment has broadened the scope of the referendum and it can now potentially relate to a large spectrum of the activities of the State such as tax, employment, health and education, albeit limited to the public services which contribute to these activities. The use of the Article 11 referendum has been quite uneven in meaning and frequency. De Gaulle used it on four occasions whether it was to amend the Constitution or deal with other prominent issues such as the troubles in Algeria.[189] This corresponded to the Gaullist approach whereby the exercise of presidential power was inseparable from consulting the people on important matters concerning the life of the Nation. Post-De Gaulle, referendums have been less frequent and have certainly lost their plebiscitary dimension.[190]

227. The provision for extraordinary powers is necessary to ensure the defence of the State and its democratic regime in case of extreme danger such as a war or an internal subversion. This is the *raison d'être* of Article 16 of the Constitution which organizes a kind of 'democratic dictatorship' aiming at protecting the Republic while allowing at the same time infringement of all of its core principles.[191] The application of Article 16 entails the absence of separation of powers hence allowing the President of the Republic to take any measure – legislative, executive or judicial – that is required under the circumstances. The use of Article 16 of the Constitution has been controversial especially since its only – and allegedly abusive – use by De Gaulle from 23 April till 29 September 1961 during the Algerian War. The 2008 constitutional amendment set new limitations to its use. The President of the Republic is free to appreciate if the substantive conditions for having recourse to Article 16 are fulfilled. These impose that, on the one hand, the independence of the Nation, the integrity of its territory or the fulfilment of its international obligations is under grave and immediate threat and, on the other, that the proper functioning of the constitutional public powers has been interrupted. Formal requirements are limited to consulting the Prime Minister, the presidents of both Houses of Parliament and the president of the Constitutional Council whose reasoned opinion is published in the

188. For example, the suppression of the mandatory military service was deemed not to fall within the scope of Art. 11 of the Constitution when the issue was discussed in the mid-90s.
189. *See* Marie-Luce Paris, 'Popular Sovereignty and the Use of the Referendum: Comparative Perspectives with Reference to France' in Eoin Carolan (ed), *The Constitution of Ireland: Perspectives and Prospects* (Bloomsbury Professional 2012) 279.
190. *Ibid.*
191. De Gaulle's concern was to avoid the repetition of the events of June 1940 when the then President of the Third Republic, Albert Lebrun, was left powerless by the circumstances which led to the demise of the Republic and the establishment of the French State (*Etat Français*).

JO. Once the conditions are fulfilled and consultations carried out, the President of the Republic informs the Nation. Other guarantees exist covering the duration of the implementation of extraordinary powers. These guarantees include the obligation to submit to the Constitutional Council for opinion the acts taken by the President of the Republic under Article 16.[192] Also, Parliament shall sit as of right and the National Assembly cannot be dissolved during the use of Article 16. Lastly, the Constitutional Council decides whether Article 16 should continue to apply at the request of either president of the Houses of Parliament, sixty deputies or sixty senators within thirty days of implementation, as of right within sixty days of implementation, and at any time after sixty days of implementation. The public opinion of the Constitutional Council is not legally binding. However, it would be politically difficult for the President of the Republic to overlook a negative opinion of the Council. Besides, an abusive use of Article 16 degenerating into a coup d'état would arguably result in the President of the Republic being impeached by Parliament.

B. Shared Powers

228. The President of the Republic shares a number of powers with other authorities. In contrast with the powers that the President exercises on his/her own, a shared power cannot be exercised unless the executive act taken by the President is also countersigned by the Prime Minister or one of the concerned ministers. The practice of countersignature was the rule under the previous Republics. It entailed a formal power since the political power was in the hands of the Head of Government. Under the Fifth Republic, the power is less formal: as much as the government may refuse to countersign acts of the Executive, the President may, in certain cases, refuse to sign these acts. Here is below a list of the shared powers.

229. The President of the Republic appoints and removes from office members of the government, on a proposal from the Prime Minister (Article 8 paragraph two Constitution). The President of the Republic plays a significant part in the selection of ministers in the areas of foreign affairs and defence in particular (*See* below). The President of the Republic chairs the Council of Ministers meetings (Article 9 Constitution); as such, s/he convenes the weekly meetings, determines the agenda, chairs the discussions and has oversight of the minutes. The President of the Republic signs two types of acts: ordinances and decrees deliberated in the Council of Ministers (*See* below). The power to sign ordinances has been interpreted as a discretionary one since the Constitution sets no time limit in this regard as opposed to the fifteen-day period stipulated for the promulgation of laws.[193] The President of the Republic also shares with the government the power to appoint top civil and

192. The opinion of the Constitutional Council is not published though.
193. During the first Mitterrand-Chirac cohabitation (1986–1988), the President of the Republic refused to sign ordinances on three occasions.

military servants (*See* below).[194] The President of the Republic may, by decree at the request of the Prime Minister or at the request of the majority of deputies, convene Parliament for an extraordinary session (Article 29 Constitution).[195] The question of whether such power is legally binding can be posed since the President refused to convene Parliament on two occasions – in 1960, De Gaulle refused to convene Parliament despite the request of the majority in the National Assembly; and in 1987, Mitterrand, during the first cohabitation, rejected in a press communiqué a request from his Prime Minister Chirac to convene an extraordinary session of the Parliament on the status of the Renault company, hereby confirming the discretionary nature of that power.[196] The President of the Republic, by decree countersigned by the Prime Minister, promulgates laws within fifteen days of their vote by Parliament (Article 10 Constitution). The President, with the approval of the Prime Minister, may request a further deliberation of an enacted law, in full or in part.[197] The President of the Republic is the guarantor of the independence of the judicial authority (Article 64 Constitution). In that role, s/he is assisted by the Superior Council of the Judiciary (*Conseil Supérieur de la Magistrature* or CSM) which is presided over by the First President of the Court of Cassation.[198] Lastly, the President of the Republic holds a regal pardon power (Article 17 Constitution). This power allows amending the effects of a judicial sentence by, for instance, suspending the criminal conviction or exempting the convicted individual from penalties. This only applies to individual convictions and is not a general right of pardon.

II. Regulatory Powers

230. A distinction is made under the Constitution between the autonomous regulatory power of the Prime Minister and the more classical regulatory power in the hands of the government for the implementation of laws. A residual regulatory power exists as regards ministers under certain conditions.

---

194. Article 13 Constitution. The enumeration contained in the Constitution may be completed by an organic law. As regards top civil and military servants whose appointment is discretionary, their appointment is proposed by the Prime Minister subject to the approval by the President of the Republic.
195. Since parliamentary ordinary sessions take place from October to June, extraordinary sessions can only be convened during the months of July, August and September.
196. It can also happen that while the President of the Republic accepts to convene an extraordinary session of Parliament, s/he may nevertheless refuse that the particular government bill be tabled before Parliament – as was the case in 1993, when Mitterrand, under the second cohabitation, accepted to convene Parliament at the request of the Balladur Government but denied the discussion on the Falloux Law on public instruction.
197. The power of second deliberation has only been used on two occasions so far.
198. Until the 2008 constitutional amendment, the President of the Republic would chair the Superior Council of the Judiciary. *See also* below Chapter 5. The Judiciary, §1. Organization of the Judiciary, II. Constitutional and Legal Status of Members of the Judiciary, A. The Independence of the Judiciary, 1. The Superior Council of the Judiciary.

A. *Autonomous Regulatory Power*

231. A significant attribution of the Prime Minister relates to the adoption of acts via his/her regulatory power (Article 37 Constitution). The exercise of this power means that the regulatory acts taken by the Prime Minister are countersigned by the relevant ministers in charge. For those acts (i.e., decrees) deliberated in the Council of Ministers, the signature of the President of the Republic is also required. A decree deliberated in the Council of Ministers can only be amended via the same procedure which has the effect of diminishing the regulatory power of the Prime Minister because of the presidential oversight.

B. *Regulatory Powers Necessary for the Implementation of Laws*

232. The government may act by way of ordinances (Article 38 Constitution). Ordinances allow the government to take, within a limited time frame, measures of legislative nature in order to implement its programme.[199] The legal regime of ordinances is specific. Parliament must vote an enabling law at the request of the government in order to trigger the power to make ordinances.[200] The enabling law must fulfil a number of substantive requirements: ordinances only aims at the implementation of the government's programme; the power to issue ordinances is limited in time with an express indication of an enabling period during which the government can act, on the one hand, and a ratification period during which the government must table a ratification bill before Parliament, on the other hand; ordinance may concern a number of areas of legislative nature but not all of them since it would be unconstitutional. Once the enabling law is enacted, ordinances are formally adopted in the Council of Ministers after an opinion of the Council of State. Ordinances are signed by the President of the Republic, albeit the President is not legally bound to do so. After the expiry of the enabling period, the government cannot have recourse to new ordinances on the basis of the enabling law concerned. Existing ordinances are either null and void, should the government fail to table them for ratification before Parliament within the ratification period, or valid, should they be expressly ratified by Parliament within such period. The legal status of ordinances therefore evolves depending on the course of action taken: originally regulatory acts which legality may be reviewed by the Council of State, ordinances acquire a legislative nature once ratified by Parliament.

C. *Regulatory Powers of Ministers*

233. Individual ministers are not entitled to exercise any regulatory power unless this power is expressly delegated to them by the Prime Minister or results from the express provisions contained in an enabling legislative or regulatory act.

---

199. Ordinances were formerly known under the previous Republics as 'decrees-laws' (*décrets-lois*).
200. The initiative cannot come from Parliament. *See* CC Decision No 2004-509 DC of 13 Jan. 2005, *Loi de programmation pour la cohésion sociale, Rec.* 33.

Ministers countersign the decrees taken by the Prime Minister in their area of action, as well as the decrees enacted in the Council of Ministers and signed by the President of the Republic.

III. Powers relating to National Defence and Foreign Affairs

234. According to the Constitution, powers relating to national defence and foreign affairs are shared between the President of the Republic and the government. There is, however, a degree of overlap in this division of powers in the areas of defence and diplomacy. In practice, these areas have traditionally been the exclusive preserve (i.e., *domaine réservé*) of the Head of State who can count on a majority in Parliament and government. Again, the situation is different in case of cohabitation where power-sharing as defined under constitutional provisions applies.[201] Nonetheless, while the idea of a '*domaine réservé*' was prevalent during De Gaulle presidency (1959–1969), it progressively lost its relevance in more recent presidencies. This was confirmed by President Chirac in his declaration of 14 July 1997. He contended that there was no presidential preserve but rather emphasized the particular role of the Head of State in preserving the role of France in the world, as well as maintaining the European and social *acquis*. Overall, those powers in the area of diplomacy and defence depend on the functioning of the regime (i.e., cohabitation or not). It also depends on the personality of the President of the Republic who might be inclined to give leeway to the government in those sensitive areas in order to avoid exposure or, on the contrary, decide to intervene in as many areas and as actively as s/he chooses fit.

A. National Defence

235. In relation to the armed forces, the President of the Republic is the Commander-in-Chief of the Armed Forces and presides over the higher councils and committees for national defence (Article 15 Constitution). However, this power overlaps to a certain extent with that of the government which has power over the armed forces (Article 20 paragraph two Constitution), on the one hand, and that of the Prime Minister who is responsible for the national defence (Article 21 paragraph one Constitution), on the other hand.

201. The 2008 constitutional amendment introduced a degree of parliamentary control over the decision to send military troops abroad. The President of the Republic must inform Parliament within three days of sending the troops. MPs may debate, but not vote, on such decision. The extension of the military intervention is subject to parliamentary approval, with the final word to the National Assembly, after four months. For example, the Serval Operation in Mali was approved by Parliament on 22 Apr. 2013. The only exception, even in case of cohabitation, is the power to resort to the nuclear power which belongs exclusively to the President of the Republic.

B. Foreign Affairs

236. In international affairs, the President of the Republic is responsible for negotiating and ratifying international agreements (Article 52 paragraph one Constitution)[202] as well as accrediting ambassadors to other jurisdictions and receiving letters of accreditation from foreign jurisdictions in respect of their ambassadors (Article 14 Constitution). The President of the Republic is in charge of foreign policy and, as such, sits in the European Council. However, there is a degree of overlap since the government, in charge of the national policy (Article 20 paragraph one Constitution), is also necessarily involved in international relations.

C. Treaty-Making Powers

237. See below Part V. Specific Issues, §2. Treaties and Foreign Affairs, II. The Treaty-Making Power.

IV. Powers regarding Parliament

238. Both the President of the Republic and the government have a role vis-à-vis Parliament. Some of these powers are shared between them.[203] In that regard, it is worth noting the primary role of the Prime Minister in the relationship between the government and Parliament. The Prime Minister leads legislative initiatives and is at the heart of the law-making process since s/he is the one who decides which amendments will be tabled before Parliament on behalf of the government (Article 44 Constitution), the one who decides to convene a joint parliamentary committee in order to solve a disagreement between the two Houses of Parliament (Article 45 Constitution), and the one who decides to activate the responsibility of the government after deliberation with the Council of Ministers (Article 49 Constitution). The Prime Minister can also refer a law to the Constitutional Council for judicial review (Article 61 Constitution).

V. Powers regarding the Judiciary

239. See above B. Shared Powers.

---

202. Also, the President of the Republic is informed of any negotiation on an international agreement which is not subject to ratification (Art. 52 para. two Constitution).

203. *See* above B. Shared Powers.

VI. Other Powers

240. The legislative referendum of Article 11 of the Constitution can be categorized as a non-shared power.[204] However, other types of referendums are shared between the two heads of the Executive, one of a European dimension, the other of a local dimension. First, the ratification of a treaty concerning the accession of a new Member State to the EU must be approved by the French people by referendum. If the government issues the bill authorizing such ratification, it is put to a referendum by the President of the Republic (Article 88-5 paragraph one Constitution).[205] The other type of referendum concerns the power of the President of the Republic, on a proposal submitted by the government (or on a joint proposal from both Houses of Parliament), to decide to consult the people of an overseas territory on a question relating to the organization, competences or governance of that territory (Article 72-4 paragraph two Constitution).

§4. The Council of Ministers

241. The government formally makes its decisions within the Council of Ministers while the preparatory work is done beforehand. The Council of Ministers is the equivalent of the Cabinet where the principle of ministerial solidarity applies. Each member of the Council of Ministers must support the decisions made, even if s/he personally disapproves of them, or must resign. As Head of the Government, the Prime Minister directs its action and, in this respect, sets out its essential political orientations which, apart from periods of cohabitation, are those defined by the President of the Republic. The Prime Minister must also ensure the coordination of government action and avoid, through arbitration, that different ministers take initiatives in opposite directions. In other words, the Prime Minister makes sure that the principle of ministerial solidarity is respected among government members. The Prime Minister is assisted in his/her role by a Cabinet and the General Secretariat of the government, the latter being in charge of preparing the agenda for the Council of Ministers in cooperation with the General Secretariat of the presidency. Other consultative bodies, such as the Council of State (in its consultative role) or the Economic, Social and Environmental Council, assist the Prime Minister in the decision-making process via their consultative or mandatory opinions.[206]

---

204. *See* above A. Discretionary Powers of the President of the Republic.
205. While the referendum route was the only route when the constitutional provision was inserted, the 2008 constitutional amendment opened the parliamentary route as well. By voting on a motion adopted in identical terms by each House of Parliament by a three-fifths majority, Parliament may authorize the adoption of the ratification bill under the procedure provided for in Art. 89 para. three of the Constitution which is when Parliament is convened as a Congress (Art. 88-5 para. two Constitution).
206. *See* below Chapter 6. Independent Advisory or Supervisory Bodies at the Legislative and Executive Levels.

§5. MISCELLANEOUS

242. Other powers of the Executive comprise nomination powers and powers in times of crisis.

I. Nomination Powers

243. Bar those ones which are of the competence of the President of the Republic under the Constitution,[207] the Prime Minister has a role in the appointment to top civil and military posts (Article 21 paragraph one Constitution).

II. Powers in Times of Crisis

244. While the President of the Republic has at its disposal extraordinary powers,[208] the government may resort to exceptional measures in order to deal with crises. The state of siege and the state of emergency are two kinds of such measures.[209]

207. *See* above A. Discretionary Powers of the President of the Republic.
208. *Ibid.*
209. *See* below Part. V. Specific Issues Chapter. 3. Emergency Powers.

Chapter 5. The Judiciary

245. The Constitution refers to a judicial *authority* rather than to a judicial *power*. The specific evolution and status of the French judiciary are reflected in its organization and judicial review mechanism.

§1. Organization of the Judiciary

246. The foundations of the French judicial system, including its dual organization between ordinary courts and administrative courts, are examined first. Further developments are concerned with the constitutional and legal status of the judiciary, including independence of its members, judicial proceedings and State liability for torts caused by the judiciary.

I. General Introduction

247. Inherited from the 1789 Revolution, the French judicial system is based on domestic general principles and laws enacted by Parliament, as well as on European and international laws. Justice fulfils a fundamental mission that the State cannot concede or alienate. Justice aims at guaranteeing individual freedoms and the rule of law. Justice is a public service rendered in the name of the French people.[210] Justice is primarily rendered by public courts. However, as has been the case in many other jurisdictions, the development of processes of alternative dispute resolution (or ADR), whereby private parties resolve their disputes without trial, has flourished in recent years, often encouraged by the French legislature. This development can be explained by both ideological and practical reasons. Ideologically, a justice which is initiated and conducted by private individuals might arguably be regarded as more legitimate and hence respected by the citizens. In this perspective, the argument is that justice conducted in the context of a courtroom often fuels more tension between the parties involved. Pragmatically, parties are attracted to the flexibility of ADR processes. These allow them to decide on the modalities of their dispute as well as avoid lengthy and costly judicial proceedings. From the perspective of the State, and given the increasing caseload of French courts, domestic authorities certainly see an advantage in this form of justice.

248. Typically, ADR processes include, in French law, arbitration, on the one hand, and other diverse processes based on mediation or other participative modes of dispute resolution, on the other. First, arbitration is the settling of a dispute between two private parties by a freely chosen impartial third party. The arbitrator may decide *ex aequo et bono* (*amiable compositeur*) but must respect the principle of due process and the right to a fair hearing. Arbitration may be envisaged even before any dispute arises and, for example, be provided for in a contract between

210. This phrase (i.e., '*Au nom du peuple français*') is mentioned on each judicial decision.

the parties (*clause compromissoire*')[211] or, after a dispute arises, for example in a specific document (*convention de compromis*').[212] The decision rendered by the arbitrator (*sentence arbitrale*) is of judicial character and, as having the authority of res judicata, must be accepted by the contending parties. However, it is only enforceable after a trial judge has delivered an execution order (*ordonnance d'exequatur*) reviewing the conformity of the arbitrator's decision to the public order.[213] The conciliation and the mediation procedures, the contractual transaction as well as the participatory procedure agreement represent other ADR means which have been encouraged by the French authorities and which, in some cases, have been made compulsory in proceedings before domestic courts. In a conciliation procedure, parties attempt to find an acceptable agreement to solve their dispute, possibly with the involvement of a third party, the conciliator. The conciliation procedure is part of the general mission of the trial judge under Article 21 of the Code of Civil Procedure. This is mandatory in a number of areas such as, for example, in labour law: any judicial proceedings before the labour court must be preceded by a judicial conciliation between the employer and the employee. In all other areas, the conciliation procedure is optional and facilitated in cases concerning petty claims and in family matters in particular. Mediation actively involves a third party, the mediator, who assists the parties in reaching an acceptable agreement to solve their dispute. The mediation may be judicial, as decided by a judge, or conventional. The mediation procedure, although optional, is widely used in French law in diverse areas such as family law as regards divorce or parental authority, consumer law, labour law and, increasingly, as regards petty offences in criminal law.[214] The contractual transaction is a contract whereby the parties settle a dispute, which has arisen or may arise, by making concessions to each other, that is by waiving their right or part of their rights.[215] The settlement agreement has force of res judicata between the parties and can only be challenged before a court in limited circumstances. The procedure is widely used in labour law and, more recently, in criminal law with the introduction of the guilty plea procedure.[216] Lastly, the participatory procedure agreement, which is written and concluded for a fixed period of time, allows parties to a dispute to work jointly and in good faith towards a friendly resolution or settlement of their dispute. Shall the parties fail to reach a

211. Such provision is only allowed in the context of professional relationships, except in international arbitration.
212. Matters pertaining to the public order, such as family matters, cannot be the object of arbitration (Arts 2059 and 2060 Civil Code).
213. The arbitrator's decision may be subject to an appeal before domestic courts under certain conditions.
214. *See* Ordinance No 2011-1540 of 16 Nov. 2011 transposing Directive 2008/52/EC of the European Parliament and of the Council of 21 May 2008 on certain aspects of mediation in civil and commercial matters. The 2011 Ordinance establishes a common regime for the conventional conciliation and mediation procedures which is now laid down under Art. 1530 of the Code of Civil Procedure. The '*Maisons de la Justice et du Droit*' are legal advice centres established within the remit of first instance courts which aim, among other tasks, at dealing with these procedures.
215. *See* Arts 2044 to 2058 Civil Code.
216. Law No 2004-204 of 9 Mar. 2004 adapting justice to the evolution of criminality.

settlement, they will be allowed to bring proceedings before a court without being required to undertake a conciliation or mediation.[217]

249. The French judicial organization is twofold and consists of ordinary courts and administrative courts. Other types of courts include a regulatory court, namely the Court of Auditors, and the so-called political courts, namely the High Court to judge the President of the Republic, and the Court of Justice of the Republic to judge the members of the government.

A. *French Dual Judicial Organization: Distinguishing Between the Ordinary and the Administrative Courts*

250. The organization of justice in France features a duality of judicial orders split between the ordinary judicial order and an autonomous administrative judicial order. Both judicial orders form two distinct and hierarchized sets of jurisdictions. While this model has been replicated in some European countries, such as Greece or Luxembourg, it remains a peculiarity compared to most other Western democracies. The separation between the ordinary and administrative courts finds its historical origin in the distrust held towards judges of the *Ancien Régime* who could, in their courts (called at the time parliaments), deliver judicial decisions of general scope and bearing binding authority on the lower courts (the so-called *arrêts de règlement*), thereby interfering with the royal power. By establishing the principle of separation of powers, not only the 1789 revolutionaries weakened the judiciary as a power but also decided to entrust the power to judge the administration to special courts (i.e., the administrative courts). Distinct from the ordinary courts and independent from the administration, administrative courts originally comprised the Council of State, created by Napoleon Bonaparte in 1799, and the prefectural councils (*Conseils de Préfecture*),[218] established in 1800. A 1953 reform instituted trial administrative courts of first instance (*Tribunaux Administratifs*), and a 1987 reform added administrative courts of appeal (*Cours Administratives d'Appel*). The existence of a dual judicial organization explains the existence of a Disputes Court (*Tribunal des Conflits*).[219] The Disputes Court is a single court which does not belong to any judicial order. It consists of an equal number of members from the two Supreme Courts of each judicial order, namely the Court of Cassation for the ordinary judicial order and the Council of State for the administrative judicial order. The role of the Disputes Court is to rule on conflicts of jurisdictions between the two judicial orders. Different types of conflicts of jurisdictions may arise, whether it is to determine which court has jurisdiction in the first place or which decision is valid in case of contrariety of final judgments. A positive conflict occurs when the administration, in the person of the representative of the State in the department, disputes

217. *See* Arts 2062 to 2067 Civil Code.
218. Prefectural councils were replaced in 1926 by the interdepartmental prefectural councils.
219. The Disputes Court was established in 1872. Its organization and rules of procedure were amended by Law No 2015-177 of 16 Feb. 2015 on the modernization and simplification of law and procedures in the areas of justice and home affairs.

the competence of an ordinary court to judge a case which has been put before it. A negative conflict is where the courts of each of the two judicial orders have irrevocably declared themselves to be incompetent on the same matter, without the latter court having referred the dispute to the Disputes Court. In that case, the interested parties may file a petition with a view to determine which court is competent to settle the dispute.[220] The Disputes Court is also competent in case of conflicting decisions, that is when the final judgments of the administrative courts and the ordinary courts, in proceedings before the two orders of jurisdiction in disputes concerning the same subject matter, present a contrariety which leads to a denial of justice.[221] Also, the Disputes Court has a special competence in case of excessive lengthy judicial proceedings. In that case, an action for damages may be brought before the Disputes Court if a claim relating to excessively long proceedings in the same litigation and between the same parties before the courts of both orders on account of the applicable rules of jurisdiction has been implicitly or explicitly rejected by the Department of Justice.

B. Subdivisions within the Courts of Ordinary Jurisdiction

251. Ordinary courts are competent to settle disputes between private parties, whether natural or legal persons before the civil courts, as well as to punish those responsible for criminal offences before the criminal courts. Civil courts and criminal courts form part of a unified system which is topped by the Court of Cassation.

1. The Courts of Ordinary Jurisdiction

a. Civil Courts Settle Disputes but Do Not Impose Penalties

252. The judicial organization and competence of civil courts are governed by the Code of Judicial Organization. The 'judicial map' which, as established in 1958 – and, for some parts, inherited from the *Ancien Régime* – had long been regarded as not meeting today's economic and demographic realities. For this reason, it was

220. There is also the possibility that a court refers a matter to be decided by a court of the other judicial order after a final judgment has been made, called a 'conflict on referral' (*conflit de renvoi*). More specifically, where a court of the ordinary or administrative judicial order has, by a decision which is no longer subject to appeal, declined the jurisdiction of the court to which it belongs on the ground that the dispute does not fall within that judicial order, any court of the other order, to which the same dispute is referred to, if it considers that the dispute arises out of the order of the court to which it was originally referred to, must, by a reasoned decision, which is not subject to appeal even in cassation, refer the matter to the Disputes Court and stay proceedings until such jurisdictional matter is resolved by the said Court. The same is true when a court has to decide on a case which involves the trial of either an action brought or an exception, a jurisdictional issue raising a serious difficulty involving the separation of the judicial orders. That court may, by a reasoned decision which is not subject to appeal, refer the matter to the Disputes Court for a decision on the question of jurisdiction.

221. A denial of justice is prohibited under Art. 4 of the Civil Code: 'The judge who refuses to rule, under the pretext of silence, obscurity or insufficiency of the law, may be prosecuted as guilty of denial of justice.'

greatly modified under the Sarkozy's presidency (2007–2012).[222] In an effort to contribute to the efficiency and quality of the judicial system, the reform led to the abolition of nearly four hundred courts and the creation of a dozen. From a total of one thousand and two hundred courts in 2009, the number of ordinary civil courts on the national territory stands now at eight hundred and nineteen courts.[223] Beyond these quantitative and geographical issues, there was also the issue of the even distribution of courts on the French territory in order to meet the right of the citizens to equal access to justice. From this perspective, the reform was quite controversial because it involved political choices as regards not only the necessity to concentrate some specialized kinds of disputes in one court but also the need to redefine the competences between various courts.[224]

253. Civil courts of first instance are trial courts of original jurisdiction. They are divided between those with general jurisdiction and those entrusted with a special jurisdiction in a particular area of law.[225] The civil court of general jurisdiction (*juridiction de droit commun*) is the Court of First Instance (*Tribunal de Grande Instance* or TGI).[226] Composed of professional judges,[227] the Court of First Instance has primary jurisdiction over all civil and commercial matters which have not been attributed to a specialized court by reason of their nature or amount claimed. In particular, the Court of First Instance is competent for all civil law disputes involving claims in excess of EUR 10,000. The Court of First Instance has also exclusive jurisdiction over a number of matters regardless of the amount of the claim. These matters are the status of persons (including marital status, filiations, change of name and nationality), family law (including matrimonial regimes, divorce, parental authority, adoption, alimony, succession), real estate (including real estate foreclosure) and patents and trademark law. In principle, the Court of First Instance shall

---

222. The reform took place between 2007 and 2011. A series of decrees published on 15 Feb. 2008 and 29 May 2008 amended the geographical jurisdictional remit of a number of first instance courts, namely *Tribunaux d'Instance*, *Tribunaux de Grande Instance*, *Tribunaux de Commerce* and *Conseils de Prud'Hommes*.
223. The implementation of this reform took place until 2011. There are now one hundred and sixty Courts of First Instance (twenty-one suppressed), three hundred and five District Courts (one hundred and seventy-eight suppressed, and seven created), two hundred and ten Labour Courts (sixty-two suppressed and one created) and one hundred and thirty-five Commercial Courts (fifty-five suppressed and five created).
224. The last reform relating to the judicial system deals with further modifications of the judicial map in a very limited way. *See* Law No 2016-1547 of 18 Nov. 2016 on the modernization of justice in the twenty-first century.
225. Local courts (*Juridictions de Proximité*) represented another category of civil ordinary courts. Composed of non-professional judges, their role was to settle petty disputes. Established in 2002, these courts were abolished in 2015 and their personnel incorporated into existing civil courts as court assessors.
226. There are now one hundred and sixty Courts of First instance in France, at least one in each department.
227. Each Court of First Instance includes professional judges, including a president and vice-presidents, as well as clerks, collaborators of judges and registry staff. Depending on its importance, a Court of First Instance may include several chambers (i.e., thirty-one in Paris, and eleven in Marseille). The president of a Court of First Instance enjoys a specific role in the context of interlocutory proceedings as well as in the function of the judge of the execution which s/he may delegate.

rule as a collegiate body, composed of three sitting judges, assisted by a judicial clerk. In certain cases, the Court rules as a single judge. This is the case in family disputes where the single judge sits as a Family Court (*Juge aux Affaires Familiales* or JAF) and in matters regarding the protection of minors in danger and young adults where the single judge sits as a Juvenile Judge (*Juge des Enfants*). Also, the Court sits as the judge of the pretrial who ensures, in civil matters, the proper conduct of the procedure and makes sure that cases are ready to be tried within a reasonable time. Lastly, the judge of the execution sits as a single judge who decides on the difficulties arising from the execution of judicial decisions (*Juge de l'Exécution des Peines*). The Public Prosecution Service may intervene in civil proceedings in order to enforce the law and ensure that the general interest of society is respected. The public prosecutor (*Procureur de la République*) and his/her deputies form the Public Prosecutor's Office (*Ministère Public*).

254. The Court of First Instance shares its civil jurisdiction with the District Court (*Tribunal d'Instance* or TI).[228] Close and accessible to the public, the District Court has jurisdiction over all civil law cases involving claims below EUR 10,000 as of 1 July 2017. Such claims may include, among others, disputes relating to traffic accidents, payment of condominium fees, unpaid debts, or claims for damages or refund of a product or service. The District Court has also exclusive jurisdiction for certain disputes whatever the amount of the claim. These disputes include, for example, disputes between landlords and tenants relating to the payment of rents or termination of the lease, disputes relating to funeral arrangements, disputes relating to tuition or boarding fees, disputes relating to tree and hedge pruning, disputes relating to the determination of properties boundaries or even disputes concerning professional elections within companies. The District Court also deals with disputes relating to consumer credit of an amount less than, or equal to, EUR 75,000. District Courts include one or more professional judges. Cases are always adjudicated by a single trial judge who presides over the hearings and makes his/her own decision, assisted by a clerk. The public prosecutor is not necessarily present at hearings but may be involved in order to enforce the law and protect the interests of society. Specialized courts of first instance have jurisdiction over a particular area of law.

255. Commercial Courts (*Tribunaux de Commerce*) are competent to decide on disputes between traders, or between traders and commercial companies, and on those disputes relating to commercial acts.[229] Commercial Courts rule either at both first and last instance (i.e., without the possibility of an appeal) or in first instance (i.e., with the possibility of an appeal) depending on the importance of the claim under dispute. Commercial Courts are composed of non-professional judges called

228. There are now three hundred and five District Courts in France.

229. There are one hundred and thirty-five Commercial Courts in France. This is the oldest type of domestic court which dates back to pre-Revolution times. Due to historical reasons, the distribution of the Commercial Courts is rather uneven on the French territory as their establishment originally used to depend on where business was done. In the absence of a Commercial Court, the Court of First Instance is competent. There are also special regimes in Alsace-Moselle, New Caledonia and French Guiana.

'consular judges' (*juges consulaires*) who are traders elected by their fellow traders and other business professionals – the idea being that lay judges are better placed than professional judges to deal with cases involving practices and customs of the trade profession. The judgment formation must include at least three judges, unless otherwise stipulated. The public prosecutor represents the interests of society before the Commercial Court and his/her representation is mandatory in cases of receivership or liquidation of companies. The registry of the Commercial Court is held by a public officer and performs various functions such as record-keeping and delivery of copies of judicial decisions for their execution; the registry also keeps the Companies Register and ensures the legality of signatures and record entries of books of traders and companies.

256. Labour Courts (*Conseils de Prud'Hommes*) settle the disputes that arise between employees (or apprentices) and their employers during the employment contract, whether these are open-ended contracts, fixed-term contracts or contract of apprenticeship.[230] Therefore, Labour Courts are competent to recognize the existence or validity of an employment contract. Labour Courts are also competent to deal with disputes relating to performance of an employment contract such as disputes concerning wages, bonuses, holidays, discrimination, training, but also as regards, among others, dismissal, compensation, non-competition clauses, legal duration of the notice of departure. The jurisdiction of Labour Courts is limited to individual disputes. Conflicts involving collective interests such as in professional elections, interruption of a strike, problems of interpretation of a collective agreement or of a collective agreement between a trade union organization and an employer do not fall within their jurisdiction. Like Commercial Courts, Labour Courts are composed of lay judges in order to ensure their connection with the reality of the business they are confronted with in litigation.[231] These *Prud'Hommes* judges are appointed for a four-year term on a joint proposal from the representatives of the trade unions and the employers' organizations according to their respective audiences.[232] In order to assist and represent the employee who so wishes before the Labour Court, the law has put in place the trade union defender (*défenseur syndical*) who benefits from paid leave of absence as well as a special protected status in order to perform his/her role. Referral to the Labour Court involves a prior conciliation procedure between the parties before the Conciliation and Guidance Office (*Bureau de Conciliation et d'Orientation*). If the parties do not

230. There are two hundred and ten Labour Courts, plus six Employment Courts in France.

231. The Labour Court is divided into five autonomous sections corresponding to the different sectors of activity, namely agriculture, industry, trade and management (i.e., managers and assimilated employees regardless of their sector of activity), and other professional sectors (i.e., liberal professions, artistic activities, education, domestic workers, caretakers, building keepers). A president and a vice-president are elected each year to manage each section. These positions are occupied alternately by an employee assessor and then by an employer assessor.

232. Labour Courts also include a registry, composed of clerks and other registry staff. In case of a tie in a decision, a professional judge will intervene and have a casting vote.

reach an agreement, they are referred to the trial office (*Bureau de Règlement*).[233] The conciliation procedure is mandatory, except in some cases. For claims in excess of EUR 4,000, appeals may be lodged within one month before the Court of Appeal. In the case of disputes the amount of which does not reach this threshold, the Labour Court rules in first and last instances and an appeal may be brought before the Court of Cassation within a period of two months on points of law only.

257. Civil Courts of Appeal re-examine cases that have already been tried in first instance in civil, commercial or social matters, coming from the Courts of First Instance, District Courts, Labour Courts, Commercial Courts and other specialized courts.[234] The Court of Appeal exercises its jurisdiction in law and in fact on the judgment submitted to it. The Court can either confirm the decision rendered by the first instance judge or may invalidate it (i.e., annul or reform it) in whole or in part. In the latter case, the Court rules on the substance of the case. Judgments of the Court of Appeal may be subject to an appeal before the Court of Cassation on points of law only. A Court of Appeal is composed solely of professional judges, namely a first president, presidents of chambers and counsels.[235] The Public Prosecutor's Office is represented at the hearings of the Court of Appeal by a professional magistrate, namely the general prosecutor or one of the general prosecutor's substitutes.

b. Criminal Courts Judge Suspected Offenders and Impose Penalties on Them

258. Criminal courts of first instance are trial courts of original jurisdiction. These courts are divided between those with general jurisdiction and those entrusted with a special jurisdiction in a particular area of law. French criminal law follows a tripartite division which is based on the seriousness of the offence committed – the so-called contraventions, offences and crimes division (*contraventions*, *délits*, *crimes*). Contraventions concern petty infractions (e.g., parking ticket fines) which are punishable by a fine of less than EUR 3,000. Offences are more serious infractions (e.g., thefts, misappropriation of company assets, manslaughter) which are punishable by a fine equal to, or of more than, EUR 3,000 and/or a jail sentence of less than ten years. Finally, crimes top the categorization to include infractions (e.g., murder, rape) which are punishable by a life sentence or jail term of more than ten years. Three types of court formations are involved in criminal proceedings, namely (1) investigating courts, (2) trial courts and (3) enforcement courts. Investigating

233. There is also the possibility of interlocutory proceedings for all sections of the Labour Court. In that case, a Labour Court may rule in cases without serious contestation and take interim measures in order to prevent further damage, or put an end to a manifestly unlawful disorder.

234. There are thirty-six Courts of Appeal in France. For their criminal competence, *see* below b. Criminal courts judge suspected offenders and impose penalties on them. For historical reasons since the location of a number of Courts of Appeal corresponded to the location of parliaments (i.e., former courts) during the *Ancien Régime*, Courts of Appeal are not present in every major city in France; there is no Court of Appeal in, for example, Marseille or Lille, but there is one in Aix-en-Provence and one in Douai.

235. Each Court of Appeal comprises specialized chambers (i.e., civil, social, commercial and criminal), each composed of three professional judges, namely a chamber president and two counsels. However, for cases to be held in a solemn hearing (e.g., on a referral from the Court of Cassation), judgments are rendered by five judges.

courts are involved in the investigation of crimes and, possibly, of the lower category of the offences. The conduct of the judicial investigation is carried out by an investigating judge (*juge d'instruction*) who belongs to the Court of First Instance. His/her investigation seeks to build a case by gathering all evidence, whether it incriminates or exonerates the defendant. The investigating judge eventually decides on whether to drop the case by issuing an order accordingly (*ordonnance de non-lieu*) or to pursue the case by formally charging the defendant (*mise en examen*). In that latter case, the investigating judge brings the case before the first instance Criminal Court (*Tribunal Correctionnel*) in relation to offences, or before the Court of Assizes in relation to crimes. The orders rendered by the investigating judge can be appealed before the court of investigation (*Chambre de l'Instruction*) which is a special formation of the Court of Appeal competent on all measures taken by the investigating judge. The formation also deals with measures taken by the judge of liberties and detention (*Juge des Libertés et de la Détention* or JLD) who is competent to rule on a deprivation of liberty of the accused offender. Trial courts of general jurisdiction replicate the three-tiered division between contraventions, offences and crimes. The Police Court (*Tribunal de Police*), which is an emanation of the District Court in its criminal formation, is competent for contraventions. The Criminal Court (*Tribunal Correctionnel*), which is an emanation of the Court of First Instance in its criminal formation, is competent as regards offences. The Court of Assizes is competent as regards crimes and is the only French court to include a jury.[236] All decisions rendered by these trial courts are subject to appeal, before the Court of Criminal Appeals for offences and contraventions, and before another formation of the Court of Assizes for crimes.[237] Enforcement courts are either sitting in a single-judge formation as the enforcement judge (*Juge de l'Application des Peines* or JAP) or in a collegial formation as the enforcement tribunal (*Tribunal de l'Application des Peines* or TAP).

259. Specialized criminal courts are competent to rule over certain types of criminal offences such as those committed by minors, military personnel, seafarers or those committed by politicians such as the President of the Republic and ministers.[238]

260. The link between civil and criminal courts is also demonstrated by the option available to the aggrieved victim to bring civil action proceedings before a criminal court in order to claim damages, instead of claiming those damages before the ordinary civil courts.

---

236. The Court of Assizes is composed of six jurors, selected by lot, and three professional judges.

237. In that case, the Court of Assizes for appeals is composed of nine jurors and three professional judges.

238. *See* below *D. Other Courts*.

2. The Court of Cassation

261. The Court of Cassation is the highest court of the ordinary judiciary. It sits in Paris and exercises its jurisdiction over the whole French territory. The Court of Cassation rules on the conformity with the law of lower courts decisions. In other words, it rules on points of law only, and does not rule on facts. The Court does not represent a third level of appeal. Proceedings are brought before the Court via the so-called cassation appeal (*pourvoi en cassation*), by a legal or natural person who has been the subject of a court ruling, or by the public prosecutor. Where the Court of Cassation considers that the contested decision was not taken in accordance with the law, it quashes (or 'breaks') the decision. The case is then referred to a lower court for retrial since the Court of Cassation is only a judge of law and does not rule on the facts of the case. If, on the contrary, the Court of Cassation dismisses the cassation appeal, it means that it upholds the impugned decision of the lower court. By its role, the Court of Cassation contributes to harmonize domestic case law. Since 2001, the Court of Cassation has also a consultative role. The procedure allows lower ordinary courts to refer to the Court of Cassation for an opinion a question on a novel point of law, which presents a serious difficulty and which arises in numerous disputes.[239] The opinion of the Supreme Court is not binding, not on the lower courts or on the Court of Cassation itself. However, by clarifying a particular point of law outside the context of a lawsuit, such opinion may influence lower judges and hence contribute to further stabilize the case law. Lastly, the Court of Cassation has a constitutional law role via its decision to refer an issue of constitutionality to the French Constitutional Council under the QPC procedure.[240]

262. The Court of Cassation is divided into chambers (*Chambres*), namely three civil chambers,[241] a commercial and financial chamber, a social chamber, and a criminal chamber. In case of conflicts of interpretation between two or more chambers, the Court may sit in a joint chambers formation which groups judges from two or more chambers known as *Chambres Mixtes*, or it may sit as in a plenary hearing of nineteen judges representing the different chambers and presided by the First President of the Court known as the *Assemblée Plénière*. Each chamber is composed of a president and counsels, all belonging to the category of the sitting judges. The public prosecutor is represented by the General Prosecutor and substitutes of the General Prosecutor.

---

239. Article L 441-1 Code of Judicial Organization. The procedure applies to all ordinary courts, including criminal courts, except investigating courts and the Court of Assizes.

240. *See* below §2. Judicial Review, II. The Constitutional Council, A. Jurisdiction.

241. The civil chambers are specialized as follows: status of the persons, conflict of laws and private international law for the first civil chamber; torts and contract law for the second civil chamber; and property law for the third civil chamber.

C. Subdivisions within the Courts of Administrative Jurisdiction

263. Administrative courts decide disputes between the administration (i.e., State, local authorities, public institutions or private bodies entrusted with a public service mission) and the citizens, or between two public bodies. These administrative courts form part of a unified system with the Council of State sitting at the top of the hierarchy.

1. The Courts of Administrative Jurisdiction

264. Administrative courts are divided between those with general jurisdiction and those entrusted with a special jurisdiction in a particular area of law.

a. General Administrative Courts

265. Administrative Courts (*Tribunaux Administratifs* or TA) are the ordinary trial courts of first instance which judge disputes between individuals and the administration, as well as labour disputes in the public service.[242] They can also be consulted by local administrative authorities for an opinion. Administrative Courts are divided into chambers (from one to seventeen) and usually sit in a formation headed by a president and two counsels, or first counsels. Administrative Courts of Appeals (*Cours Administratives d'Appel* or CAA) are competent to decide on appeal, at the request of a private party or at the request of the administration, about judgments rendered by the Administrative Courts, save a few exceptions in which appeals are directly referred to the Council of State. This is the case of referrals from the ordinary judiciary, of litigation on local elections, and of judicial review appeals.[243] Administrative Courts of Appeals are headed by a member of the Council of State and are divided into chambers (three or four). The judgment formation is headed by the president of the chamber and four counsels, namely two chamber counsels, one counsel from another chamber and one counsel rapporteur.

b. Specialized Administrative Courts

266. A number of specific disputes fall under the jurisdiction of specialized administrative courts, at first instance and then on appeal. Their decisions may then be referred to the Council of State, which is the cassation court of the administrative judicial order. Some courts are specialized to rule on disciplinary matters of certain professions, such as the Superior Council of the Judiciary (*See* below II.

242. There are forty-two Administrative Courts in France, at least one per region. *See* Law No 53-611 of 11 Jul. 1953 relating to economic and financial recovery, and Decree No 53-934 of 30 Sep. 1953 on reforming administrative litigation.

243. There are eight Administrative Courts of Appeals in France. *See* Law No 87-1127 of 31 Dec. 1987 on reforming administrative litigation.

Constitutional and Legal Status of the Members of the Judiciary; Judicial Independence, *A. The Independence of the Judiciary*, 1. The Superior Council of the Judiciary), and disciplinary sections of professional bodies such those concerning architects, auditors, veterinarians, doctors, dental surgeons, pharmacists or midwives. Other courts are specialized in the litigation of foreign nationals with the task of granting, refusing or withdrawing refugee status and subsidiary protection (i.e., The National Court of Asylum); others are competent in social matters (i.e., departmental committees and central welfare commissions as well as departmental and regional courts for military invalidity pensions), or in financial matters (i.e., regional courts of auditors and the national Court of Auditors, as well as the enforcement committee of the Financial Markets Regulator).

2. The Council of State

267. The Council of State is the highest administrative court in France.[244] It sits in Paris and exercises its jurisdiction over the whole French territory. Being the supreme administrative jurisdiction, its role is pivotal to maintaining the relationship between citizens and public authorities. Only an administrative judge can quash or reform the decisions made by authorities exercising executive powers such as the central administration or entities that exercise delegated powers.[245] The Council of State has competence to rule on cassation, on appeal, or in first and last instances (which means, in that latter instance, that it is the only court hearing the case).[246] The disputes before the Council of State range from disputes concerning public liberties, to disputes on administrative police, taxes, public contracts, the civil service, public health, competition rules, environmental law, and urban and regional development just to name a few. First, the Council of State is the judge of cassation of the judgments delivered by the Administrative Courts of Appeals. It does not judge the dispute a third time but verifies compliance with the rules of procedure and the correct application of the law by the Administrative Courts and the Administrative Courts of Appeals. In that role, and like the Court of Cassation for the ordinary judicial order, the Council of State contributes to the unity of the case law. Second, the Council of State is, exceptionally, an appellate judge particularly in electoral matters at local level as regards municipal and cantonal elections.[247] Finally, the Council of State has a judicial review competence in the first and last instances as regards a number of administrative acts, including decrees and regulatory acts of ministers

244. Formally installed in 1799, the Council of State reprised the role of the Council of the King which, composed of close advisers to the monarch, dealt with the administration of the Kingdom. Post-Revolution, the Council was sought to implement the principle of the separation of powers by having a special judicial order to judge the administration.
245. With the evolving politico-socio context, administrative law disputes have correspondingly increased by an average of 10% in recent years.
246. In addition to its judicial competence, the Council of State has also an advisory role. *See* below Chapter 6. Independent Advisory Bodies at the Legislative and Executive Levels, §1. The Council of State.
247. The Council of State was relieved of much of this appellate competence with the creation of the Administrative Courts of Appeals.

(e.g., circulars), as well as challenges against EU and regional elections results.[248] Also, the Council of State has a constitutional law role via its decision to refer an issue of constitutionality to the French Constitutional Council under the QPC procedure.[249]

268. Administrative law has developed as a judge-made law based on seminal decisions by the Council of State, as well as the Disputes Court. The legislative and regulatory powers have later codified key principles and rules found in the case law of the Council of State.[250] The Council of State is divided up into sections which reflect the two main roles – (1) judicial and (2) advisory – of the court, namely a judicial section (*section du contentieux*) and a number of administrative sections (*sections administratives*).[251] Members of the Council of State sit in the two formations, either in a judicial capacity to rule on cases or in an advisory capacity to give opinions, the aim being to allow the emergence of a unified position between the twofold role of the supreme administrative court. The judicial section is composed of ten chambers – formerly known as subsections (*sous-sections*) – which are themselves specialized in different areas of public law. The plenary chamber (*Assemblée du Contentieux*) is competent to rule on difficult legal issues of principle.

D. *Other Courts*

269. Other types of courts include a regulatory administrative court, namely the Court of Auditors, and the so-called political courts, namely the High Court which is competent to judge the President of the Republic, and the Court of Justice of the Republic which is competent to judge members of government.

1. The Court of Auditors

270. The Court of Auditors is the supreme body which audits the use of public funds in France.[252] The Court has financial jurisdiction and is in charge of auditing, issuing rulings and certifying the State and Social Security accounts, as well as contributing to the evaluation of public policies. The Court's organization will be presented after a brief description of its guiding principles and missions.

---

248. While it might not be that relevant in English, the terminology in the French language is important. Judicial decisions of Administrative Courts as well as those of Administrative Courts of Appeals are formally called *judgments*. However, we talk about *decisions* for the Council of State.

249. *See* below §2. Judicial Review, II. The Constitutional Council, A. Jurisdiction.

250. Marceau Long, Prosper Weil, Guy Braibant, Pierre Devolvé, Bruno Genevois (eds), *Les grands arrêts de la jurisprudence administrative* (21st ed, Dalloz 2017).

251. For a description of the administrative sections, *see* below Chapter 6. Independent Advisory Bodies at the Legislative and Executive Levels, §1. The Council of State.

252. Developments inspired by the website of the Court of Auditors. *See* <https://www.ccomptes.fr/en> (accessed 10 Jun. 2018).

a. Guiding Principles

271. The work of the Court of Auditors follows a number of principles, namely independence (in the programming and conduct of audits and the choice of action to be undertaken subsequently), collegiality and the adversarial procedure, all of which guarantee the quality and impartiality of its observations. Independence from both the government and Parliament is a key feature of the Court of Auditors. This independence is based on its status as a Court, which has been the case since it was founded in 1807.[253] This was reinforced when the Court became self-governing and took charge of certifying the State's accounts thus making inappropriate for it to continue to be managed by the Department of Finance which produces these accounts. The independence of the Court also stems from the independence of its members who are permanent judges.[254] The independence is also a state of mind and practice which is now firmly established within the institution owing it to its prestige and long-standing existence. In its procedure, the Court of Auditors respects the principle of fair hearing (i.e., *audi alteram partem* principle) which is a general principle in legal proceedings guaranteed under Article 6 of the European Convention on Human Rights (ECHR). Members of the Court carry out their audit based on documents and on-site investigations. The audited party has the right to give their point of view on the provisional document supplied to them by the Court. Methods for applying the fair hearing principle to the Court have changed over the years thanks to successive reforms which have sought to strike a balance between the obligation to hear the point of view of the individual being investigated, and the need to conduct an audit within a reasonable time frame in the interest of efficiency in the conduct of the Court's work. Auditing is an individually focused process. The magistrate investigates 'for the prosecution and for the defence' and simply suggests what outcome his/her observations should lead to and whether there may be legal or non-legal consequences. However, ruling on auditing matters is a collegial decision – this is in order to eliminate personal preferences. Moreover, each person's position is covered by the confidentiality of proceedings. Even though it is not regarded as a general procedural principle in French law, the principle of collective responsibility is therefore another important principle in the procedure of the Court which has proven necessary for the legitimacy and credibility of the Court.

---

253. *See* CC Decision No 2001-448 DC of 25 Jul. 2001, *Loi organique relative aux lois de finances*, *Rec.* 99, pt 106: 'Considering that under the Code of Financial Jurisdictions, the Court of Auditors is an administrative court; that, as stated above, the Constitution guarantees its independence from the legislative and executive powers; whereas, although some of its tasks, notably auditing and management, are not of a judicial nature, they may reveal irregularities calling for the implementation of court proceedings.'

254. Their statutory guarantees have been reinforced since 2006. These are supplemented by a code of practice which also applies to non-judicial inspection staff (i.e., rapporteurs, experts and assistants). This independence results from legislation governing the level of recruitment, methods of appointment, promotion and pay.

b. Missions

272. The Court of Auditors ensures the proper, efficient and effective use of public funds.[255] In order to fulfil its missions, the Court assesses audits, evaluates and certifies. First, the Court assesses the accounts of public accounting officers (i.e., civil servants or public officers accredited to manage public funds) in order to check that income and expenditure are correct.[256] The Court then releases the accountant from liability if the accounts are correct or declares them in default if income has been lost or improper expenditure has been made. Although its activity as a court is the Court's longest-standing mission, it no longer represents the major part of its activity.[257] Second, in its auditing role, the Court ensures the proper (i.e., controlling the conformity of management actions with legislation and regulations, including EU legislation and regulations), efficient (i.e., ensuring that the relationship between activities and the related resources used or mobilized is as good as possible), and effective (i.e., checking that the results obtained by public action comply with the stated objectives) use of public funds. Third, the Court of Auditors helps evaluate public policies, either praising the positive aspects of a particular policy or drawing attention to its negative impact. When these policies are conducted both nationally and locally, the Court conducts joint enquiries with the Regional and Territorial Chambers of Accounts (*Chambres Régionales et Territoriales des Comptes*).[258] Fourth, far from being a solely technical matter, certification represents a new field of competence for the Court. The objective is to provide a more reliable, transparent and comprehensive financial and accounting information of the financial reality of the State, as well as of the Social Security general regime.[259] In addition, the Court of Auditors is called to assist the government and Parliament, a role which was reinforced in recent years.

c. Organization

273. The Court of Auditors is composed of members, appointed by decree of the President of the Republic, and other auditing staff, including private sector experts,

255. As specified and extended in Art. 47-2 of the Constitution. *See also* Art. 15 of the 1789 Declaration: 'Society has the right to call any public official to account for their administration.'
256. The Court of Auditors also assesses de facto accountants (i.e., persons who improperly handle public funds). All in all, the Court has jurisdiction for over some one thousand accounts.
257. The Court's procedures were thoroughly modernized in 2005, 2006 and 2008 and its jurisdictional authority strengthened in 2011. However, the Court still does not have authority to assess the authorizing officer that is the person who gives the instruction to pay or receive payment to the accountant.
258. Since the Law No 2011-140 of 3 Feb. 2011 to strengthen Parliament's means of controlling the government's action and evaluating public policies, the president of the National Assembly and the president of the Senate may request the Court to provide for evaluation reports, handed in within one year of their request.
259. Since 2013, the Court certifies the accounts of both Houses of Parliament by transmitting to their respective president an annual report on the regularity of the accounts thereof.

as well as civil servants assigned to help with auditing and administrative management.[260] The first president, who is a judge, presides over the Court. There are also chief auditors (*conseillers-maîtres*), senior auditors (*conseillers référendaires*) and junior auditors (*auditeurs*). The Court is divided into seven chambers and has a General Prosecutor's Office.

2. The High Court

274. The role of the High Court (*Haute Cour*) is to pronounce the removal of the President of the Republic from office in case of breach of his/her duties that is manifestly incompatible with the exercise of his/her mandate (Article 68 Constitution).[261] This is the only court that can deal with the situation of the President of the Republic during the exercise of his/her mandate. The High Court is more a political body than a criminal court.[262] It is composed of members of the National Assembly and members of the Senate presided over by the president of the National Assembly. The procedure for dismissal is as follows. The proposed meeting of the High Court must be voted by a two-thirds majority of each House of Parliament. The High Court, chaired by the president of the National Assembly, shall then rule within one month and by a two-thirds majority of its members on the removal of the President of the Republic from office. The vote is personal and secret. Proxy voting is not permitted in that situation. The decision of the Court is of immediate effect. The procedure is similar to that of the impeachment procedure of the President of the USA.

3. The Court of Justice of the Republic

275. The Court of Justice of the Republic (*Cour de Justice de la République*) decides on criminal liability cases for offences committed by members of the government while in office.[263] Offences unrelated to the conduct of the Nation's policy fall within the jurisdiction of ordinary criminal courts. This special court competent to deal with ministerial responsibility is made up of fifteen judges, namely twelve

---

260. In 2018, seven hundred and forty-six staff are employed by the Court of Auditors. One thousand and thirty-one staff are employed by the Regional and Territorial Chambers of Accounts, of which thirteen are located in metropolitan France and four overseas.
261. Title IX Of The High Court (Arts 67–68 Constitution). *See* above Chapter 2. The Head of State, §2. Legal Status.
262. The High Court was put in place by Constitutional Law No 2007-238 of 23 Feb. 2007 amending Title IX of the Constitution, in order to replace the High Court of Justice (*Haute Cour de Justice de la République*). The former Court was composed of MPs and was entrusted by the Constitution to try the President of the Republic in the case of a crime of 'high treason'. The Senate was competent to try the President under the Third Republic, and the National Assembly under the Fourth Republic, to pronounce indictment as well as to determine guilt in the case.
263. Title X Of The Criminal Liability of Members of Government (Arts 68-1 to 68-3 Constitution). *See* above Chapter 4. The Executive, §2. Legal Status, II. Criminal Liability of Members of Government. The Court was established in 1993 in line with the proposals of the committee chaired by Dean Vedel instituted at the initiative of President Mitterrand in 1992 and as a consequence of the

MPs (i.e., three deputies elected by the National Assembly, and three senators elected by the Senate),[264] and three sitting judges from the Court of Cassation with one of them presiding over the Court. Proceedings before the Court of Justice of the Republic are brought by any individual, whether French or foreign, who claim his/her rights have been infringed by a government official in the performance of his/her duties. A complaints commission consisting of professional judges from the Court of Cassation, the Council of State and the Court of Auditors may decide either to dismiss the case or to refer it to the Court of Cassation for formal referral to the Court of Justice of the Republic. This filter mechanism, via the complaints commission, avoids that the remedy offered to individuals become a political weapon against governmental action. If the complaint is declared admissible, an inquiry committee composed of three Court of Cassation judges shall hear the persons charged and those who declare themselves victims. The committee then decides whether or not to refer the case to the Court of Justice of the Republic. The Court shall rule by absolute majority and by secret ballot on the guilt of the accused and then, in case of guilt, on the application of the sentence imposed. Judgments of the Court may be appealed to the Court of Cassation. In the event of its decisions being rejected, the Court must be reconstituted before the case is rejected.

276. While the possibility of initiating judicial proceedings is an improvement for the victim of governmental criminal action, the procedure has been criticized in a number of respects.[265] One criticism has been about the impossibility for individual parties to take part in the proceedings, while another criticism has been in respect of the separation of cases concerning top administrators which are dealt with before ordinary administrative courts and the difficulty of bringing these administrators to testify. Numerous calls have been made for the demise of the Court of Justice of the Republic, including by a number of candidates in the 2017 presidential election and recently by President Macron as announced by the Philippe Government in April 2018 as part of a major constitutional and institutional reform currently (June 2018) under discussion in Parliament. The Court indeed represents a privilege for ministers which has no longer any *raison d'être*. Members of the government should be tried by the ordinary criminal courts, including for acts performed in the exercise of their functions.

---

dramatic contaminated blood case which started in the mid-1980s. *See* Constitutional Law No 93-952 of 27 Jul. 1993 revising the Constitution of 4 Oct. 1958 and amending its Titles VIII, IX, X and XVIII.

264. MPs are elected after each renewal of the Houses of Parliament.

265. The Court of Justice of the Republic has dealt with several cases such as, for example, the tragic contaminated blood case which started in the mid-1980s. The case ended up with the conviction of one government official, Edmond Hervé, former Secretary of State for Health. Two other higher ranked members were acquitted, namely Georgina Dufoix, former Minister for Social Affairs and Laurent Fabius, former Prime Minister (1984–1986) and president of the Constitutional Council (2016-present). The famous quote from Dufoix (i.e., 'I certainly feel responsible; however, this does not mean that I feel guilty') illustrates the kind of disconnect that exists between the actions of government members and their actual responsibility.

II. Constitutional and Legal Status of Members of the Judiciary

277. The French judicial system aims at ensuring the application of the law and guaranteeing the respect of each individual's rights and freedoms. Referred to as the 'judicial *authority*' (*autorité judiciaire*), rather than referred to as the judicial *power*, the judiciary encompasses all civil, commercial, criminal and social courts which, under the authority of the Courts of Appeal and the Court of Cassation, rule on private law disputes. To ensure impartiality, the Constitution affirms the independence of the judicial authority from the executive (government) and legislative (Parliament) powers. The President of the Republic is entrusted with the task of guaranteeing the independence of the judiciary (Article 64 Constitution). Given the prominent powers of the President of the Republic, this has been problematic as regards the separation of powers which is one of the fundamental principles of the French constitutional order. However, the Constitutional Council has clarified that 'the independence of the courts [both ordinary and administrative] is guaranteed as well as the specific nature of their functions which neither the legislature nor the government can encroach upon'.[266] In other words, the legislative and executive powers cannot overrule court's rulings, or issue an order against them, or substitute their own judgment for that of the domestic courts.

A. The Independence of the Judiciary

278. The independence of the judicial authority is enshrined in the Constitution. It results not only from the separation of powers but also from the statutory guarantees which protect judges from the pressures or threats that might weigh on their ability to judge. Independence entails impartiality of the judges. As another fundamental feature of the judiciary, the importance of which is in particular guaranteed under the ECHR, the principle refers to the absence of prejudice which must characterize judges. This rather concerns the relations of judges with the other powers and constitutes a condition, necessary but not sufficient, of their impartiality in their relations with the litigants. Also, in order to guarantee the impartiality of judges, the law provides for certain inability to judge, for example in the case of a relationship between several judges of the same court or between a judge and a lawyer or a party. There is also a specific procedure which allows the parties to challenge the suspected bias of a judge. The independence enshrined in the Constitution concerns the sitting judges (*magistrats du siège*) only and does not extend to prosecuting judges (*magistrats du parquet*). Indeed, due to their role as public prosecutors representing the interest of society, prosecutors have an organic link with the Executive. They may thus have to follow the instructions of their hierarchical authority (i.e., the Department of Justice) in their written submissions. The independence of public prosecutors is a recurring issue in France.[267] A number of lawyers and politicians

266. CC Decision No 80-119 DC of 22 Jul. 1980, *Loi portant validation d'actes administratifs*, *Rec*. 46, pt 6.

267. On the general issue of the independence of the public prosecutors, *see* the case law of the ECtHR (ECtHR, *Moulin v. France*, app. No 37104/06, 23 Feb. 2011), the Court of Cassation (C. cass.,

have suggested aligning their status on that of ordinary judges. By contrast, judges do not bear the same obligation. Although they are public officials, judges are not civil servants and are therefore not subject to the hierarchical authority of a minister. They are irremovable and, as such, cannot be transferred, even as a promotion, to another court without their consent. Their decisions can only be challenged in the context of the exercise of judicial remedies.

1. The Superior Council of the Judiciary

279. The Superior Council of the Judiciary (*Conseil Supérieur de la Magistrature* or CSM) is the body responsible for the appointment and career development of members of the judiciary. Originally established under the 1946 Constitution, the CSM was re-established under the current Constitution with a prominent role afforded to the President of the Republic. The President of the Republic was initially charged with presiding over the institution and appointing all of its members in all categories. Two constitutional reforms, in 1993 and 2008 respectively, contributed to diminish the role of the Executive in that respect.[268] The CSM is composed of two formations: one formation which is competent as regards sitting judges, on the one hand, and another formation which is competent as regards public prosecutors, on the other hand. The First President of the Court of Cassation (equivalent to the Chief Justice) presides over the formation of the CSM which is competent as regards judges, while the General Prosecutor of the Court of Cassation presides over the formation of the CSM which is competent as regards public prosecutors. Each formation consists of fifteen members: the president (i.e., the First President of the Court of Cassation as regards judges, and the General Prosecutor of the Court of Cassation as regards prosecutors), six judges, a member of the Council of State, a legal practitioner, as well as six external highly qualified persons appointed respectively by the President of the Republic, the president of the National Assembly and the president of the Senate. The CSM's role is to intervene in the appointment and career of members of the judiciary. Concerning judges, the CSM makes proposals concerning high ranked judges and only gives its assent as regards all other ranked judges. As far as prosecutors are concerned, the CSM only gives an advisory opinion with the exception of the most prominent prosecutors whose appointment is decided in the Council of Ministers. The constitutional amendment, under discussion in Parliament at the time of writing (June 2018), is

Crim., 15 Dec. 2010, *Bull. crim.* I, 2010, No 207), and the Constitutional Council (CC Decision No 2011-125 QPC of 6 May 2011, *Mr Abderrahmane L. [Transfer into the custody of the Public Prosecutor], Rec.* 218, pt 8*).

268. Constitutional Law No 93-952 of 27 Jul. 1993 revising the Constitution of 4 Oct. 1958 and amending its Titles VIII, IX, X and XVIII, and Constitutional Law No 2008-724 of 23 Jul. 2008 on the modernization of the institutions of the Fifth Republic.

proposing, among other changes, that the CSM gives its assent, rather than an advisory opinion, to the appointment of prosecutors. The CSM also deals with disciplinary issues. In that case, the CSM sits in full capacity as a disciplinary body as far as judges are concerned, and delivers an opinion on the penalty to be imposed as far as prosecutors are concerned.

2. The Independence of Administrative Judges

280. The judges of the administrative judicial order have a status and a formation which differ from the judges of the ordinary judicial order. The Constitutional Council enshrined the existence and independence of the administrative jurisdiction as being part of the Fundamental Principles recognized by the Laws of the Republic.[269] The judges of the administrative judicial order thus benefit from a special status which guarantees their independence, notably by ensuring their immutability.[270] They are often graduates of the National School of Administration who are recruited through specific selective procedures. Disciplinary procedures and appointments are ensured by the Superior Council of Administrative Courts and Administrative Courts of Appeal, which is established on the example of its judicial counterpart, namely the Superior Council of the Judiciary. Administrative judges are under the supervision of the Vice-President of the Council of State, and not of the Department of Home Affairs, which represents an additional guarantee of their independence.

B. Limited Interference by the Executive with the Functions of the Judiciary

281. The independence of the judicial authority is enshrined in the Constitution. It results not only from the separation of powers but also from legal guarantees that protect judges from pressures or threats that could affect their ability to judge.

1. The President of the Republic and the Judiciary

282. Under the Constitution, the President of the Republic has a prominent role in the field of justice, which has, however, been progressively limited by several constitutional amendments. S/he is in charge of ensuring the independence of the judicial authority and is assisted in that role by the Superior Council of the Judiciary (Article 64 Constitution). Originally, the President of the Republic chaired the Superior Council of the Judiciary and appointed all of its members. This function seemed to allow the Head of State to exercise a certain influence over the judicial authority. The constitutional amendment of 27 July 1993 put an end to the power of

269. CC Decision No 80-119 DC of 22 Jul. 1980, *Loi portant validation d'actes administratifs*, *Rec.* 46, pt 6.
270. Law No 86-14 of 6 Jan. 1986 laying down the rules guaranteeing the independence of the members of the Administrative Courts and Administrative Courts of Appeals.

appointment by the President of the Republic. Moreover, since the 2008 constitutional amendment, the President of the Republic no longer chairs the Superior Council of the Judiciary. However, the President of the Republic retains the power to appoint professional judges (Article 13 paragraph two Constitution).[271] The President of the Republic exercises this prerogative on a proposal from the Superior Council of the Judiciary in the case of the appointment of sitting judges. His/her power is still significant as regards the appointment of prosecutors since the Superior Council of the Judiciary issues a simple opinion in that case – which is, however, usually respected. In addition, the President of the Republic holds a regal pardon power (Article 17 Constitution). This 'presidential pardon' is a shared power and must be countersigned by the Prime Minister and the Minister for Justice. This power allows amending the effects of a judicial sentence by, for instance, suspending the criminal conviction or exempting the convicted individual from penalties. This presidential prerogative is limited to individual grace and is not a general right of pardon.

2. The Public Prosecutor's Office

283. The Public Prosecutor's Office (or *Parquet*) groups all the judges who are in charge of requesting the application of the law and conducting criminal proceedings on behalf of society. At the level of each Court of First Instance, the Public Prosecutor's Office includes a public prosecutor, possibly assisted by assistant prosecutors and substitutes. All the judges of the same Public Prosecutor's Office are interchangeable and substitutable, which means that each one of them can represent indifferently the Public Prosecutor's Office in ordinary judicial proceedings. Each public prosecutor is under the hierarchy of the Executive through the control of the Minister for Justice.

III. Judicial Proceedings

284. Three types of judicial proceedings exist in French courts, namely civil proceedings, criminal proceedings, and administrative proceedings.

A. *Civil Proceedings*

285. Once a case is regularly brought before a Court of First Instance, civil proceedings take place in several stages, namely the investigation, the proceedings, and the judgment itself. The investigation stage is called the pretrial whereby the parties exchange their observations and conclusions that summarize their claims and arguments. This is an application of the principle of adversarial proceedings. During pretrial, the judge may also order certain measures of inquiry such as experts' opinions

271. *See also* Ordinance No 58-1270 of 22 Dec. 1958 on the Organic Law on the status of the judiciary (Arts 26 and 28).

which are supposed to be relevant to the outcome of the dispute at hand. After a final exchange of arguments and evidence and if the case is deemed ready for trial, the judge issues an order to close the trial and the case is remitted for pleading. The procedure before the Court of First Instance is written and representation by a lawyer is compulsory. Therefore, the pleading can be limited to a simple filing by lawyers of their final conclusions. Except where provided for by law (e.g., in family matters), hearings in civil proceedings before the Court of First Instance are public. At the end of the deliberations, which may last several months in case the dispute raises complex legal issues, the court gives a judgment summarizing the facts of the dispute, the parties' claims and arguments as well as the ratio decidendi. The judgment has the authority of res judicata and, unless one of the parties decides to appeal, it shall definitively terminate the dispute.

B. Criminal Proceedings

286. Criminal proceedings before criminal courts are subject to the fundamental principles common to all trials, namely the principle that trials are public, that the procedure is oral and must respect the right of defence, including the right to a counsel. Collegiality is also in principle applied in criminal proceedings, but many cases, considered to be the least serious ones, are dealt with by a single judge. Criminal hearings start with the appeal of the parties. The court then proceeds to read its act of referral, which recalls the nature and circumstances of the alleged offence against the accused. The latter can then take the floor to submit his/her arguments in defence. The judges, as well as also the parties, may ask questions. Witnesses and experts may be called and heard at this stage. This phase of explanation and interrogation is called 'instruction at the hearing'. Finally, the president of the court gives the floor, in a specific order, to the aggrieved party, then to the representative of the public prosecutor and finally to the defendant himself/herself or his/her counsel. The court then withdraws to deliberate. There also exists a specific procedure allowing for immediate trial (*comparution immédiate*) which makes it possible to bring instantly to justice an identified accused so that s/he may be tried in custody without being released. This procedure falls within the competence of the collegiate formation of the criminal court. It implies the presence of a lawyer, and presupposes that the accused agrees to be tried on the same day. Such procedure concerns only certain offences only. Despite its effectiveness, the procedure has often been denounced as an illustration of an expeditious criminal justice.

C. Administrative Proceedings

287. Proceedings before administrative courts are different from that of judicial proceedings in many respects. In the main, administrative proceedings are inquisitorial, written and contradictory. The inquisitorial nature before the administrative courts is mainly due to the importance of the role of the judge; indeed, immediately after the enrolment of the case with the court's registry, the president of the court appoints a judge rapporteur who will be responsible for examining the case. The judge rapporteur will challenge the applicant's adversary and act as an intermediary in the communication of documents and pleadings of the parties. S/he will also intervene in all the incidents of the proceedings and ensures that the parties respect the principle of adversarial proceedings. This interventionism of the judge is explained by the need to rebalance the respective situation of the parties, which is still very unequal in administrative proceedings since these involve an individual facing a public authority. The procedure is entirely written meaning that the parties must present their findings and arguments in the form of written submissions in French. While oral submissions are admitted at the hearing, the judge may rule only on written evidence. At the hearing, which is in principle public, the judge rapporteur first makes a report summarizing the facts and the legal issue(s) involved, before the parties make their oral observations. Then, the Public Rapporteur (formerly known as the Government's Commissioner) presents, publicly and independently, his/her findings which constitute an informed legal opinion on what s/he thinks ought to be the outcome of the dispute at hand. The court then withdraws to deliberate and renders its judgment.

IV. State Liability for the Torts of Judges or of Members of the Public Prosecutor's Office

288. Judges' professional misconduct can only be sanctioned following a conviction by the State. The law lays down the conditions to commit the responsibility of a public authority with regard to users of the public service of justice in those terms: '[T]he State is obliged to repair the damage caused by the defective functioning of the public service of Justice'; however, 'this responsibility is only engaged by a gross error or a denial of justice'.[272] Traditionally, gross error or negligence meant a serious mistake revealing the intent to harm or a judge's contempt of the basic duties of his/her office. In a judgment of 23 February 2001,[273] which concerned the so-called Little Grégory case in which procedural errors had multiplied, the Court of Cassation broadened this notion to include 'any malfunction characterized by a fact or a series of facts reflecting the inability of the public service of Justice to fulfil [its] mission'.

289. In addition, some special regimes of State responsibility have been put in place in the area of criminal justice. The Law of 17 July 1970 instituted a system of compensation for unjustified custodial detention whereby any individual who has been acquitted or who has been freed despite being placed in pretrial detention has an automatic right to compensation without having to prove the existence of the

272. Law No 72-626 of 5 Jul. 1972 establishing a judge of the execution and relating to the reform of the civil procedure.

273. C. cass, Ass. plén, 23 Feb. 2001, *Bull. Ass. plén.* 2001, No 5. The 'Little Grégory' case refers to the horrendous murder of a four-year old boy in the East of France in 1984. The case has sparked a lengthy police investigation and a judicial saga which has attracted considerable domestic media coverage over the years. The killer has never been found to this day and the case remains open.

damage.[274] Similarly, the Law of 30 December 2000 allows the victim of a miscarriage of justice, which has been revealed by a new fact and after having been the subject of judicial review, to obtain full compensation for the material and moral damage resulting from his/her conviction.[275] Finally, the functioning of the public service of administrative justice can also result in the State being held liable in the case of a simple wrong which, in a seminal case of 2002 by the Council of State, was regarded as being the non-respect of the right to be tried within a reasonable time.[276]

§2. Judicial Review

290. The notion of judicial review in French constitutional law will be explained before describing the Constitutional Council which has jurisdiction in the matter.

I. Judicial Review in French Constitutional Law

291. The current meaning of judicial review in domestic law is the result of a long history about the progressive and relatively recent emergence of judicial review of legislation in particular.

A. The Meaning of Judicial Review

292. The general expression of 'judicial review' means 'that a judge can examine a legal decision or norm, or another object of scrutiny, and check its compatibility with a higher norm'. In other words, it is 'a court's power to detect conflicts in law, and possibly to attach consequences to resolve the conflict'.[277] Judicial review is aimed at reviewing executive and legislative acts by the courts, possibly leading to the invalidation of such acts. In its administrative meaning, judicial review is a procedure through which the courts may question the lawfulness of the action by public bodies. In other words, judicial review ensures that any delegated legislation is consistent with the scope of power granted by Parliament and ensures the legality of government action and the actions of other public bodies. In its constitutional meaning, judicial (constitutional) review is the review by a court of the

274. Law No 70-643 of 17 Jul. 1970 to strengthen the guarantee of the individual rights of citizens.
275. Law No 2000-1354 of 30 Dec. 2000 to facilitate the compensation of convicts recognized as innocent and relating to diverse coordination provisions in criminal procedure.
276. CE, Ass., 28 Jun. 2002, *Ministre de la Justice c/Magiera*, app No 239575.
277. Aalt Willem Heringa, Constitutions Compared: An Introduction to Comparative Constitutional Law (4th ed, Intersentia 2016) 159.

conformity of legislation enacted by Parliament to the Constitution. Constitutional review has now become 'a dominant feature of modern constitutionalism' and 'is now clearly a global phenomenon'.[278]

293. The Constitution represents the supreme act in the French legal order organizing the existence and relations of the public authorities and setting the rules for the exercise of political power. Both the administrative and ordinary judges have considered that the supremacy conferred to international agreements on the laws by the Constitution (Article 55 Constitution) cannot, in the internal order, be extended 'to the provisions of constitutional nature'.[279] In the domestic hierarchy of norms, the Constitution is at the top. Consequently, all other legal norms must conform to the Constitution which is the *raison d'être* of the judicial constitutional review whereby the conformity of laws to the Constitution will be ensured. Furthermore, the review concerns the conformity to not only the text of the Constitution but also to a range of norms of constitutional value which, together with the Constitution, has formed what is called the 'block of constitutionality' (*See* above Part I. Sources of Constitutional Law, Chapter 2. The Constitution, §1. The Characteristics of Constitutional Norms, II. The Extent of the Constitution: The Block of Constitutionality). The block of constitutionality includes all constitutional provisions, the 1789 Declaration, the Preamble to the 1946 Constitution, the 2004 Charter for the Environment, as well as a number of principles derived from the case law of the Constitutional Council (i.e., 'Principles of Law Particularly Necessary to our Time', 'Fundamental Principles recognized by the Laws of the Republic').

B. Judicial Review of Legislation in French Constitutional History

294. A proper mechanism of constitutional review has not been firmly established before the Fifth Republic in 1958, further enhanced by the 2008 constitutional amendment and the introduction of a posteriori review. The reluctance to establish constitutional review in domestic law is explained by the specific place of the law in the French legal order: from being an 'inviolable' norm, the law has been progressively undermined with the advancement of constitutionalism.

1. The Principle of the 'Inviolability of the Law'

295. The history of judicial review of legislation in France has been full of paradoxes and failures. Despite early provisions in the 1789 Declaration which posed the principle of constitutional justice and attested of the limits of the law, France

278. Albert HY Chen and Miguel Poiares Maduro, 'The judiciary and constitutional review' in Mark Tushnet, Thomas Fleiner and Cheryl Saunders (eds), *Routledge Handbook of Constitutional Law* (Routledge 2013) 97, 100.

279. CE, Ass., 30 Oct. 1998, *Sarran, Levacher et autres, Rec. Lebon* 368; C. cass., Ass. plén., 2 Jun. 2000, *Fraisse, Bull. Ass. plén.* 2000, No 4.

had come to 'sacralize' the law. Inherited from Rousseau's legal theory, an idealized conception of the law started to emerge. As an 'expression of the general will', the law was considered as a supreme, irreproachable and indisputable act and perceived as the best way to reconcile the exercise of power with the protection of citizens' liberties by limiting the action of the Executive. In strictly legal terms, it meant that the law was regarded as unlimited in its scope (i.e., no restriction on its scope), indivisible (i.e., no delegation of the power to make law) and unquestionable (i.e., judicial immunity as judges were supposed to 'serve' the law and not sanction it). *Légicentrisme* (i.e., the doctrine which places the law at the centre of the hierarchy of norms) combined with an historical hostility towards judges made it difficult to envisage judicial review of legislation.[280]

2. The Principle Undermined

296. The excesses of the governments during the twentieth century led to unstable regimes in which the Legislative dominated the Executive and resulted, most notably in the case of a number of European jurisdictions, into totalitarian practices. The consequential acknowledgment that the law was unable to fulfil its role in securing individual and collective rights and freedoms, and in providing for political stability, led to a shift in favour of the constitution. Envisaged as the supreme norm, the constitution was henceforth regarded as the norm capable of acting as a more solid bulwark against these risks. The Fifth Republic is the regime which definitely broke from the previous tenets relating to the sovereignty of the law by curtailing the sovereignty of Parliament. The weakening of the law and the ensuing recognition of the political and judicial authority of the constitution was embodied in several provisions of the Constitution, namely Article 34 (i.e., delimitation of the scope of the law), Article 55 (i.e., supremacy of international law), and Article 61 (i.e., limited review of legislation).[281] This is, however, the establishment of the Constitutional Council which, by its evolution as an institution and its progressive case law, has drastically changed the outlook of judicial review in French constitutional law.

II. The Constitutional Council

297. The jurisdiction, composition, organization and operation of the Constitutional Council will be briefly examined. Further references will be provided about what has become a fully fledged constitutional court.

---

280. *See* Marie-Luce Paris, 'The French System of Rights-Based Review: From Exceptionalism to Parochial Constitutionalism' in John Bell and Marie-Luce Paris, *Rights-Based Constitutional; Review: Constitutional Courts in a Changing Landscape* (Edward Elgar 2016) 302, 308–309.
281. *Ibid.* 309.

A. Jurisdiction

298. The substance of the review as well as the proceedings before the Constitutional Council are described below in order to fully grasp the extent of its jurisdiction in the matter of judicial review.

1. The Substance of the Review

299. The powers of the Constitutional Council are set out in the Constitution and completed by a set of organic laws and decrees. The principle is that the Council's powers are limited to those powers which have been expressly conferred upon it. This principle of limited constitutional jurisdiction was first expressed in a 1961 Decision when the Council considered that its competence in giving consultative advice was a limited and not a general one.[282] In respect of its judicial review competence, the Council has repeatedly asserted that Article 61 of the Constitution does not confer upon it 'a general or particular discretion identical with that of Parliament, but simply empowers [the Council] to rule on the constitutionality of [laws] referred to it'.[283] Some of the Council's well-known decisions are indeed decisions of incompetence. One example is the 1962 Decision on the 28 October 1962 Referendum on the Election of the President of the Republic by Direct Universal Suffrage. The Council refused to rule on the constitutionality of the law adopted by referendum because it regarded such law as 'the direct expression of national sovereignty' which the Council could not challenge.[284]

300. The power of judicial review of the Constitutional Council is part of its judicial powers, the other being its power as an electoral judge.[285] Because the Constitution established a distinction between the legislative area (Article 34 Constitution) and the regulatory area (Article 37 Constitution), and endowed the government with a normative power (i.e., the power to issue regulations), the task of the Council has primarily been to make sure that this division is respected and that Parliament does not infringe upon the regulatory competence of government. However, the task of the Council is mostly to review the constitutionality of legislation (Article 61 Constitution), as well as the constitutionality of international agreements (Article 54 Constitution). The Council exercises two types of review in this

282. CC Decision No 61-1 AUTR of 14 Sep. 1961, *Demande d'avis présentée par le Président de l'Assemblée nationale (Recevabilité de la motion de censure)*, *Rec.* 55, pt 1: 'Considering that the Constitution has strictly defined the competence of the Constitutional Council; that the latter may be called upon to give a ruling or issue an opinion only in the cases and according to the procedures [the Constitution] has set.'

283. CC Decision No 74-54 DC of 15 Jan. 1975, *Loi relative à l'interruption volontaire de grossesse*, *Rec.* 19, pt 1*.

284. CC Decision No 62-20 DC of 6 Nov. 1962, *Loi relative à l'élection du Président de la République au suffrage universel direct, adoptée par le référendum du 28 octobre 1962*, *Rec.* 27, pt 2.

285. The Constitutional Council has also consultative powers. *See* Marie-Luce Paris, 'The French Constitutional Council: Another "Work in Progress"' in Emmanuel Guinchard et Marie-Pierre Granger, *The New EU Judiciary: An Analysis of Current Judicial Reforms* (Kluwer 2017) 47, 56.

regard, namely a priori review (as it puts the voted legislation on hold until the outcome of the review of constitutionality) and a posteriori review (as it occurs after the law is promulgated). Judicial review is the area which has most transformed the role and dynamic of the Council. Notably, in its 1971 Decision on Freedom of Association the Council declared, for the first time, the unconstitutionality of a law for breach of fundamental rights, hereby marking the start of its judicial empowerment.[286] From then onwards, the Council decided to exercise an effective review, not only from a procedural point of view by reviewing the conformity of laws to procedural and institutional rules pertaining to the functioning of public powers but also from a substantive perspective.

2. Proceedings Before the Constitutional Council

301. Proceedings before the Constitutional Council have greatly evolved since its inception. These have become increasingly judicial in nature. The decisions are taken by a simple majority, in plenary sessions, with a quorum of seven members, which is essential to ensure the authority of the rulings. While the length of judicial proceedings is a negative trait of most Supreme Courts in Europe, including the European Court of Human Rights (ECtHR), the Council has been quite exemplary in rendering justice within prescribed time frames and has always managed to respect the strict time frame of one month in a priori review proceedings. Although proceedings before the Council do not display the classic features that one might expect to find in judicial proceedings (i.e., the adversarial principle, the right to be heard and the publicity of court hearings) since its proceedings have traditionally been of an inquisitorial type, mostly conducted in writing, with limited involvement of parties, and limited publicity, some incremental changes have greatly remediated that.[287] Furthermore, two constitutional amendments further empowered the Constitutional Council in its judicial review role, one concerning its a priori review and the other its a posteriori review.

a. A Priori Review

302. The 1974 constitutional amendment[288] was a turning point which granted to sixty deputies or sixty senators, the right to challenge a law a priori, while this right was reserved before to only the President of the Republic, the Prime Minister and the president of either House of Parliament. By de facto opening the review to the MPs of the opposition, the reform notably increased the activity of the Constitutional Council and raised its profile in the political landscape. A priori referrals, although optional, have become quite systematic testing the constitutionality of

286. CC Decision No 71-44 DC of 16 Jul. 1971, *Loi complétant les dispositions des articles 5 et 7 de la loi du 1er juillet 1901 relative au contrat d'association*, *Rec.* 25*.

287. *See* Marie-Luce Paris, 'The French Constitutional Council: Another "Work in Progress"' in Emmanuel Guinchard et Marie-Pierre Granger, *The New EU Judiciary: An Analysis of Current Judicial Reforms* (Kluwer 2017) 47, 62 et seq.

288. Law No 74-904 of 29 Oct. 1974 on the revision of Art. 61 of the Constitution.

many laws touching upon some of the most significant political and societal issues of modern France such as the termination of pregnancy, immigration, bioethics, civil partnership, headscarf ban, decentralization, nationalizations and privatizations, and the participation of France to the European integration. A priori review is either mandatory or facultative, depending on the type of norms concerned. Organic laws before their promulgation, rules of procedure of both Houses of Parliament before coming into force, and, under certain conditions, parliamentary bills before they are submitted to referendum, *must* be referred to the Constitutional Council (Article 61 paragraph one Constitution), whereas ordinary laws *may* be referred before their promulgation (Article 61 paragraph two Constitution). A finding of unconstitutionality leads to the censure of all, or part of, the law (i.e., not its annulment since it is not in existence yet).

b. A Posteriori Review (QPC Procedure)

303. The introduction of the procedure for 'Priority Preliminary Rulings on an Issue of Constitutionality' (*Question Prioritaire de Constitutionnalité* or QPC) on the occasion of the 2008 constitutional amendment[289] added another constitutional remedy in the form of a posteriori review (Article 61-1 paragraph one Constitution). If, during pending proceedings before a French court, it is argued that a legislative provision infringes the rights and freedoms guaranteed by the Constitution, the Constitutional Council may be seized of this issue by the Council of State or the Court of Cassation, which can decide on the matter within a specified period of time. So, the general mechanism of the QPC is that it is, first, raised before a first instance court, an appeal court or one of the Supreme Courts (i.e., Court of Cassation or Council of State); second, it is filtered by one of the Supreme Courts if coming from lower instances; eventually, it is decided upon by the Constitutional Council. A QPC is declared admissible, by a first instance or appeal judge, under four conditions: if (i) the allegedly unconstitutional provision is of legislative nature; (ii) its application is necessary for the outcome of the case; (iii) it has not been previously declared compatible with the Constitution by the Council (except for a change of circumstances of fact or law); and (iv) the issue of constitutionality presents a 'serious character'. If declared admissible, the ordinary judge will then suspend the proceedings until a decision is reached by the Council. In the eventuality that an issue of conventionality (i.e., an issue about the compatibility of the challenged law with the ECHR, or any other international convention), is raised during the same proceedings, the QPC should be dealt with by priority. A provision declared unconstitutional on that basis is repealed from the publication of the decision of the Constitutional Council, or from a later date fixed by this decision.

c. Effects of Rulings

304. The rulings of the Constitutional Council are binding on all public authorities (Article 62 Constitution) encompassing, beyond those authorities involved in the particular case, political authorities, the administration and courts at all levels.

289. Law No 2008-724 of 23 Jul. 2008 on the modernization of the institutions of the Fifth Republic.

However, no actual enforcement procedure exists. The authority of res judicata works in its strongest form here. The authority of the ruling does not only concern the operative part of the rulings but also its ratio decidendi. It also means that decisions of the Council cannot be appealed or subject to other judicial remedy, except a complaint before the ECtHR to the extent that it forms part of the exhaustion of domestic remedies in a particular case.

B. Composition

305. The Constitutional Council is composed of nine members appointed for a non-renewable term of nine years. Members of the Council are appointed by political authorities: three are appointed by the President of the Republic, three by the president of the National Assembly, and three by the president of the Senate. One-third of the Council is replaced every three years, meaning that the President of the Republic and the president of each of the appointing House of Parliament each appoint one member to the Council every three years. In addition to these appointed members, former Presidents of the Republic are members of the Council ex officio – de facto for life. This brings to twelve the total number of members although the latter type of membership is more contentious given that most former Heads of State are not actually sitting.[290] The constitutional amendment, under discussion in Parliament at the time of writing (June 2018), is proposing, among other changes, to end the presence of former Presidents of the Republic in the Constitutional Council. The president of the Council is appointed by the President of the Republic who may choose among appointed members or ex officio members, although no president has been appointed in the latter category so far. The current president of the Council, who took office in March 2016, is Laurent Fabius.[291]

C. Organization and Operation

306. The Constitutional Council enjoys a 'triple autonomy', namely an administrative, regulatory and budgetary autonomy.[292] First, the Council is in charge of its administrative organization under the leadership of its president. The other key figure is the Secretary-General. Often dubbed the 'tenth member' of the Council, the Secretary-General is generally a lawyer of the highest standing. S/he manages the different services of the Council, namely the Legal Service, including the Registry attached to it, the Research and Documentation Service which runs legal research, the Administrative and Financial Service responsible for the management of the institution, and the Press or External Relations Service in charge of the Council's

---

290. Only Giscard d'Estaing has currently been sitting, since 2004, in the Constitutional Council. Chirac, who sat from 2007, retired for health reasons in 2011. Sarkozy was quick to decide, in January 2013, not to be a member. Hollande chose not to sit as a member.

291. For more, *see* Marie-Luce Paris, 'The French Constitutional Council: Another "Work in Progress"' in Emmanuel Guinchard et Marie-Pierre Granger, *The New EU Judiciary: An Analysis of Current Judicial Reforms* (Kluwer 2017) 47, 50-53.

292. *Ibid.* 60 et seq.

publications, relations with other courts, universities and French institutions, and international relations. Aside from these administrative functions, the Secretary-General directs the preparation of the work of the Council and liaises with the different government departments. The Council's size, which consists of a team of between sixty and seventy staff, is relatively modest compared to other equivalent courts. For example, members of the Council do not have personal advisers or collaborators apart from their secretariat. However, the Council has made adjustments to expand at the margins, liaising with other institutions and for various purposes. For instance, the Council is assisted by delegates and rapporteurs during elections. Legal Service staff are generally hired from among members of the Council of State as well as a few coming from the top ordinary court (i.e., Court of Cassation); it may also comprise clerks on secondment from Parliament and law academics; also, some charges de mission may be hired to deal with the QPC cases (generally academics at non-professorial level), and some *stagiaires* hired among the best students in (mostly Parisian) law schools for specific research tasks. Second, the regulatory autonomy of the Constitutional Council is provided for in a number of constitutional and organic laws which have left a certain margin of appreciation to the Council since all these laws, except Organic Law of 7 November 1958 (1958 Organic Law), were referred to it for review. Until the 2008 constitutional amendment, the regulatory framework was quite loose with only one rule of court (adopted without mention of a date) on the basis of the 1958 Organic Law. This is only in 2010, on the occasion of the entry into force of the QPC, that the Council decided to adopt proper rules of court but limited, to date, to the QPC procedure. Third, in terms of financial autonomy, the Constitutional Council sets its own budget which, despite comparing quite modestly with other constitutional courts, still represents a substantial sum of EUR 11,719,229 million for 2018. Again, the Council benefits from a certain leeway in that matter. Indeed, its budget, the funding of which is stipulated in the Finance Bill as part of the 'Public Powers' mission, is not only voted, without any amendment nor discussion, by Parliament but also it does not entail financial accountability for the Council which has no obligation to justify its expenses before the government or Parliament.

D. *Critical Assessment*

307. *See* Marie-Luce Paris, 'The French System of Rights-Based Review: From Exceptionalism to Parochial Constitutionalism' in John Bell and Marie-Luce Paris, *Rights-Based Constitutional; Review: Constitutional Courts in a Changing Landscape* (Edward Elgar 2016) 302, and Marie-Luce Paris, 'The French Constitutional Council: Another "Work in Progress"' in Emmanuel Guinchard et Marie-Pierre Granger, *The New EU Judiciary: An Analysis of Current Judicial Reforms* (Kluwer 2017) 47.

Chapter 6. Independent Advisory Bodies at the Legislative and Executive Levels

308. The Council of State, the Economic, Social and Environmental Council, and the Defender of Rights are the independent bodies which have an advisory role with the government and Parliament.

§1. The Council of State

309. After introductory remarks about its origin and composition, the powers of the Council of State will be examined.

I. General

310. *See* above Chapter 5. The Judiciary, §1. The Organization of the Judiciary, I. General Introduction, C. Subdivisions within the Courts of Administrative Jurisdiction, 2. The Council of State.

II. Powers

311. In addition to its judicial role,[293] the Council of State has an advisory role. The Council of State *must* be consulted before the enactment of ordinances and before the deliberation of government bills within the Council of Ministers (Article 38 paragraph two and Article 39 paragraph two Constitution). The opinions of the Council of State are not legally binding on the government although they are, to a large extent, followed by in practice. The Council of State *may* also be consulted, at the request of the president of the National Assembly or the president of the Senate, on any private member's bill (Article 39 Constitution). The government may also request an opinion from the Council of State on any proposal and on any legal issue of interest or on an administrative matter. In its advisory formation responsible for reviewing drafts prepared by the government, the Council of State is divided up into five specialized sections, namely the section on the Administration, the section on Internal Affairs, the section on Public Works, the section on Finance, and the section on Social Matters. The section on Reports and Studies, which was added later on, is in charge of preparing the annual report, coordinating research projects, keeping up-to-date with developments in EU law and monitoring issues related to the

293. *See* above Chapter 5. The Judiciary, §1. The Organization of the Judiciary, I. General Introduction, C. Subdivisions within the Courts of Administrative Jurisdiction, 2. The Council of State.

enforcement of the Council's decisions.[294] The procedure is as follows. A rapporteur is assigned to gather the relevant legal documentation and to study the relevant case. The officials and top civil servants from the ministerial departments, also known as Government Commissioners, provide the Council of State with the necessary clarifications concerning the general scope of a text, the conditions of its elaboration and the reasons for the choices made by the ministerial departments. The rapporteur then submits the case to the relevant department for discussion and the department votes on any potential amendments.

§2. The Economic, Social and Environmental Council

312. After introductory remarks about its origin and composition, the role and working methods of the Economic, Social and Environmental Council will be examined.

I. General

313. The Economic, Social and Environmental Council (*Conseil Economique, Social et Environnemental* or CESE) is an advisory body to the government which status is enshrined in the Constitution (Articles 69 and 70 Constitution).[295] Its composition and role were enhanced by the 2008 constitutional amendment in an effort to improve its representativity and accessibility.[296] The CESE represents key economic, social and environmental fields, promoting cooperation between different socio-professional interest groups and ensuring that they are part of the process of shaping and reviewing public policy.

314. The CESE consists of two hundred and thirty-three members, comprising eighteen groups of civil society representatives appointed for a term of five years. Members cannot serve more than two consecutive terms. Members are appointed according to different rules which were amended in 2010 to include representatives for environmental and nature conservation along with representatives for youth and student interests. Other measures have improved the representativity of the CESE such as ensuring the respect of gender balance as regards organizations which appoint more than one member to the Council, lowering the minimum age from

294. Attached to this section is the international relations delegation which coordinates the cooperative efforts of the Council of State, both bilateral and multilateral, with foreign jurisdictions or international associations, such as the International Association of Supreme Administrative Courts and the Association of the Councils of State and Supreme Administrative Courts of the EU.

295. Title XI on The Economic, Social and Environmental Council.

296. *See* Ordinance No 58-1360 of 29 Dec. 1958 on the Organic Law concerning The Economic and Social Council, as amended by Organic Law No 2010-704 of 28 Jun. 2010 on The Economic, Social and Environmental Council. The Council was established, originally as the Economic and Social Council, in 1925 under the Third Republic. Its existence was constitutionalized under the Fourth Republic as an advisory body at the disposal of the National Assembly and Council of Ministers.

twenty-five to eighteen to become a Council member, and prohibiting more than two consecutive terms of office to ensure a more frequent renewal of the membership. Most members represent employees and employers appointed by representative professional organizations and trade associations. Membership is split between the following three categories: first, one hundred and forty members for economic matters and social dialogue, including employee representatives, representatives of private industry, trade and services, representatives of farmers and agricultural activities, representatives of craft industry, representatives of liberal professions, and qualified individuals chosen for their experience in economics, including two from public corporations and one representative of French economic interests abroad; second, sixty members for social and territorial cohesion and community life, including representatives of the non-agricultural areas of the economy based on mutuality, cooperation and solidarity, representatives of mutual organizations and agricultural production and processing cooperatives, representatives of family associations, representatives of other associations and foundations, representatives of economic and social activities in French overseas departments and regions, overseas territories (including New Caledonia), representatives of youth and students, as well as qualified individuals chosen for their experience in social, cultural, sports and scientific fields, in social housing, or in promoting the interests of disabled citizens and pensioners; third, thirty-three members for environmental and nature conservation including representatives of associations and foundations active in the field of environmental and nature conservation as well as qualified individuals chosen for their expertise in sustainable development and the environment, including at least three business leaders from companies highly active in these fields. Other members are individual experts appointed by the government. The government may also request that up to seventy-two public figures chosen based on their respective skills join one of the CESE's sections for a specific period and mission. These temporary members bring additional expertise and enhance the efforts of their respective working groups. The Philippe Government has announced in April 2018, as part of a major constitutional and institutional reform currently (June 2018) under discussion in Parliament, its plan to reduce by half the number of members of the CESE and transform it into 'a civil society assembly' which will be consulted on 'future plans for French society'.

II. Role and Working Methods

315. The CESE has five main roles. First, the Council advises the government and Parliament, as well as participates in the development of economic, social and environmental policies. Second, the Council promotes dialogue between socio-professional groups which might initially display different concerns but have to cooperate to shape proposals in the public interest. Third, the Council contributes to the review of public policy on economic, social and environmental issues. Fourt, the Council promotes constructive dialogue and cooperation with advisory bodies created within local governments and with its counterparts in the EU and other countries. Lastly, the Council helps inform citizens. The government may consult the CESE on any government bill or any private member's bill, as well as on proposals of regulatory acts (i.e., ordinances and decrees). The government may also consult the Council on any issue of economic, social or environmental nature. The opinion of the Council is mandatory regarding any planning or programming law of an economic, social or environmental nature. The president of each House of Parliament may also ask the Council's opinion, as can the citizens by way of petition of more than 500,000 signatures.[297] The Council must deliver its opinion within one year of receiving a valid petition. The opinion on a petition is notified to the Prime Minister, the president of the National Assembly and the president of the Senate, as well as to the representative of the citizens and published in the *JO*.

316. The CESE working methods are similar to those of the Houses of Parliament. The Council sits permanently with plenary sessions twice a month. The Council's working groups, which include sections, delegations and temporary commissions, are tasked with preparing studies and draft opinions within their respective field as established by decree. The two hundred and thirty-three members of the Council vote on the opinions prepared by the sections.[298] Members of the government may attend plenary sessions of the Council and take part in the debate on an opinion falling into their area. Opinions issued by the Council enjoy a significant authority although they are not legally binding on the government.

§3. The Defender of Rights

317. After introductory remarks about its origin and general role, the powers and independence of the Defender of Rights will be examined.

I. General

318. The Defender of Rights is an independent administrative single authority enshrined in the Constitution (Article 71-1 Constitution).[299] It refers both to the institution and to the person who directs it. The Defender of Rights was established by the 2008 constitutional amendment[300] with the aim of providing a nonjudicial remedy to citizens for the protection of their rights and freedoms against the action of the State, local authorities, and any public body or other body entrusted with a public service mission. The institution was modelled on equivalent authorities in other European jurisdictions such as the Ombudsman in Sweden and Finland, the *Defensor del Pueblo* in Spain, or the *Provedor de Justiça* in Portugal. From 2011,

297. Other conditions exist as regards citizens' petitions in order to filter them. Petitions are limited to issues of general interest falling within the remit of the Council's areas of competence. Formally, petitions must be written in French, signed by a minimum of 500,00 citizens of over eighteen years of age, and of French nationality or legally residing in France. Petitions must be received by a representative who acts as the link between the citizens and the Council.
298. The Council issues between twenty-five and thirty opinions per year.
299. Title XI *bis* on The Defender of Rights.
300. As completed by Organic Law No 2011-333 of 29 Mar. 2011 and Law No 2011-334 of 29 Mar. 2011 on The Defender of Rights.

the areas of competence of the French Mediator (*Médiateur de la République*), the Children's Ombudsman (*Défenseur des Enfants*), the Equality and Anti-Discrimination Authority (*Haute Autorité de Lutte contre les Discriminations et Pour l'Égalité*, or HALDE), and the National Commission on Security Ethics (*Commission Nationale de Déontologie de la Sécurité*, or CNDS) have been joined together within the area of competence of the Defender of Rights in the interest of facilitating and simplifying access by citizens.[301] The Defender of Rights is assisted by deputy defenders of rights who are responsible, under the supervision of the main Defender of Rights, for their respective area of competence, namely children's rights, anti-discrimination and equality, and security ethics. The Defender of Rights is appointed by the President of the Republic for a non-renewable and irrevocable six-year term.[302] S/he shall report to the President of the Republic and Parliament.

II. Powers and Independence

319. The role of the Defender of Rights is to oversee the protection of citizens' rights and freedoms, promote equality and ensure greater access to rights. Any natural or legal person may refer a case to the Defender of Rights directly and free of charge. The Defender of Rights may also initiate a case on his/her own initiative. The Defender of Rights has powers of investigation and intervention. First, under powers of investigation, the Defender of Rights can request, subject to criminal prosecution, to receive all information or useful documents to investigate the case before him/her. S/he can also conduct all necessary interviews and carry out all necessary on-site verifications and examinations. S/he may also refer questions of interpretation of legal texts regarding administrative law to the Council of State. Second, the Defender of Rights has powers to intervene in settling a dispute and can work to resolve a conflict by mutual agreement by making recommendations, including as regards possible legislative or regulatory changes, or through mediation. Also, the Defender of Rights can impose a binding solution in cases of misconduct or of proven wrongdoing by intervening in support of a civil or criminal transaction, or requesting disciplinary action against a public agent, or making observations before a court in support of a claimant, or recommending administrative sanctions against an individual or legal entity at the origin of a discrimination.

320. In his/her role, the Defender of Rights is totally independent from the administration and the government. The autonomy and independence of the

301. Other authorities, such as the office of the Controller-General for Places of Deprivation of Liberty (*Contrôleur Général des Lieux de Privation de Liberté*), the Commission on Access to Administrative Documents (*Commission d'Accès aux Documents Administratifs* or CADA), and the National Agency for Information Technology and Civil Liberties regulating data protection (*Commission Nationale de l'Informatique et des Libertés* or CNIL), were not merged within the competence of the Defender of Rights because of their particularity. Such an overall concentration of authorities would have been regarded as an arguably harmful rationalization in terms of rights protection.

302. Jacques Toubon is the current Defender of Rights (2014–2020) preceded by Dominique Baudis (2011-until his death in 2014).

Defender of Rights, which are guaranteed by law, mean that s/he shall not accept instructions from any authority, party to the case, or other individual or pressure group. His/her duties cannot be terminated prematurely, except in case of an unexpected obstacle ascertained by the highest courts. Legal proceedings cannot be instituted against the Defender of Rights and s/he cannot be arrested or tried on the basis of his/her opinions or acts connected with the performance of his/her duties.[303] The Defender of Rights cannot hold any electoral mandate or any other public office, nor can s/he exercise any other professional activity while in office.

Selected Further Reading

On Political Parties Lobbies and Interest Groups

Pierre Avril, *Essais sur les partis politiques* (Payot 1990).
Jean-Pierre Camby, *Le financement de la vie politique* (Montchrestien 1995).
Yves-Marie Doublet, *Le financement de la vie politique* (2nd ed., PUF 1997).
Maurice Duverger, *Les partis politiques* (Collection Points 1981, A. Colin 1951).
Maurice Duverger, *La monarchie républicaine, ou comment les démocraties se donnent des rois* (Robert Laffont 1974).
Jacques Le Bohec and Christophe Le Digol, *Gauche/Droite: Genèse d'un clivage politique* (PUF 2012).

On the President of the Republic

Marie-Anne Cohendet, *Le président de la République* (2nd ed., Dalloz 2012).
Charles Debbasch, 'Le président de la République et le Premier ministre dans le système politique de la Ve République: duel ou duo?' RDP, 1982, 1175.
Le président, Pouvoirs No°91 (1987).
Jean Massot, *Chef de l'Etat et chef de gouvernement. Dyarchie et hiérarchie* (La Documentation française 1993).
Marcel Morabito, *Le chef de l'Etat en France* (LGDJ 1996).
Pierre Servent, *Les présidents et la guerre 1958–2017* (Perrin 2017).

On the Legislature

Michel Ameller, *L'Assemblée nationale* (2nd ed., PUF 2000).
Pierre Avril, Jean Gicquel and Jean-Eric Gicquel, *Droit parlementaire* (5th ed., Montchrestien 2014).
Jean-Pierre Camby, *Le Conseil constitutionnel, juge électoral* (7th ed., Dalloz 2017).
Jean-Pierre Camby et Pierre Servent, *Le travail parlementaire sous la Ve République* (5th ed., Montchrestien 2010).

303. The legal immunity of the Defender of Rights is similar to that enjoyed by MPs under Art. 26 of the Constitution.

Selected Further Reading

Le renouveau du Parlement, Pouvoirs No 146 (2013).
Le Parlement, Pouvoirs No 64 (1993).
Le Sénat, Pour quoi faire?, Pouvoirs No°159 (2016).
Le Sénat, Pouvoirs No°44 (1988).
Benjamin Morel, *Le Sénat et sa légitimité: l'institution interprète de son rôle constitutionnel* (Dalloz 2018).
François Pillet, *Le Sénat, gardien des libertés* (Mare & Martin 2017).

On the Executive

Philippe Ardant, *Le Premier ministre en France* (Montchrestien 1997).
José Delfont, *Responsabilité pénale et fonction politique* (LGDJ 2006).
Jacques Fournier, *Le travail gouvernemental* (Dalloz 1987).
Richard Ghevontian, Xavier Magnon and Marthe Stéfanini (eds), *Pouvoir exécutif et Parlement: de nouveaux équilibres?* (PUAM 2012).
Pascal Jan, *Le gouvernement* (La Documentation française 2005).
La responsabilité des gouvernants, Pouvoirs No 92 (2000)
Le Ministre, Pouvoirs No 36 (1986).
Le Premier ministre, Pouvoirs No 83 (1997).
Olivier Schramek, *Dans l'ombre de la République: les cabinets ministériels* (Dalloz 2006).
Qui gouverne la France?, Pouvoirs No°68 (1994).

On the Judiciary

Jean-Jacques Bienvenu et alii (eds), *La Constitution administrative de la France* (Dalloz 2012).
Jean-Paul Branlard, *L'essentiel de l'organisation judiciaire en France* (5th ed., Gualino 2015).
René Chapus, 'Dualité de juridictions et unité de l'ordre juridique', RFDA (1990) 739.
Thierry Debard, Serge Guinchard and André Varinard, *Institutions juridictionnelles* (14th ed., Dalloz 2017).
Hugues Fulchiron and Laurent Eck, *Introduction au droit français* (LexisNexis 2016).
Fabrice Hourquebie, *Le pouvoir juridictionnel en France* (LGDJ 2010).
Marceau Long, *Les grands arrêts de la jurisprudence administrative* (21st ed., Dalloz, 2017).
Thierry-Serge Renoux, *La justice en France* (La Documentation française 2013).
Bernard Stirn, *Quelques réflexions sur le dualisme juridictionnel*, 3 Justices: Revue générale de droit processuel 41 (Janv.-Juin 1996).

On Judicial Review

Pierre Avril and Jean Gicquel, *Le Conseil constitutionnel* (6th ed., Montchrestien 2011).

Julien Bonnet and Pierre-Yves Gahdoun, *La question prioritaire de constitutionnalité* (PUF 2014).
Louis Favoreu, *La politique saisie par le droit* (Economica 1988).
Patrick Gaïa et alii [Louis Favoreu and Loïc Philip], *Les grandes décisions du Conseil constitutionnel* (19th ed., Dalloz 2018).
Léo Hamon, *Les juges de la loi: Naissance et rôle d'un contre-pouvoir* (Fayard 1987).
La question prioritaire de constitutionnalité, Pouvoirs No°137 (2011).
Bertrand Mathieu et alii, *Les grandes délibérations du Conseil constitutionnel* (Dalloz 2014).
Bertrand Mathieu and Dominique Rousseau, *Les grandes décisions de la question prioritaire de constitutionnalité* (LGDJ 2013).
Christine Maugüe and Jacques-Henri Stahl, *La question prioritaire de constitutionnalité* (3rd ed., Dalloz 2017).
Marie-Luce Paris, 'The French Constitutional Council: Another "Work in Progress"', Emmanuel Guinchard et Marie-Pierre Granger, *The New EU Judiciary: An Analysis of Current Judicial Reforms* (Kluwer 2017) 47.
Marie-Luce Paris, 'The French System of Rights-Based Review: From Exceptionalism to Parochial Constitutionalism', in John Bell and Marie-Luce Paris, *Rights-Based Constitutional; Review: Constitutional Courts in a Changing Landscape* (Edward Elgar 2016) 302.
Dominique Rousseau, *Droit du contentieux constitutionnel* (11th ed., LGDJ 2016).
Henri Roussillon and Pierre Espuglas, *Le Conseil constitutionnel* (8th ed., Dalloz 2015).
Michel Verpeaux, *Contentieux constitutionnel* (Dalloz 2016).
Michel Verpeaux and Betrand Mathieu (eds), *L'autorité des décisions du Conseil constitutionnel* (Dalloz 2010).

On the Council of State

Florence Chaltiel Terral, *Le Conseil d'Etat, acteur et censeur de l'action publique* (LGDJ 2017).
Bruno Latour, *La fabrique du droit: Une ethnographie du Conseil d'Etat* (La Découverte 2004).
Le Conseil d'Etat, Pouvoirs No 123 (2007/4).

On the Defender of Rights

Dominique Grandguillot, *Le Défenseur des droits* (Gualino 2011).
Le Défenseur des droits, RFAP No 139 (2011/3).

Part III. The State and Its Subdivisions

321. This Part is concerned with a presentation of the structure of the French State. France is the unitary State *par excellence* which organization has been, however, recognized as decentralized into different local authorities.

Chapter 1. The Structure of the State, a Decentralized Unitary State

322. France is a centralized State. For historical reasons due to internal wars on the metropolitan territory as well as external wars and conquests, France was built in the face of 'localist' tendencies, some of which remain today. French centralism is often illustrated by using the expression 'French Jacobinism', which refers to the Jacobin revolutionary party and its programme aimed at centralizing power. Beyond the 1789 revolutionary ideals, what was then apparent was the willingness to achieve the unity of the French social body and the belief in the ability to generate universal rules which could be applicable to each and every territory. Paradoxically, the heterogeneity of the French people, and the diversity of its territory and geography, might have contributed to the development of a strong central authority over the course of history. For a long time, the question of how to organize State power at local level was a question of 'deconcentration' – the concept being developed after the phenomenon. A change happened in this approach in the 1980s with the development of a 'decentralized' administration which effect was to endow locally elected authorities the power to freely self-administer. Before then and with the important exception of the municipalities in particular under the *Ancien Régime*, local authorities were mainly under the tutelage of the State. Since then, the decentralization process has continued to deepen. Local authorities in metropolitan France and overseas territories have been granted more autonomy and the responsibility of new competences as evidenced by the 2003 constitutional amendment (*See* below), as well as by the subsequent and ongoing reforms of the General Code of Local Authorities.

§1. Unity and Indivisibility of the Republic

I. Principles

323. The principle of indivisibility of the Republic is laid out in the first paragraph of the First Article of the Constitution: 'France is an indivisible, secular, democratic and social Republic'. The paragraph thereof also states that: 'Its organization is decentralized'. Indivisibility and decentralization are not incompatible. While the regime of the Fifth Republic authorizes the existence of local authorities that are freely administered, this is within the limits of, and in compliance with, the law and, more so, the Constitution. The indivisibility of the Republic is related to the indivisibility of the sovereign French people to the extent that the State is only the legal projection of this indivisible sovereign which is the equivalent of the principle of unity of the French people manifested in the existence of universal suffrage in particular. The indivisibility of the sovereign power is contained in Article 3 of the Constitution, which in its first two paragraphs, states that: 'The national sovereignty belongs to the people who shall exercise it through their representatives and by way of referendum. No fraction of the people or any individual may arrogate to themselves the right to exercise [that sovereignty]'.

324. The Constitutional Council recognized the constitutionality of the concept of the 'French people' in its 1991 Decision on the Status of the Island of Corsica.[304] The Council ruled that 'under the first paragraph of the Preamble to the 1958 Constitution "the French people" solemnly proclaim their attachment to human rights and the principles of national sovereignty as were defined by the Declaration of 1789, confirmed and complemented by the Preamble to the 1946 Constitution; that the Declaration of the Rights of Man and of the Citizen of 1789 to which reference is hereby made, emanated from representatives "of the French people"; that the Preamble to the 1946 Constitution, reaffirmed by the Preamble to the 1958 Constitution, states that "the French People proclaims again that every human being without distinction of race, religion or belief, possess inalienable and sacred rights"; that the 1958 Constitution distinguishes the French People from overseas people who have a right to self-determination; that the reference to the "French people" has appeared elsewhere over two centuries in a number of constitutional texts; that thus the legal concept of "French people" has a constitutional value'.[305] The Constitutional Council has confirmed this principle in subsequent decisions. For example, in its 1999 Decision on The European Charter for Regional or Minority Languages in which it declared that: 'The result of these combined provisions is that the European Charter for Regional or Minority Languages, in so far as it confers specific rights to "groups" of users of regional or minority languages, within "territories" in which those languages are spoken, violates the constitutional principles of the indivisibility of the Republic, of equality before the law, and of unity of the French people'.[306] The indivisibility of the French people is reflected in the central action of the State and specifically in the hierarchy of norms.

II. Unity of Action of the State

325. This unity is first expressed in the monopoly of the State as regards the legislative and constitutional powers, as well as in the conduct of external relations.

A. The Legislative and Constitutional Monopoly

326. The legal regime applicable to acts of local authorities is that of administrative acts, subject to the principle of legality. There is a requirement to comply with the norm of a higher rank that is the law which, under Article 6 of the 1789 Declaration, 'is the expression of the general will'. Decentralized authorities shall comply with the principle of legality. In particular, the principle of self-government

304. CC Decision No 91-290 DC of 9 May 1991, *Loi portant statut de la collectivité territoriale de Corse*, *Rec.* 50*. The mention of Corsica in the Constitution as is proposed in the constitutional amendment, currently (June 2018) under discussion in Parliament, is likely to be a bone of contention in this regard.

305. *Ibid.* pt 12.

306. CC Decision No 99-412 DC of 15 Jun. 1999, *Charte européenne des langues régionales ou minoritaires*, *Rec.* 71, pt 10*.

of local authorities is limited by law which is itself subject to constitutional provisions. Local authorities are represented in Parliament. The Senate 'shall represent the local authorities of the Republic' (Article 24 paragraph four Constitution). Senators are elected by indirect universal suffrage by an electoral college made up of locally elected officials including elected officials of the municipalities.

327. However, the legislative monopoly has two exceptions, albeit of limited practical relevance. First, the constitutional regime applicable to New Caledonia established the 'laws of the land' (*lois du pays*) which are local texts of legislative value.[307] In a limited number of areas, the Assembly of New Caledonia may pass such laws which derogate from domestic laws. These laws are reviewed by the Constitutional Council before their promulgation. French Polynesia may also resort to laws of the land although these are only regarded as administrative acts and, as such, subject to review by the Council of State. Second, the 2003 constitutional amendment introduced the possibility for local authorities to derogate from domestic laws for a limited object and a determined period, referred to as the 'experimental procedure'. The fourth paragraph of Article 72 of the Constitution states as follows: 'Under the conditions prescribed by the organic law, and save where the essential conditions for the exercise of a public freedom or of a constitutionally guaranteed right are at issue, local authorities or their groupings thereof may, as prescribed, as the case may be, by law or regulation, derogate, on an experimental basis and for a limited purpose and duration, from the legislative or regulatory provisions which govern the exercise of their competences'. The 'experimental procedure' has been granted to local authorities, on a very conditional basis, with the result of distinguishing between the unity of the law and its consistency. While the legislature ultimately retains the monopoly of making laws, it does not necessarily have to impose the same rules on all authorities. Some local authorities may well 'experiment' with rules suitable for their territory by temporarily derogating from the legislation common to all other authorities. Such experiment may also be, if successful, a model that will then be extended to other authorities on the territory.

B. External Relations

328. The unity of the French State is also reflected in the conduct of external relations. The French Government does not grant to domestic local authorities the power to maintain diplomatic relations with other States since this is a sovereign prerogative attached to the central State. However, since the 1982 legislation on decentralization (*See* below), the French Government has allowed its local authorities to conduct actions of decentralized cooperation, namely the possibility of concluding cooperation agreements between local authorities of different countries in

307. Constitutional Law No 98-610 of 20 Jul. 1998 on New Caledonia and Organic Law No 99-209 of 19 Mar. 1999 on New Caledonia.

the areas of culture, education, sustainable development or related to economic matters.[308] Articles L. 1115-1 et seq. of the General Code of Local Authorities, as amended,[309] now provide for different forms of external action by local authorities such as, for example, cross-border management cooperation through the creation of an organization with legal personality: 'In the context of cross-border cooperation, local authorities and their groupings may establish with foreign local authorities and their groupings a local cross-border cooperation consortium called a European District, with legal personality and financial autonomy' (L. 1115-4-1). This can also be the case that a French local authority takes part in the activities of a foreign consortium (L. 1115-4). Local authorities may only exercise this power in compliance with international agreements signed by the French State.

III. The Integrity of the Territory

329. The indivisibility of the Republic and of the French people does not prohibit certain territories from claiming and taking their independence. This was the case, for example, of Algeria which was a French department up until 1962, or of the Comoros – except the island of Mayotte – up until 1975. Under the last paragraph of Article 53 of the Constitution, a right to self-determination is recognized in the following terms: 'No transfer, no exchange or no addition of territory shall be valid without the consent of the people concerned'. In its 1975 Decision on The Self-Determination of the Comoros Islands, the Constitutional Council ruled that: '… the provisions of this Article [Article 53] shall be interpreted as being applicable not only in the event that France would transfer to, or acquire from, a foreign State a territory, but also in the event that a territory would cease to belong to the Republic in order to form an independent State or be attached to it'.[310] However, there are conditions attached to the right of self-determination. Only the French State can proceed to consult with the inhabitants of the territory concerned. This consultation must then be carried out, not in accordance with any norm of international law, but in accordance with French constitutional law. Finally, Parliament must authorize the change in status of the territory in question. In the event of a refusal of the people to accede to independence, Parliament is obliged to comply with their will by refusing any transfer or secession of their territory.

---

308. Law No 82-213 of 2 Mar. 1982 on the rights and freedoms of municipalities, departments and regions.
309. *See* Law No 2008-352 of 16 Apr. 2008 aiming to reinforce the cross-border, transnational and interregional cooperation by the bringing into conformity of the General Code of the Local Authorities with the European regulation on a European grouping of territorial cooperation, and Law No 2014-773 of 7 Jul. 2014 of orientation and programming relating to the policy of development and international solidarity.
310. CC Decision No 75-59 DC of 30 Dec. 1975, *Loi relative aux conséquences de l'autodétermination des îles des Comores*, *Rec.* 26, pt 2.

§2. THE PROCESS OF DECENTRALIZATION

330. In a centralized country like France, decentralization has been a slow and cautious political and legal process. At the time of writing, the process is still undergoing thereby showing how it is neither completed nor, for some, satisfactory.

331. What is meant by 'completed' decentralization? The issue has to do with the search for a balance between national democracy and local democracy, between effectiveness of the action of the State and the action of local government. The seminal Law of 2 March 1982 on the Rights and Freedoms of Municipalities, Departments and Regions (hereafter the 1982 Law)[311] is often presented as the first act of decentralization in France, despite the fact that municipalities and departments were already in existence, albeit without a comparable autonomy, long before that time. The 1789 Revolution contributed to the development of the power of local institutions. In particular, the Law of 14 December 1789 created municipalities, and the Law of 22 December 1789 created departments, each level endowed with its own powers and elected representatives. In contrast, the post-revolutionary period from 1792 witnessed a movement of centralization which was subsequently confirmed with the shaping of a strong State power particularly under Napoleonic times. For example, the Law of 28 Pluviôse VIII (17 February 1800) on the Division of the Territory of the Republic and the Administration allowed Napoleon Bonaparte to deprive municipalities of their modest local autonomy in favour of a State hierarchy based on the local authority of the prefect. Apart from the Law of 10 August 1871 on General Councils (dealing with departmental affairs) and the Law of 5 April 1884 on the Organization of Municipalities (which recognized their autonomous power to manage their own affairs), it was only after the Second World War that decentralization came back to the fore. Laws relating to cooperation between municipalities, or on the creation of regions were passed, but it is the 1982 Law which, following the change in presidential orientation after the 1981 election, marked the most significant progress in the decentralization process.

I. The 1982 Legislation

332. The 1982 legislation profoundly altered the relationship between local authorities and the State. While previously this relationship was one of supervisory nature, the 1982 Law gave local authorities legal, political, and fiscal autonomy. Discussed during the presidential election of 1981, decentralization was one of the major acts of the start of the first seven-year term of François Mitterrand. The instigator of the legislation, Gaston Defferre,[312] had already proposed back in the 1950s when he was then Minister for Overseas France, the so-called Defferre Framework

311. Law No 82-213 of 2 Mar. 1982 on the rights and freedoms of municipalities, departments and regions.

312. The 1982 Law is referred to as the 'Defferre Law' since Gaston Deferre was its instigator as Minister of the Interior and Decentralization at the time.

Law allowing for the adoption of measures regarding the development of overseas territories which would later result into the decolonization process of French Black Africa.

333. The decentralization reform is not contained in a single law. While the 1982 Law set out the main principles of decentralization, several subsequent legislative texts quickly followed to complement it, in particular two laws of 1983,[313] and a law creating a local civil service in 1984.[314] The 1982 Law lays down in its first article that 'municipalities, departments and regions are freely administered by elected councils'.[315] The legislation on decentralization in effect replaced the supervisory role of the State with an autonomy granted to local authorities whose acts can only be reviewed a posteriori – that is after their adoption – by the administrative judge, possibly on a referral by the prefect whose role is to ensure the respect of the legality of administrative acts. The 1982 legislation established regions as local authorities endowed with the full exercise of local power, as well as devolved the executive power to the president of the General Council as regards departments, to the president of the Regional Council as regards regions. Lastly, it also removed the control of the State in financial matters. The whole legislation on decentralization was further complemented by several provisions on cooperation between municipalities, and groupings of municipalities, as well as provisions regarding the electoral process to the Regional Council. The whole legislation is now codified in the General Code of Local Authorities which includes a legislative part enacted in 1996,[316] and a regulatory part enacted in 2000.[317]

II. The 2003 Constitutional Amendment

334. What has sometimes been presented as 'Act Two' of the French decentralization, primarily aimed at entrenching it. Confirming the relevance of the previous 1982 reform, the newly elected majority in 2002 – and on the opposing political side to that of 1982 – following the re-election of President Jacques Chirac, wished to firmly establish decentralization at the highest level of the hierarchy of norms, as well as extend it. Certainly, one would not go without the other. Continuing the process of devolution or empowerment of local authorities would require a revision of the Constitution as is now evidenced under its First Article which refers to the decentralized nature of the Republic in the following terms: 'France is an indivisible, secular, democratic and social Republic. [The Republic] shall ensure equality

313. Law No 83-8 of 7 Jan. 1983 on the distribution of powers between the municipalities, the departments, the regions and the State, and Law No 83-663 of 22 Jul. 1983 supplementing Law No 83-8 of 7 Jan. 1983 on the distribution of powers between the municipalities, the departments, the regions and the State.
314. Law No 84-53 of 26 Jan. 1984 on statutory provisions relating to the territorial civil service.
315. This provision is now codified in Art. L. 1111-1 of the General Code of Local Authorities.
316. Law No 96-142 of 21 Feb. 1996 on the legislative part of the General Code of Local Authorities.
317. Decree No 2000-318 of 7 Apr. 2000 on the regulatory part of the General Code of Local Authorities.

under the law of all citizens without discrimination based on origin, race or religion. [The Republic] respects all beliefs. *Its organization is decentralized* (emphasis added).' The entrenchment of decentralization also includes the entrenchment of the regions which, unlike departments and municipalities, were not included in the Constitution. Article 72 now provides in its first paragraph that: 'The local authorities of the Republic are the municipalities, the departments, the regions, the local authorities with special status and the overseas territories governed by Article 74.'

335. The overall objective of the 2003 constitutional amendment was to grant greater autonomy to local authorities. First, it recognized the power of the legislature to allow local authorities to adopt special derogatory regimes as regards their governing laws and regulations.[318] This is consistent with the second paragraph of Article 72 of the Constitution which purportedly establishes a principle of subsidiarity as follows: 'Local authorities shall aim at making decisions concerning all powers that can be best implemented at their level.'

336. Second, the 2003 constitutional amendment increased local autonomy as regards financial matters which is developed under the four points laid down in Article 72-2:

- Local authorities draw their own resources from local taxes in relation to which they may, if the law allows, fix the base and rate.
- This tax revenue 'represents, for each category of [local authorities], 'a determining share of their overall resources' which entails a corresponding decrease in State endowment.
- 'Any transfer of powers between the State and local authorities shall be accompanied by the allocation of resources equivalent to those devoted to their exercise. Any creation or extension of powers thereof which results in an increase of the expenses of the local authorities shall be accompanied by resources as prescribed by law.'
- In order to avoid widening inequalities between the richest and poorest local areas of the territory, the law establishes an equalization scheme between them, which is a redistribution regime which is aimed at limiting the differences in wealth between local authorities. The underlying idea here is to prevent the financial autonomy of the poorest local authorities from turning into an abandonment of them.

337. Third, the 2003 constitutional amendment concerned the organization of the action of local authorities. Still prohibiting one local authority exerting supervision over another, the Constitution provides for the possibility of a local authority being in charge or leading in a particular subject area. Under the fifth paragraph of

318. *See* Art. 72 para. 4: 'Under the conditions prescribed by the organic law, and save where the essential conditions for the exercise of a public freedom or of a constitutionally guaranteed right are at issue, local authorities or their groupings thereof, where law or regulation has so provided, derogate, on an experimental basis and for limited purposes and duration, from the legislative or regulatory provisions which govern the exercise of their powers.'

Article 72, '[n]o local authority shall exercise guardianship authority over another. However, where the exercise of a power requires the joint action of several local authorities, the law may allow one of the authorities or groupings thereof to organize the terms of their joint action'. While proving difficult to put into practice, this provisions has been justified less by a question of autonomy of local authorities than by a concern to make their action more efficient and visible in the public sphere.

338. Finally, the 2003 constitutional amendment strengthened the role of the Senate and local populations. The Senate, which represents the different territories at national level, has been given priority as regards the scrutiny of 'government bills whose main object relates to the organization of local authorities'. (Article 39 paragraph two Constitution). Also, the right of citizens to participate in the development of local politics has been recognized through their right of petition and of local initiative referendum under the first paragraph of Article 72-1 of the Constitution: 'The law shall lay down the conditions under which the electors in each local authority may, by the exercise of their right to petition, request the inclusion on the agenda of the deliberative assembly of the local authority of a matter of concern which falls within its competence'.

339. Under the conditions provided for by organic law, draft bills or acts within the jurisdiction of a local authority may, on its own initiative, be submitted by way of referendum to the decision of the local voters. Under the last paragraph of Article 72-1 of the Constitution, when it is proposed to create a local authority with a special status, or to change its organization, it may be decided by law to consult with the voters registered in the local authority concerned. Changes to the limits of local authorities can also lead to the consultation with electors as provided by law.

III. Latest Reforms

340. Since 2003, the territorial organization of France has been the subject of further reforms. These reform projects have notably focused on clarifying the powers of local authorities. For instance, a 2010 reform initiated under the presidency of Nicolas Sarkozy aimed at four objectives in this regard: first, the creation of large metropolitan areas; second, the simplification of the network of intermunicipalities; third, the specialization of the powers of the departments and regions (and therefore the removal of their general powers clause); and fourth, the merger of departmental councillors (elected by the deliberative forum of the department) and regional councillors (elected by the assembly of the regional council) to create a single 'territorial councillor'.

341. If this particular reform was not taken up by the new majority after Sarkozy's defeat, other reforms were initiated under the presidency of François Hollande. These were threefold. First, one project concerned the 'modernization of local government action and affirmation of the metropolises (sic)'. Initiated in 2012, the project resulted in the adoption of the Law of 27 January 2014 of the same name[319] which restores the general power of the regions and departments – which is eventually suppressed in the second and third parts of the reform hereof, but was supposed to be removed by the entry into force in 2015 of the 2010 reform. The new legislation also establishes the so-called leader local authorities (*collectivités 'chefs de file'*) which would lead the local administration in certain areas of competence. Thus, the region aims to become a leader in economic development, and subsidies provider to businesses and transport networks; the department to become a leader in social matters, digital development of territories and territorial solidarity; and municipalities to become leaders in 'sustainable mobility and air quality' (i.e., emissions reduction from traffic pollution in cities). In relation to municipalities, the new legislation confirms the creation of the so-called metropolises which would have industrial, tourist and housing powers. Shaping a sort of enhanced inter-municipality, the effect of the legislation should allow the implementation of more coherent economic and social policies for and around major French cities such as the Grand Paris Metropolis, and the Lyon Metropolis. The second part of the reform aimed at 'the clarification of the territorial organization of the Republic' primarily concerning the regions, with a merger of a number of these resulting, in mainland France, in a decrease from twenty-two to thirteen regions. In addition, this part of the reform aimed at strengthening the power of the regions in economic matters which appears to be in contradiction with the first part of the reform. Besides the provisions specific to the regions, several other provisions relate to the financial responsibility of local authorities, the transfer of power from the department to the metropolises, the network of inter-municipalities, the deliberative process in Corsica, or the fight against the 'digital divide' (i.e., the fact that some areas are better equipped than others – most often urban versus rural areas – in terms of access to electronic technology and communication, the access to Internet in particular). The third and final part of the territorial reform is the Law on the New Territorial Organization of the Republic which was passed into law in August 2015.[320] It is aimed at permanently replacing the general competence clause with specific powers conferred by law on a specific local level. This particular point was the subject of intense parliamentary debates which can be explained by the fact that several MPs often combine their parliamentary mandate with local executive mandates – which is no longer allowed from March 2017. Despite hesitations and contradictions, the general sense of these latest reforms – from 2010 to 2015 at least – seems to be that of a specialization of powers of local authorities in order to increase both the transparency and effectiveness of their actions.

319. Law No 2014-58 of 27 Jan. 2014 of modernization of the territorial public action and affirmation of the metropolises.
320. Law No 2015-991 of 7 Aug. 2015 on the new territorial organization of the Republic (or 'NOTRe' Law as in '*Nouvelle Organisation Territoriale de la République*').

Chapter 2. The Different Local Authorities in the Republic

342. France is composed of ordinary local authorities (i.e., municipalities, departments and regions) and local authorities with a special status, mainly in overseas territories.

§1. Ordinary Local Authorities

I. Data on Municipalities

343. In July 2017, France had 35,414 municipalities, 35,285 in France and 129 in overseas territories. This significant figure – the highest in Europe – is the result of several factors of historical (i.e., the redistribution of *Ancien Régime* parishes into municipalities back in 1789), geographical (i.e., the geographical diversity of the French territory), and cultural (i.e., the deep attachment of the French people to this level of proximity) nature. Regarding this last aspect, the mayor would often be regarded, along with the President of the Republic, as the most identifiable politician and often the most appreciated. For this reason, the municipality is considered a key territory for the democratic life of the country. History also explains the attachment of a citizen to their locality as is exemplified by the presence, in almost all French municipalities, of war memorials which recall the significance of these national past events and their impact at local level. The mixed result of the ongoing merging of municipalities also explains this high number which is bound to decrease, albeit very slowly.[321] Over 86% of these municipalities have less than 2,000 inhabitants and only 41 municipalities have more than 100,000 inhabitants. Eleven have more than 200,000 inhabitants, and Paris counts about 2.2 million inhabitants. This places France as one of the EU Member States with municipalities which are on average less populated. The average size of these municipalities is about 15 km^2.

II. Data on Departments

344. France is divided into ninty-five departments in Metropolitan France, five overseas departments, namely Guadeloupe, Martinique, French Guiana, Réunion, and Mayotte. The departments were established by the Decree of 26 February 1790 and have, in the main, not changed as regards their boundaries except for the old region of Paris which was reorganized by the Law of 10 July 1964,[322] and Corsica which was divided into two departments by the Law of 15 May 1975.[323] The departments are relatively homogenous in terms of their superficies in mainland

321. France had about 40,000 municipalities in the early nineteenth century.
322. Law No 64-707 of 10 Jul. 1964 reorganizing the Paris area. The area of Paris consists of the city of Paris, the *Hauts-de-Seine*, *Seine-Saint-Denis*, *Val-de-Marne*, *Essonne*, *Yvelines*, *Val-d'Oise* and *Seine-et-Marne* departments. The departments of *Seine* and *Seine-et-Oise* ceased to exist.
323. *See* below. Law No 75-356 of 15 May 1975 reorganizing Corsica.

France.[324] However, outside the department of Ile-de-France[325] and the territory of Belfort, which is the result of the dismantling of Alsace in 1871,[326] the departments have a very uneven population. For instance, the Nord department and the department of Paris have each more than 2 million inhabitants with, respectively, 2.58 and 2.25 million, whereas the department of Lozère, the least populated of France, counts only 77,000 inhabitants.

III. Data on Regions

345. The regions represent the most recent subnational level and also the most reformed – which is actually correlated. The recent reform relating to the clarification of the territorial organization of the Republic reduces the number of regions from twenty-two to thirteen in mainland France. Previously, France was divided into the following areas: in the mainland (and by alphabetical order), Alsace, Aquitaine, Auvergne, Burgundy, Brittany, Centre, Champagne-Ardenne, Corsica, Franche-Comté, Ile-de-France, Languedoc-Roussillon, Limousin, Lorraine, Lower Normandy, Midi-Pyrénées, Nord-Pas-de-Calais, Pays de la Loire, Picardie, Poitou-Charentes, Provence-Alpes-Côte d'Azur, Rhône-Alpes, and Upper Normandy; and overseas (and by alphabetical order), Guadeloupe, Guiana, Réunion Island, Martinique, and Mayotte. The 2015 reform[327] merges the Nord-Pas-de-Calais and Picardy regions; the Alsace, Champagne-Ardenne and Lorraine regions; the Upper Normandy and Lower Normandy regions; Burgundy and Franche-Comté regions; Aquitaine, Limousin and Poitou-Charentes regions; Auvergne and Rhône-Alpes regions; and Languedoc-Roussillon and Midi-Pyrénées regions. The regions of Brittany, Centre, Corsica, Ile-de-France, Pays de la Loire, and Provence-Alpes-Côte d'Azur are not changed. While increasing the size of the regions, the reform has maintained disparities between them in terms of size, population, and even economic weight. Apart from Corsica, the Ile-de-France region, which includes Paris, remains the smallest region at about 12,000 km^2. It is, however, also the most populated with about 12 million people across eight departments and the wealthiest with a gross domestic product of about EUR 612 billion in 2012 – slightly less than a third of the national GDP that year. The region of Corsica, however, has only 322,000 inhabitants.

IV. Observations on Inter-Municipality and the Metropolitan Cities

346. The grouping of municipalities, or inter-municipalities, do not represent local authorities but groupings in which a number of municipalities will jointly exercise their competence in a particular area. These are called 'public institutions for

324. Overseas, French Guiana, with 83,534 km^2 of territory, is almost fifteen times larger than the national average.
325. The city of Paris represents only 105 km^2.
326. The territory of Belfort has a superficy of 609 km^2.
327. Law No 2015-29 of 16 Jan. 2015 on the delimitation of the regions, on regional and departmental elections, and on modifying the electoral calendar.

inter-municipal cooperation' (*Etablissements Publics de Coopération Intercommunale*, abbreviated *EPCI*). Enjoying legal personality, they are not independent of their members and have a specific, as opposed to a general, competence. Their legal regime may vary depending on the intensity of their legal obligations within the grouping. One such form of *EPCI* is the 'municipal syndicate' (*syndicat de communes*) which has been in existence since 1890. Such syndicates are freely created by the municipalities in order to manage one or more areas of competence. In contrast, an 'urban municipality' (*communauté urbaine*) will be based on a more constrained agreement. Designed to facilitate the management of large urban areas, such municipalities can be agreed only between public authorities representing at least 500,000 inhabitants, and are granted mandatory powers, in planning and development in particular such as the management of planning deeds, zoning planning, and urban transportation planning. Without being fully fledged local authorities, these public institutions for inter-municipal cooperation are becoming increasingly important, especially since they prevent the fragmentation of responsibilities between too small municipalities. In 2017, there are 1,266 such *EPCI* with their own taxation regime, and more than 9,106 municipal syndicates with no independent tax regime.[328] Such cooperation allows to rationalize the action of local government which would otherwise be much less efficient between sparsely populated municipalities (often also with weak finances). This arguably represents the first step towards more groupings of municipalities which are clearly insufficient today despite being regularly encouraged, most recently by the Law of 16 December 2010 on the reform of local authorities, for example.[329] For the first time in the municipal elections of March 2014, the so-called municipal councillors (*conseillers communautaires*), who represent the member municipalities of *EPCI*, have been elected by direct universal suffrage, thereby reinforcing the democratic nature and legitimacy of such institutions which increasingly assert themselves as genuine local authorities with extended powers.

347. Metropolises or metropolitan cities, established by the Law of 16 December 2010, as amended by the Law of 27 January 2014,[330] participate in the same movement of rationalization of local government action. Now codified in Article L. 5217-1 of the General Code of Local Authorities, the law provides: 'The metropolis is a Public Institution for Inter-Municipal Cooperation with its own taxation regime which groups several contiguous municipalities within a space of solidarity to develop and lead together an economic, environmental, educational, cultural and social development project in their territory in order to improve cohesion and competitiveness and to contribute to sustainable and inclusive development of the regional territory. [The metropolis] values local economic activity, its transport networks and its academic research and innovation resources, in a spirit of regional and interregional cooperation and with the aim of a balanced territorial development.'

---

328. Bulletin d'Information Statistique (BIS) de la DGCL (Direction Générale des Collectivités Territoriales), <https://www.collectivites-locales.gouv.fr/files/files/statistiques/bis_113.pdf> accessed on 13 Nov. 2017.
329. Law No 2010-1563 of 16 Dec. 2010 of the reform of the local authorities.
330. Law No 2014-58 of 27 Jan. 2014 of modernization of the territorial public action and affirmation of the metropolises.

From 1 January 2018, there are nineteen of these metropolitan cities, seventeen with ordinary status and two of them with special status. The metropolitan cities with special status are: the Grand Paris Metropolis and the Metropolis of Aix-Marseille-Provence, both established on 1 January 2016. The metropolitan cities with common status are: the metropolis of Nice-Côte d'Azur, established in 2011, and the metropolises of Bordeaux, Brest, Grenoble, Lille, Montpellier, Nantes, Rennes, Rouen, Strasbourg, and Toulouse, all created on 1 January 2015. The city of Lyon is a local authority with special status created in 2014.

§2. Local Authorities with Special Status

348. Under the provisions of Article 72 paragraph one of the Constitution, '[t]he local authorities of the Republic are the municipalities, the departments, the regions, the local authorities with special status and the overseas territories governed by Article 74. Any other local authority shall be established by law, where appropriate, in place of one or more local authorities mentioned in the present paragraph'. There are several local authorities with special status which represent adaptations of French law to local characteristics inherited from history or linked to geography. Strictly speaking, only Corsica is currently a 'special status local authority' within the meaning of Article 72 of the Constitution. However, there are other local authorities, in both mainland France and overseas territories, which status is derogatory. The capital city of Paris has a special status for reasons of economic importance and results in the accumulation of municipal and departmental functions. As with Lyon (nine districts) and Marseille (sixteen districts), Paris is divided into districts or *arrondissements* (twenty districts) in which there are 'district councils' (*mairies d'arrondissement*) exercising executive authority on part of the municipality. The high population in these three cities, which are the most populated of France, explains this subdivision.[331] Overseas territories aside, Corsica is the only local authority with its own institutional organization which is characterized by an extensive deliberative power granted to the local assembly and the responsibility of the local executive before it. As regards overseas territories, there is a great diversity and some territories, such as Mayotte, are now departments while New Caledonia, for example, possesses an independent status.

I. Corsica

349. The status of the island of Corsica has evolved from being that of a local authority attached to the ordinary regime towards that of a special institutional organization organized in order to address local specificities and claims. The Law of 2

331. The 20th district of Paris has a population of about 200,000 inhabitants; the 3rd district of Lyon of about 100,000 inhabitants, and the 8th district of Marseille of approximately 78,000 inhabitants.

March 1982 on the special status of Corsica and relating to its administrative organization,[332] as amended by the Law of 30 July 1982 on the special status of Corsica and relating to its competences,[333] first gave the island the status of 'Region of Corsica'. Article 1 of that law provided: 'The local authorities of Corsica exercise the powers that the laws, in so far as not contrary to the provisions of the present law, attribute to all municipalities, departments and regions. In addition, and in accordance with Law No 82-214 of 2 March 1982 on the special status of the Region of Corsica: administrative organization, the region of Corsica exercises the powers that this law aims to define and that its specific nature requires.' The Law of 13 May 1991 on the status of the local authority of Corsica[334] allowed for a special institutional organization which would derogate from local authorities of ordinary status. By establishing a deliberative assembly and an executive power which shall be responsible before it,[335] the 1991 regime is a sui generis institutional organization applicable to the island of Corsica which is akin to an operational parliamentary system – which should reinforce democratic life at the level of this territory. In line with previous institutional changes, the Law of 22 January 2002 transferred new powers to the island of Corsica, in particular in terms of deliberative powers in the areas of land use, transportation, housing, economy, environment, culture and education.[336] Finally, the Law of 7 August 2015 on the New Territorial Organization of the Republic contains several provisions relating to Corsica. The island is no longer a 'local authority' but constitutes, from 1 January 2018, a special status local authority within the meaning of Article 72 of the Constitution. It is called the 'collectivity of Corsica' (*collectivité de Corse*) in lieu of the departments of *Corse-du-Sud* and *Haute-Corse* and replaces its ordinary status of local authority. The most recent developments on the issue are contained in the Mastor Report of 18 January 2018 which argues in favour of new constitutional status for Corsica, a status which would grant the island authorities legislative autonomy in certain matters without infringing the principle of invisibility of the Republic, thereby conforming to the decentralizing trend at domestic and European level. The addition of a new Article 74-2 to the Constitution is proposed to this end.[337]

---

332. Law No 82-214 of 2 Mar. 1982 on the special status of the region of Corsica: administrative organization.
333. Law No 82-659 of 30 Jul. 1982 on the special status of the region of Corsica: competences.
334. Law No 91-428 of 13 May 1991 on the status of the local authority of Corsica.
335. Article 38 of the 1991 Law.
336. Law No 2002-92 of 22 Jan. 2002 on Corsica. Art. 4 of the 2002 Law, now Art. L. 4424- 1 of the General Code of Local Authorities, states: 'The Corsican authorities shall provide the representative of the State, after consultation of the Economic, Social, and Cultural Council of Corsica and after taking account of the guidelines set by the plan, with the predictive scheme for training colleges, high schools, vocational institutions, art schools, special education institutions, professional maritime colleges, and agricultural schools mentioned in Article L. 811-8 of the Rural Code and information and referral centres.'
337. *Pour un statut constitutionnel de la Corse*, Rapport remis à monsieur le Président de l'Assemblée de Corse, 18 Jan. 2018, accessed at <https://www.corse.fr/assembleecorse/docs/Rapport%20statut%20constitutionnel%20de%20la%20Corse%20%20version%20definitive.pdf> on 30 Jan. 2018.

II. Overseas Departments and Regions, Overseas Territories, and New Caledonia

350. Article 72-3 of the Constitution is the foundational text in respect of overseas territories: 'The Republic shall recognize, as part of the French people, the overseas populations, in a common ideal of freedom, equality and fraternity.' Guadeloupe, French Guiana, Martinique, the islands of Réunion, Mayotte, Saint Barthélemy, Saint Martin, Saint Pierre and Miquelon, Wallis and Futuna, and French Polynesia are governed by Article 73 as regards those which are overseas departments and regions, and by Article 74 as regards other local authorities. The status of New Caledonia is governed by Title XIII of the Constitution. In addition, the law determines the legal system and special organization of the French Southern and Antarctic Territories and Clipperton.

A. *Overseas Departments and Regions*

351. The overseas departments and regions are local authorities that have, in principle, the same status as departments and regions in mainland France. As such, the same rules of law apply and only in exceptional cases may the law derogate. The first three paragraphs of Article 73[338] are the legal basis in this regard:

- Laws and regulations shall be automatically applicable in overseas departments and regions. They may be adapted to the particular characteristics and constraints of these overseas territories.
- The adaptations thereof may be decided by these local authorities in matters under their remit and if they have been enabled to do so, as the case may be, by law or regulation.
- By way of derogation from the first paragraph and to take into account their specificities, local authorities governed by the present Article may be enabled, as the case may be, by law or by regulation, to lay down the rules applicable in their territory, in a limited number of matters that may fall within the legislative or regulatory area.

352. Generally, exemptions granted by the State are set out in the final provisions of laws or regulations. For example, with regard to the organization of administrative courts, the Decree of 13 May 2008 provides a chapter III entitled 'Provisions on Administrative Tribunals Overseas Departments and Regions of Mayotte, Saint Barthélemy, Saint Martin and Saint Pierre and Miquelon', and similarly, with regard to labour law rules, the Labour Code contains a Book V entitled 'Provisions on Overseas' – as is the case with several other areas.

338. The fourth paragraph of Art. 73 lists a number of areas in which these exceptions are not possible, namely nationality, civil rights, guarantees of public freedoms, status and legal capacity of persons, the administration of justice, criminal law, criminal procedure, foreign policy, defence, public security and order, currency, credit and foreign exchange matters, and electoral law.

1. Guadeloupe, Réunion and Mayotte

353. These three territories are former French colonies which became French departments with the Law of 19 March 1946 leading to the classification as French departments of Guadeloupe, Martinique, Réunion and French Guiana.[339] Article 2 of the 1946 Law provides that '[t]he laws and decrees currently in force in metropolitan France and which are not yet applied to these colonies will be, before 1 January 1947, the subject of implementing decrees to these new departments'. Under the provisions of Article 76 of the 1946 Constitution, the laws applicable in these departments should be, except as determined by law, the same as in the metropolitan departments. This legislative status has been maintained under Article 73 of the current Constitution. Guadeloupe became a French region after the decentralization reform of 1982. As is the case with Réunion, Guadeloupe is now both a region and a single department and, as such, cumulates departmental and regional functions, hence the reference to the acronym DROM standing for '*Départements et Régions d'Outre-Mer*' (Overseas Departments and Regions). Unlike Guadeloupe and Mayotte, Réunion does not benefit from the opportunity offered by the third and fourth paragraphs of Article 73 of the Constitution to be empowered by law or regulation to set its own territorial rules to reflect its specificities. The fifth paragraph of the provision thereof expressly excludes Réunion from what constitutes a flexible framework afforded to other local authorities. Mayotte became a French department – the one hundred and first department – following the referendum of 29 March 2009, which entered into force on 31 March 2011, making Mayotte both a department and a region of overseas territories. Since the independence of the Comoros in 1974 (and the subsequent referendum in which Mayotte people chose to stay under French sovereignty), the status of Mayotte has been challenged before the United Nations (UN) by the Comorian State which has claimed that the territory should be ceded to them.

2. French Guiana and Martinique

354. As a result of two referendums held in 2010, French Guiana and Martinique were made into so-called single local authorities. These referendum consultations were held in accordance with the last paragraph of Article 73 which states: 'The establishment by law of a local authority replacing an overseas department and an overseas region or the establishment of a single deliberative assembly for the two local authorities shall not intervene until the consent of the registered voters within the jurisdiction of the local authorities concerned has been obtained, in the manner prescribed by the provisions of the second paragraph of Article 72-4.' The first consultation held on 10 January 2010 focused on increasing the autonomy of these two territories, particularly in the transition towards a status of overseas local authority or collectivity governed by the provisions of Article 74 of the Constitution. The people of Guiana and Martinique responded in the negative. A second consultation

339. Law No 46-451 of 19 Mar. 1946 tending to classification as French departments of Guadeloupe, Martinique, Réunion and French Guiana.

was then held on 24 January 2010 in order for these people to vote on the following question: 'Do you approve of the creation [in Martinique and Guiana] of a single local authority exercising the powers vested in the department and the region while still being governed by Article 73 of the Constitution?'. To this second question the people of Guiana and Martinique responded positively.

355. These two territories thus abandoned the duality of their functions (i.e., both departmental and regional) to become each a 'single local authority' which combines powers and is managed by a single deliberative assembly. Articles L. 7111-1 et seq. of the General Code of Local Authorities provides in the case of Guiana that 'Guiana is a local authority of the Republic governed by Article 73 of the Constitution which shall exercise the powers conferred to an overseas department and an overseas region and all the powers conferred on it by law taking account of its special characteristics and constraints (...). The bodies of the local authority of Guiana include the Assembly of Guiana and its President, assisted by the Economic, Social, Environmental, Cultural, Educational, and Economic Council of Guiana'. Equivalent provisions concern Martinique. As a result of this, the elections to the two local assemblies were organized by a single vote in December 2015, whilst in the ordinary local authorities a consultation for the election of departmental councillors was scheduled for March 2015 and another for the election of regional councillors in December 2015. This new status brings together these single local authorities with the newly created metropolitan cities under the same aim of visibility and efficiency of local public action.

B. *Overseas Territories*

356. The so-called overseas territories are governed by Article 74 of the Constitution, as amended by the 2003 constitutional amendment:[340] 'The overseas territories governed by the present Article shall have a status which takes into account the interests of each of them within the Republic.' Their status is laid down in organic laws enacted after consultation with the relevant local deliberative assemblies. These overseas territories are the following ones:

- Saint Pierre and Miquelon, territory located in the North Atlantic Ocean below Newfoundland, with a population of about 6,000 inhabitants.
- Wallis and Futuna, territory located in the southern Pacific Ocean, east of Australia and north of New Zealand, with a population of about 12,000 inhabitants.
- French Polynesia, located in the centre of the southern Pacific Ocean, and equidistant from eastern Australia and western South America, with a population of about 270,000 inhabitants.
- Saint-Barthélemy, territory located in the Caribbean, with a population of about 9,000 inhabitants; and

340. Constitutional Law No 2003-276 of 28 Mar. 2003 on the decentralized organization of the Republic.

– Saint Martin, also located in the Caribbean with a population of about 35,000 inhabitants.

357. Article 74 provides for two distinct types of overseas territories, and for both require 'taking into account the specific interests of each [of these types of territories] within the Republic'. As regards the first type of overseas territories, their particular status lays down, amongst others, the conditions under which laws and regulations apply within their respective territory, the powers exercised by the local authorities thereof, the rules of organization and functioning of local institutions and the electoral system of their deliberative assemblies, as well as the conditions under which the overseas territories thereof are consulted on draft laws, ordinances, decrees or international agreements which might affect their area of competence. As regard the second type of overseas territories, these enjoy a wider autonomy as reflected under Article 74 which refers to 'self-governing overseas territories'. Concerning in particular French Polynesia, this translates into a meaningful autonomy of local norms vis-à-vis national laws. Article 74 in its eighth paragraph allows, for example, for an organic law to lay down a specific review of certain acts of these autonomous authorities;[341] its ninth paragraph allows deliberative assemblies to 'amend a law promulgated after the entry into force of the status of the overseas territory, where the Constitutional Council ... finds that the law herein falls within this territory's jurisdiction'; and its tenth paragraph allows overseas authorities to adopt derogating measures in the areas of access to local employment, professional activity, and protection of property rights. In short, these provisions allow varying degrees of autonomy in the governance of decentralized entities addressing local interests and related political demands.

358. Two territories are not subject to the above-described status, namely Clipperton and the French Southern and Antarctic Lands or Territories. These territories are governed by the Law of 6 August 1955 on the status of French Southern and Antarctic Territories and Clipperton Island.[342] Clipperton Island, located in the East Pacific off the Mexican coast, has no permanent local population and is under the jurisdiction of a High Commissioner for the Republic in French Polynesia. EU law does not apply to this territory. French Southern and Antarctic Territories (i.e., St Paul and Amsterdam Islands, Crozet Islands, Kerguelen Islands, and *Terre Adélie*) do not have a local population either and are under the authority of a senior administrator prefect. Unlike Clipperton Island, French Southern and Antarctic Lands are listed in Appendix II of the Treaty on the Functioning of the European Union (TFEU) which lists the countries and territories to which the provisions of Part IV of the Treaty apply. As such, EU law is applicable thereof under Part Four of the TFEU entitled 'Association of the Overseas Countries and Territories'.

---

341. 'The Council of State shall exercise a specific judicial review of certain categories of acts by the deliberative assembly [of an overseas territory] when acting within its legislative competence.'
342. Law No 55-1052 of 6 Aug. 1955 on the status of French Southern and Antarctic Lands and Clipperton Island.

C. New Caledonia

359. New Caledonia is not governed by Articles 72 to 75-1 under Title XII on 'Local Authorities', but by Articles 76 and 77 under Title XIII, entitled 'Of Transitional Provisions on New Caledonia'. New Caledonia is certainly a 'local authority' of the Republic but its exclusion from the main title clearly sets it apart in French law. Carcassonne even commented that Title XIII stands less as a set of particular constitutional provisions than as a new Constitution in itself which the Constitution 'incorporates in its Title XIII in a Russian dolls type of way'.[343] As is often the case with particular constitutional regimes, the status of New Caledonia is the result of historical events and upheavals. Since at least the 1980s, New Caledonia has been halfway between independence and autonomy, although there is now an irreversible path towards independence.

360. The relevant constitutional provisions reveal a difficult evolution overall – between violence and compromise – concerning the status of New Caledonia. These provisions, which constitutionalize a set of laws and organic laws, include various matters relating to the composition of the Caledonian electorate, the transfer of powers from the central State, the institutional organization of the territory, as well as the scheduling of local consultations and referendums. Article 76 thus provides that: 'The people of New Caledonia shall be called upon to vote before 31 December 1998 on the provisions of the Agreement signed in Nouméa on 5 May 1998 and published on 27 May 1998 in the Official Journal of the French Republic (paragraph one). Individuals who meet the requirements prescribed by Article 2 of Law No. 88-1028 of 9 November 1988 shall be eligible to take part in the vote (paragraph two).' This was intended to guarantee that the Agreement reached in 1988,[344] after severe episodes of violence at local level, would be respected in particular with regard to the consultation of the Caledonians on the independence process. Provisions on the composition of the electorate were aimed at to reassuring the Caledonian population, the Kanaks in particular, that changes in the local demographic balance would not entail any change in the composition of the electorate invited to vote in a referendum. Following the 1998 local consultation, the Organic Law No 99-209 of 19 March 1999 was adopted which essentially lays down the legal regime of New Caledonia. Without dispelling the ambiguity about independence, the 1999 Law lays down in its Article 3 that '[t]he provinces and municipalities of New Caledonia are local authorities of the Republic' which are 'freely administered by assemblies elected by direct universal suffrage'. Under Article 99 of the 1999 Law, the Congress of New Caledonia adopts provisions – the so-called laws of the land (*lois du pays*) – on various matters, including the distribution of powers between the State and New Caledonia; the institutional organization of the territory; locally

343. Guy Carcassonne and Marc Guillaume, *La Constitution* (12th ed., Points Seuil 2014) 369.

344. The Matignon Agreement was reached in June 1988, a month after an uprising in Ouvéa which resulted in the death of nineteen separatists and two soldiers. The Agreement was approved by referendum on 6 Nov. 1988. Ten years after this dramatic episode, another agreement was reached between the French State, the independentists and the loyalists – the so-called Nouméa Agreement – which defined the new constitutional status of New Caledonia.

applicable property law; legally binding force of the laws of the land; electoral issues; the powers of the High Commissioner for the Republic who is responsible in particular for ensuring 'the proper exercise of powers by the institutions and provinces of New Caledonia as well as the legality of their acts'; State supervision (i.e., judicial review, financial audit, and tax control); and budgetary rules. These laws of the land represent the most significant element of this special constitutional regime as, under Article 107 of the 1999 Law, they have the force of law in the area defined in Article 99 – which constitutes a real exception to the hierarchy of legislative and administrative norms. Proposed concurrently at the initiative of the government and Caledonian Congress, the laws of the land may concern any of the areas which fall within the jurisdiction of New Caledonia. They may be submitted for opinion to the French Council of State before their adoption, and may be subject to a further deliberation at the request of the High Commissioner for the Republic, the government, the president of the Caledonian Congress, the president of an assembly of province, or eleven members of the Caledonian Congress. The Constitutional Council may also, on a referral, review such laws as regard their conformity to the Constitution and in particular the provisions on the distribution of powers between the State and New Caledonia.

361. In law, New Caledonia currently enjoys a broad autonomy but not a true constitutional sovereignty. The Nouméa Agreement set a transitional period of 15–20 years after which the Caledonian people would decide by referendum on independence. The current Congress, elected in 2014, has the task of determining the date of the self-determination referendum. If the members of the local assembly fail to reach, by a three-fifths majority, an agreement on a date by November 2018 (which is the end of the Congress's term of office), it will then be up to the French Government to decide on a date for the referendum.

Chapter 3. Decentralized Local Authorities

362. Decentralization, which is the transfer of powers from the State to elected local authorities, has aimed at revitalizing democracy by bringing public decision-making closer to the citizens, and by subjecting decision makers to the vote of their constituents. This transfer of powers is referred to as 'territorial decentralization'. 'Functional decentralization' is another kind of decentralization involving the transfer of central State power to other authorities and concerns specialized public institutions. This form of decentralization does not involve a transfer of general powers to locally elected authorities, but rather the assignment of particular functions to specialized and autonomous institutions in their management and operational roles such as, for example, universities or hospitals. Although significant in practice, such transfer, unlike 'territorial decentralization', does not affect the territorial organization of the Republic.

363. Local authorities are governed by the principle of free administration which is core to their autonomy and protects them against encroachments by both the State and another local authority. Such principle does not prohibit the exercise of a degree of supervision by central State authorities.

§1. The Principle of Free Administration of Local Authorities

364. The constitutional principle of free administration is intended to prevent the State from establishing a legal or factual form of supervision on local authorities. This principle ensures that elected local bodies enjoy decisional autonomy in matters within their area of competence and that they enjoy, in principle, budgetary independence.

I. A Constitutional Principle

365. Under Article 72 of the Constitution, '[l]ocal authorities shall aim at making decisions concerning all powers that can be best implemented at their level (paragraph two). Under the conditions prescribed by law, the authorities thereof shall freely administer themselves through elected councils and shall have regulatory power to exercise their competences (paragraph three)'. This is otherwise formulated in Article 34: 'The Law shall lay down the fundamental principles: (…) – With respect to the free administration of local authorities, powers and resources.' On numerous occasions, the Constitutional Council has affirmed the constitutional value of the principle of free administration and its significance in relation to the law. In its Decision of 29 May 1990, the Council stated that if, by virtue of Article 72 of the Constitution, local authorities freely administer through elected councils, they do so in accordance with the law.[345] The primary implication is that only a law can limit the free administration of local authorities. In principle, it is not for the Executive to encroach on the powers of decentralized local authorities.[346] Another implication is to be found in the balance between the intervention of the legislature and the effectiveness of the free administration of local authorities. The Constitutional Council has ruled that the law could not intervene in an area under the jurisdiction of local authorities to the point of preventing them from freely administering.[347] This is in that sense that the lawmaker must find a balance and that would not be the case if the lawmaker was to impose 'undue hardship, without justification'.[348]

366. In any event, a margin of appreciation must be left to local authorities. The legislature may establish a legal framework, but shall not replace the local authorities in the decisions they must be free to make. One example is the above-mentioned 1984 Decision of the Constitutional Council in relation to the local civil service.[349] According to the Council, the lawmaker may lay down the rules governing the local civil service applicable to incumbent agents of the municipalities, departments or regions. However, the legal regime may only be consistent with the Constitution if it is also consistent with the free administration of the local authorities in the terms that follow: 'A local authority is to decide freely on the creation and loss of jobs, to appoint to the relevant scales in the local civil service, to resolve the statutory positions of the appointments and their advancement in scale and grade, and to exercise, under the normal rules of the Civil Service, any relevant disciplinary powers which might result, after due process of law, in dismissal for incompetence'.[350] This freedom of administration of local authorities is a prerequisite for local democracy since, without it, there would be no point in the election of their representatives.

345. CC Decision No 90-274 DC of 29 May 1990, *Loi visant à la mise en œuvre du droit au logement, Rec.* 61, pt 12.
346. CC Decision No 83-168 DC of 20 Jan. 1984, *Loi portant dispositions statutaires relatives à la fonction publique territoriale, Rec.* 38, pt 19.
347. CC Decision No 90-277 DC of 25 Jul. 1990, *Loi relative à la révision générale des évaluations des immeubles retenus pour la détermination des bases des impôts directs locaux, Rec.* 70, pt 14.
348. CC Decision No 92-316 DC of 20 Jan. 1993, *Loi relative à la prévention de la corruption et à la transparence de la vie économique et des procédures publiques, Rec.* 38, pt 43.
349. CC Decision No 83-168 DC of 20 Jan. 1984, *Loi portant dispositions statutaires relatives à la fonction publique territoriale, Rec.* 38.
350. *Ibid.*, pt 5.

II. The Elections of Local Authorities

367. Unlike 'deconcentrated' local authorities which merely represent the central State at local level and derive from it,[351] decentralized local authorities – which legitimacy rests on the democratic revitalization of public action – come into existence upon local elections.

A. *Local Elections in the Municipality*

368. Municipal bodies are first the mayor and his/her deputies, and the Municipal Council.[352]

1. The Elections of the Municipal Council, Mayor and Deputies

369. Members of the Municipal Council are elected by direct universal suffrage by a list system[353] with the following features: the vote is by proportional representation and includes a majority bonus for the leading list,[354] and there are two ballots (maintaining only the lists involving more than 12.5% of the votes, which further tempers the proportionality of the election). Under the second paragraph of the First Article of the Constitution, electoral lists must comply with the principle of gender equality according to which'[t]he law shall promote equal access by women and men to electoral mandates and elective functions, as well as equal access to professional and social responsibilities'. Since the Law of 17 May 2013 on the election of departmental councillors, municipal councillors and inter-municipal councillors, and amending the electoral calendar,[355] this voting system is applicable in all municipalities of France of over a thousand people, including in the three largest cities, namely Paris, Lyon and Marseille where elections are conducted at district level (i.e., the level of the *arrondissement*). In municipalities with less than 1,000 inhabitants, the poll is not by proportional representation but on a majority vote with two ballots. The lists are multi-member lists with the possibility of mixing by the voter (i.e., the voter may change the names on the list by crossing out names, hence the idea of 'mixing' or *panachage*). One counts the votes cast for each name. Unless one candidate obtains an absolute majority of voters – and over 25% of the votes of registered voters – councillors are elected in the second ballot by the number of seats to be filled at the Municipal Council. Accrued lists do not have to respect the

351. Deconcentration and decentralization are the two forms of local government in France. Deconcentration is the weakest form of transfer of powers from the central State to the local level. In this system, the appointed local representative, generally the prefect, represents the State.
352. The Municipal Council is the equivalent of the City Council.
353. In practice, each candidate for the office of mayor comes top of the list which also includes his/her fellow candidates who intend to become local councillors.
354. The leading list gets an advantage in the number of people elected in order to obtain a clear and stable municipal majority.
355. Law No 2013-403 of 17 May 2013 on the election of departmental councillors, municipal councillors and community councillors, and modifying the electoral calendar.

gender equality principle. These differences with the ballot applicable in municipalities with more than 1,000 inhabitants can be explained by the desire to simplify the local electoral process in the many small towns of France that sometimes encounter difficulties in establishing a Council. As for the mayor and his/her deputies, they are elected by indirect universal suffrage by the Municipal Council. According to the General Code of Local Authorities and the Electoral Code, the mayor is elected by the Municipal Council for the same term as the Council thereof, namely six years. The vote is secret and the mayor candidate must obtain an absolute majority of the votes cast in the first ballot or in the second ballot. If there is no majority in the second ballot, the election is made by a relative majority. Each deputy mayor is elected in the same way, on an individual basis.

2. The Functions of the Municipal Council, Mayor and Deputies

370. The Municipal Council is the deliberative body of the municipality. Under Article L. 2121-29 of the General Code of Local Authorities, 'the Municipal Council governs, through its deliberations, the matters pertaining to the municipality. The Council gives its opinion whenever this opinion is required by law and regulatory provisions, or is requested by the State representative in the department. When the Municipal Council, which is regularly required and summoned, refuses or neglects to give its opinion, it can be overridden. The Council give recommendations on all objects of local interest'. The Council votes on the local budget. It meets at least once every quarter and may do so whenever the mayor asks.

371. The mayor and his/her deputies represent the local executive power. The mayor, as head of the local executive, does not simply 'execute' the deliberations of the Municipal Council. First, s/he is responsible for the local administration (i.e., all of the town officials). Second, s/he has a large number of powers that s/he exercises in his/her own name such as powers with regard to the administrative police in the town (especially in respect of public security and health and safety matters), powers of judicial nature, and powers in relation to civil registers – all powers which make him/her an agent of the State. Third, s/he is responsible for preparing the deliberations of the Municipal Council, which may delegate to the mayor to rule alone in a number of areas. The mayor's deputies are responsible for specific areas such as planning and development, finances, charities regulation, on which local authority has been delegated by the mayor in accordance with Article L. 2122-18 of the General Code of Local Authorities which states: 'The mayor is solely responsible for the administration, but s/he can, under his/her own supervision and responsibility, delegate by decree some of his/her powers to one or more of his/her deputies, and, in case of the absence or impeachment of deputies or when deputies are all exercising a delegation of power already, [the mayor can delegate by decree some of his/her powers] to ordinary members of the Municipal Council.'

B. Local Elections in the Department

372. The department is administered by a Departmental Council[356] and a president assisted by a standing committee.

1. The Elections of the Departmental Council, President and Standing Committee

373. For a long time, bodies at departmental level held a variety of names forming quite a motley ensemble. The deliberative body of the department was called the General Council, the local councillors were named general councillors, and their electoral districts in the department were called '*cantons*'. The Law of 17 May 2013 on the election of departmental councillors, municipal councillors and intermunicipal councillors, and amending the electoral calendar (hereafter the 2013 Law),[357] put some order into this terminology, transforming the General Council in a Departmental Council, general councillors into departmental councillors – only the *canton* has remained unchanged. The departmental councillors are elected for six years by direct universal suffrage. Their mode of election has been substantially amended by the 2013 Law, which applied for the first time at the March 2015 departmental elections. In accordance with the principle of gender equality as regards access to elective mandates and elected offices, voting is now done in pairs consisting of a woman and a man presented in each *canton*. Each pair shall be deemed elected on obtaining an absolute majority of the votes cast in the *canton* representing at least 25% of registered voters. Failing to obtain such a majority in the first round, a second ballot is held between the pairs who received at least 12.5% of the votes cast in the first ballot.[358] The president of the Departmental Council is elected by departmental councillors for a three-year renewable term. Similarly to the election of the mayor at municipal level, s/he is elected by an absolute majority vote of departmental councillors in the first or second ballot. If no absolute majority is obtained after these two ballots, there shall be a third ballot upon which the president shall be deemed elected by a relative majority. The president of the Departmental Council is assisted by a standing committee elected by the Council and composed of the president and a number of vice-presidents.

356. The Department Council is the equivalent of the County Council.
357. Law No 2013-403 of 17 May 2013 on the election of departmental councillors, municipal councillors and community councillors, and modifying the electoral calendar.
358. If only one pair raised more than 12.5% of the votes, its successor may nevertheless present itself. If no candidate pair received more than 12.5% of the votes, the two top entry lists are maintained in the second ballot.

2. The Functions of the Departmental Council, President, Standing Committee and Vice-Presidents

374. Under Article L. 3211-1 of the General Code of Local Authorities, '[t]he Department Council governs, through its deliberations, the matters pertaining to the department. The Council shall act on all matters on which it is called to deliberate by laws and regulatory provisions and all matters of departmental interest before it. The Council has jurisdiction to promote solidarity and territorial cohesion within the territory of the department, respecting the integrity, independence and powers of the regions and municipalities'. The Council votes on the budget of the department. The Departmental Council meets at least once a quarter and whenever its president so requests. The Council may delegate some of its powers to the standing committee.

375. The president of the Departmental Council is the head of the local executive which powers are governed under Articles L. 3221-1 et seq. of the General Code of Local Authorities. In particular, the president of the Council 'shall prepare and execute the deliberations of the Departmental Council'; as the 'authority on expenditure in the department', s/he shall call for the implementation of departmental revenue; s/he shall be the sole responsible for the administration, which s/he may delegate to his/her vice-presidents; last, s/he shall also exercise policing powers in the department such as those related to traffic matters for example, and s/he shall be responsible for certain staff appointments at the level of the department.

C. Local Elections in the Region

376. As with the French departments, regions are administered by an elected council headed by a president.

1. The Elections of the Regional Council and of the President of the Regional Council

377. Pursuant to Article L. 366 of the Electoral Code, '[r]egional councillors are elected for six years; they may be re-elected. Regional Councils are renewed in full. [Regional] Elections are held at the same time as the general renewal of Departmental Councils'. The voting system applicable to the election of regional councillors is partly codified in Article L. 338 of the Electoral Code and is as follows: 'Regional councillors are elected in each region via a two-round list system which does not allow any addition or deletion of names nor any change in the order of presentation. Each list consists of as many sections as there are departments in the region.' This election is on the basis of proportional representation with a majority bonus for the leading list. Each list must alternate between a female candidate and a male candidate to meet the gender equality requirement. The division by departments of the election of regional councillors is aimed at bringing the candidate closer to his/her electorate. The president of the Regional Council is elected by the Council thereof for the same term of six years. As with the Departmental Council and the Municipality Council, the election of the president of the region is carried out by an absolute majority of votes cast. If this majority is not constituted in the first two ballots, a relative majority is sufficient in the third ballot.

2. The Functions of the Regional Council and of its President

378. Under Article L. 4221-1 of the General Code of Local Authorities, 'the Regional Council governs, through its deliberations, the matters pertaining to the region. [The Council] shall act on all matters on which it is called to deliberate by laws and regulatory provisions and all matters of regional interest before it. [The Council] is responsible for promoting the economic, social, health, cultural and scientific life of the region and the development of its territory, as well as for ensuring the preservation of its identity and the advancement of its regional languages, while respecting the integrity, autonomy and respective responsibilities of departments and municipalities. [The Council] may engage in actions complementing those of the State, of other local authorities and of public institutions in the region, within the limits and under the conditions laid down by laws determining the division of powers between the State, municipalities, departments and regions'. The Regional Council also must vote on the budget of the region.

379. The president of the Regional Council is the head of the local executive. Under Articles L. 4231-1 et seq. of the General Code of Local Authorities, '[s/h]e prepares and executes the deliberations of the Regional Council'; s/he is 'the authority on expenditure in the region and calls for the implementation of regional revenue'; s/he is 'the sole one responsible for the administration', unless s/he chooses to delegate to the vice-presidents; s/he 'manages the territory of the region'; s/he enters contracts for the region. The president of the Regional Council is assisted by a standing committee, elected by a list system within the Regional Council, as well as a bureau which is made up of the president, vice-presidents and, where appropriate, members of the standing committee who have received a delegation of power.[359]

D. Incompatibilities and Ineligibility

380. All candidates to the above-described elective positions shall meet a number of general requirements. First, a candidate must meet formal eligibility conditions. S/he must be over eighteen years of age, of French nationality or a national of one of the EU Member States, have fulfilled his/her military obligations, and be registered on the electoral roll or the role of contributions from the place where s/he stands for election (i.e., list of local taxpayers). In addition, s/he must not have been declared ineligible (i.e., not have been criminally convicted to a term of ineligibility, or have been legally declared incapacitated). Second, a candidate should not be

359. Article L. 4133-8 General Code of Local Authorities.

in a situation of incompatibility of office. A prefectural office, military position, leadership in the police, membership of the administrative judiciary or of the Constitutional Council are, among others, incompatible with a local elected position. The holding of several functions is also subject to restrictions. The prohibition of holding several elective mandates concurrently has been a recurring issue. It is a rather common practice in France as it is not unusual to find individuals who are, at the same time, member of the Senate, mayor of a large city, as well as member of a Regional or Departmental Council. While, for some, such accumulation of mandates reinforces the experience and authority of the particular elected individual, for others, this represents a disturbing trend towards the constitution of some kind of 'local aristocracy' which should be incompatible with the requirements of time and integrity required by each elected office. The Organic Law of 14 February 2014[360] prohibiting the holding of several local executive functions concurrently with the office of deputy or senator was adopted with a view to curtail such practice. The 2014 Organic Law prohibits the holding of local executive functions (i.e., mayor, president of the Departmental Council or Regional Council, president of the Assembly of Corsica, president of the Assembly of French Polynesia) with a parliamentary mandate.[361] It also limits the possibility for an MP to be a member of a local assembly. An MP can be a member of only one local assembly (i.e., Municipal, Departmental or Regional Council). The accumulation of allowances is also prohibited.

III. The Decision-Making Autonomy

381. Local authorities are free to take measures they deem appropriate in matters within their jurisdiction and, even beyond, as regards any matter that is of a local interest. To that effect, they enjoy budgetary autonomy and possess their own property and staff.

A. The General Jurisdiction Clause and Conferred Powers

382. Local authorities have a number of powers conferred on them by law as well as a general decision-making power based on a so-called general jurisdiction clause which has been removed as regards departments and regions under the 'NOTRe' Law of 7 August 2015 on the new territorial organization of the Republic (hereafter the 2015 Law).[362]

360. Organic Law No 2014-125 of 14 Feb. 2014 prohibiting the cumulation of local executive functions with the mandate of deputy or senator.

361. Another law extends this principle to mandates of the EP. *See* Law No 2014-126 of 14 Feb. 2014 prohibiting the cumulation of local executive functions with the mandate of representative in the European Parliament.

362. Law No 2015-991 of 7 Aug. 2015 on the new territorial organization of the Republic, or the 'NOTRe' Law as in '*Nouvelle Organisation Territoriale de la République*'.

1. The General Jurisdiction Clause

383. The General Jurisdiction Clause was coined by the doctrine by reference to the provisions of the General Code of Local Authorities which provide:

- With respect to municipalities, the Municipal Council regulates by its deliberations the business of the city.
- With respect to departments, the Departmental Council regulates by its deliberations the business of the department.
- With respect to regions, the Regional Council regulates through its deliberations the business of the region.[363]

384. The meaning of these provisions phrased in general terms seems to suggest that a local authority can act in all matters affecting its territory, which is somewhat confirmed under the second paragraph of Article 72 of the Constitution: 'Local authorities shall aim at making decisions concerning all powers that can be best implemented at their level.' However, this general jurisdiction is limited, on the one hand, by the powers exclusively conferred upon other local authorities or upon the State and, on the other hand, by the requirement of an actual local interest justifying the action of the local authority. This general jurisdiction has been criticized for rendering public action difficult to anticipate as well as making it inefficient since any local authority may act in all areas of interest. Supporters of such jurisdiction argue, on the contrary, that the principle of free administration of local authorities necessarily implies the power to act in all matters of particular interest to their territory. After some dithering, the government eventually decided to remove the general jurisdiction from departments and regions in favour of specific powers – which is not the case for municipalities which retain the right to act as regard any matter of local interest.

2. Conferred Powers

385. Municipalities have subsidiary powers that make them both visible and valued in their action at local level. They are in charge, on a mandatory basis or not, of a number of public services including, in the first place, the management of elementary schools (called 'primary schools' or *écoles primaires*) and pre-elementary schools (called 'kindergarten' or *écoles maternelles*), as well as the management of extracurricular activities (i.e., all educational activities outside the classroom). Municipalities can also intervene in social matters (i.e., crèches, nurseries, training centres), in culture (i.e., libraries, museums, theatres, tourism), or matters relating to sports facilities (i.e., swimming pools, stadiums, gymnasiums). Municipalities have also a conferred jurisdiction in the area of town planning and are competent to issue planning permissions, and draft and vote on most of the planning deeds. Municipalities also have competence regarding local roads, which they

363. Articles L. 2121-29, L. 3211-1, and L. 4221-1, respectively, of the General Code of Local Authorities.

are responsible for maintaining. Last, the mayor is the administrative police authority on behalf of the municipality endowed with general policing powers on its territory in order to maintain law and order.

386. Departments have a conferred power primarily in the area of social action and are responsible for managing social benefits, children's social welfare, elderly's social welfare, and disabled's social welfare. More recently, they have acquired jurisdiction to assist with families which cannot afford to meet their basic energy needs such as heating and electricity, in an effort to tackle the so-called fuel poverty. Departments are also responsible for the construction, maintenance and equipment of first-cycle secondary schools (*collèges*), and school transportation in the department. Departments can also intervene in support of the municipalities to achieve, for example, public facilities projects. If the geography of the department so requires, departmental authorities are also in charge of maritime fishing ports.

387. Regions are primarily conferred power over economic matters. Being responsible for economic development projects such as the development of planning agreements, which are economic planning instruments, regions have competence over economic assistance to businesses as well as in the area of vocational training. Regions also have a special competence as regards regional transport equipment, including railways and airports, and now as regards digital equipment in the regional territory. Finally, regions are responsible for the construction, maintenance and equipment of second-cycle secondary schools (*lycées*). The 2015 Law has strengthened the economic competence of the regions.

B. Public Property and the Local Civil Service

388. To carry out their missions, local authorities have material and human resources. First, with regard to their property, local authorities may own property in a public[364] or private capacity – called respectively 'public domain' and 'private domain' of local authorities. For example, municipalities are the owners of such elementary school buildings, local roads, city halls, and equipment for local public services. These assets, assigned to the public service or on direct public use and which have been specifically deployed for the operation of the public service, belong to the public domain. As such, a protective legal regime applies to them. The applicable regime protects the inalienability, imprescriptibility and unseizability of the public domain, as well as protects it through the imposition of special penalties in case of infringements to the property and any related domain (*contraventions de grande voirie*). This legal regime is binding on local authorities which do not possess, in this sense, the same property rights as those that private individuals enjoy over their property. However, such regime does not prevent local authorities from increasing the value of the public domain by resorting to private investment.

364. CC Decision No 94-346 DC of 21 Jul. 1994, *Loi complétant le code du domaine de l'état et relative à la constitution de droits réels sur le domaine public*, *Rec.* 96.

389. Second, with regard to human resources, local authorities operate through public servants belonging to the local civil service, as well as through non-tenured staff employed on a contract basis. In France, there are three categories of public servants: those who belong to the State public service (*fonction publique d'Etat*), those who belong to the hospital public service (*fonction publique hospitalière*), and those who belong to the local civil service (*fonction publique territoriale*). The latter, aimed at local authorities, does not therefore depend on the State in the recruitment of their servants. While local authorities abide by the status common to all public service, including competitive recruitment, they are free to determine their staffing needs and conduct recruitment on their own budget.

C. *Budgetary Autonomy*

390. The budgetary autonomy of local authorities is crucial for their free administration.[365] The 2003 constitutional amendment took into account this obvious fact by constitutionalizing the rules of budgetary autonomy of local authorities which are now laid down in Article 72-2 of the Constitution on local finances:

- Local authorities shall benefit from resources freely available to them under the conditions prescribed by law.
- They shall be entitled to receive all or part of the proceeds of taxes of all types. The tax base and rate of the taxation thereof may be authorized by law within the limits it prescribes.
- Tax revenue and other own resources of local authorities shall represent, for each category of authorities thereof, a determining share of their overall resources. An organic law shall determine the conditions under which this rule is implemented.
- Any transfer of powers between the State and local authorities shall be accompanied by the allocation of resources equivalent to those devoted to their exercise. Any creation or extension of the powers thereof which result in an increase of the expenses of the local authorities shall be accompanied by resources as prescribed by law.
- The law shall provide for equalization schemes designed to promote equality between local authorities.

1. Local Taxes

391. If local authorities can freely dispose of income tax, they cannot establish the tax themselves. The Constitution reserves this power to the legislature under Article 34 of the Constitution: 'The Law shall lay down the fundamental principles: (...) – With respect to the free administration of local authorities, powers and resources.' However, local authorities have some scope in the matter since, under Article 72-2 of the Constitution, they can fix the base and rate of local taxes. Direct

365. CC Decision No 2000-442 DC of 28 Dec. 2000, *Loi de finances pour 2001*, *Rec.* 56.

local taxes consist of three household taxes, namely the housing tax, the tax on developed land, and the tax on undeveloped land, as well as of a professional tax, namely the local economic contribution, which replaced the business tax since 2010. Indirect local taxes are variable and could consist of, for example, taxes on household waste, on commercial property, or on rolling stock used on the national rail network. The law divides the revenue from these taxes among local authorities and their public institutions – for example, the revenue generated by the housing tax is dedicated to municipalities and public institutions for inter-municipal cooperation, and the revenue generated by the land tax on developed property is distributed between departments and municipalities. In any event, the own revenue of local authorities shall constitute the determining share of all their resources.

2. The 'Determining Share' of the Budget of Local Authorities and Transfers of Powers

392. The financial relationships between the State and local authorities are the object of conflicting issues. On the one hand, while local authorities are generally inclined to exercise new powers, they may nevertheless be wary of burdensome additional powers which are being transferred without new resources to exercise them. On the other hand, while local authorities expect the State to ensure adequate resources, they also expect to retain their budgetary autonomy. Therefore, the balance is hard, if at all, to find.

393. The principle laid down in the 2003 constitutional amendment and codified in Article 72-2 of the Constitution enshrines the notion of 'determining share' of the budget of local authorities: 'Tax revenue and other own resources of local authorities shall represent, for each category of authorities thereof, a determining share of all their overall resources.' This notion tends to limit the direct involvement of the State in the constitution of the budget of local authorities through State endowments. Such endowments are paid directly by the State to local authorities which, while being essential to their functioning, imply an element of financial supervision. These are intended to offset the transfer of powers from the State to local authorities. There exist several kinds of endowments, the most important one being the 'overall operating endowment' (*dotation globale de fonctionnement*) which represents over 20% of the budget of municipalities, public institutions for inter-municipal cooperation, departments and regions.[366] This overall operating endowment is calculated for each level of local authority on the basis of several types of endowments. For municipalities, the endowment thereof is composed of a fixed endowment to which must be added, if necessary, the endowment of urban solidarity and social cohesion, the rural solidarity endowment, and the national

366. In 2017, it represents EUR 30.9 billion, compared with EUR 32.2 billion in 2016 and another EUR 40 billion in 2014. This particularly strong and rapid decline demonstrates the State's policy of reducing its endowments.

equalization endowment. In addition to this overall budget, there are several specific endowments that can top up the accounts of local authorities such as the urban development endowment, the equipment for rural areas endowment, the endowment for municipalities in difficulty, etc.

394. In view of these State endowments, local authorities' own resources must form a 'determining share' of their budget. These resources do not consist only of local taxes since other types of resources must be included such as, for example, tariff revenues of local public services (i.e., fees paid by users of public services for various services such as school canteens, nurseries, sports facilities), products related to the public domain (i.e., fees paid by private users of the public domain), urban interests, any financial products, potential donations and legacies.[367] EU structural funds can also bolster the budget of local authorities such as the European Regional Development Fund in particular. Finally, loans are among the possible resources of local authorities, but are not counted as own resources within the meaning of Article 72-2 of the Constitution.[368] The sum of these products, apart from loans, should be the 'determining share' of the local authorities' budgets. Article LO 1114-3 of the General Code of Local Authorities gives a criterion for calculating this 'determining share' in considering that: 'For each category of local authorities, the share of own resources is calculated by dividing the amount of the latter into that of the totality of their resources, excluding loans, resources corresponding to the funding of powers transferred on an experimental basis or implemented by delegation, and financial transfers between local authorities of the same category. (...) For each category, the share of own resources cannot be lower than level recorded for 2003 [year of the constitutional revision].' As a convenient benchmark, the share observed in 2003 is the ratio that the Constitutional Council will review annually when reviewing the finance law for the year and represents approximately 61% for the budget of the municipalities, 59% for the budget of the departments, and only 42% for the budget of the regions.

3. Equalization

395. Equalization is a redistribution device of financial resources among local authorities which aims at ensuring a minimum of equality between territories. In particular, it aims at offsetting the imbalance in terms of revenues generated by the local economic contribution since companies and businesses are being unevenly installed on the national territory. There are two types of equalization mechanisms: one is called 'vertical equalization' when the State itself modulates the endowments, and one is called 'horizontal equalization' when redistribution takes place between local authorities. Equalization is bound to be enhanced in the coming years,

367. Article 3 of the Organic Law No 2004-758 of 29 Jul. 2004 on the financial autonomy of local authorities, now codified in Art. LO 1114-2 of the General Code of Local Authorities.
368. Article 4 of the Organic Law of 29 Jul. 2004.

through the creation of equalization funds in particular.[369] This equalization device has been criticized. While for its proponents, it certainly reduces the structural imbalances between local territories which the poorest areas would be unable to fill whatever the implementation policy, for others, it penalizes territories which have made efforts to attract business investments and activity.

§2. The Principle of Non-guardianship of One Local Authority over Another

396. The principle of free administration of local authorities not only ensures that they are independent from the State in the conduct of their business but also aims at ensuring that each local authority will not be subject to the supervision of another local authority. The fifth paragraph of Article 72 of the Constitution states in this regard: 'No local authority shall exercise guardianship authority over another.' This principle is, however, immediately followed by one exception, which is the principle of the so-called leader local authority (*collectivité chef de file*): 'However, where the exercise of a power requires the joint action of several local authorities, the law may allow one of the authorities or groupings thereof to organize the terms of their joint action.' Article L. 1111-9 of the General Code of Local Authorities, as amended in 2017, specifies the regime of this derogation – which is in reality quite limited – by determining so-called leaders for certain subject matters. Thus, as regards the regions, the law states: 'II. – The region is responsible for organizing, as the leader, the terms of the joint action of local authorities and their public institutions for the exercise of powers relating to: 1. Planning and sustainable development of the area; 2.°The protection of biodiversity; 3. Climate, air quality and energy; 4. Economic development; 5. Support for innovation; 6. Business globalization; 7. Intermodality and complementarity between modes of transport; 8. Support to higher education and research.' As regards departments, the law establishes that: 'III. – The department is responsible for organizing, as a leader, the terms of joint action between local authorities and their public institutions for the exercise of powers relating to: 1. Social action, social development and the tackling of fuel poverty; 2. The autonomy of persons; 3. Local solidarity.' As regards municipalities, the law provides that: 'IV. – The municipality, or the public institution for inter-municipal cooperation with its own taxation regime to which the municipality has transferred powers, is responsible for organizing, as the leader, the terms of the joint action of local authorities and their public institutions for the exercise of powers relating to: 1. Sustainable mobility; 2. The organization of local public services; 3. Local territorial planning; 4. Local development.' However, the scope of these provisions remains limited since it is conditional upon a local authority expressly consenting to the establishment of a leader. In any event, the organization of the

369. Such funds include the National Equalization Fund of Inter-Municipal and Municipal Resources, the National Equalization Fund on Value Added to Businesses for Departments and Regions, the National Equalization Fund for Pecuniary Transaction Tax for Departments, or the Solidarity Fund for the Municipalities in the Ile-de-France Region.

cooperation between local authorities under the authority of a leader can be established only contractually which, in respect of the principle of non-guardianship, cannot compel any local authority.

§3. State Supervision

397. The State has the sole authority to supervise the activity of local authorities. It does so through a control over their executive organs as well as through a power of judicial review of their acts.

I. State Supervision over Local Authorities

A. *Dissolution of the Municipal Council, Suspension and Revocation of the Mayor or Deputies*

398. In case of malfunction of a local authority, the State retains a power of control which can lead to the dissolution of the local authority thereof and its placement under State supervision. In this regard, Article L. 2121-6 of the General Code of Local Authorities provides in relation to the municipalities that 'a Municipal Council can be dissolved only by reasoned decree issued by the Council of Ministers and published in the *JO*. In case of urgency, [the Council] may be provisionally suspended by reasoned order of the State representative in the department. The duration of the suspension may not exceed one month'.[370] The possible reasons for such dissolution are not specified in the text, but the case law gives an indication of the situations envisaged. These might be cases of disagreement between members of a Municipal Council of such a nature as to preclude the normal administration of the municipality and particularly the vote of its budget. In such case, the dissolution results in the appointment by the prefect of a 'special delegation' in the following terms: 'In case of dissolution of a Municipal Council or resignation of all its members in office, or in case of definitive cancellation of the election of all its members, or when a Municipal Council cannot be constituted, a special delegation performs its functions.(…) The special delegation is appointed by decision of the State representative in the department within eight days of the dissolution, the definitive cancellation of elections, the acceptance of resignation or the finding of inability to constitute the council thereof.'[371] As for the mayor and his/her deputies, the legislature has provided for sanctions in case of serious breaches of their duties. In addition to criminal prosecution, Article L. 2122-16 of the General Code of Local Authorities provides that: 'The mayor and his/her deputies, having been heard or asked to provide a written explanation as regards the alleged breach, may be suspended by reasoned ministerial decree for a period not exceeding one month. They can be dismissed only by reasoned decree issued by the Council of Ministers. (...)

370. Identical provisions apply to the department (Art. L. 3121-5 of the General Code of Local Authorities) and to the region (Art. L. 4132-3 of the General Code of Local Authorities).
371. Articles L. 2121-35 and L. 2121-36 of the General Code of Local Authorities.

The dismissal thereof shall automatically entail ineligibility for the office of mayor and for the office of those concerned deputies for a period of one year after the dismissal decree unless it is carried out before the general renewal Municipal Councils.' This provision applies where, for example, a mayor is deprived of moral authority because of various criminal convictions for fraud and forgery or corruption.

B. State Supervision over the Budget

399. A local authority may be supervised by the prefect when warranted by its budgetary situation. This supervision is provided for, in law, under Article L. 1612-14 of the General Code of Local Authorities and relies on the expertise of the regional audit body in the following terms:

- When the closing of accounts of a local authority displays in the execution of the budget, after verification of the accuracy of the listings of revenue and expenditure, a deficit equal to or more than 10% of revenues from the operation section if it is a municipality of less than 20,000 residents and 5% in other cases, the regional audit body, after referral by the State representative, suggests to the local authority the necessary measures in order to restore fiscal balance, within a period of one month of such referral.
- When the budget of a local authority has been the subject of the remedies provided for in the preceding paragraph, the State representative in the department shall forward to the regional audit body the initial budget accounts relating to the following exercise.
- If, in consideration of the initial budget, the regional audit body finds that the local authority has not taken sufficient steps to eliminate this deficit, it shall propose the necessary measures to the State representative in the department within a period of one month from the transmission specified in the preceding paragraph. The State representative sets the budget and makes it enforceable... .

II. Judicial Review of Acts of Local Authorities

400. Judicial review of administrative acts of the local authorities is a constitutional requirement which provides under the sixth paragraph of Article 72 of the Constitution, as amended by the 2003 constitutional amendment, the following: 'Within the local authorities of the Republic, the State representative, representing each of the members of the Government, shall be responsible for national interests, administrative control and compliance with laws.' The Constitutional Council interpreted this provision by ruling that: '[I]t follows from the aforementioned provisions of Article 72 of the Constitution that, while the law may set the conditions for the free administration of local authorities, it is subject to reservation that the law thereof respects the prerogatives of the State set out in the third paragraph of the provision thereof; that these prerogatives cannot be restricted or rendered ineffective, even temporarily; that the intervention of the legislator is thus subject to the condition that administrative review under the third paragraph of Article 72, makes it possible to ensure compliance with the laws and, more generally, the safeguarding of the national interests which, moreover, relates to the implementation of international commitments to this end.'[372] Before 1982, the prefect exercised a real power of review over administrative acts according to which s/he could annul such acts before their entry into force. Following the 1982 reform on decentralization (*See* above), such a review was made no longer possible. Nevertheless, the principle of the unity of the State combined with the respect of the hierarchy of norms could only lead the constituent power to adopt a modified form of judicial review of the administrative acts of local authorities. In marked contrast to the previous regime, the new form of review has implied a limited role for the prefect who can only act after the entry into force of the administrative acts and may refer, if in doubt about their legality, to the administrative court which may decide on their annulment. A number of administrative acts of the local authorities must therefore be referred to the prefect – namely the most serious acts such as procurement contracts above a certain amount, loan agreements, or acts of the administrative police – who may, in turn, refer them to the administrative judge who has sole authority to annul them in case of illegality.

Selected Further Reading

Emmanuel Auber, Delphine Cervelle, *Les collectivités territoriales: Une approche juridique et pratique de la décentralisation* (3rd ed., Armand Colin 2015).

Julie Benetti, *Les collectivités territoriales et le principe d'égalité* (L'Harmattan 2016).

Cour des Comptes, Chambres régionales et territoriales des comptes, *La départementalisation de Mayotte: Une réforme mal préparée, des actions prioritaires à conduire* (La Documentation Française 2016).

Bertrand Faure, *Droit des collectivités territoriales* (4th ed., Dalloz 2016).

Bertrand Faure and Antoinette Hastings-Marchadier (eds), *La décentralisation à la française* (LGDJ 2015).

Patrick Gérard, 'Premier point sur la réforme de l'Etat territorial', 8 AJDA 432 (2015).

Gis-Grale-Cnrs, *Droit et gestion des collectivités territoriales: Les territoires de l'Etat* (Le Moniteur Editions 2017).

Christophe Guettier, *Institutions administratives* (6th ed., Dalloz 2015).

Laetitia Guilloud, 'Transferts de compétences et pouvoir normatif des collectivités territoriales: Splendeur et misère de la décentralisation sous la Ve République', 138 Les Petites Affiches 51 (10 July 2008).

La Constitution et les collectivités territoriales, 42 Les nouveaux Cahiers du Conseil constitutionnel (2014/1).

---

372. CC Decision No 82-137 DC of 25 Feb. 1982, *Loi relative aux droits et libertés des communes, des départements et des régions, Rec.* 38, pt 4.

Selected Further Reading

Marie-Aimée Latournerie, 'Les collectivités territoriales de la République dans la Constitution: Quel retour sur le dernier siècle pour quelles orientations?', RDP 895 (2017).

Gilles Le Chatelier, *La Constitution et les relations entre les collectivités*, 42 Les Nouveaux Cahiers du Conseil Constitutionnel 53 (2014/1).

Anne-Marie Le Pourhiet, *Départements d'outre-mer: L'assimilation en questions*, 12 Les Cahiers du Conseil Constitutionnel 107 (2002/1).

Yves Luchaire, *Réforme territoriale: Des métropoles aux grandes régions* (Economica 2016).

François Luchaire and Yves Luchaire, *Décentralisation et Constitution* (Economica 2003).

Wanda Mastor, *Pour un statut constitutionnel de la Corse*, Rapport remis à monsieur le Président de l'Assemblée de Corse, 18 January 2018.

Ferdinand Mélin-Soucramanien, *Le principe d'égalité entre collectivités locales*, 12 Les Cahiers du Conseil Constitutionnel 93 (2002/1).

Alexis Niepceron, *La place des régions dans la décentralisation française* (L'Harmattan 2017).

Jacques-Henri Stahl, *Le principe de libre administration a-t-il une portée normative?*, 42 Les Nouveaux Cahiers du Conseil Constitutionnel 40 (2014/1).

Michel Verpeaux, Christine Rimbault, Franck Waserman, *Les collectivités territoriales et la décentralisation* (10th ed., La Documentation française 2017).

Part IV. Citizenship and the Administration of Justice

401. This Part is concerned with the rules concerning French citizenship, fundamental rights and liberties, and the constitutional problems of minorities. It also deals with the judicial control of administrative action and the rights and status of foreigners.

Chapter 1. French Citizenship

402. After some general considerations about the evolution and conception of French nationality law, the obtention of French nationality, the effects attached to it, and the loss thereof will be examined.

§1. Introduction

403. The conception of French citizenship has evolved over time reflecting a certain political conception of the Nation. Nationality law has fluctuated between a voluntarist conception of the Nation, backing onto the right of the soil (*jus soli*) and a more ethnic approach to it, based on the right of blood (*jus sanguinis*). In any case, it has been a matter of favouring either openness or parochialism. For example, the Constitution of 3 September 1791, which was based on the idea of voluntary adherence to the Nation, and enacted at a time when the aim was to grow the French citizen body, established principles such as:

> Article 2: French citizens are: Those born in France of a French father; Those born in France to a foreign father, who have established their residence in the Kingdom; Those born in a foreign country to a French father, who have come to settle in France and have taken the civic oath; Finally, those who, born in a foreign country and descending from, to any degree whatsoever, a Frenchman or a Frenchwoman expatriated due to religion, coming to live in France and taking the civic oath.
> Article 3: Those who, born outside the Kingdom to foreign parents, reside in France, become French citizens after five years of continuous residence in the Kingdom, if they have also acquired property or married a French person or formed an agricultural or commercial trade, and if they have taken the civic oath.
> Article 4: The legislative power may, for important considerations, give a foreigner an act of naturalization, without any conditions other than to take up residence in France and to take the civic oath.

404. In order to meet the recruitment needs of the army at that time and to submit equally all residents in France to military obligations, the Law of 28 June 1889 attributed French citizenship to any child born on French soil, even born of foreign parents. Likewise, in order to overcome the consequent demographic deficit in the Second World War, the Ordinance of 19 October 1945 allowed any child born on French soil to acquire French nationality by simple declaration during his minority.[373] In addition to the above examples favouring the application of a territorial criterion for the acquisition of French nationality, the 1804 Civil Code lays down the

373. Ordinance No 45-2441 of 19 Oct. 1945 on the French Nationality Code.

principle of the transmission of nationality by descent. Under Article 18 of the Code, a 'legitimate or illegitimate child, whose one or both parents are French, is himself/herself French'.

405. Today, Article 34 of the Constitution gives the legislature the power to lay down 'the rules with respect to: (...) – Nationality (...)'. The essence of these rules is now found in Articles 17 et seq. of the Civil Code, under Title I A entitled 'On French Nationality'.

§2. Obtaining French Nationality

406. Following the general provisions, Title I A of the Civil Code on nationality contains a Chapter 2 on 'French Nationality of Origin' and a Chapter 3 on 'The Acquisition of French Nationality'. The attribution of nationality at birth is supplemented by various acquisition modes during life.

I. The Attribution of French Nationality

407. French nationality is granted to a child regardless of the place of his/her birth if at least one of his/her parents has French nationality. This is the first rule of attribution of French nationality, established under Article 18 of the Civil Code which reflects the application of the principle of *jus sanguinis* (i.e., the attribution of French nationality by French descent). However, the right of blood not only concerns a child born to a French parent. Under Article 19-3 of the Civil Code, 'a child born in France to parents, at least one of whom is also born there, is [also] French'. This allows nationality to be granted to the children of immigrants, or rather to the grandchildren of immigrants, whose parents are already born on French soil without necessarily having acquired French nationality. This is a mode of attribution of nationality involving both the right of soil and the right of blood, or rather a method of attribution which rebalances the right of blood with the right of soil. This mode should be extended to children of parents born in the territory of the States which were formerly under French sovereignty (i.e., Comoros, Ivory Coast, Senegal). The Law of 22 July 1993 reforming nationality law[374] has, however, limited this possibility to children born before 31 December 1993, which therefore no longer currently concerns minor children. As regards children of Algerian parents to whom the birth limit of 31 December 1993 does not apply, the date of the independence of Algeria is decisive – the independence was proclaimed on 3 July 1962, with the possibility for locals to opt for French nationality until 1 January 1963. Three cases – which relevance is not as significant today though – must be distinguished in this regard. First, there is the case of children (now adults) born before the independence of Algeria whose nationality depends on the choice made in 1962 by their own parents to become, or not, French citizens. Second, there is the case of children

374. Law No 93-933 of 22 Jul. 1993 reforming the law of nationality.

of parents born in Algeria before independence and having chosen Algerian nationality: these children can benefit from the provisions of Article 19-3 of the Civil Code since, pre-independence, Algeria was a French department. Conversely, the children of parents born on Algerian territory after independence cannot benefit from Article 19-3 of the Civil Code since Algeria was no longer a French territory but had then become an independent State.

408. Mirroring the acquisition of nationality on the basis of parental filiation, the Civil Code offers the possibility of acquiring French nationality based on the absence of filiation. Articles 19-2 and 58 of the Civil Code provide for the particular case of a child which is newborn, found, and without filiation. In such a case, the child is presumed to be French under Article 19-2 which provides: 'The child whose birth has been presented in accordance with Article 58 of this Code is presumed to be French'; and Article 58 of the same states: 'Anyone who finds a newborn child is required to make a declaration to the State civil registrar of the place of discovery. If [the person who has found the child] does not agree to take care of the child, s/he needs to hand in the child, as well as clothes and other effects found with her, to the registrar. A detailed report (...) records the date, time, place and circumstances of the discovery, as well as describe the apparent age and sex of the child, all particularity that can contribute to the child's identification and the authority or person to whom the child is entrusted. This report is registered to date on the civil status register. Following this report, and separately, the registrar establishes a deed in lieu of a birth certificate'. This legal regime allows the child found to be granted a nationality in accordance with the requirements of the Convention on the Rights of the Child of 26 January 1990. It also prevents statelessness in accordance with the objectives of the European Convention on Nationality adopted by the Council of Europe on 6 November 1997. Pursuing the same objective, the Civil Code provides in Article 19 that '[a] child of unknown parents is French' and in Article 20 that '(...) 1. [a] child born in France of stateless parents is French; 2. [a] child born in France to foreign parents for whom foreign nationality laws do not in any way allow the passing of nationality of either of his/her parents (...) is French'.

409. In all these situations, and contrary to the logic of the *acquisition* of French nationality, a child who is given French citizenship is deemed French from birth. In other words, the child is regarded as a native as expressed under Article 20 of the Civil Code: '[a] child who is French under the provisions of this Chapter [i.e., Articles 18 to 20-5 of the Civil Code] is deemed to have been French from birth, even though the conditions required by law for granting French citizenship are established only later.'

II. The Acquisition of French Nationality

410. The acquisition of French nationality may result from different personal events. Subject to conditions, one may acquire French nationality, first, as a result of marriage, second, on reaching the age of majority, or, before that age, by a child whose parents are foreign, and third, by naturalization. Contrary to the attribution of French nationality by law, the acquisition of French nationality does imply rights and obligations only from the day it is lawfully acquired.

A. *Acquisition by Marriage*

411. French citizenship is not acquired automatically by virtue of marrying a French citizen. Under Article 21-1 of the Civil Code, '[m]arriage shall have no effect as of right on nationality'. The spouse of a French national acquires French nationality on making a statement, and upon meeting a number of conditions. In particular, since the Law of 16 June 2011 relating to matters of immigration, integration and nationality,[375] the spouse of a French man or French woman must prove an effective community life in France for at least four years from the date of marriage, or five years if the presence on the French territory has not been continuous. In this regard, Article 21-2 of the Civil Code specifies that the community of life must be 'both emotional and material' and should not have 'ceased between spouses since the marriage'. It is also necessary for the French spouse to have retained his/her French nationality as this was regarded by the 2011 legislature as an important requirement to curtail so-called marriage of convenience. In addition, Article 21-2 of the Civil Code states that 'the foreign spouse must also prove a sufficient knowledge, according to his/her circumstances, of the French language, which level and means of assessment are laid down by decree in the Council of State'.

412. The government may oppose the acquisition of French nationality within two years of its granting on grounds of 'unworthiness or lack of assimilation'. Article 21-4 of the Civil Code states that the lack of assimilation or integration may result, for example, from a criminal conviction for polygamy. In that regard, a circular of 24 August 2011 on the monitoring of the condition of assimilation in the procedures for acquiring French nationality clarifies that:

> a failure to assimilate includes revealing the elements of an intolerant or discriminatory attitude based, in particular, on sex, race, religion or nationality, such as denigration of certain communities or membership of radical movements advocating violence. Similarly, [a failure to assimilate includes] a radical practice of religion or a lifestyle which does not comply with customs and traditions as would, for example, be home confinement, or limiting social relationships with people of the opposite sex, and a fortiori a conduct contrary to public order (e.g., polygamy, genital mutilation practices).

B. *Acquisition by a Child Born to Foreign Parents*

413. Under Article 21-7 of the Civil Code, '[e]very child born in France to foreign parents acquires French nationality at his/her majority if, at that date, s/he

375. Law No 2011-672 of 16 Jun. 2011 on immigration, integration and nationality.

resides in France and has been an ordinarily resident in France for a continuous or discontinuous period of at least five years, since the age of eleven'. Prior to the amendment of Article 21-7 by the Law of 16 March 1998,[376] the minor child had to demonstrate his/her desire to become French. Restoring a form of automatic acquisition of French nationality on reaching eighteen years of age, the 1998 legislature instructed the authorities to widely circulate and ensure the respect of this legal regime: 'Local courts, local authorities, organizations and public services, including educational institutions, are obliged to inform the public, especially the persons to whom the first paragraph of [Article 21-7] applies, of the provisions in force concerning nationality'. In that context, the child has the right to declare his/her willingness to acquire French nationality at the age of sixteen, without the need for parental consent. The acquisition of French nationality may be brought forward at the age of thirteen on parental request when the child has been a resident in France from the age of eight. In addition, Article 21-12 of the Civil Code provides for the possibility of making a declaration of nationality in relation to a child who was adopted (under the simple adoption procedure) by a French national. The provision thereof extends this possibility to a child 'raised in France and reared by a French national or who has been, for at least three years, in the care of social services; [as well as to] a child raised in France and reared in conditions allowing her to receive, for at least five years, a French education be it by a public institution, or a private institution as defined under a decree in the Council of State'.

414. Although the acquisition of French nationality under these conditions does not require any particular formality, proving it can be problematic. When establishing a certificate of nationality, the minor, or the just-over-eighteen years old adult, must prove that s/he fulfils the requirements of Articles 21-7 et seq. of the Civil Code. In particular, s/he must provide evidence of his/her birth in France (e.g., via civil status documents) as well as proof of residence in France for the required duration (school certificates would, for example, constitute prima facie written evidence).

C. *Naturalization*

415. Unlike other modes of acquisition of the French nationality, naturalization is always a discretionary act decided by public authorities as an expression of a sovereign prerogative. In other words, a person applying for naturalization is never entitled to a right to be naturalized, even though s/he fulfils the conditions required by the Civil Code. In addition to the general requirement that the person applying for naturalization should have reached the age of majority – with the exception of the case, under Articles 21–22 of the Civil Code, of the minor child in relation to whom at least one parent has been naturalized – several other conditions must be met as regards the admissibility of an application for naturalization.

376. Law No 98-170 of 16 Mar. 1998 on nationality.

416. First, a common condition of residence in France is required. Under Article 21-16 of the Civil Code, the foreign national must reside in France at the time of his/her application for naturalization, and must, under Article 21-17, have resided therein for, at least, the five previous years. This period is referred to as the 'internship' period. A number of derogations exist in that respect whereby this period is reduced to two years. Under Article 21-18 of the Civil Code, this is the case when a foreign national has successfully completed two years of graduate studies at a university or at another domestic higher educational institution; or has rendered 'by his/her abilities and talent important services to France'; or 'has followed an exemplary integration path, assessed in light of activities or actions undertaken in the civic, scientific, economic, cultural or sports areas'. Exemptions to the internship period are provided for under Article 21-19 of the Civil Code such as, for example, when a foreign national has accomplished his/her military service in a unit of the French army or who has signed up voluntarily, in time of war, to the French or allied armies.

417. Second, the applicant to naturalization must meet the condition as regards assimilation. This is the same condition encountered above regarding the spouse of a French national who applies to acquire French nationality. Under Article 21-24 of the Civil Code, 'one may not be naturalized unless s/he proves his/her assimilation into the French community, which includes demonstrating, according to his/her own circumstances, sufficient knowledge of the French language, history, culture and society, the level and means of assessment of which shall be fixed by a decree in the Council of State, and of the rights and duties conferred by French nationality, as well as adherence to the principles and core values of the Republic'. Illustrating the idea expressed by academic Hennette-Vauchez that 'establishing the criteria relating to the acquisition of nationality means defining a national identity and unveiling a political project',[377] the legislature sought to impose on naturalized persons the signing of 'a charter of rights and duties of the French citizen'. Under the provisions of Article 21-24 of the Civil Code, 'the charter, approved by decree in the Council of State, recalls the main principles, values and symbols of the French Republic'. The first paragraph of the charter thus refers to the 1789 Declaration, as well as to the 'democratic principles inherited' from French history.

418. Third, the foreign national applying for citizenship must satisfy a condition of personal and stable source of income which should be, in whole or mainly, of French origin. A circular of 16 October 2012 tempers this requirement by stating that 'if professional integration is an essential condition of assimilation, it cannot, in a context of economic and social crisis affecting a large number of citizens, systematically prevent the naturalization of persons who suffer from difficult employment situations, a period of non-employment or a lack of prior training'.

419. Fourth and finally, the naturalization of a foreigner must meet the obligation of 'good character' which means, under Articles 21–23 of the Civil Code, an

377. Stéphanie Hennette-Vauchez and Diane Roman, *Droits de l'homme et des libertés fondamentales* (Hypercours Dalloz 2013) 26.

obligation of 'loyalty towards the French institutions'. The fulfilment of this requirement is assessed through a police investigation. The applicant must not have been the subject of a criminal conviction, or must not have remained illegally on the French territory. Under Articles 21–27 of the Civil Code, '[n]o one can acquire French nationality or be reinstated in that nationality if s/he has been the subject either of a conviction of crimes or offences constituting a violation of the fundamental interests of the Nation or an act of terrorism, or, in relation to whatever offence at issue, s/he has been sentenced to a non-suspended six-month, or longer, jail term. The same applies to the applicant who is the subject of either an unsuspended and unrevoked deportation order, or of a partially executed ban from the French territory. The same applies to the applicant who has been illegally residing in France under the law and conventions relating to the stay of foreigners in France'.

§3. The Effects Attached to French Nationality

420. A certain number of effects are attached to the French nationality. These concern the status and personal effects of the French citizen. The acquisition of French nationality also confers political rights and entails civic duties from the part of the French national.

I. The Principle of Equality

421. In accordance with the constitutional principle of equality and the principle of the indivisibility of the Republic,[378] no distinction can be made between French nationals on the basis of how they have acquired their nationality – though there is a probationary period during which the public authority may, subject to conditions, revoke its decision to grant nationality to a foreign national. Under the provisions of Article 22 of the Civil Code, the 'person who acquires French nationality enjoys all the rights, and is bound by all the obligations, attached to being of French nationality, from the date of the acquisition thereof'. The principle of acquisition of French legal heritage has an effect on the civil status of the newly French national as well as on his/her family.

II. Personal Effects

422. As far as his/her civil status is concerned, the foreigner who acquires French nationality may choose to change his/her name, as well as those of his/her children, to make the name French-sounding. S/he can also retain his/her nationality of origin as French law does not object, in principle, to the existence of dual nationality. With regard to the effect of the acquisition of French nationality on the

378. *See* the first two sentences of Art. 1 of the Constitution: 'France is an indivisible, secular, democratic and social Republic. [The Republic] shall ensure equality of all citizens under the law without discrimination based on origin, race or religion.'

family of the foreign national, the so-called collective effect means that when a parent becomes French, his/her children have the right to also become so. In that regard, Article 22-1 of the Civil Code provides as follows:

> A minor child, one parent of whom acquires French nationality, is French by right if s/he has the same habitual residence of that parent or resides alternately with that parent in the event of separation or divorce.

III. Political Rights and Civic Duties

423. The acquisition of French nationality also confers political rights and entails civic duties. As far as political rights are concerned, the quality of French citizenship is indivisible from that of the voter (and from that of the person eligible to run for election). The Constitutional Council ruled that 'the quality of citizenship opens the right to vote and stand for election under similar conditions to all those who are not excluded by reason of age, disability or nationality, or for some reason designed to preserve the freedom of the voter or the independence of the person elected; these constitutional principles preclude any division into categories of voters or people eligible to stand for election'.[379] This principle refers to the universal nature of the electoral suffrage in France. As such, the French citizen, who also has European citizenship, participates in ballots for the European elections. In addition, the quality of French citizenship gives entitlement, in political matters, to the exercise of public freedoms such as freedom of speech, freedom of assembly, freedom of association, as well as trade union freedoms, and the right to strike. Finally, it should be noted that French nationality gives entitlement to the benefit of diplomatic protection of France. As far as civic obligations are concerned, these were for a long time of military nature. In particular, the French citizen had the obligation to perform military service. Compulsory military service was abolished in 1995 – leaving an exclusively professional army – and replaced, for the rest of the citizens, by an annual 'Defence and Citizenship Day'. However, the idea of restoring a civic service in a more or less obligatory form for young French citizens reaching the age of majority has been an object of continuous debate ever since.

§4. Loss of French Nationality

424. The loss of French nationality may result from a voluntary decision or from a decision imposed by the public authority.

379. CC Decision No 82-146 DC of 18 Nov. 1982, *Loi modifiant le code électoral et le code des communes et relative à l'élection des conseillers municipaux et aux conditions d'inscription des Français établis hors de France sur les listes électorales ('Quotas par sexe')*, *Rec.* 22, pt 7*.

I. The Voluntary Loss of French Nationality

425. The voluntary loss of French nationality is a possibility offered to the child to whom it was granted under Articles 18 or 19-2 of the Civil Code, or to the child who has acquired it on the basis of Article 22-1 thereof. It is also an option open to a French national who acquires the nationality of his/her foreign spouse.

A. *Renunciation of French Citizenship*

1. Renunciation by a Child Whose One Parent only is French

426. The attribution by right of French nationality does not bar its recipient from renouncing it. The Civil Code refers in that case to the notion of 'renunciation' (*répudiation*), which characterizes the willingness to waive a right. Nevertheless, the objective of the fight against statelessness requires that the waiving of such right is conditioned on the acquisition by the child of the nationality of the foreign parent. Under Article 18-1 of the Civil Code, '[i]f only one of the parents [of the child referred to in Article 18 of the Civil Code] is French, the child who was not born in France has the option to renounce his/her French citizenship within the six months preceding his/her majority and within twelve months following it'. In the same vein, as regards the granting of French nationality to a child whose foreign parent was himself/herself born in France, Article 19-4 of the Civil Code provides that 'if only one of his/her parents was born in France, then the French child, pursuant to Article 19-3, has the right to renounce his/her citizenship within the six months before reaching his/her majority and the twelve months following it'.

2. Renunciation by the Spouse of a Foreign National

427. Article 23-5 of the Civil Code entitles a French citizen who marries a foreign national the opportunity to renounce his/her nationality of origin: 'In case of marriage to a foreigner, the French spouse may renounce his/her French nationality (...) on condition that s/he has acquired the foreign nationality of his/her spouse and that the habitual residence of the household has been established abroad.' In addition to the conditions of residence abroad and the acquisition of the nationality of the foreign spouse, the provision thereof provides that 'French nationals under thirty-five years old of age may exercise their right of renunciation only insofar as they comply with the obligations set out in Book II of the National Service Code [which, as indicated above, are now only formal].'

B. *Loss of French Nationality by Government Authorization*

428. Article 23-4 of the Civil Code provides that any French national who has acquired another nationality may request the French Government the authorization to renounce his/her French citizenship – an act which is often referred to as a request to be 'freed from all ties of allegiance to France'.[380] Under Article 54 of the Decree of 30 December 1993, '[t]he application [for the authorization to renounce French citizenship], the civil status documents and the documents justifying that the applicant holds foreign citizenship are filed with the authority designated in the preceding article and addressed to him/her, together with a report and a reasoned opinion to the minister responsible for naturalization through, where appropriate, the Minister for Foreign Affairs or the Minister for Overseas Departments and Territories'.[381] The authorization thereof is granted at the discretion of the government.

II. The Imposed Loss of French Nationality

429. Besides the voluntary loss of French nationality, there are cases where such loss is imposed by a decision of the public authority. These may consist of a decision by the government aimed at punishing a particular behaviour, or taking into account the disappearance of one of the conditions necessary to naturalization, or may consist of a judgment declaring the lack of de facto possession of French citizenship. In any event, the loss of French nationality must not have the effect of rendering a person stateless.

A. *Loss of French Nationality Imposed by a Decision of the Government*

1. Loss of Nationality Based on Articles 23-7 and 23-8 of the Civil Code

430. This concerns the situation of French natives (i.e., those who have acquired French nationality at birth). Under Article 23-7 of the Civil Code, '[a] French national who behaves de facto like the national of a foreign country may, if s/he has the nationality of that country, be declared, by a decree decided in the Council of State, to have lost French citizenship'. This provision aims at sanctioning disloyal attitudes towards France displayed by binationals. Article 23-8 of the Civil Code adds to the reasons which might justify the loss of French nationality by a government decree: 'French citizenship is lost by a French national who, occupying a position in a foreign army or in a foreign public service or in an international organization of which France is not a part or more generally to which France is not providing assistance, has not resigned his/her employment or has continued assistance despite a government order to do so. The national concerned will be, by decree in the Council of State, declared to have lost his/her French nationality if, within the period set by the order, which period may not be less than fifteen days and no more than two months, s/he has not terminated his/her activity'. This touches upon cases susceptible to being qualified as criminal offences.

380. *See*, e.g., CE, Sect., 26 Apr. 2006, *M. A.*, *Rec. Lebon* 255.
381. Decree No 93-1362 of 30 Dec. 1993 relating to declarations of nationality, decisions of naturalization, reinstatement, loss, revocation and withdrawal of French nationality.

2. Deprivation of Nationality

431. The deprivation of nationality applies only to non-natives (i.e., those nationals who have acquired French nationality other than by birth). It punishes acts of disloyalty towards France, or nationals who would have been convicted of the offence of 'national unworthiness' (*indignité nationale*). Article 25 of the Civil Code provides the conditions upon which the deprivation of nationality may be pronounced:

> The individual who has acquired French nationality may, by decree in the Council of State, be deprived of his/her French nationality, unless this deprivation renders him/her stateless:
>
> 1. If s/he has been convicted of a criminal act or offence constituting a violation of fundamental interests of the Nation or of a crime or offence constituting an act of terrorism;
> 2. If s/he has been convicted of a criminal act or offence punishable under Chapter II of Title III of Book IV of the Criminal Code;
> 3. If s/he has been convicted of evading his/her obligations under the National Service Code;
> 4. If s/he has been carrying out acts deemed incompatible with French citizenship and detrimental to the interests of France to the benefit of a foreign State.

432. On a referral for a priority preliminary ruling on the issue of constitutionality, the Constitutional Council has ruled on the conformity of the provision thereof with the constitutional principle of equality of citizens before the law and, recalling its earlier case law, it held that 'nationals who have acquired French nationality and those to whom French nationality was attributed at birth are in the same situation';[382] in an earlier ruling, the Constitutional Council ruled that given the objective of further strengthening the fight against terrorism,[383] the legislature was able to make provision, for a limited time, for the administrative authority to deprive those who have acquired it of their French nationality, 'without the resulting difference in treatment violating [the principle of equality]'.[384] This deprivation of nationality applies only if the alleged acts were committed prior to the naturalization of the individual concerned, or within ten years after his/her naturalization. Under Article 25-1 of the Civil Code, a limitation period of ten years, or fifteen years for

382. CC Decision No 96-377 DC of 16 Jul. 1996, *Loi tendant à renforcer la répression du terrorisme et des atteintes aux personnes dépositaires de l'autorité publique ou chargées d'une mission de service public et comportant des dispositions relatives à la police judiciaire*, *Rec.* 66, pt 23*. *See also* CC Decision No 2014-439 QPC of 23 Jan. 2015, *M. Ahmed S. [Déchéance de nationalité]*, *Rec.* 26*.

383. This was due to the terrorist attacks which occurred in the mid-1990s in Paris.

384. CC Decision No 96-377 DC of 16 Jul. 1996, *Loi tendant à renforcer la répression du terrorisme et des atteintes aux personnes dépositaires de l'autorité publique ou chargées d'une mission de service public et comportant des dispositions relatives à la police judiciaire*, *Rec.* 66, pt 23*.

the acts mentioned under the first paragraph of Article 25 of the Civil Code, shall apply from the commission of the acts thereof.

3. Revocation of a Naturalization Certificate

433. Under Article 27-2 of the Civil Code, the revocation of a decision of naturalization can be pronounced, within two years of its granting, if the administrative authorities find out that the individual concerned does not actually meet the conditions required by law, or if that individual has obtained his/her naturalization by fraud. This might be the case, for example, where a lack of integration would have been concealed from the authorities, or if false documents would have been produced.

B. Other Cases of Loss of French Nationality

434. The loss of French nationality may be pronounced by a judgment which states that an individual holding French nationality presents de facto none of its practical implications. This is referred to as the rare occurrence of a lack of 'possession of status' or *possession d'état* (i.e., the enjoyment of a particular status based on factual elements) of French citizenship. Under Article 23-6 of the Civil Code, '[t]he loss of French nationality may be ascertained by a judicial decision where the individual concerned, who holds French nationality of origin by birth, does not de facto enjoy the status of a French national and has never had his/her habitual residence in France, if his/her ascendants from whom s/he obtained French nationality, do not themselves enjoy the status of French citizens, nor have they had a residence in France over the previous fifty years. The judgment determines the date of the loss of French nationality thereof. The judgment may decide that that nationality was lost by his/her ascendants and that the individual concerned could, in fact, never have been regarded as being a French national'. Finally, under Article 53 of the Constitution, the loss of French nationality may result from the transfer of, or the accession to independence of, a part of the French territory.

435. In light of these multiple scenarios as regards the loss of French nationality, the Civil Code provides for the possibility of the reintegration, by decree, of French nationality under Articles 24 et seq.

Chapter 2. Fundamental Rights and Liberties

436. Fundamental rights and liberties are traditionally divided between civil and political rights, on the one hand, and economic, social and cultural rights, on the other. The recognition and implementation of these different rights are done through a common framework in French law.

§1. General

437. Different rules and mechanisms govern the recognition, implementation and protection of fundamental rights and liberties in French law.

I. Sources of Fundamental Rights and Liberties

438. The sources of fundamental rights and liberties in French law results from the domestic application of international and European norms as well as from national norms.

A. *International and European Sources*

439. France has acceded to numerous international conventions for the protection of human rights. These international conventions have a supra-legislative value (Article 55 Constitution). At international level, France has ratified different UN treaties as well as general treaties such as the International Covenant on Civil and Political Rights and the International Covenant on Economic, Social and Cultural Rights. France is also bound by a number of specific instruments such as, for instance, the Convention on the Rights of the Child, or the Convention on the Rights of Persons with Disabilities.

440. The protection of human rights at European level has made a great impact on French law, notably due to advanced systems of judicial enforcement, with the ECHR at the forefront. France ratified the ECHR in 1974 while accepting individual applications before the ECtHR in 1981, a mechanism that has since been made mandatory. The protection of human rights has also gained an unprecedented importance in the EU. Having initially an economic scope, EU law was not primarily dedicated to their protection, even though the establishment of the internal market involved protection against discrimination, on the basis of nationality in particular. The protection of human rights has been developed by the CJEU (formerly the ECJ) as general principles of EU law, the inspiration of which is to be found in the constitutional traditions common to the Member States as well as in the international instruments to which they partake, and in particular the ECHR.[385]

385. ECJ, 4/73 *Nold KG v. Commission* (14 May 1974), [1974] ECR 491.

Since the 1992 Treaty of Maastricht, the protection of human rights found a basis in the treaties which led to the drafting of the EU Charter of Fundamental Rights in 2000. The 2007 Treaty of Lisbon made the Charter legally binding and of the same legal value as EU primary law.[386] The TFEU also provides for the membership of the EU itself to the ECHR.[387]

B. Domestic Sources

441. At domestic level, fundamental rights have primarily their source in the Constitution and in the different norms that are constitutive of the block of constitutionality (*See* Part I Sources of Constitutional Law). This includes, first, the provisions of the Constitution. For instance, Article 3 recognizes the right of suffrage and Article 66 makes of the judicial authority the 'guardian of individual freedom'. Nonetheless, the protection of fundamental rights is primarily guaranteed by instruments referred to in the Preamble to the Constitution, since the Constitution itself does not contain a catalogue of rights. The Preamble first refers to the 1789 Declaration. It also refers to the Preamble to the 1946 Constitution from which two categories of principles are derived, namely the Principles of Laws Particularly Necessary to our Time and the Fundamental Principles recognized by the Laws of the Republic. As regards the first category, the Constitutional Council gave judicial recognition notably to the principle of equality between men and women (paragraph 3 of the Preamble to the 1946 Constitution),[388] the right of asylum (paragraph 4 idem),[389] or the right to strike (paragraph 7 idem).[390] In relation to the second category, the Constitutional Council included, for instance, the freedom of association,[391] the freedom of conscience,[392] or the independence of university teacher-researcher[393] among Fundamental Principles recognized by the Laws of the Republic. The Charter for the Environment of 2004, which is also referred to in the Preamble to the Constitution, also contains a number of fundamental rights. Its Article 1 recognizes 'the right to live in a balanced environment that respects health' while its Article 7 provides for a right to information on environmental matters.

386. Article 6 TEU.
387. Protocol No 8 TFEU relating to Art. 6(2) TEU on the accession of the Union to the European Convention on the Protection of Human Rights and Fundamental Freedoms.
388. CC Decision No 81-133 DC of 30 Dec. 1981, *Loi de finances pour 1982*, *Rec.* 41.
389. CC Decision No 79-109 DC of 9 Jan. 1980, *Loi relative à la prévention de l'immigration clandestine et portant modification de l'ordonnance n° 45-2658 du 2 novembre 1945 relative aux conditions d'entrée et de séjour en France des étrangers et portant création de l'office national d'immigration*, *Rec.* 29.
390. CC Decision No 79-105 DC of 25 Jul. 1979, *Loi modifiant les dispositions de la loi n° 74-696 du 7 août 1974 relatives à la continuité du service public de la radio et de la télévision en cas de cessation concertée du travail*, *Rec.* 33.
391. CC Decision No 71-44 DC of 16 Jul. 1971, *Loi complétant les disposition des articles 5 et 7 de la loi du 1er juillet 1901 relative au contrat d'association*, *Rec.* 25*.
392. CC Decision No 77-87 DC of 23 Nov. 1977, *Loi complémentaire à la loi n° 59-1557 du 31 décembre 1959 modifiée par la loi n° 71-400 du 1er juin 1971 et relative à la liberté de l'enseignement*, *Rec.* 42.
393. CC Decision No 83-165 DC of 20 Jan. 1984, *Loi relative à l'enseignement supérieur*, *Rec.* 30; and CC Decision No 2010-20/21 QPC of 6 Aug. 2010, *M. Jean C. et autres [Loi Université]*, *Rec.* 203.

442. In addition, fundamental rights have also been developed by the case law of the Constitutional Council which, in the absence of textual basis, has referred to constitutional principles, constitutional requirements, or objectives of constitutional value as, for example, the safeguard of public order, the respect for the freedom of others, and the preservation of pluralism in sociocultural expressions[394] The case law of the Council of State has also been associated with the judicial development of fundamental rights. Many of the general principles of law developed by the administrative courts are related to the protection of human rights. This is the case, for example, in connection with the principle of equality before public services[395] or equality before the courts.[396]

II. Implementation of Fundamental Rights and Liberties

443. A number of authorities are in charge of ensuring the implementation of fundamental rights and liberties in French law through mainly two different regimes. In addition, special circumstances can justify restrictions being put on protected fundamental rights.

A. *Authorities in Charge of the Implementation of Fundamental Rights and Liberties*

444. In light of the division of normative competences established in French law, both legislative and administrative authorities participate in the implementation of fundamental rights and liberties.

1. Legislative Implementation

445. The Constitution entrusts the legislative power with a primary role as regards the implementation of fundamental rights and liberties. Several articles of the 1789 Declaration refer to laws in order to implement the rights recognized therein. The same principle is also expressed in the Preamble to the 1946 Constitution in relation to the Principles of Laws Particularly Necessary to our Time, notably in its paragraphs 3 and 7. This general capacity of the legislative power in the field of fundamental rights finds its expression in Article 34 of the Constitution which defines the legislative areas of competence by affirming that '[t]he Law shall lay down the rules with respect to: (…) – Civil rights and fundamental guarantees granted to citizens for the exercise of their public freedoms'. Others provisions of the Constitution apply this general principle of legislative competence to specific questions as, for example, the right to vote under Article 3, or the prohibition of arbitrary detention entrusted to the judicial authority as the guardian of individual

394. CC Decision No 82-141 DC of 27 Jul. 1982, *Loi sur la communication audiovisuelle*, *Rec.* 48.
395. CE, Sect., 9 Mar. 1951, *Société des concerts du Conservatoire*, *Rec. Lebon* 151.
396. CE, Ass., 12 Oct. 1979, *Rassemblements des nouveaux avocats de France*, *Rec. Lebon* 371.

freedom under Article 66. The recognition of fundamental rights at constitutional level is not sufficient to ensure their effectiveness. Legislation is necessary to determine the modalities of their exercise and especially their limitations as specified under Article 4 of the 1789 Declaration.[397] These limitations are justified by the necessary conciliation between the various fundamental rights, as well as the balance to be found between the exercise of these rights and the safeguard of public order. While the legislative power enjoys a margin of appreciation, its competence is not unfettered. Courts ensure that laws implement rather than infringe fundamental rights. The review exercised by the Constitutional Council ensures the respect of laws for constitutionally protected rights. The conformity of legislation with fundamental rights defined at international level is guaranteed by the review of conventionality exercised by domestic courts or through the control of supranational judicial bodies.

2. Administrative Implementation

446. The government has competence as regards the implementation of fundamental rights through the exercise of its regulatory power to implement laws. The government is also competent when it exercises the autonomous regulatory power provided for by Article 37 of the Constitution, even though in the field of fundamental rights this competence is merely residual. More generally, administrative authorities are concerned with the implementation of fundamental rights through the exercise of their powers of administrative police. These powers have a preventive function aimed at protecting public order, hereby affecting fundamental rights and their exercise. Traditionally, public order encompasses public security, tranquillity and salubrity. [398] It has been extended by courts to also cover public morality and human dignity.[399] At national level, the powers of administrative police are exercised by the Prime Minister. Prefects are competent in departments, in association with the presidents of the Departmental Councils, and mayors at municipal level. Besides these powers of general administrative police, special administrative police powers are established by law and concern specific activities, and thus specific fundamental rights. For instance, freedom of expression and communication is concerned by the police of cinema that issues broadcast licences and which is exercised by the Minister for Culture. The acts of the administrative police are subject to the review of the administrative courts where freedom is the rule and restrictions the exception. The primary purpose of such acts must be solely to maintain public order. Furthermore, these acts must be appropriate, necessary and proportionate,[400] in light of specific local circumstances.[401]

397. 'Freedom consists in being able to do all that does not harm others: thus, the exercise of the natural rights of every man has no bounds other than those that to the other members of society the enjoyment of these same rights. These bounds may be determined only by the Law.'

398. Article L. 2212-2 General Code of Local Authorities.

399. CE, Ass., 27 Oct. 1995, *Commune de Morsang-sur-Orge*, *Rec. Lebon* 372.

400. CE, 19 May 1933, *Benjamin*, *Rec. Lebon* 541.

401. CE., Sect., 18 Dec. 1959, *Société 'Les Films Lutétia'*, *Rec. Lebon* 693.

B. Regimes of Implementation of Fundamental Rights and Liberties

447. Two regimes are distinguished as regards the implementation of fundamental rights, namely the repressive regime and the preventive regime. The repressive regime, as the most liberal one, is based on the free exercise of fundamental rights by the individual in accordance with Articles 4 and 5 of the 1789 Declaration.[402] Sanctions will intervene once infringements, exceeding the limits of the exercise of these rights set by law, have been determined. The preventive regime is more coercive since it subjects the exercise of fundamental rights to the approval by public authorities. This approval can take two different forms. First, it may consist of a prior *authorization* as, for instance, the broadcast licence for the screening of a movie or the delivery of a driving licence as the condition for the exercise of the freedom to come and go with a motor vehicle. Due to the seriousness of its impact on fundamental rights, prior authorization can only be established by law. Second, the prevention regime can take the form of a prior *declaration*. The individual has to inform the administration of the exercise of a fundamental right but public authorities cannot oppose this exercise. For instance, the constitution of an association requires a declaration at the prefecture. This declaration allows the administrative authorities to take the necessary measures, if necessary, to safeguard public order.

C. Limitations to Fundamental Rights and Liberties

448. Limitations to fundamental rights and liberties may be necessary in order to reconcile different rights as well as to address considerations pertaining to the protection of public order. This pertains, as matter of principle, to the legislature as expressed under Article 4 of the 1789 Declaration.[403] The powers of administrative police also play an important role in the appreciation of the compatibility of the exercise of fundamental rights with the protection of public order. In addition to these restrictions which depend on the very nature of fundamental rights, certain regimes are especially designed to allow derogations to liberties in case of exceptional circumstances and periods of crisis.

449. The first derogation concerns the extraordinary powers granted under Article 16 of the Constitution to the President of the Republic (*See also* Part II Form of Government and Part V Specific Problems). Under such circumstances, the President of the Republic may take any acts designed 'to ensure that the constitutional public powers are promptly in a position to carry out their mission'. Even though

402. Article 4: 'Freedom consists in being able to do all that does not harm others: thus, the exercise of the natural rights of every man has no bounds other than those that to the other members of society the enjoyment of these same rights. These bounds may be determined only by the Law.'; Article 5: 'The Law has the right to defend only actions harmful to society. All that is not defended by the Law cannot be prevented, and no one can be compelled to do what it does not order.'

403. *Ibid.*

Article 16 of the Constitution does not directly concern fundamental rights, it primarily affects them since acts taken on its basis often depart from the regular protection of fundamental rights and liberties. Article 16 has only been applied once, from April to September 1961, following the putsch of the generals in Algeria. It led notably to the creation of emergency courts, changes in criminal procedure, the authorization of administrative detention, and a stricter control of publications. Article 16 constitutionalized earlier case law. During the First World War, the Council of State had developed a theory of exceptional circumstances whereby certain decisions could be considered as valid, even though they would be sanctioned in normal circumstances.[404] This theory has not been abandoned and still exists in parallel to the regimes established by law or by the Constitution. It does not imply the suspension of judicial review. However, once recognized, the exceptional circumstances will affect the assessment of the necessity and proportionality of administrative acts.[405]

450. The second derogation concerns the state of siege, which finds its origin in legislative provisions.[406] It is now provided for by Article 36 of the Constitution. It applies in case of armed conflicts. Article L. 2121-1 of the Code of Defence specifies that it can only be implemented 'in case of imminent danger resulting from a foreign war or an armed insurrection'. Police powers and the powers vested in the civil authority for the maintenance of order are transferred to military authorities and extended, which result in increased restrictions on fundamental rights. For instance, publications and public meetings that endanger public order can be prohibited.[407]

451. The third derogation to fundamental rights is the state of emergency, which is governed by law.[408] By virtue of its Article 1, the state of emergency can be declared 'on the whole metropolitan territory, or part of it, in overseas departments, in overseas territories governed by Article 74 of the Constitution and in New Caledonia, either in case of imminent danger resulting from serious breaches of public order, or in case of events having, by their nature and their gravity, the character of a public calamity'. Under the regime of the state of emergency, police powers remain exercised by civil authorities but they are extended. Notably, this regime allows restrictions on fundamental rights and liberties of individuals suspected of being a threat to public security. For example, the state of emergency allows the prefect or the Minister for Home Affairs to limit or prohibit traffic in certain places, to prohibit certain public meetings or temporarily close certain public places, to authorize administrative searches, or to pronounce house arrests. Following the attacks

---

404. CE, 28 Jun. 1918, *Heyriès*, *Rec. Lebon* 651.
405. CE, 28 Feb. 1919, *Dames Dol et Laurent*, *Rec. Lebon* 651.
406. *See* Law of 9 Aug. 1849 on the state of siege and Law of 3 Apr. 1878 on the state of siege. *See* below Part V Specific Issues, Chapter 3. Emergency Powers, §2. The State of Siege.
407. Notwithstanding the state of siege, all the rights guaranteed by the Constitution continue to be exercised when their enjoyment is not suspended under the provisions relating to the state of siege under the Code of Defence. *See* Arts L. 2121-1 to L. 2121-8 Code of Defence.
408. Law No 55-385 of 3 Apr. 1955 on the state of emergency (as lastly amended in July 2017). *See* below Part V Specific Issues, Chapter 3. Emergency Powers, §3. The State of Emergency.

perpetrated in Paris and Saint-Denis in November 2015, the state of emergency was declared at a Council of Ministers meeting on the night of Friday 13 November to Saturday 14 November.[409] Prolonged six times by the French Parliament, the state of emergency ended on 1 November 2017, when the Law of 31 October 2017 came into effect, strengthening domestic security and the fight against terrorism.[410]

III. The Protection of Fundamental Rights and Liberties

452. The protection of human rights may require going beyond what is legally enforceable. Article 2 of the 1789 Declaration affirms that '[t]he aim of every political association is the preservation of the natural and imprescriptible rights of Man' and recognizes the right to resistance to oppression to that purpose. However, fundamental rights are primarily enforced by legal channels, both at domestic and international level.

A. *The Protection of Fundamental Rights and Liberties at Domestic Level*

453. At domestic level, nonjudicial and judicial institutions are entrusted with the protection of fundamental rights and liberties.

1. Nonjudicial Protection of Fundamental Rights

454. The protection of fundamental rights by nonjudicial institutions is primarily entrusted to independent administrative authorities. For instance, the National Commission for Data Protection and Liberties CNIL (*Commission Nationale de l'Informatique et des Libertés* or CNIL) controls the protection of personal data in relation to new technologies, and the HADOPI (*Haute Autorité pour la Diffusion des Œuvres sur Internet*) ensures the distribution and protection of creative works on the Internet. However, the principal independent administrative authority in relation to fundamental rights is the Office of the Defender of Rights established in 2008 as the merging of different pre-existing independent administrative authorities.[411] The Defender of Rights, as an individual, is appointed by the President of the

---

409. Before November 2015, the state of emergency was declared five times: three times in relation to the Algerian troubles – in 1955 in the departments which formed the French Algeria, in 1958 and 1961 in the metropolitan territory; one time in 1984 in relation to overseas troubles in New Caledonia; and one time in 2005 to put an end to riots in a number of French suburbs which concerned twenty-five departments, including the entire Ile-de-France (suburban areas outside Paris).

410. Law No 2017-1510 of 30 Oct. 2017 strengthening domestic security and the fight against terrorism. Some of the several laws which prolonged the state of emergency from November 2015 till November 2017 also amended some aspects of the regime. *See* Laws of 20 Nov. 2015, of 21 Jul. 2016, and of 19 Dec. 2016.

411. It is now governed by Art. 71-1 of the Constitution which forms the single provision of Title XI Bis on The Defender of Rights. The Defender of Rights is regulated by Organic Law No 2011-333 of 29 Mar. 2011 on The Defender of Rights and Law No 2011-334 of 29 Mar. 2011 on The Defender of Rights.

Republic according to the procedure governed by Article 13-5 of the Constitution. His/her independence is guaranteed by a number of measures. His/her mandate of six years is irrevocable and non-renewable. S/he benefits from criminal immunity and cannot receive instructions. S/he is assisted by deputies who are nominated on his/her proposal by the Prime Minister. The primary mission of the Office of the Defender of Rights is to 'ensure the respect of rights and freedoms by the State administrations, local authorities, and public institutions, as well as anybody entrusted with a public service mission or upon which competences are conferred by an organic law'. (Article 71-1 Constitution). More particularly, these missions reflect those of the previous independent administrative authorities it regroups. They concern the protection of fundamental rights in relation with the administration, the protection of the rights of children, the fight against discrimination and the promotion of equality, the guarantee of the respect of deontology by officials engaged in security activities. Any individual, who claims a breach of his/her fundamental rights in the field of competence of the Defender of Rights, may refer a case to the Defender of Rights who can also act on his/her own initiative. The Defender of Rights benefits from wide powers to fulfil his/her missions. S/he can resort to friendly settlements as well as intervene before courts to protect fundamental rights. The Defender of Rights also enjoys wide powers of investigation and can suggest settling a dispute on the basis of equity rather than legality. Lastly, s/he has recommendation powers and produces an annual report in relation to fundamental of rights where s/he can propose normative reforms.

2. Judicial Protection of Fundamental Rights

455. Courts are the primary forum for the protection of fundamental rights and liberties. Judicial protection of fundamental rights depends on the existence of a right to an effective remedy. In French law, the right to an effective judicial remedy is grounded in Article 16 of the 1789 Declaration which states that '[a]ny society in which the guarantee of rights is not ensured nor the separation of powers determined, has no constitution'.[412] As a result, judicial institutions must present certain features. In this regard, French law has been greatly influence by the case law relating to the right to a fair trial provided for under Article 6 paragraph one of the ECHR.

456. First, the judiciary must be independent. Under Article 64 of the Constitution, the President of the Republic, assisted by the Superior Council of the Judiciary, is entrusted with the independence of the ordinary judicial order. The Superior Council of the Judiciary is competent as regards the career and disciplinary sanctions of judges of the ordinary judicial order. One of the main guarantees of the independence of judges is the principle of immovability according to which judges cannot be assigned to a new position, even a promotion, without their consent. As

412. CC Decision No 96-373 DC of 9 Apr. 1996, *Loi organique portant statut d'autonomie de la Polynésie française*, *Rec.* 43*.

regards, the administrative judicial order, the independence of members of administrative tribunals and of administrative courts of appeal, and notably their immovability, is ensured by legislation.[413] A High Council of Administrative Tribunals and Administrative Courts of Appeal is entrusted with their career. The independence of members of the Council of State results primarily from tradition. Nonetheless, the independence of the administrative courts has been affirmed by the Constitutional Council as a Fundamental Principle recognized by the laws of the Republic.[414] Second, judges must show impartiality towards litigants. This impartiality must be subjective but also objective. Justice must be *seen* as impartial. The obligation for justice to appear impartial, notably on the basis of Article 6 paragraph one of the ECHR, prompted reforms of the administrative procedure. For instance, the role of the *Commissaire du Gouvernement* was amended and became the institution of the *Rapporteur Public* in 2009.[415] Lastly, judicial proceedings must be public, respect the adversarial principle and ensure the equality of arms between litigants. Litigants also have the right to a hearing within a reasonable time. In addition, some principles are specific to criminal proceedings. These consist primarily of the presumption of innocence, which is protected by Article 9 of the 1789 Declaration, Article 9-1 of the Civil Code and Article 6 of the ECHR, as well as of the respect for the rights of the defence which are notably protected by Article 6 of the ECHR and that the Constitutional Council has derived from Article 16 of the 1789 Declaration.[416]

457. The protection of fundamental rights is one the central missions of the judiciary which it exercises through a range of mechanisms. First, the protection of fundamental rights is ensured by the Constitutional Council through its review of constitutionality of legislation. Such review may intervene before the law comes into force (i.e., preventive review or a priori review) (Article 61 Constitution), or once the law has been come into force and been applied (i.e., curative review or a posteriori review) in the form of the priority preliminary ruling on the issue of constitutionality (Article 61-1 Constitution). This second form of review, which has been introduced only a decade ago, enables litigants, 'during proceedings pending before a court of law', to challenge a legislative provision that infringes upon the 'rights and freedoms guaranteed by [the] Constitution'. Second, courts of the ordinary judicial order are entrusted with a special role as regards the protection of fundamental rights and liberties. Article 66 of the Constitution defines the judicial authority as the 'guardian of individual freedom', hereby empowering ordinary courts to sanction administrative actions that infringe fundamental rights. This competence is subject to the competences of the administrative judicial order in this matter and thus only concerns common assaults (*voie de fait*) and, until recently, the

413. Articles L. 231-1 et seq. Code of Administrative Justice.
414. CC Decision No 80-119 DC of 22 Jul. 1980, *Validation d'actes administratifs*, *Rec.* 46.
415. Decree No 2009-14 of 7 Jan. 2009 on the public rapporteur before administrative courts and the proceedings thereof. Same for the Disputes Court: *See* Decree No 2015-233 of 27 Feb. 2015 concerning the Disputes Court and the preliminary rulings.
416. CC Decision No 2006-535 DC of 30 Mar. 2006, *Loi pour l'égalité des chances*, *Rec.* 50. For the definition of the rights of the defence as a Fundamental Principle recognized by the Laws of the Republic, *see* CC Decision No 95-360 DC of 2 Feb. 1995, *Loi relative à l'organisation des juridictions et à la procedure civile, pénale et administrative*, *Rec.* 195.

irregular right-of-way (*emprise*).[417] Also, by virtue of Article 66, the protection of fundamental freedoms by the judicial authority is an absolute principle in criminal matters. In criminal proceedings, the ordinary criminal courts are thus competent to interpret and assess the legality of administrative, regulatory or individual acts when the outcome of the criminal proceedings before them is dependent on such acts.[418] Third, fundamental rights and liberties can be enforced by administrative courts, primarily in relation to powers of administrative police, and in other various areas such as regards, for instance, psychiatric hospitalization or computerized data. Administrative courts are also provided with interlocutory or summary proceedings that litigants may use pending, where appropriate, a judgment on the merits.[419] One of these interlocutory proceedings concerns the protection of fundamental rights, namely the 'petition for safeguard of fundamental liberties' (*référé-liberté*). According to Article L. 521-2 of the Code of Administrative Justice, an administrative judge, acting as the interlocutory judge, can, within forty-eight hours, implement 'any measures necessary to safeguard a fundamental freedom that could have been affected seriously and in a manifestly illegal manner by a legal person governed by public law or by a legal person governed by private law entrusted with a mission of public service, in the exercise of one of its powers'.

B. The Protection of Fundamental Rights and Liberties at International Level

458. The protection of fundamental rights and liberties at international level can take the form of nonjudicial mechanisms such as referrals to the UN Human Rights Committee in relation to the International Covenant on Civil and Political Rights. This protection can also be ensured by judicial means such as international criminal courts. The judicial enforcement of fundamental rights is particularly developed at European level and is exercised by the ECtHR and the CJEU. The competence of the former jurisdiction as regards the ECHR is subsidiary and individual applications are only admissible after the exhaustion of domestic remedies. The protection of fundamental rights defined in international instruments is also enforced by domestic courts. According to Article 55 of the Constitution, international treaties have a supra-legislative value and the review of conventionality is exercised by

417. *See* the decisions of the Disputes Court which have redefined the notion of assault in this context with the result of giving a broader competence to administrative courts: TC, 17 Jun. 2013, *MB c. Société ERDF Annecy*, app. No 3911, and TC, 9 Dec. 2013, *M et Mme P. c. Commune de Saint-Palais-sur-Mer*, app. No 3931.
418. Article 111-5 Criminal Code.
419. Law No 2000-597 of 30 Jun. 2000 on interlocutory proceedings before administrative courts. *See also* below Chapter 4. Judicial Control of Administrative Action.

ordinary courts. This interpretation of the Constitution results from the case law of the Constitutional Council[420] and is applied by both ordinary courts[421] and administrative courts.[422]

§2. Civil and Political Rights

459. Civil and political rights are traditionally divided into two categories, namely physical freedoms and intellectual freedoms.

I. Physical Freedoms

A. *The Right to Life, Integrity and Human Dignity*

460. The principle of human dignity has emerged as the prevalent principle structuring the protection of fundamental rights and liberties. It is closely associated with the right to life and physical integrity, especially in a medical context.

1. Human Dignity

461. In contrast with provisions found in international instruments and other domestic constitutions, the principle of human dignity is not expressly mentioned in the Constitution. It is nonetheless expressed in Article 16 of the Civil Code. Its constitutional value has been recognized by the Constitutional Council as derived from the first paragraph of the Preamble to the 1946 Constitution.[423] The Council of State, for its part, considers that human dignity is a component of the public order.[424] Despite its importance, the principle of human dignity remains difficult to define precisely. To some extent, human dignity is not a fundamental right to be balanced with other rights and liberties but rather stands as an overarching principle which serves to assess other fundamental rights and reconcile them.

---

420. CC Decision No 74-54 DC of 15 Jan. 1975, *Loi relative à l'interruption volontaire de grossesse, Rec.* 19*.
421. C. cass., Ch. mixte, 24 May 1975, *Administration des Douanes c. Sociétés 'Cafés Jacques Vabre', Bull. Ch. mixte* 1975, No 4.
422. CE, Ass., 20 Oct. 1989, *Nicolo, Rec. Lebon* 190.
423. CC Decision No 94-343/344 DC of 27 Jul. 1994, *Loi relative au respect du corps humain et loi relative au don et à l'utilisation des éléments et produits du corps humain, à l'assistance médicale à la procréation et au diagnostic prénatal, Rec.* 100, pt 2*: 'The preamble to the 1946 Constitution reaffirmed and proclaimed rights, freedoms and constitutional principles, declaring in its opening paragraph: 'In the morrow of the victory achieved by the free peoples over the regimes that had sought to enslave and degrade humanity, the people of France proclaim anew that each human being, without distinction of race, religion or creed, possesses sacred and inalienable rights'; it follows that the protection of human dignity against all forms of enslavement or degradation is a principle of constitutional status.'
424. CE, Ass., 27 Oct. 1995, *Commune de Morsang-sur-Orge, Rec. Lebon* 372.

2. The Right to Life and Physical Integrity

462. The 'respect for every human being from the beginning of life' has been first affirmed in Article 1 (now abrogated) of the Law of 17 January 1975 on the Voluntary Termination of Pregnancy.[425] This principle is now included in Article 16 of the Civil Code which declares that: 'The law ensures the primacy of the person, prohibits any harm on his/her dignity and guarantees respect for every human being from the beginning of his/her life'. In French law, legal personality, which is the condition to the enjoyment of fundamental rights in general and to the right to life in particular, is attributed to any infant who is born alive and viable.[426] The right to life and individual integrity, and its necessary protection, implies numerous negative and positive obligations for public authorities. One of these negative obligations is the prohibition of death penalty which was abrogated in France by the Law of 9 October 1981.[427] Since 2007, the prohibition of the death penalty has a constitutional value as provided for by Article 66-1 of the Constitution.[428] However, this prohibition is not absolute and is tolerated in relation to acts of war and operations of peacekeeping. Nonetheless, domestic courts assess its application by enforcing a strict necessity test.[429] The right to life and physical integrity also forbids torture as well as inhuman and degrading treatment.[430] As for positive obligations upon the State in relation to the protection of the right to life and physical integrity, this is by means of the creation of effective criminal offences deterring from violating these rights.

3. Medical Issues Related to the Right to Life

463. The development of medical technology has had unprecedented consequences on the right to life, whether in relation to procreation or the ending of life. Medically assisted reproduction is only authorized, under French law, to remedy the infertility of a couple or to prevent the transmission of a particularly severe disease.[431] The donation of gametes is allowed and is conditional upon the consent and anonymity of the donor. In contrast, surrogate motherhood is prohibited by Article

425. Law No 75-17 of 17 Jan. 1975 on the voluntary termination of pregnancy.
426. C. cass, Ass. plén., 29 Jun. 2001, *Bull. Ass. plén.* 2001, No 8.
427. Law No 81-908 of 9 Oct. 1981 abolishing the death penalty.
428. 'No one shall be sentenced to the death penalty.'
429. *See*, e.g., CE, 4/5 SSR, 2 Sep. 2009, *Association Réseau d'alerte et d'intervention pour les droits de l'homme*, apps No 318584/321715.
430. *See*, e.g., ECtHR, *Tomasi v. France*, Series A 241-A, app. No 12850/87, 27 Aug. 1992; ECtHR, *Selmouni v. France*, app. No 25803/94, 28 Jul. 1999.
431. Article L. 2141 Code of Public Health.

16-7 of the Civil Code.[432] Traditionally, research on human embryos was prohibited, as matter of principle, save for the exceptions provided for by law. The situation was reversed under the Law of 6 August 2013 which posits that such research is, in principle, authorized under the conditions determined by law.[433]

464. The voluntary termination of pregnancy (abortion) is allowed in France since 1975.[434] It can take place during the first twelve weeks of the pregnancy. The requirement of a situation of distress resulting from the pregnancy has been suppressed in 2014 to be replaced by a requirement of a woman 'who does not want to continue a pregnancy'.[435] Termination can also be decided for medical reasons if two physicians attest that the pregnancy can severely endanger the health of the woman or if the unborn child is likely to suffer from an incurable and particularly severe illness.[436]

465. Organs donation is allowed under French law provided that three principles of the law of bioethics are respected, namely the presumed consent of the donor, the gratuity of the donation, and the anonymity between the donor and the recipient. Organs donation stands as an exception to the inalienability of the human body with the impossibility to treat the human body as a property right due to being not for trade by nature under Article 16-1 of the Civil Code.[437] As regards the donation of the organs of a living person, the donor can only be a member of the recipient's family or a person who can prove two years of living as if married with the recipient. Removal of organs from a deceased person is allowed as a matter of principle, unless a refusal has been expressed during their lifetime.[438]

466. As a matter of principle, Article 16-3 of the Civil Code requires the consent of the patient to any medical treatment.[439] A patient can thus oppose medical treatment, even if this endangers his/her own life. Nonetheless, the judiciary has been reluctant to sanction physicians who administer a vital treatment, such as blood

---

432. 'Any convention relating to procreation or pregnancy on behalf of others is null and void.'
433. Law No 2013-715 of 6 Aug. 2013 amending Law No 2011-814 of 7 Jul. 2011 relating to bioethics by authorizing under certain conditions the research on embryos and embryonic stem cells.
434. Law No 75-17 of 17 Jan. 1975 on the voluntary termination of pregnancy.
435. Law No 2014-873 of 4 Aug. 2014 for the substantive equality between women and men.
436. Article L. 2213-1 Code of Public Health.
437. 'Everyone has the right to respect for his/her body. The human body is inviolable. The human body, its elements and its products can not be the object of a patrimonial right.'
438. The conditions for refusing to agree on organs removal after death have been simplified by Decree No 2016-1118 of 11 Aug. 2016 on the terms of expression of the refusal of organ removal after death. Three ways of refusal are possible: first, the main way is to register, possibly online as matter of further simplification, in the national register of refusals; secondly, an individual may also file his/her refusal of removal in writing and leave this dated and signed document with a relative; thirdly, an individual may communicate orally his/her opposition to relatives who will have to certify it with the medical team. Moreover, the refusal can now be partial and only concern certain organs or tissues.
439. 'The integrity of the human body can be impaired only in the case of medical necessity for the person or exceptionally in the therapeutic interest of others. The consent of the person concerned must be obtained beforehand except when his/her condition necessitates a therapeutic intervention to which s/he is not in a position to consent.'

transfusion, against the will of the patient.[440] To that extent, domestic case law might contrast with the position adopted by the ECtHR.[441] Euthanasia, in its active form, as well as any form of assisted suicide, are prohibited under French law. Instead the focus of domestic legislation is on palliative care. In this regard, the so-called Leonetti Law introduced the notion of 'unreasonable obstination'.[442] A person in an advanced or terminal phase, of a serious and incurable disease can decide to limit or halt any (medical) treatment.[443] In addition, the Leonetti Law provides for mechanisms in case a patient is not in a position to express his/her will. Advance directives regarding the end of life, especially concerning the pursuit of the medical treatment, its limitation, termination or refusal, may be written by a patient over eighteen years of age should s/he be unable to express his/her will in the future.[444] A trusted person may also be designated should such impossibility occur.[445] The cessation of treatment may also be decided after a collegiate decision of physicians and the consultation of the designated person, the family, a close relation, or the advance directives.[446]

B. The Right to Individual Safety

467. The right to safety protects against arbitrary arrest and forms part – together with the right to liberty, property and resistance to oppression – of the four fundamental rights mentioned in Article 2 of the 1789 Declaration. The right to safety concerns criminal law and procedural law, either criminal or administrative, which involves a deprivation of liberty.

1. Principles of Criminal Law and the Right to Individual Safety

468. The right to safety could not be preserved without the correlative protection of the principle of legality of criminal offences and penalties, the principle of non-retroactivity of criminal law, and the principle of proportionality and necessity of penalties. The principle of the legality of criminal offences and penalties, affirmed under Article 7 and Article 8 of the 1789 Declaration,[447] means that these can only

440. CE, Ass., 26 Oct. 2001, *Mme Catherine Senanayake*, *Rec. Lebon* 514.
441. ECtHR, *Pretty v. United Kingdom*, app. No 2346/02, 29 Apr. 2002.
442. Law No 2005-370 of 22 Apr. 2005 on the rights of the patients and the end of life, as amended by Law No 2016-87 of 2 Feb. 2016 creating new rights for sick people and people at the end of life.
443. Article L. 1111-10 Code of Public Health.
444. Article L. 1111-11 Code of Public Health.
445. Article L. 1111-6 Code of Public Health.
446. Article L. 1111-4 Code of Public Health.
447. Article 7: 'No man may be accused, arrested or detained except in the cases determined by the Law, and following the procedure that it has prescribed. Those who solicit, expedite, carry out, or cause to be carried out arbitrary orders must be punished; but any citizen summoned or apprehended by virtue of the Law, must give instant obedience; resistance makes him guilty'; Article 8: 'The Law must prescribe only the punishments that are strictly and evidently necessary; and no one may be punished except by virtue of a Law drawn up and promulgated before the offence is committed, and legally applied.'

be enforced on the basis of a legal rule. Furthermore, the Constitutional Council has competence to ensure that criminal offences are defined with sufficient clarity.[448] Article 34 of the Constitution reserves to the legislative power the task of defining the most serious criminal offences (i.e., crimes and misdemeanours) while the autonomous regulatory power is competent as regards petty offences (i.e., contraventions). Retroactive laws in criminal matters are prohibited. The non-retroactivity of criminal law is protected at constitutional level under Article 8 of the 1789 Declaration. Nonetheless, this prohibition only applies to substantive laws and not to legal instruments related to criminal procedure. By way of exception, criminal laws which are more lenient may be applied retroactively. The principle of the necessity and proportionality of penalties is guaranteed under Article 8 of the 1789 Declaration. The Constitutional Council exercises a limited review in this regard by sanctioning penalties that are manifestly disproportionate.[449] This principle also entails that the Criminal Code only determines maximum sanctions and that criminal courts are free to decide on the appropriate penalty in light of the specifics of the case. This principle also justifies the development of penalties that are alternative to imprisonment, such as community work or suspended sentences with probation. Since 1997, a measure of surveillance by means of electronic bracelet permits the sentence to be served at home.[450] Recent developments have seen the introduction of a penalty known as criminal coercion.[451] It consists of a sentence of probation, alternative to imprisonment, that involves reinforced measures of monitoring and control whereby the offender is submitted to obligations and prohibitions which are directly related to the offence committed.

469. In addition, a range of precautionary security measures have been introduced under domestic law. However, these measures have been criticized for infringing the right to safety since they involve a deprivation of liberty that does not constitute the penalty related to the commission of a criminal offence. They are primarily justified by the prevention of recidivism and are implemented after the sentence for the commission of a crime or a misdemeanour has been served. Among these measures, the procedures of judicial surveillance and secure surveillance apply to offenders who have been convicted respectively to a sentence of at least ten years for the commission of a misdemeanour or a crime, and to a sentence of at least fifteen years for the commission of certain crimes. The risk of reoffending has to be medically certified. These procedures consist of certain obligations of surveillance and assistance and may include supervision by means of mobile electronic

448. CC Decision No 80-127 DC of 20 Jan. 1981, *Loi renforçant la sécurité et protégeant la liberté des personnes*, *Rec.* 65, pt 7.
449. *Ibid.* pt 11.
450. Law No 97-1159 of 19 Dec. 1997 devoting electronic surveillance as a means of enforcing custodial sentences as amended by Law No 2004-204 of 9 Mar. 2004 adapting justice to the evolution of criminality.
451. Law No 2014-896 of 15 Aug. 2014 on the individualization of sentences and reinforcing the effectiveness of criminal sanctions.

surveillance in particular. The measure of secure surveillance can only be implemented after the execution of another security measure. Security detention[452] is another precautionary measure which was introduced as regards offenders who have been convicted to a sentence of more than fifteen years for a limited list of crimes and who represent a serious dangerousness characterized by a very probability of recidivism due to a severe personality disorder. Once they have served their sentence, these individuals can be placed in a socio-forensic centre and such placement has to be provided for from the initial conviction.[453]

2. Procedural Guarantees of the Right to Safety

470. The procedural guarantees required under the protection of the right to safety relate to both criminal and administrative procedures.

a. Criminal Procedure

471. Criminal procedure in relation to the right to safety includes identity checks, police custody and detention on remand. These guarantees increase with the seriousness of the infringement on the right to safety. Identity checks can be of two kinds. First, identity checks can be made in the context of an operation of the judicial police and, in this case, have to be ordered by an officer of the judicial police and must concern individuals who are suspected of having committed or attempted to commit an offence, or who can provide information relevant to a judicial investigation. Second, identity checks can be made in the context of an operation of administrative police. These checks are of a preventive nature and used in order to maintain public order. The Constitutional Council requires that the administrative authorities justify of the particular circumstances that present a potential breach to the public order.[454] The individual who cannot, or refuse to, justify of his/her identity can be detained for a maximum duration of four hours until his/her identity has been verified. Police custody is a measure of deprivation of liberty that has to be ordered by an officer of the judicial police and concerns individuals who are suspected of a crime or misdemeanour. It has to be the only means to achieve a number of listed objectives such as the preservation of evidence or preventing the influence on witnesses.[455] The domestic legal regime governing police custody has long been criticized, notably by the ECtHR,[456] and by the Constitutional Council which declared such regime, in particular due to the absence of the assistance of a

452. Law No 2008-174 of 25 Feb. 2008 on security detention and the declaration of criminal irresponsibility on account of mental disorder.
453. Article 706-53-13 Code of Criminal Procedure.
454. CC Decision No 93-323 DC of 5 Aug. 1993, *Loi relative aux contrôles et vérifications d'identité*, *Rec.* 213, pt 10.
455. Article 62-2 Code of Criminal Procedure.
456. *See*, e.g, ECtHR, *Tomasi v. France*, Series A 241-A, app. No 12850/87, 27 Aug. 1992; ECtHR, *Selmouni v. France*, app. No 25803/94, 28 Jul. 1999; ECtHR, *Brusco v. France*, app. No 1466/07, 14 Oct. 2010.

lawyer, was repugnant to the Constitution.[457] The Court of Cassation reached a similar conclusion on the basis of Article 6 paragraph one of the ECHR.[458] Eventually, this resulted in an overhaul of the law on police custody in 2011.[459] Under the new regime,[460] the offender detained in police custody benefits from a number of improved procedural guarantees such as the right to the assistance of a lawyer from the beginning of the custody, or the right to remain silent. Police custody lasts for a maximum of twenty-four hours. A further extension of twenty-four hours can be authorized by the public prosecutor. Longer periods of police custody apply to serious crimes and can amount to six days in case of a serious risk of an imminent terrorist attack. Pretrial detention is the most serious threat to the right to safety since it involves the deprivation of liberty of a presumed innocent individual. The judge of liberties and detention (*Juge des Libertés et de la Détention* or JLD), a special judge created in 2000,[461] is competent for that matter and rules on such detention under the conditions defined by law. The principle is that pretrial detention pending trial stands as an exceptional measure which use should be limited in case no lesser coercive measure would achieve a number of objectives such as the preservation of evidence, the preventing the individual from fleeing, the protection of witnesses and victims.[462]

b. Administrative Procedure

472. The right to safety also pertains to administrative decisions that involve deprivation of liberty. These may include psychiatric hospitalizations or removal orders from the national territory. The legal regime governing the involuntary internment of individuals suffering from a mental disorder was modified by the Law of 5 July 2011 on the rights and protection of persons in psychiatric care and the modalities of their treatment.[463] While psychiatric care may result from a voluntary

457. CC Decision No 2010-14/22 QPC of 30 Jul. 2010, *M. Daniel W. et autres [Garde à vue], Rec.* 179*.
458. C. cass., Ass. plén., 11 Apr. 2011, *Bull. crim.* 2011, No 1–4.
459. Law No 2011-392 of 14 Apr. 2011 on police custody.
460. Articles 63-1 et seq. Code of Criminal Procedure.
461. Law No 2000-516 of 15 Jun. 2000 reinforcing the protection of the presumption of innocence and the rights of the victims.
462. Article 144 Code of Criminal Procedure: 'Pre-trial detention may only be ordered or extended if it can be shown, given the precise and detailed circumstances of the proceedings, that it is the only means of achieving one or more of the following objectives and that those cannot be achieved in the case of placement under judicial surveillance or house arrest with electronic surveillance: 1. to preserve evidence, including material evidence, which are necessary for the manifestation of the truth; 2. to prevent pressure on witnesses or victims, as well as on their families; 3.°to prevent fraudulent consultation between the individual under investigation and his/her co-perpetrators or accomplices; 4. to protect the individual under investigation; 5.°to guarantee that the individual under investigation will remain at the disposal of the courts; 6.°to end the offence and prevent its reoccurrence; 7.°to put an end to the exceptional and persistent disturbance to the public order caused by the gravity of the offence, the circumstances of its commission or the extent of the damage it has caused. This trouble cannot result only from the impact that the case has on the media. However, this paragraph is not applicable in correctional matters.'
463. Articles L. 3211-1 et seq. Code of Public Health, as modified by Law No 2011-803 of 5 Jul. 2011 on the rights and the protection of persons in psychiatric care and the modalities of their treatment.

decision, it can also be imposed at the request of a third party or by a decision of the prefect. In case of involuntary internment, the individual is subject to an observation period of seventy-two hours during which two medical certificates must confirm the need for psychiatric care. If the care requires full hospitalization, the judge of liberties and detention reviews the legality of such decision within the first fifteen days, and every six months thereafter. The absence of judicial review, at the required intervals, of the full hospitalization decision will automatically result in it being lifted. Decisions on deprivation of liberty can also concern foreigners – subject to the specific regimes applicable to nationals of a Member State of the EU, of the European Economic Area (EEA) or of the Swiss Confederation – whose admission to the national territory is refused or who are requested to leave the national territory. Such decisions may happen in three instances. First, following a refusal of entry into the domestic territory, foreigners can be placed in 'areas for persons whose case is pending'. The initial decision can be made for a maximum period of four days, that can be extended for a further period of eight days, renewable once, by the judge of liberties and detention. Second, the administrative detention for verification of residence concerns foreigners who cannot justify their right of residence. Such decision can be decided for up to six hours, and renewed for ten hours, by an officer of the judicial police after informing the public prosecutor, but without the decision being susceptible of judicial review. Lastly, the administrative detention of foreigners awaiting removal can be decided in different situations, notably in case of an obligation to leave the French territory, an escort to the frontier or an expulsion. The prefect is competent to take the initial decision of detention for a maximum of five days. It can be prolonged for a period of twenty days, renewable once, by the judge of liberties and detention. In certain cases, administrative detention can be replaced by a measure of house arrest.

C. The Right to Privacy

473. While it is included in numerous international instruments,[464] the right to privacy is not formally recognized in the Constitution. It is affirmed by Article 9 of the Civil Code. However, the Constitutional Council recognized its constitutional status as part of individual freedom on the basis of Article 66 of the Constitution[465] and Article 2 of the 1789 Declaration.[466] The right to privacy has two sides. First, the right consists in a right to respect for private life. Second, the right reflects the right to make choices for one's personal life and to have those choices being legally recognized.

464. Article 17 International Covenant on Civil and Political Rights, Art. 8 ECHR; and Art. 7 EU Charter of Fundamental Rights.
465. CC Decision No 94-352 DC of 18 Jan. 1995, *Loi d'orientation et de programmation relative à la sécurité*, *Rec.* 170, pt 2.
466. CC Decision No 99-419 DC of 9 Nov. 1999, *Loi relative au pacte civil de solidarité*, *Rec.* 116, pt 73.

1. The Right to Respect for Private Life

474. The right to respect for private life offers a wide range of protection to individuals, even though it has to be balanced with other fundamental rights and liberties, mainly with freedom of expression. This balance has concerned, in more recent years, considerations of security as well as the development of new technologies in particular.

a. General

475. The right to respect for private life corresponds to the right to be left alone and develop one's life without external interferences, notably from public authorities. It first concerns the protection of the home which encompasses the free choice of residence and the inviolability of the dwelling.[467] The inviolability of the dwelling protects against nuisance from individuals but also from undue interferences by public authorities. Searches and seizures are subject to strict legal rules and can, save a few exceptions, only take place between 6 am and 9 pm. Some professions, for reason of confidentiality, enjoy a stronger protection in this regard which is the case, for example, of solicitors and barristers, as well as medical doctors and media companies.

476. The right to respect for private life also corresponds to the confidentiality of private life which protects against the divulgation of information in the public sphere. This principle has numerous applications. It includes the protection of the use of one's image. Public use of one's image requires a consent without which the right to respect for private life is violated which has to be balanced with the right to information and freedom of the press. The confidentiality of private life also applies in relation to medical confidentiality, a duty imposed on physicians but also on third parties. Furthermore, the confidentiality of private life concerns political opinions and religious beliefs as well as the sentimental life and sexual orientation. Discrimination on such grounds constitutes a criminal offence.[468] Another aspect is the confidentiality of the correspondence which concerns mail (or postal) and electronic communication, including communication by telephone and email. Infringement of such confidentiality, whether by private individuals or by public authorities, is criminally sanctioned.[469] The protection of the confidentiality of the correspondence can be wider as regards certain individuals by reason of their profession (e.g., solicitors, barristers) while, in some instances, this protection can be narrower, notably for security reasons such as, for example, in the case of prisoners. More generally, such protection of confidentiality can be reduced during criminal investigations.

477. Related to this right is the issue of the interception of electronic communications. Under domestic law, there has traditionally been a distinction between

467. CC Decision No 83-164 DC of 29 Dec. 1983, *Loi de finances pour 1984*, *Rec.* 67, pt 28.
468. Articles 225-1 et seq. Criminal Code.
469. Respectively Art. 226-15 and Art. 432-9 Criminal Code.

judicial interceptions and interceptions of security.[470] Judicial interceptions are permitted in relation to certain criminal investigations. They have to be requested by the investigating judge (*juge d'instruction*) for a maximum period of four months, a period which is renewable.[471] Interceptions of security aim at collecting information pertaining, notably 'to national security, to the safeguard of elements which are essential to the scientific and economic potential of France, or to the prevention of terrorism, of criminality and of organized crime'.[472] These interceptions have to be authorized by the Prime Minister, for a period of four months, on a proposal from the Minister for Defence, the Minister for Home Affairs, the Minister for Justice or the Minister for the Economy, Budget and Customs. Interceptions of security are subject to different rules as regards the information that can be transcribed and the duration of their conservation. The respect for rules governing such interceptions is controlled by an independent administrative authority, namely the National Commission for the Control of Intelligence Techniques (*Commission Nationale de Contrôle des Techniques de Renseignement* or *CNCTR*), formerly known as the National Commission for the Control of Interceptions of Security (*Commission Nationale de Contrôle des Interceptions de Sécurité* or *CNCIS*).[473] The president of this Commission has to be informed within forty-eight hours of a decision to proceed to an interception of security. If the president is in doubt as to the legality of such interception, the Commission is convened. If the Commission considers that the interception is repugnant to the law, it can address a recommendation to the Prime Minister, recommendation which is, however, not binding. The Commission can also act on a referral or on its own initiative to review the legality of interceptions of security.

b. New Technologies

478. The right to respect for private life is increasingly affected by the development of new technologies and by the strengthening of provisions to protect public security. This concerns, in particular, the collection of computerized data and the development of the use of video surveillance.

i. The Control of Computerized Data

479. The development of computerized files containing private data, with the amount of information that can be collected and the facility of communication it involves, has led to the creation of an independent administrative authority, namely the National Commission for Data Protection and Liberties (*Commission Nationale*

470. Law No 91-646 of 10 Jul. 1991 on the secrecy of correspondence transmitted by means of telecommunications.
471. Articles 100 et seq. Code of Criminal Procedure.
472. Article L. 241-2 Code of Homeland Security.
473. Law No 2015-912 of 24 Jul. 2015 on intelligence. *See also* CC Decision No 2017-648 QPC of 4 Aug. 2017, *La Quadrature du Net et autres [Accès administratif en temps réel aux données de connexion]**.

de l'Informatique et des Libertés or CNIL) in 1978.[474] Its role is to protect personal data and preserve individual liberties, as well as support innovation in the area of computerized data. Its general mission is to inform and educate individuals of the rights afforded to them under domestic legislation on data protection. The CNIL also aims at regulating and advising in the area via different tools, at inspecting computerized data, including video surveillance systems, and sanctioning its abusive use. The 1978 Law creating the CNIL also set the principles governing the treatment of computerized data. First, the collection of computerized data must obey the principle of loyalty by addressing explicit and legitimate objectives. Computerized data have to be used in accordance with the purpose that justified its initial collection. Furthermore, data that is collected must be exact. Last, computerized data of a personal nature require, in principle, the consent of the person concerned. Exceptions are possible, notably for reasons of public interest.

480. The legal regime of data protection also provides for the protection of a number of rights in relation to an individual's right to privacy. The individual benefits from a right to be informed and a right to access computerized data. S/he also has a right to ask for rectification if the data is erroneous, as well as a right 'to be forgotten' since the conservation of computerized data cannot exceed the period necessary to fulfil the finality that has justified its collection.[475] The right to be forgotten has also been recently affirmed by the CJEU in the context of the information available on the Internet.[476] The CNIL ensures the respect of the aforesaid principles. In particular, it ensures the enforcement of the principle of finality by controlling that the data collected is appropriate and relevant to this finality. The modalities of this control take the form, as a matter of principle, of a prior declaration to the CNIL for the collection of computerized data. By exception, computerized data may require a prior authorization by the CNIL. It is the case, for instance, when the collection of data pertains to committed offences or to convicted persons, when it concerns the administrative interconnection of computerized files, or in relation to genetic data. A special regime governs computerized data created for the State and that relate to specific information such as defence, public security or biometric data for the purpose of identification. In these instances, authorization is given by the relevant ministry or by means of a decree in the Council of State after consultation of the CNIL.

ii. Video Surveillance

481. The right to respect for private life can be endangered by video surveillance. The development of such technology led to the creation of a specific legal

474. Law No 78-17 of 6 Jan. 1978 on informatics, computerized data and freedoms, as lastly amended by Law No 2016-1321 of 7 Oct. 2016 for a Digital Republic, to be entered into force on 25 May 2018.

475. *Ibid.* Art. 6.

476. ECJ, C-131/12 *Google Spain SL, Google Inc. v Agencia Española de Protección de Datos (AEPD), Mario Costeja González* (13 May 2014) (unreported).

regime in 1995, as amended and supplemented in 2006, 2011 and 2016.[477] The latter evolution substituted the term 'video protection' for that of 'video surveillance' when the system is installed in public places or in places open to the public. The installation of a system of video protection can be justified, among others, by the protection of public buildings and facilities, the safeguard of facilities that are useful to national defence, the regulation of transport networks, the prevention of attacks against individuals and property in places particularly exposed to risks, the prevention of terrorism. The installation of a system of video protection in public places, or in places open to the public, by legal persons governed by public or private law, requires the authorization of the prefect after consultation of a departmental commission which is chaired by a judge. The authorization is valid for five years and renewable. When the system of video protection involves the recording of data that can be used for the purpose of identification of individuals, it has to be authorized by the CNIL. The installation of systems of video surveillance in places not open to the public only requires a prior declaration to the CNIL. Where relevant, representative of employees also have to be informed and consulted. In addition, the CNIL has consultation and evaluation missions in relation to video protection. The Constitutional Council has clarified a number of issues, including the impossibility for legal persons governed by private law to instal video protection devices beyond the immediate surroundings of their buildings and facilities, as well as the impossibility to entrust private operators with the installation of systems of video protection in public places. The Council ruled that these situations would be tantamount to vesting in private legal persons powers of general administrative police inherent in the exercise of the public order force. Such an outcome would be in contradiction with Article 12 of the 1789 Declaration.[478]

482. The legal regime of video protection also provides for the protection of a number of individual rights. First, individuals must be informed in a clear and permanent manner of the existence of a system of video protection, as well as about the public authority or the private individual that is responsible for this system. Second, individuals have a right, when concerned, to access the recordings and require their destruction once the period of retention has expired. In principle, the retention of images cannot exceed one month.

2. The Right to Personal Autonomy

483. The right to respect for private life also consists of the possibility of making choices as regards one's own life and have these choices legally recognized,

477. Law No 95-73 of 21 Jan. 1995 on the policy pertaining to security as amended by Law No 2006-64 of 23 Jan. 2006 on the fight against terrorism and containing various provisions relating to security and border controls, Law No 2011-267 of 14 Mar. 2011 on the policy for the achievement of homeland security, and Law No 2016-731 of 3 Jun. 2016 reinforcing the fight against organized crime, terrorism and their financing, and improving the efficiency and the guarantees of criminal procedure. The regime is now included in Arts L. 251-1 et seq of the Code of Homeland Security.

478. CC Decision No 2011-625 DC of 10 Mar. 2011, *Loi d'orientation et de programmation pour la performance de la sécurité intérieure*, *Rec.* 122, pt 19*.

what the ECtHR qualifies as the 'right to personal autonomy' on the basis of Article 8 of the ECHR.[479] This has implication primarily on the civil status of individuals as well as on their freedom to marry and have a family.

a. The Right to Personal Autonomy and Civil Status

484. Traditionally, the civil status, which consists of the elements of individualization of a person in the society, was considered as immutable, imprescriptible and inalienable. These principles have been altered to take into consideration the right to personal autonomy. One application concerns the surname. Since 2002,[480] the name of a child is not necessarily the patronymic surname (i.e., the surname of the father). Parents have the choice to give either of their names, or both, in the order they choose, to their child.[481] Another important change in the French conception of the civil status has concerned the determination of sex. After the ruling of the ECtHR in the *B* case,[482] domestic law gave recognition to transsexuality and allowed, on the basis of the right to respect for private life, the modification of their civil status by transsexual persons to reflect their identity.[483]

b. The Right to Personal Autonomy and the Family

485. Article 12 of the ECHR recognizes the right to marry while the Constitutional Council regards the liberty to marry as a component of personal freedom on the basis of Articles 2 and 4 of the 1789 Declaration.[484] The legislature can nonetheless take measures to prevent marriages of convenience that are contracted for purposes not related to the matrimonial union as long as constitutional principles related to the right to marry are not deprived of legal guarantees.[485] Before 2013, French law interpreted provisions relating to marriage as being exclusive to heterosexual couples.[486] In 1999, the introduction of a regime a civil partnership, regardless of gender, permitted the legal recognition of homosexual couples.[487] Then, in 2013, the Law on Same-Sex Marriage suppressed the difference of sex as a condition of marriage.[488] Article 143 of the Civil Code now affirms that: 'Marriage is contracted by two persons of different sex or of same sex.' The right to have a family is not recognized as such in domestic law. Nonetheless, the protection of the family

479. ECtHR, *Pretty v. United Kingdom*, app. No 2346/02, 29 Apr. 2002, para 61: 'Although no previous case has established as such any right to self-determination as being contained in Art. 8 of the Convention, the Court considers that the notion of personal autonomy is an important principle underlying the interpretation of its guarantees.'
480. Law No 2002-304 of 4 Mar. 2002 on the surname.
481. Article 311-21 Civil Code.
482. ECtHR, *B. v. France*, Series A 232-C, app. No 13343/87, 25 Mar. 1992.
483. C. cass., Ass. plén., 11 Dec. 1992, *Bull. Ass. plén.* 1992, No 13.
484. CC Decision No 2003-484 DC of 20 Nov. 2003, *Loi relative à la maîtrise de l'immigration, au séjour des étrangers en France et à la nationalité*, *Rec.* 438, pt 37.
485. CC Decision No 2012-261 QPC of 22 Jun. 2012, *M. Thierry B. [Consentement au mariage et opposition à mariage]*, *Rec.* 312, pt 5.
486. C. cass., Civ. 1re, 13 Mar. 2007, *Bull. civ.* I, 2007, No 13.
487. Law No 99-944 of 15 Nov. 1999 on the Solidarity Civil Pact.
488. Law No 2013-404 of 17 May 2013 opening marriage to couples of persons of the same sex.

is constitutionally guaranteed and is mentioned in the tenth paragraph of the Preamble to the 1946 Constitution which is part of the block of constitutionality. This principle has several implications, notably in the area of immigration law, through the right to family reunification (*See* below Chapter 5 Status and Rights of Foreigners). The introduction of same-sex marriage entails the possibility for homosexual couples to have a family through adoption.[489] For that purpose, Article 6-1 of the Civil Code affirms that rules related to marriage and to adoptive filiation apply in the same manner, whether the spouses or the parents are of a different sex or the same sex.

II. Intellectual Freedoms

A. *Freedom of Opinion and Expression*

486. Even though it is not an absolute right, the right to freedom of opinion and expression has a special value in French law. Its implementation implies positive obligations on the part of the State.

1. Constitutional Basis and Scope of Freedom of Opinion and Expression

487. Article 10 of the 1789 Declaration provides for the right to freedom of opinion as long as its manifestation does not disturb the public order.[490] Pertaining to the intellectual autonomy of the individual, freedom of opinion is widely protected. Nonetheless, it is also a strong guarantee in cases involving instances of indoctrination.

488. Freedom of opinion implies in itself the manifestation of such opinion. Article 11 of the 1789 Declaration provides for the correlative right to freedom of expression and concerns the right to speak, write and publish freely.[491] In addition, freedom of expression is considered as being 'one of the most precious rights of man'. Other constitutional provisions mention the right to freedom of expression such as Article 4 of the Constitution which affirms that law shall guarantee the pluralistic expression of opinions, and Article 34 which attributes to law the competence to ensure the 'freedom, pluralism and independence of the media'. Its importance for democracy explains the special value recognized to this right, a right that constitute the foundation of the freedom of the press and of the right to information. This particular significance has been explicitly recognized by the Constitutional Council which affirmed, in a series of rulings, that 'the requirement of

489. CC Decision No 2013-669 DC of 17 May 2013, *Loi ouvrant le mariage aux couples de personnes de même sexe*, *Rec.* 721*.
490. 'No one may be disturbed on account of his/her opinions, even religious ones, as long as the manifestation of such opinions does not interfere with the established law and order.'
491. 'The free communication of ideas and of opinions is one of the most precious rights of man. Any citizen may therefore speak, write and publish freely, except what is tantamount to the abuse of this liberty in the cases determined by the Law.'

pluralism of currents of ideas and opinions (…) constitutes the foundation of democracy',[492] and that freedom of expression is 'all the more valuable that its exercise is one of the essential guarantees of the respect of other rights and liberties and of national sovereignty'.[493] Nonetheless, constitutional provisions on freedom of expression do not adopt an absolute definition of this right and expressly provide for limitations to be determined by law. Such limitations must be necessary, appropriate and proportional to the objective being pursued.[494] These limitations are justified by the respect of other fundamental rights or the preservation of public order. These competing requirements to be taken into account as regards the implementation of freedom of expression find a specific expression in the Law of 29 July 1881 (as amended) on Freedom of the Press that governs expression in the public sphere.[495] Freedom of expression is first limited by the protection of the honour of other individuals which is protected through actions in defamation, libel and slander in particular.[496] Furthermore, freedom of expression is limited by the right to privacy. The balance between these two fundamental rights is assessed in the light of the general interest and the right to information that can justify infringements to the privacy of the individual.[497] Lastly, freedom of expression can be restricted for reason of public order. In this respect, criminal incitement and incitement to racial hatred,[498] or apology of terrorism,[499] constitute criminal offences.

2. Protection of Freedom of Expression

489. The protection of freedom of expression requires the State to be neutral towards the diversity of opinions, on the one hand, and to take measures to ensure their pluralism, on the other hand. The principle of neutrality of the administration is the corollary of the principle of equality. As a consequence, the administration must not favour groups of citizens on the ground of their opinions and must treat all opinions in an unprejudiced manner. This principle also applies to civil servants in the performance of their official duties and they must so refrain from expressing their political or religious opinion.[500] Outside their service, freedom of expression of civil servants remains the principle.[501] Nonetheless, some categories of civil servants are submitted to a duty of reserve, even outside the performance of their

492. CC Decision No 89-271 DC of 11 Jan. 1990, *Loi relative à la limitation des dépenses électorales et à la clarification du financement des activités politiques*, *Rec.* 21, pt 12.
493. CC Decision No 84-181 DC of 11 Oct. 1984, *Loi visant à limiter la concentration et à assurer la transparence financière et le pluralisme des entreprises de presse*, *Rec.* 73, pt 37.
494. CC Decision No 2012-647 DC of 28 Feb. 2012, *Loi visant à réprimer la contestation de l'existence des génocides reconnus par la loi*, *Rec.* 139, pt 5*.
495. Law of 29 Jul. 1881 on the freedom of the press.
496. *Ibid.* Art. 29 et seq.
497. Articles 226-1 et seq. Criminal Code.
498. Articles 24 et seq. 1881 Law.
499. Article 421-2-5 Criminal Code.
500. CE, Sect., 3 Mar. 1950, *Demoiselle Jamet*, *Rec. Lebon* 247.
501. Article 6 of Law No 83-634 of 13 Jul. 1983 on the rights and obligations of civil servants (as amended).

duties. This is, for instance, the case of members of the judiciary,[502] or members of the military force.[503] The protection of freedom of expression does not only consist of the negative obligation of neutrality. The State has also the obligation to promote the principle of pluralism of opinions which is expressed in Articles 4 and 34 of the Constitution in relation to political parties and the media respectively. More generally, the Constitutional Council considers pluralism as an objective of constitutional value,[504] meaning that the State has to prevent media concentration in the audiovisual field,[505] and in the press.[506] The State must also guarantee pluralism of political parties. As a result, while financial assistance is legal, it cannot lead, notably on the basis of the threshold to trigger the reimbursement of campaign expenses, to disregard the requirement of pluralism.[507] Similarly, the Superior Council of the Audiovisual (*Conseil Supérieur de l'Audiovisuel* or hereafter *CSA*) controls that political parties benefit from an equitable media exposure, in particular during election campaigns. While the use of the French language is an obligation bearing upon legal persons governed by public law by virtue of Article 2 of the Constitution, the principle of pluralism implies that private individuals should be allowed to use regional languages and foreign language expressions.[508] Since 2008, linguistic diversity has been recognized in the Constitution which provides that '[r]egional languages belong to the heritage of France'. (Article 75-1 Constitution).

490. The rules governing the right to freedom of expression depend on the type of media concerned. As regards the press, freedom of expression is regulated by a regime of the repressive type whereby the exercise of the right is of principle and sanctioned a posteriori if it exceeds the boundaries set by law. Accordingly, the publication of a newspaper or periodical only requires a prior declaration to the public prosecutor. By exception, publications intended for young people are regulated by a regime of the preventive type.[509] The repressive regime also applies to the Internet. Due to its increased significance in the technologies of communications, the Constitutional Council deduced from Article 11 of the 1789 Declaration on freedom of expression, the freedom to access the Internet.[510] In contrast, audiovisual communication is governed by a preventive regime and requires prior authorization. As a result, the diffusion of cinematographic work is submitted to the granting of a screen certificate that specifies the condition of its diffusion in terms of age groups.

502. Article 10 of Ordinance No 58-1270 of 22 Dec. 1958 on the Organic Law on the status of the judiciary.
503. Article L. 4121-2 Code of Defence.
504. CC Decision No 82-141 DC of 27 Jul. 1982, *Loi sur la communication audiovisuelle*, *Rec*. 48.
505. CC Decision No 2004-497 DC of 1 Jul. 2004, *Loi relative aux communications électroniques et aux services de communication audiovisuelle*, *Rec*. 107.
506. CC Decision No 86-210 DC of 29 Jul. 1986, *Loi portant réforme du régime juridique de la presse*, *Rec*. 110.
507. CC Decision No 89-271 DC of 11 Jan. 1990, *Loi relative à la limitation des dépenses électorales et à la clarification du financement des activités politiques*, *Rec*. 21.
508. CC Decision No 94-345 DC of 29 Jul. 1994, *Loi relative à l'emploi de la langue française*, *Rec*. 106.
509. Law No 49-956 of 16 Jul. 1949 on publications intended for the youth (as amended).
510. CC Decision No 2009-580 DC of 10 Jun. 2009, *Loi favorisant la diffusion et la protection de la création sur Internet*, *Rec*. 107*.

Mayors, when exercising their powers of administrative police, can also prevent the diffusion of films given the specific local circumstances.[511] Radio and television broadcasting are not, since 1981[512] and 1982[513] respectively, subject to State monopoly anymore. Nonetheless, radio and television broadcasting are submitted to the prior authorization of the *CSA* due to technical constraints and in order to enforce the principle of pluralism.

B. Freedom of Religion and Freedom of Education

491. Freedom of religion, under French law, is dependent on the importance and specific understanding given to the secular nature of the State. Besides, the development of the French Republic explains the particular relationship between freedom of religion and freedom of education.

1. Freedom of Religion

492. Freedom of religion is affirmed by Article 10 of the 1789 Declaration. Its protection under French law is conditioned by the secular nature of the French Republic as enshrined in the First Article of the Constitution and whereby the State ensures equality before the law without distinction of religion and respects all beliefs. The particular approach to secularism in domestic law finds its origin in the Law of 9 December 1905 (the 1905 Law),[514] which involves two principles, namely the neutrality of the State towards religions and the guarantee of freedom of religion for the individual. The departments of *Haut-Rhin*, *Bas-Rhin* and *Moselle*, that were German territories in 1905, are still governed by the Concordat of 1801, which constitutes a special agreement derogating from the principle of secularism. However, this derogation has been considered by the Constitutional Council as being in conformity with the Constitution.[515] This specific understanding of the relationship between freedom of religion and secularism may create difficulties with its definition at European level.[516]

a. The Religious Neutrality of the State

493. The negative principle derived from the secular nature of the State entails that domestic law should be indifferent as regards the various creeds and religions.

511. CE., Sect., 18 Dec. 1959, *Société 'Les Films Lutétia'*, *Rec. Lebon* 693.
512. Law No 81-994 of 9 Nov. 1981 derogating from the State monopoloy on radiodiffusion.
513. Law No 82-652 of 29 Jul. 1982 on audiovisual communication.
514. Law of 9 Dec. 1905 on the separation of the Churches and State (as amended). *See* below Part V. Specific Issues, Chapter 4. The Constitutional Relationship between Church and State.
515. CC Decision No 2012-297 QPC of 21 Feb. 2013, *Association pour la promotion et l'expansion de la laïcité [Traitement des pasteurs des églises consistoriales dans les départements du Bas-Rhin, du Haut-Rhin et de la Moselle]*, *Rec.* 293*.
516. CC Decision No 2004-505 DC of 19 Nov. 2004, *Traité établissant une Constitution pour l'Europe*, *Rec.* 173*.

Religion is considered as a private matter and is not taken into consideration in the public sphere. Article 2 of the 1905 Law declares that the Republic neither recognizes nor subsidizes any religion. First, this entails the strict neutrality of public law entities as regards religion and the prohibition of discrimination on this basis. Public servants cannot manifest their religious beliefs in the fulfilment of their professional duties.[517] Conversely, public servants cannot be discriminated on the basis of their religion.[518] This prohibition of discrimination on the basis of religion also extends to the relationships between private individuals, notably in relation to employment.[519] The State has the obligation to protect religious beliefs and provide for appropriate criminal offences in relation to such discrimination[520] and, more generally, to behaviours that would constitute a violation of the freedom of religion.[521] Second, the principle of neutrality of the State prevents direct or indirect subsidies of religious orders.[522] Nonetheless, religious buildings in existence prior to 1905 are publicly owned and public collectivities (i.e., State or local authorities) are responsible for their maintenance. Two exceptions apply to this prohibition of financial support on the basis of the positive obligation bearing on the State to protect freedom of religion. Article 2 of the 1905 Law provides for the possibility of public funding in the case of chaplaincy offices in schools, mental hospitals and prisons. The second exception concerns the funding assistance granted to private schools. Under this positive obligation, domestic courts have adopted a less strict interpretation of the prohibition of financial support to religious bodies on the condition that such funding should be justified as regard to the public interest and involve the payment of a fee. For instance, under those conditions, a municipality can make a venue available to be used as a place of worship or for ritual practices.[523]

b. The Exercise of Freedom of Religion

494. Freedom of conscience and freedom of religious worship are protected by Article 10 of the 1789 Declaration, as well as specifically enshrined in Article 1 of the 1905 Law. In that respect, the State neither appreciates whether religious beliefs are legitimate nor intervenes in the functioning of the Churches. In contrast, public authorities are under the obligation to ensure that individuals can exercise their religion freely. For instance, changing one's first name in order to reflect one's religious belief is considered as fulfilling the condition of a 'legitimate interest' as mentioned in Article 60 of the Civil Code.[524] The same principle applies in relation

517. CE, 4/6 SSR, 3 May 2000, *Mademoiselle Marteaux*, app No 217017.
518. CE, 28 Apr. 1938, *Demoiselle Weiss*, *Rec. Lebon* 379; CE, 8 Dec. 1948, *Demoiselle Pasteau*, *Rec. Lebon*, 464.
519. *See* the fifth paragraph of the Preamble to the 1946 Constitution.
520. Articles 225-1 et seq. Criminal Code.
521. Article 31 of the 1905 Law.
522. CE, 3/8 SSR, 15 Feb. 2013, *Association Grande Confrérie de Saint-Martial et autres*, apps No 347049/347050.
523. CE, Ass., 19 Jul. 2011, *Commune de Montpellier*, app No 313518; CE, Ass., 19 Jul. 2011, *Communauté urbaine du Mans-Le Mans Métropole*, app No 309131.
524. 'Anyone can ask the State civil registrar to change their name.' (first sentence of first paragraph).

to funeral.[525] Secularism has traditionally consisted of the principle of neutrality of public authorities and of the principle of individual freedom of religion. Lately, it has arguably become a positive principle justifying limitations being put on the freedom of religion. Since 2004, the principle of secularism proscribes primary and secondary schools students to conspicuously manifest their religious affiliation through the wearing of symbols and clothing.[526] Since 2011, the same approach has been relied upon on the occasion of the adoption of the law prohibiting the wearing of full-face clothing in the public space.[527] The ECtHR held that this domestic law was compatible with the ECHR in the *SAS* case of 2014.[528] While dismissing a number of arguments, including that relating to public safety, the ECtHR recognized that the interference with Articles 8 and 9 of the ECHR was justified under the need to protect the rights and freedoms of others due to the fact that social interaction could be viewed as important in a democratic society where people were 'living together' (the so-called respect for the minimum requirements of life in society referred to by the French Government),[529] and that a veil concealing the face could interfere with this in the sense that it could be perceived as 'breaching the right of others to live in a space of socialization which makes living together easier'.[530] After careful examination of the necessity of the impugned limitation, and having regard in particular to the breadth of the margin of appreciation afforded to France in the present case, the ECtHR concluded that the ban was not disproportionate to the aim pursued, namely the preservation of the conditions of 'living together' as an element of the 'protection of the rights and freedoms of others'.[531] Freedom of religion can also be curtailed by the fight against sectarian movements. This led to the creation, in the late 1990s, of the Interministerial Mission for Monitoring and Fighting against Sectarian Drifts (*Mission Interministérielle de Vigilance et de Lutte contre les Dérives Sectaires* or MIVILUDES). In 2001, legal instruments to fight sectarian movements have been expanded, notably through the adoption of a specific piece of legislation against harmful cults.[532]

---

525. Article 3 of Law of 15 Nov. 1887 on the freedom of funerals (as amended): 'Any adult or emancipated minor, who has capacity to make his/her will, may freely establish the conditions of his/her funeral, particularly as regards the civil or religious character to be given to it and the mode of his/her burial.' (first paragraph).
526. Law No 2004-228 of 15 Mar. 2004 regulating, in accordance with the principle of secularism, the wearing of symbols of clothing displaying a religious affiliation in public primary and secondary schools.
527. Law No 2010-1192 of 11 Oct. 2010 prohibiting the concealment of the face in the public space.
528. ECtHR, *S.A.S.v. France*, app. No 43835/11, 1 Jul. 2014.
529. *Ibid.* para. 121.
530. *Ibid.* para. 122.
531. *Ibid.* paras 157-158.
532. Law No 2001-504 of 12 Jun. 2001 reinforcing the prevention and repression of sectarian movements violating human rights and fundamental liberties.

2. Freedom of Education

495. Freedom of education depends on the recognition of education as a right and on the rules governing the educational system within which this right is exercised.

a. The Right to Education

496. The right to education is of constitutional value, as enshrined under the thirteenth paragraph of the Preamble to the 1946 Constitution. The State is under the obligation to take measures in order to ensure that the protection of this right is effective. The right to education goes beyond instruction. Considering that 'education is the first national priority', the Education Code also affirms that '[i]n addition to imparting knowledge, the Nation sets as the first mission of schools to share the values of the Republic with pupils'.[533] Education is not only a right but also an obligation as it is mandatory for any child, French nationals or non-nationals, from six to sixteen years of age. Education is, in general, provided for in a (public or private) educational institution, but can also be provided at home. Parents (or guardians) bear the responsibility for ensuring the compulsory part of the education of their offspring and will incur penalties should they not comply.[534]

b. Freedom of Education and the Educational System

497. The French system of education is governed by a number of general principles, namely that education is a right and an obligation and that public schooling is free and secular. In accordance with freedom of education, education can be provided for either in public or private institutions. However, the State has the sole power to award degrees.

i. Public Education

498. The Preamble to the 1946 Constitution, in its thirteenth paragraph, states that '[t]he organization of free and secular public education at all levels is a duty of the State'. The Ministry of Education represents the largest French administration. Free education applies to nursery schools (preschool) as well as to primary level and secondary level education. In contrast, tuition fees apply at higher education institutions. Dating back from the end of the nineteenth century, the secular nature of French public education has preceded the 1905 separation of the Churches and State. More generally, public education is governed by the principle of neutrality, which is compulsory as regards both teachers and students, from a political and philosophical (religious) perspective.[535] Moreover, the independence of university

533. Article L. 111-1 Education Code.
534. Articles L. 131-1 et seq Education Code.
535. Article L 511-2 Education Code.

teacher-researcher (often referred to as the principle of academic freedom) is constitutionally guaranteed as a Fundamental Principle recognized by the Laws of the Republic.[536]

ii. Private Education

499. The possibility of providing for education in private institutions has been progressively recognized for primary, secondary and higher educational institutions in, respectively, 1833, 1850 and 1875, and has subsequently been recognized by the Constitutional Council as being one of the Fundamental Principles recognized by the Laws of the Republic.[537] The creation of a private educational institution requires a declaration to be made to the mayor at primary level and to the rector of academy at secondary level,[538] the receipt of which has to be communicated to a number of authorities. Since 1959, a system based on relationships of contractual nature between the State and private educational institutions has been established,[539] which was later amended a number of times in order to allow the public financing of these institutions. Although all private educational institutions are under the control of the State, this particular system of contractual relationships enables the State to exercise an extended control over the administration, pedagogy and finance of such institutions. The modalities of this control depend on whether the private educational institution is bound to the State by a simple contract – which is only available at primary level (or for specialized institutions) – or by a contract of association – which may concern primary schools and apply to secondary schools.

C. Collective Freedoms

500. While the 1789 Declaration recognized freedom of expression to the individual, freedom of collective expression finds its foundation in the laws of the Third Republic. Freedom of collective expression mainly concerns freedom of association, freedom of assembly, as well as the right to protest and the right to address petitions. In addition to these, the Constitutional Council has also given a constitutional status to the right of collective expression itself.[540]

536. CC Decision No 83-165 DC of 20 Jan. 1984, *Loi relative à l'enseignement supérieur*, *Rec.* 30 and CC Decision No 2010-20/21 QPC of 6 Aug. 2010, *M. Jean et autres [Loi Université]*, *Rec.* 203.
537. CC Decision No 7-87 DC of 23 Nov. 1977, *Loi complémentaire à la loi n° 59-1157 du 31 décembre 1959 modifiée par la loi n° 71-400 du 1er juin 1971 et relative à la liberté de l'enseignement*, *Rec.* 42.
538. Respectively, Art. L. 441-1 and Art. L. 441-5 Education Code.
539. Law No 59-1157 of 31 Dec. 1959 on the relationships between the State and private educational institutions.
540. CC Decision No 94-352 DC of 18 Jan. 1995, *Loi d'orientation et de programmation relative à la sécurité*, *Rec.* 170.

1. Freedom of Association

501. Freedom of association is laid down in the Law of 1 July 1901 (the 1901 Law).[541] This particular freedom has been regarded as a Fundamental Principle recognized by the Laws of the Republic since the 1971 Decision of the Constitutional Council in which was shaped the notion of block of constitutionality.[542] Under the 1901 Law, associations may be formed freely without requiring any prior authorization or declaration, except for a declaration to the prefecture (i.e., to the representative of the State in the department where the association will have its registered office) in order to acquire legal capacity.[543] This, in that respect, allows associations to bring proceedings before a court of law and receive donations. Associations can be recognized as being of public utility (*associations reconnues d'utilité publique*) by decree in the Council of State which entails a number of specific rights, such as the possibility of receiving gifts and bequests. This possibility is also recognized to another special type of associations, namely the associations of worship (*associations cultuelles*) created by the 1905 Law, which cannot receive public funding due to the separation of the Churches and State (*See* above). Associations can be dissolved by a court decision, notably if their cause or activities are illicit, or contrary to the laws and morality, or which would aim to undermine the integrity of the national territory and the republican form of the government.[544] In addition to judicial dissolution, an administrative dissolution can be pronounced by the government. Initially provided for by the Law of 10 January 1936 on Combat Groups and Private Militia, this power of dissolution is now included in the Code of Homeland Security.[545] In addition to combat groups and private militia, administrative dissolution also concerns associations that incite to discrimination or hatred on the basis of, among others, religion or origin, or associations that have terrorist activities. Administrative dissolution can also apply to sports associations, and in particular to groups of supporters (to fight against hooliganism).[546]

2. Freedom of Assembly, Right to Protest and Right to Address Petitions

a. Freedom of Assembly

502. The regime of freedom of assembly under French law also finds its origin in the legislation of the Third Republic.[547] As a liberal regime, it allows the public to freely gather without requiring any prior declaration or authorization. However, a number of conditions are posed, namely that assemblies cannot continue after 11 pm, that a committee of at least three persons has to be designated to ensure the smooth progress of the assembly, and that an administrative or judicial official can

541. Law of 1 Jul. 1901 on the contract of association (as amended).
542. CC Decision No 71-44 DC of 16 Jul. 1971, *Loi complétant les dispositions des articles 5 et 7 de la loi du 1er juillet 1901 relative au contrat d'association*, *Rec.* 25*.
543. Article 2 of the 1901 Law.
544. Article 3 of the 1901 Law.
545. Article L. 212-1 Code of Homeland Security.
546. Article L. 332-18 Code of Sport.
547. Law of 30 Jun. 1881 on freedom of assembly (as amended).

attend the gathering. Public authorities endowed with a power of administrative police can oppose public reunions to protect the public order. However, administrative courts may exercise a power of judicial review over such administrative decisions as regards whether they are appropriate, proportionate and justified in light of local circumstances.[548]

b. The Right to Protest

503. Until 2012, a decree-law provided for the law governing protests and demonstrations, until its incorporation into the Code of Homeland Security.[549] Demonstrations are submitted to a prior declaration to the town hall of the municipalities concerned[550] which should be made no less than three days and no more than fifteen days before the demonstration. By exception, demonstrations that are consistent with local practice do not require a declaration.[551] Demonstrations can be forbidden by public authorities for reason of public order. Such decisions, similarly to those in the context of freedom of assembly, may be judicially reviewed by administrative courts which apply the same principles as those used in relation to public assemblies. Demonstrations have to be distinguished from unlawful gatherings that are spontaneous and potentially endanger the public order. Unlawful gathering is sanctioned by criminal law.[552]

c. The Right to Address Petitions

504. Petitions correspond to a request which is addressed by an individual to a public authority with the view of making the authority exercise its competences in a specific manner. An Ordinance of 17 November 1958 provides for such a right as regards petitions addressed to Parliament.[553] Since 2003, Article 72-1 of the Constitution also permits to address petitions to local authorities and to ask for the inclusion on the agenda of their deliberative assembly of a matter of concern falling within their competence.

§3. ECONOMIC, SOCIAL AND CULTURAL RIGHTS

505. When compared with civil and political rights, the introduction of economic, social and cultural rights into French law is more recent. The importance of these rights depends on their status in the domestic constitutional order.

---

548. CE, 19 May 1933, *Benjamin*, *Rec. Lebon* 541.
549. Decree-Law of 23 Oct. 1935 regulating measures pertaining to the reinforcement of the safeguarding of public order, now included in the Code of Homeland Security (Arts L. 211-1 to L. 211-4).
550. In Paris, the declaration is made to the Police Prefecture.
551. Articles L. 211-1 et seq Code of Homeland Security, dealing with public manifestations.
552. Articles 431-3 to 431-12 Criminal Code, dealing with criminal participation in a protest, as well as illicit demonstrations and criminal participation in a public event or public meeting.
553. Ordinance No 58-1100 of 17 Nov. 1958 on the functioning of parliamentary assemblies (as amended).

I. The Constitutional Status of Economic, Social and Cultural Rights

506. At domestic level, the recognition of economic, social and cultural rights primarily proceeds from the Preamble to the 1946 Constitution, which is part of the block of constitutionality. In contrast with the liberal rights included in the 1789 Declaration, the Preamble to the 1946 Constitution is of social inspiration and lists in the category of the Principles of Laws Particularly Necessary to our Time a number of different economic and social rights, among which the principle of equality between men and women (paragraph 3), the right to asylum (paragraph 4), employment rights (paragraphs 5, 6, 7 and 8), the right to family life (paragraph 10), the right to health (paragraph 11), and the right to education (paragraph 13). These rights, such as the right to education, also pertain to political and civil rights. For the Constitutional Council, the 1789 Declaration and the Preamble to the 1946 Constitution have the same constitutional value. The latter instrument does not oppose but completes the former in that it merely and solemnly reaffirms the rights and freedoms enshrined on the 1789 Declaration and only tends to supplement them and allow their realization by the formulation of more modern principles.[554]

507. The particularity of economic, social and cultural rights lies in the measures to be taken by the State for their implementation. Their effectiveness is further guaranteed when the Constitutional Council is in a position to enforce their negative element and sanction the legislature for infringing on these rights. Their enforcement is more problematic when they require positive actions to be taken by Parliament. In any case, although the Constitutional Council is entrusted with exercising a review of the implementation of these rights, the Council does not have, following the now standard formulation, 'a general power of appreciation and decision that is identical to that of Parliament'.[555] The task of the Council is to ensure that the power of appreciation and decision of Parliament does not denature nor impair those constitutional rights, hereby primarily sanctioning manifest errors of appreciation. The recognition of cultural rights is more problematic under French law since these rights can be seen as a challenge to the indivisibility of the Republic that is affirmed in the First Article of the Constitution. This state of affairs has led to difficulties in relation to the recognition of collective rights at European level.[556] Today, the recognition of cultural rights has been introduced in the 'NOTRe' Law of 7 August 2015 on the New Territorial Organization of the Republic which specifies that 'the responsibility in the matter of culture is exercised jointly by the local authorities and the State in respect of the cultural rights set forth in the Convention on the Protection and Promotion of the Diversity of Cultural Expressions of 20 October 2005'.[557]

---

554. CC Decision No 81-132 DC of 16 Jan. 1982, *Loi de nationalisation*, *Rec.* 18, pt 15.
555. *See*, e.g., CC Decision No 74-54 DC of 15 Jan. 1975, *Loi relative à l'interruption volontaire de grossesse*, *Rec.* 19, pt 1*.
556. CC Decision No 2004-505 DC of 19 Nov. 2004, *Traité établissant une Constitution pour l'Europe*, *Rec.* 173, pt 16*.
557. Law No 2015-991 of 7 Aug. 2015 on the new territorial organization of the Republic, or the 'NOTRe' Law as in '*Nouvelle Organisation Territoriale de la République*' (Art. 103).

II. The Implementation of Economic, Social and Cultural Rights

508. Specific developments about the implementation of economic, social and cultural rights in French law concern the right to property, employment rights, the right to asylum, and rights relating to family life, health and housing.

A. *The Right to Property*

509. The right to property is the basis of economic rights. It is mentioned twice in the 1789 Declaration, in Articles 2 and 17 respectively. Despite being a right of constitutional value,[558] it is not an absolute right and can be limited in light of the public interest as expressed, for example, in the ninth paragraph of the Preamble to the 1946 Constitution which affirms the common property of public services and de facto monopolies. Any limitation to the right of property for reasons of public interest has to be proportionate to the objective pursued,[559] and, if such limitation entails a deprivation of property, fair compensation must be made to the aggrieved party prior to the deprivation thereof.[560]

B. *Employment Rights*

510. The right to employment is enshrined in the Preamble to the 1946 Constitution as well as the right to participate in the determination of one's working conditions and management of the workplace, the right to strike and the right to form trade unions. The Constitutional Council has expressly recognized the constitutional value of the right to employment on the basis of the fifth paragraph of the Preamble to the 1946 Constitution. The reduction by the legislature of the maximum weekly working hours (the thirty-five hours) could be justified in order to protect this right on that basis.[561] The right to form trade unions has been recognized by the Waldeck-Rousseau Law of 21 March 1884 which was later elevated to constitutional status by virtue of its inclusion in the sixth paragraph of the Preamble to the 1946 Constitution.[562] Trade unions are considered as having a 'natural vocation to defend, in particular through collective bargaining, the rights and interests of workers',[563] and, as a matter of principle, workers cannot be subject to discrimination on the ground of their membership to a union. Likewise, the right to strike is of constitutional value as enshrined in the seventh paragraph of the Preamble to the

558. CC Decision No 81-132 DC of 16 Jan. 1982, *Loi de nationalisation*, *Rec.* 18, pt 16.
559. CC Decision No 2010-60 QPC of 12 Nov. 2010, *M. Pierre B. [Mur mitoyen]*, *Rec.* 321, pt 3.
560. CC Decision No 81-132 DC of 16 Jan. 1982, *Loi de nationalisation*, *Rec.* 18, pt 44.
561. CC Decision No 98-401 DC of 10 Jun. 1998, *Loi d'orientation et d'incitation relative à la réduction du temps de travail*, *Rec.* 258, pts 24-29.
562. CC Decision No 89-257 DC of 25 Jul. 1989, *Loi modifiant le code du travail et relative à la prévention du licenciement économique et au droit à la conversion*, *Rec.* 59, pt 10.
563. CC Decision No 96-383 DC of 6 Nov. 1996, *Loi relative à l'information et à la consultation des salariés dans les entreprises et les groupes d'entreprises de dimension communautaire, ainsi qu'au développement de la négociation collective*, *Rec.* 128, pt 8.

1946 Constitution.[564] Nonetheless, this paragraph also mentions the competence of Parliament to regulate this right. In particular, it can be limited to take into account other principles of constitutional value, such as the continuity of the public service since 'where public services are concerned, recognising the right to strike should not result in precluding Parliament from determining the necessary limits of such a right in order to ensure the continuity of public service which, like the right to strike, is a principle of constitutional status'.[565] Lastly, the eighth paragraph of the Preamble to the 1946 Constitution recognizes the right of workers to participate, through their representatives, in the determination of their working conditions and in the management of their workplace.

C. The Right to Asylum

511. The right to asylum, which is mentioned in the fourth paragraph of the Preamble to the 1946 Constitution, has been recognized as being of constitutional value in 1980.[566] In 1993, the Constitutional Council interpreted this provision as making mandatory for administrative and judicial authorities to examine asylum requests,[567] which resulted in a constitutional amendment whereby Article 53-1 of the Constitution defines asylum as a right of the State – which may *grant* asylum – rather than a right of aliens – who may *claim* asylum. Nonetheless, the Constitutional Council has maintained the prevalence of its interpretation of the Preamble to the 1946 Constitution over this constitutional provision by affirming that 'the legislature must at all times secure the legal guarantees' included in the fourth paragraph of the Preamble to the 1946 Constitution.[568] The domestic legal regime of asylum has been amended a number of times, notably to take into account a number of imperatives stemming from the immigration policy of the successive governments, from the recognition of a right to territorial asylum in 1998,[569] later replaced

564. CC Decision No 79-105 DC of 25 Jul. 1979, *Loi modifiant les dispositions de la loi n° 74-696 du 7 août 1974 relatives à la continuité du service public de la radio et de la télévision en cas de cessation concertée du travail*, *Rec.* 33, pt 1.

565. *See*, e.g., CC Decision No 2007-556 DC of 16 Aug. 2007, *Loi sur le dialogue social et la continuité du service public dans les transports terrestres réguliers de voyageurs*, *Rec.* 319, pt 10*.

566. CC Decision No 79-109 DC of 9 Jan. 1980, *Loi relative à la prévention de l'immigration clandestine et portant modification de l'ordonnance n° 45-2658 du 2 novembre 1945 relative aux conditions d'entrée et de séjour en France des étrangers et portant création de l'office national d'immigration*, *Rec.* 29, pt .1. The right to asylum is also recognized in international (i.e., 1948 Universal Declaration of Human Rights, 1951 Geneva Convention, as amended in 1967) and European (i.e., EU Charter of Fundamental Rights) texts. *See also* below Chapter 5. Status and Rights of Foreigners.

567. CC Decision No 93-325 DC of 13 Aug. 1993, *Loi relative à la maîtrise de l'immigration et aux conditions d'entrée, d'accueil et de séjour des étrangers en France*, *Rec.* 224, pt 4*.

568. CC Decision No 97-389 DC of 22 Apr. 1997, *Loi portant diverses dispositions relatives à l'immigration*, *Rec.* 45, pt 25*; CC Decision No 2003-485 DC of 4 Dec. 2003, *Loi modifiant la loi n° 52-893 du 25 juillet 1952 relative au droit d'asile*, *Rec.* 455, pt 2.

569. Law No 98-349 of 11 May 1998 on the entry and residence of foreigners in France and the right to asylum.

by the subsidiary protection,[570] to the last upheaval in 2015. The current regime aims at improving the situation of individuals in need of international protection, on the one hand, and at better fighting against ill-founded claims to asylum from migrants who misuse this right, on the other hand.[571]

D. Rights to Family Life, Health and Housing

512. The Preamble to the 1946 Constitution affirms, in its tenth paragraph, that '[t]he Nation shall provide the individual and the family with the conditions that are necessary to their development', while its eleventh paragraph adds that the Nation 'shall guarantee to all, notably to children, mothers and elderly workers, protection of their health, material security, rest and leisure'. From these provisions, and their combination, the Constitutional Council has deduced a number of rights in relation to family life, health and housing with paying due respect, however, to the margin of appreciation of the legislature in these areas. In that respect, the right to health, as recognized on the basis of the eleventh paragraph of the Preamble to the 1946 Constitution,[572] may be limited due to objectives of constitutional value related to public finances.[573] In relation to the right to family life, the Constitutional Council has recognized that the tenth and eleventh paragraphs of the Preamble to the 1946 Constitution require implementing a policy of national solidarity in favour of the family.[574] The right to family life has also implications as regards immigration since it entails a right to family reunification.[575] It is also on the basis of the tenth paragraph of the Preamble to the 1946 Constitution that the Constitutional Council has affirmed that an adoption must be compatible with the child's best interests.[576] From the combination of the tenth and eleventh paragraphs of the Preamble to the 1946 Constitution, as well as the recognition of human dignity as a principle of constitutional value, the Constitutional Council has ruled that the possibility for any individual to have decent housing is an objective of constitutional value,[577] with the legislature emphasizing, on a number of occasions, the fundamental nature of the right to housing.[578] However, an increased consideration has been recently given to

570. Law No 2003-1176 of 10 Dec. 2003 modifying Law No 52-893 of 25 Jul. 1952 on the right to asylum.
571. Law No 2015-925 of 29 Jul. 2015 on the reform of the right to asylum.
572. CC Decision No 90-283 DC of 8 Jan. 1991, *Loi relative à la lutte contre le tabagisme et l'alcoolisme*, *Rec.* 11, pt 2.
573. CC Decision No 2002-463 DC of 12 Dec. 2002, *Loi de financement de la sécurité sociale pour 2003*, *Rec.* 540, pt 18.
574. CC Decision No 98-405 DC of 29 Dec. 1998, *Loi de finances pour 1999*, *Rec.* 326, pt 12.
575. CC Decision No 93-325 DC of 13 Aug. 1993, *Loi relative à la maîtrise de l'immigration et aux conditions d'entrée, d'accueil et de séjour des étrangers en France*, *Rec.* 224, pt 70*. *See also* below Chapter 5. Status and Rights of Foreigners.
576. CC Decision No 2013-669 DC of 17 May 2013, *Loi ouvrant le mariage aux couples de personnes de même sexe*, *Rec.* 721, pt 46*.
577. CC Decision No 94-359 DC of 19 Jan. 1995, *Loi relative à la diversité de l'habitat*, *Rec.* 176, pt 7.
578. *See*, e.g., Law No 82-526 of 22 Jun. 1982 on the rights and obligations of tenants and landlords.

the effectiveness of this right in, for instance, the Law of 5 March 2007 which introduced an 'enforceable right to housing' to the benefit of disadvantaged people.[579] Similarly, in 2009, a right to emergency accommodation was introduced in French law in favour of homeless people in a situation of medical, mental and social distress.[580]

579. Law No 2007-290 of 5 Mar. 2007 instituting the enforceable right to housing and concerning miscellaneous measures in favour of social cohesion.
580. Law No 2009-323 of 25 Mar. 2009 of mobilization for housing and fight against exclusion.

Chapter 3. Constitutional Problems of Minorities

513. The question of the protection of minorities and group rights is closely linked to the principle of equality. The particular understanding of this principle under French law has impaired the express recognition of minorities' rights. Nonetheless, the requirement of differentiation, even if limited, has gained an increasing importance in domestic constitutional law.

§1. The Principle of Equality

514. The domestic approach to equality constitutes the framework within which minorities are protected and the extent to which their rights are limited.

I. The Constitutional Principle

515. The fundamental principle of equality was first recognized by the Constitutional Council in 1973 on the basis of the 1789 Declaration[581] which, under its First Article, affirms that '[m]en are born and remain free and equal in rights'. In that respect, equality underlies all the provisions of the 1789 Declaration and is also mentioned in its Articles 6 and 13. Article 6 indicates that the law 'must be the same for all, whether it protects or it punishes' and specifies that all citizens are equal in its eyes, while Article 13 concerns equality before public charges. The 1789 Declaration displays a formal understanding of the principle equality whereby citizens are constructed as abstract entities. It follows an impossibility to acknowledge any differences among categories of citizens as emphasized under its Article 6. The Constitution reflects the same conception as under its First Article, France 'shall ensure equality of all citizens under the law without discrimination based on origin, race or religion'. As a result, the State is under the duty 'to show indifference to differences'. One example concerns equality in relation to public employment whereby civil servant can be appointed only according to their capacities, virtues and talents.[582] The principle of equality extends beyond citizens and also concerns foreigners. The Constitutional Council has developed, in that respect, a constitutional status of foreigners where equality is the principle. Respect for fundamental rights and liberties applies to all residents on the territory of the Republic and differences concerning foreigners can only be justified on the basis of the constitutional objective of preserving the public order.[583] In contrast, the Preamble to the 1946 Constitution arguably offers an alternative approach to equality since it refers to a substantive definition of this principle whereby social differences must be taken into account in order to ensure an effective equality among citizens. Thus, it states the

581. CC Decision No 73-51 DC of 27 Dec. 1973, *Loi de finances pour 1974*, *Rec.* 25.
582. CC Decision No 82-153 DC of 14 Jan. 1983, *Loi relative au statut général des fonctionnaires*, *Rec.* 35.
583. CC Decision No 93-325 DC of 13 Aug. 1993, *Loi relative à la maîtrise de l'immigration et aux conditions d'entrée, d'accueil et de séjour des étrangers en France*, *Rec.* 224*.

principle of equality between men and women (second paragraph) and among workers (fifth paragraph) in particular, as well as the protection of health, material security, rest and leisure which is guaranteed 'to all, notably to children, mothers and elderly workers' (eleventh paragraph).

II. The Absence of Recognition of Group Rights

516. The formal conception of equality is linked to two other constitutional principles, namely the indivisibility of the Republic and the unity of the French people (*See also* Part III The State and its Subdivisions). Together, they oppose any segmentation of society. While the First Article of the Constitution ensures that all citizens are equal without distinction of origin, race or religion, it also states that 'France is an indivisible (…) Republic.' Similarly, Article 3 proclaims that '[t]he national sovereignty belongs to the people who shall exercise it through their representatives or by way of referendum (paragraph one). No fraction of the people or any individual may arrogate to themselves the right to exercise [that sovereignty] (paragraph two)'. Thus, equality involves the indifference and neutrality of the State towards social diversity which is circumscribed to the private sphere.

517. The case law of the Constitutional Council reflects the systemic relationship between formal equality, one the one hand, and the indivisibility of the Republic and the unity of the French people, on the other hand. Hence, the Constitutional Council has found repugnant to the Constitution the legislative reference to 'the Corsican people, a component of the French people' since, in its words, 'the legal concept of "the French people" is of constitutional status' and 'the Constitution recognizes only the French people, made up of all French citizens regardless of origin, race or religion'.[584] Similarly, the Constitutional Council has considered that the 1992 European Charter for Regional or Minority Languages was incompatible with the Constitution – which prevented its ratification by France – since the recognition of group rights on the basis of culture, language or belief is contrary to the principles above-mentioned, namely equality, indivisibility of the Republic and unity of the French people.[585] In conclusion, the formal conception of equality, as informed by the principles of indivisibility of the Republic and unity of the French people, prevents, in principle, the positive recognition of minorities. As ruled by the Constitutional Council, 'Articles 1 to 3 of the Constitution (…) proscribe any recognition of collective rights of any group defined by origin, culture, language or beliefs.'[586]

---

584. CC Decision No 91-290 DC of 9 May 1991, *Loi portant statut de la collectivité territoriale de Corse*, *Rec.* 50*.
585. CC Decision No 99-412 DC of 15 Jun. 1999, *Charte européenne des langues régionales ou minoritaires*, *Rec.* 71*.
586. CC Decision No 2004-505 DC of 19 Nov. 2004, *Traité établissant une Constitution pour l'Europe*, *Rec.* 173*.

§2. Minorities and the French Approach to Equality

518. Given the formal understanding of equality under French law, the protection of minorities is primarily realized in a negative manner. Nonetheless, acknowledgements of differences as such have recently emerged in domestic law.

I. Equality and the Protection of Minorities

519. Formal equality as a guarantee of the indivisibility of the Republic and of the unity of the French people entails the prohibition of discrimination. When French law allows for a limited acknowledgement of social differences, substantive equality is perceived as a means to achieve formal equality.

A. The Protection Against Discrimination

520. Formal equality protects minorities through the principle of non-discrimination. This principle of non-discrimination is notably affirmed by Article 225-1 of the Criminal Code and Article L. 1132-1 of the Labour Code. In both instances, the prohibition of discrimination covers an extensive range of criteria including origins, sex, family status, pregnancy, physical appearance, surname, place of residence, health, disabilities, genetic characteristics, sexual orientation, age, political opinions, union activities, membership of an ethnic group, people or religion. In 2004, an independent administrative authority, the High Authority of Fight against Discriminations and for Equality (*Haute Autorité de Lutte contre les Discriminations et pour l'Egalité* or *HALDE*) was created.[587] Its missions encompassed the fight against discriminations prohibited by law, supporting victims of discrimination and promoting the principle of equality. Since 2008, its competences have been transferred to the Defender of Rights that has been created under Article 71-1 of the Constitution.

B. Substantive Equality Through the Recognition of Differences

521. Formal equality is not an absolute principle. The Constitutional Council has affirmed that this principle 'neither prevents the legislator from treating different situations in a different manner, nor from departing from the principle of equality for reasons of general interest, provided that in both cases the resulting difference of treatment is directly connected to the purpose of the statute establishing it'.[588] As a result, while the principle of equality commands similar situations to be treated in the same manner, it does not prevent different situations to be governed by different

587. Law No 2004-186 of 30 Dec. 2004 creating the high authority of fight against discriminations and for equality.
588. CC Decision No 87-232 DC of 7 Jan. 1988, *Loi relative à la mutualisation de la Caisse nationale de crédit agricole*, *Rec.* 17.

rules. However, treating different situations differently is not an obligation, what can lead the French understanding of equality to be at odds with EU law.[589]

522. The recognition of social differences, in contrast with the prevalent abstract representation of citizens, can be made to take into account obstacles to the effectiveness of the principle of equality. Often seen as temporary measures to compensate differences, mechanisms of substantive equality participate in promoting formal equality. The legal regime applicable to disabled people is an example of this implementation of substantive equality. According to a Law of 2005,[590] French law affirms their right to compensation for the consequences of their disability.[591] Similarly, the Constitutional Council has recognized that differentiated measures in order to support the employment of youth represented a constitutionally valid instance of the possibility for the legislative power 'to come to the assistance of categories of disadvantaged people'.[592] The third paragraph of the Preamble of 1946 affirms the equality between men and women. The affirmation of a substantive conception of equality participates in the promotion of women's rights. It has enabled the dismantling of inequalities generated by the legal system itself. For instance, in 1965, legislation put an end to the legal incapacity of married women, and to the impossibility for them to have an employment and open a bank account without the authorization of their husband.[593] Since the reforms of 1970 and 1985, married women have equal rights as regards parental authority as well as the management of family property.[594] Substantive equality also requires to take into consideration and to remediate concrete differences so that men and women can be placed on an equal footing. This notably applies in the professional field. The prohibition of discriminations on the basis of sex in the private sector was introduced in 1983.[595] In the public sector, the equality between men and women was established by case law,[596] and reaffirmed by legislation.[597] Legislative instruments have also aimed at establishing equal remuneration between men and women.[598]

589. CE, Ass., 8 Feb. 2007, *Société Arcelor Atlantique et Lorraine et autres*, *Rec. Lebon* 56; ECJ, C-127/07 *Société Arcelor Atlantique et Lorraine and others v. Premier ministre and others* (16 Dec. 2008), [2008] ECR I-9895.
590. Law No 2005-102 of 11 Feb. 2005 for the equality of rights and opportunities, the participation and the civic rights of disabled people.
591. Article L. 114-1-1 Code of Social Action and of Families.
592. CC Decision No 2006-535 DC of 30 Mar. 2006, *Loi pour l'égalité des chances*, *Rec.* 50.
593. Law No 65-570 of 13 Jul. 1965 reforming matrimonial regimes.
594. Law No 70-459 of 4 Jun. 1970 on parental authority; Law No 85-1372 of 23 Dec. 1985 on the equality of spouses in matrimonial regimes and of parents in the management of the goods of minor children.
595. Law No 83-635 of 13 Jul. 1983 modifying the Labour Code and the Criminal Code as regards the professional equality between women and men.
596. CE, Ass., 3 Jul. 1936, *Damoiselle Bobard et autres*, *Rec. Lebon* 721.
597. Law No 83-634 of 13 Jul. 1983 concerning rights and obligation of civil servants.
598. *See*, e.g., Law No 2006-340 of 23 Mar. 2006 on the equal pay between women and men.

II. Equality and the Limited Recognition of Social Differences

523. Despite the prevalence of a formal conception of equality and the refusal to recognize collective rights, French law has recently seen the emergence of mechanisms of affirmative action. This could be the sign of an attenuation of the principles of indivisibility of the Republic and of unity of the French people.

A. Gender Equality

524. While the right to vote was granted to women in 1944, national and local representatives are (still) overwhelmingly men. The first attempt to remediate this situation was made in 1982 by attempting to ensure that 25% of candidates for municipal elections would be women. The Constitutional Council, in accordance with its traditional formal understanding of the principle of equality, relying on Article 6 of the 1789 Declaration and Article 3 of the Constitution, considered that 'any division of persons entitled to vote and stand for election into separate categories' was repugnant to the Constitution.[599] The Council reiterated this position in 1999 as regards a new attempt to introduce gender equality in the electoral system.[600] This decision led to an amendment to the Constitution. The provision that is now included in the First Article of the Constitution affirms that 'law shall promote equal access by women and men to electoral mandates and elective functions, as well as equal access to professional and social responsibilities', while Article 4 mentions that political parties contribute to the implementation of this principle. These modifications to the Constitution allowed the legislative implementation of gender equality as regards political elections.[601] In elections using the list system, the lists must have the same number of male and female candidates, with a maximum difference of one, and these candidates must be alternatively a male and a female. In single-member constituency elections, gender equality is promoted through a financial incentive of political parties. A law of 2013 has deepened this requirement as regards elections of departmental councillors.[602] From 2015 onwards, elections will concern pairs of candidates of different gender.

525. When compared to other forms of recognition of social differences, the question of gender equality has created more difficulties. In relation to representation, this can be explained by the conflict with Article 3 of the Constitution that

599. CC Decision No 82-146 DC of 18 Nov. 1982, *Loi modifiant le code électoral et le code des communes et relative à l'élection des conseillers municipaux et aux conditions d'inscription des Français établis hors de France sur les listes électorales ('Quotas par sexe'), Rec.* 22*.
600. CC Decision No 98-407 DC of 14 Jan. 1999, *Loi relative au mode d'élection des conseillers régionaux et des conseillers à l'Assemblée de Corse et au fonctionnement des Conseils régionaux, Rec.* 21.
601. Law No 2000-493 of 6 Jun. 2000 promoting equal access of women and men to electoral mandates and elective offices.
602. Law No 2013-403 of 17 May 2013 on the election of departmental councillors, municipal councillors, and community councillors, and modifying the electoral calendar.

affirms that '[n]o fraction of the people or any individual may arrogate to themselves the right to exercise' of sovereignty. However, these difficulties may have also originated in the different logic introduced by gender equality in the political field when compared to other forms of recognition of differences in the French legal order. The question of the gender equality may not only be limited to a temporary consideration being given to substantive equality, and its disruption, as a means to achieve formal equality. In contrast, gender equality could be seen as a requirement to recognize diversity as such. It reflects a representation of the social fabric that differs from the unity of the French people and the indifference to social distinctions that is traditionally proclaimed by French law. A second constitutional amendment supports this latter interpretation. Since 2008, the requirement of gender equality has exceeded the boundaries of the political realm. The First Article of the Constitution proclaims that the law must also promote equal access of women and men to 'professional and social responsibilities'. Different laws have contributed to the implementation of this new constitutional objective. For instance, in the private sector, the Law of 2011 on the balanced representation of women and men in administration and supervisory boards has promoted professional equality,[603] while another law adopted in 2012 has ensured the implementation of the same principle in the senior public service.[604] Eventually, a law of 2014 has aimed at broadening this concern and offering a holistic approach to gender equality of women and men.[605]

B. *The Constitutional Development of Differentiation*

526. While French law enforces some form of affirmative action, this does not amount to the recognition of group rights. In particular, differences that can be recognized are not based on ethnocultural specificities. In this regard, the case law of the Constitutional Council has restrained the possibility of identifying such minorities and thus of implementing specific legal measures. It has explicitly considered that studies concerning the diversity of people's origins, discrimination and integration can be based on objective data, such as surnames, the geographical origins or nationalities. Nonetheless, the collection of data as regards ethnicity or race would be contrary to the First Article of the Constitution that affirms the indivisibility of the Republic and 'equality of all citizens under the law without distinction of origin, race or religion'.[606]

603. Law No 2011-103 of 27 Jan. 2011 on the balanced representation of women and men in administration and supervisory boards and on professional equality (as amended).
604. Law No 2012-347 of 12 Mar. 2012 on the access to tenured employment and the improvement of the employment conditions of contractual agents in the public service, to the fight against discrimination and containing miscellaneous provisions pertaining to public service (as amended).
605. Law No 2014-873 of 4 Aug. 2014 for the substantive equality between women and men.
606. CC Decision No 2007-557 of 15 Nov. 2007, *Loi relative à la maîtrise de l'immigration, à l'intégration et à l'asile*, *Rec.* 360*.

527. By exception to the indivisibility of the Republic, however, the recognition of cultural differences can proceed from territorial specificities. First, the departments of *Haut-Rhin*, *Bas-Rhin* and *Moselle*, which were German territories from 1871 to 1919, have retained some legal specificities, as regards the separation of the Churches and State in particular (*See* below Part V Specific Issues). For the Constitutional Council, this local particularism is a Fundamental Principle recognized by the Laws of the Republic.[607] More generally, the French Republic has developed as a unitary State, in opposition to local particularisms (*See* above Part III The State and its Subdivisions). However, since 2003, the First Article of the Constitution states that '[i]ts organization is decentralized'. The Constitution was also amended so that local authorities may benefit from experimental powers in legislative and regulatory matters (Article 72 Constitution). Prior to the constitutional recognition of the decentralized organization of the Republic, the Constitutional Council considered that the attribution of experimental powers was repugnant to Article 3 of the Constitution.[608] These new powers granted to local authorities can thus be seen as a mitigation of the indivisibility of the Republic in light of local specificities. The status of regional languages reflects the same dynamics. The Constitutional Council considered that, by providing for collective rights and by being contrary to its Article 2 that affirms that '[t]he language of the Republic is French', the European Charter for Regional or Minority Languages was incompatible with the Constitution.[609] However, despite this constitutional requirement of linguistic unity, Article 75-1, which was introduced in 2008, affirms that '[r]egional languages belong to the heritage of France'. The recognition of local specificities is even more affirmed in relation to overseas territories. While unity is still the rule, the French Republic 'shall recognize, as part of the French people, the overseas populations'. (Article 72-3 paragraph one Constitution). On this basis, derogations in light of local specificities have been gradually acknowledged. In overseas departments and regions, the principle is the application of the law of the Republic. However, derogations may be permitted to take their specificities into account, except in the island of the Réunion (Article 73 third paragraph Constitution). As for overseas local authorities, derogations in order to reflect their specificities are of principle (Article 74 Constitution). Moreover, the same constitutional provision provides for the autonomous status of some of these overseas local authorities and the extension of their derogatory status. The derogatory regime of New Caledonia, which is provided for by Title XIII of the Constitution, is even greater. Its most emblematic feature is the possibility of adopting the so-called laws of the land (*lois du pays*) on various matters as provided for by Article 99 et seq. of the Organic Law of 1999 (Article 77 Constitution).[610] This constitutes a constitutional transfer of legislative competence. Since 2004, French Polynesia, an overseas territory, can also pass laws of the land albeit

607. CC Decision No 2011-157 QPC of 5 Aug. 2011, *Société SOMODIA [Interdiction du travail le dimanche en Alsace-Moselle]*, *Rec.* 430.

608. CC Decision No 2001-454 of 17 Jan. 2002, *Loi relative à la Corse*, *Rec.* 70.

609. CC Decision No 99-412 DC of 15 Jun. 1999, *Charte européenne des langues régionales ou minoritaires*, *Rec.* 71*.

610. Organic Law No 99-209 of 19 Mar. 1999 on New Caledonia (as amended).

of a different nature from the ones concerning New Caledonia.[611] As acts of an administrative nature, the laws of the land of French Polynesia are subject to judicial review by the Council of State, rather than by the Constitutional Council as in the case of the laws of the land of New Caledonia.

611. Organic Law No 2004-193 of 27 Feb. 2004 completing the autonomous status of French Polynesia (as amended).

Chapter 4. Judicial Control of Administrative Action

528. After some general considerations, the independence of the administrative judge and the mechanism of judicial review will be examined.

§1. Introduction

529. The control of administrative action is in principle vested in an administrative judge who provides guarantees of independence in relation to the administration. Judicial review of administrative action has been beyond the reach of the ordinary courts since the 1789 Revolution due to the separation of executive and judicial powers. The Law of 16–24 August 1790 had the effect of removing administrative action from the remit of the ordinary judicial order, in as much as, according to a standard formula, 'to judge the administration is still to administer'. Article 13 of the 1790 Law thus established that: 'Judicial functions are distinct and will always remain separate from administrative functions. Judges may not, on pain of forfeiture, disturb, in any manner whatsoever, the actions of the administrative body, nor may they summon administrators before them for reasons of their duties.' This text was confirmed five years later by the Decree of 16 Fructidor Year III (2 September 1795).

530. While the prohibition of judicial review of administrative acts by the ordinary courts has an express textual basis, the possibility of review by an administrative judge results, in contrast, from a more empirical construction. During the Consulate, Napoleon Bonaparte established in the Constitution of the year VIII (13 December 1799) a so-called Council of State whose function was to work with the Executive. Article 75 of the 1799 Constitution stipulated in this regard that '[g]overnment agents, other than ministers, may be prosecuted for acts relating to their duties, only by virtue of a decision of the Council of State: in this case, the matter proceeds in the ordinary courts'. Therefore, the Council of State originally assumed the role of a filter in the initiation of legal proceedings against a government official. It is precisely this modest role that allowed the Council of State to develop judicial review of the acts of the administration. The Decree of 11 June 1806 established a complaints commission within the Council of State, which is now regarded as the first embryo of a truly specialized administrative court. At that time, the Council was not yet independent of the Executive and the Council was regarded as exercising a so-called justice retained (*justice retenue*), meaning a justice rendered under the supervision of the minister as head of the administration. The minister then exercised his/her review over the decisions of the Council of State under what was called the 'minister-judge theory'. Furthermore, the decisions of the Council of State would only become enforceable after being signed by the Head of State.

531. It was only with the renewal brought about by the Third Republic after the defeat of France against Prussia in 1870, and the subsequent fall of the Second Napoleonic Empire, that guarantees of independence were recognized to administrative courts. Article 9 of the Law of 24 May 1872 first recognized the sovereignty of the Council of State under the following terms: 'The Council of State rules independently on appeals in contentious administrative matters, and in proceedings for annulment in relation to the acts of the administrative authorities on grounds of excessive powers [ultra vires]'. The competence of the executive power in terms of granting enforceability to decisions of the Council of State thereby disappeared from then on. The Council of State went onto to develop its case law so as to deny the minister's jurisdiction over administrative disputes put before him. In particular, in the *Cadot* ruling of 13 December 1889,[612] the Council claimed that it had jurisdiction over administrative disputes and, in so doing, definitely stripped of the minister of his/her office as judge – thereby marking the end of the 'minister-judge theory'. Such development has been described as the transition from a system of 'justice retained' (*justice retenue*) to a system of 'delegated justice' (*justice déléguée*), since what was at stake, at the time, was precisely the development of the independence of the administrative judicial order. This independence vis-à-vis the administration and the Executive was subsequently entrenched at constitutional level, as was the extent of the jurisdiction of administrative courts.

§2. The Independence of the Administrative Judge

532. Guaranteeing the existence of an actual court in charge of administrative litigation requires protecting not only its independence vis-à-vis the executive power but also its sphere of competence.

I. Constitutionally Guaranteed Independence

533. The Constitution expressly guarantees the independence of ordinary courts (Article 64 Constitution). By contrast, the independence of the administrative judge was constitutionally established through a decision of the Constitutional Council. In its decision of 22 July 1980, the Council identified a Fundamental Principle recognized by the Laws of the Republic based on the aforementioned Law of 24 May 1872 in the following terms: '[It] follows from the provisions of Article 64 of the Constitution with regard to the judiciary and from the Fundamental Principles recognized by the Laws of the Republic in relation to, since the Law of 24 May 1872, the administrative judicial order, that the independence of the judiciary is guaranteed as is the specific nature of their functions upon which neither the Parliament nor the government may encroach.' [613] The decision of the Constitutional Council had the effect of barring the legislature and the executive power from any interference in the functions of the administrative judge and thus in any judicial review of administrative acts.

---

612. CE, 13 Dec. 1889, *Cadot*, *Rec. Lebon*. 1148.
613. CC Decision No 80-119 DC of 22 Jul. 1980, *Loi portant validation d'actes administratifs*, *Rec*. 46, pt 6.

II. Constitutionally Guaranteed Jurisdiction

534. Entrenching the jurisdiction of the administrative courts in the French judicial order was regarded as important as recognizing and entrenching its existence. Yet, the issue of its jurisdiction has raised, and still raises, vibrant doctrinal discussions and interesting judicial developments. The issue of the administrative judge's jurisdiction (i.e., the issue of the rule of competence of the administrative judge's) refers to the distinction, in French law, between civil law stricto sensu, as a branch of private law, and administrative law, as a branch of public law. Since the *Blanco* case of 8 February 1873,[614] the administrative judge has fleshed out an autonomous sphere of civil law. Like the criminal judge applies and develops criminal law, and the civil law judge applies and develop civil law, the extent of the jurisdiction of the administrative judge determines the sphere of application of administrative law – which does not prohibit the application of one type of law by the judge of the other judicial order and vice and versa (i.e., the ordinary courts applying standards of administrative law, and the administrative courts applying civil law standards). The delimitation of the administrative judge's jurisdiction therefore poses the issue of the criterion (of application) of administrative law: What are the acts subject to review by the administrative courts and which are governed by administrative law? This issue of the delimitation of the two spheres of law is not neutral since administrative law is, in principle, more protective of the public interest, which public authorities are supposed to protect, than civil private law which holds its subjects to equal rights.

535. Two historic schools of thought argued for opposite views on the issue in the late nineteenth and early twentieth century, namely the school of thought of Dean Maurice Hauriou (of the Faculty of Law of Toulouse), on the one hand, and the so-called school of 'the public service', on the other hand, the origin of which is attributed to Dean Léon Duguit (of the Faculty of Law of Bordeaux) and later supported by successors such as Professor Gaston Jèze. According to Dean Hauriou, the determining feature of the sphere of administrative law should be, putting it simply, that of the 'prerogative of public power' – in other words, only acts in relation to public order should be governed by administrative law which is protective of the interest thereof. The rest of public acts, which subsequently developed at the time, namely acts relating to public service that did not involve the exercise of any specific public power, or acts that did not present a regalian character, should remain in the sphere of civil law. On the contrary, according to the alternative school of thought centered on the notion of public service, all public law acts – in other words, those which aim at protecting the general public interest – should benefit from the application of a special law, namely administrative law. This dichotomy relates to the fundamental distinction between liberal and interventionist theories.

536. Without providing a definitive answer to these doctrinal questions, the Constitutional Council has opted to constitutionalize certain areas of competences of the administrative judge, leaving to the legislature the option to determine others. The

614. TC, 8 Feb. 1873, *Blanco*, *Rec. Lebon* 61.

somehow puzzling answer to the doctrinal issue is that administrative acts, which involve a number of multifaceted authorities, may be reviewed by either administrative courts, or ordinary courts. For instance, in its decision of 23 January 1987,[615] the Council held that the power to annul or review an act of the executive power taken in the exercise of its public powers was vested exclusively in the remit of the administrative courts. The Council regarded the French principle of the separation of powers as the constitutional legal basis for recognizing such competence of the administrative courts, thereby acknowledging the view proposed by Dean Hauriou. Alongside this 'hardcore' – in the words of Bruno Genevois, former Secretary-General of the Constitutional Council – competence of the administrative judge, and outside the matters belonging by nature to the ordinary courts (such as private property law and individual freedoms), the Council has left it to the legislature to determine other matters that could be assigned to the jurisdiction of administrative courts. The legislature has had therefore all latitude, as inspired by the 'public service' doctrine, to submit entire areas of non-regalian public activity to administrative law.

§3. Judicial Review

537. Under French administrative law,[616] an action for judicial review is lodged by means of an application or appeal on the ground of 'excess of power' referred to as *recours pour excès de pouvoir*. This remedy aims at reviewing acts of the administration in cases where a violation of the principle of legality is alleged. Non-observance of such principle may give rise to a violation of any one or more of the four grounds of review which the Council of State has developed doctrinally throughout the years, namely the lack of competence (*incompétence*), the infringement of an essential procedural requirement (*vice de forme*), the infringement of any rule of law (*violation de la loi*), and the misuse of power (*détournement de pouvoir*).

I. Appeal for Excessive Use of Power

538. The French administration is subject to judicial review by the administrative judge whether the administrative authority in question has acted by way of an administrative contract or by way of a unilateral administrative act. Judicial review, which aims at reviewing the conformity of an act of the Executive with the law or, when appropriate, with any norm of higher value – such as norms of EU law, international law, constitutional law, etc. – was first developed as a general principle of law before being entrenched as a constitutional principle.

---

615. CC Decision No 86-224 DC of 23 Jan. 1987, *Loi transférant à la juridiction judiciaire le contentieux des décisions du Conseil de la concurrence*, *Rec.* 8, pt 15.

616. For judicial constitutional review by the Constitutional Council, *see* above Part II. Form of Government, Chapter 5. The Judiciary, §2. Judicial Review.

A. *Constitutional Value of the Right to Appeal on Ground of Excessive Use of Power*

539. In its *Dame Lamotte* ruling,[617] the Council of State established the general principle of law according to which every administrative act may be subject, even without it being expressly providing for in a text, to judicial review on the ground that the act was ultra vires. This right of review is granted so as to provide for a general mechanism of protection whereby the legality of administrative acts can be reviewed and the effectiveness of the hierarchy of norms ensured. As regards acts of local authorities, judicial review is also provided for in the form of a 'prefectural application (or appeal)' (*déféré préfectoral*) whereby the prefect is entitled to review the acts which are transmitted to him/her by local authorities – in some cases on a mandatory basis – and to, when in doubt as to their legality, refer these acts to the administrative judge. The right of review against administrative acts is entrenched in constitutional texts and particularly in Article 16 of the 1789 Declaration relating to the guarantee of rights and the principle of the separation of powers. The Constitutional Council has ruled on the issue, and on the constitutional value of the right of review in particular, in the following terms: 'Article 16 of the 1789 Declaration reads "[a]ny society in which the guarantee of rights is not assured nor the separation of powers defined, has no Constitution" … it follows from that provision that as matter of principle there may be no substantial encroachment on the right of interested individuals to enjoy an effective remedy before the courts.'[618] This includes an action on the ground of ultra vires.

B. *Scope of the Right to Appeal on Ground of Excessive Use of Power*

1. Fair Trial

540. As in any court of law, guarantees of a fair trial under Article 6 paragraph one of the ECHR are applicable to administrative proceedings. The well-known dispute about the presence of the Public Rapporteur (*Rapporteur Public*), formerly called Government Commissioner (*Commissaire du Gouvernement*), in the deliberations of the administrative courts represents a vivid illustration thereof.[619] Proceedings against an administrative act must be brought before a court which presents guarantees of independence and impartiality, which is the case of the administrative court (*tribunal administratif*) acting as the ordinary Court of First Instance.[620] The first instance judgment is, as a matter of principle, susceptible of review before one of the administrative courts of appeal (*cour administrative*

617. CE, Ass., 17 Feb. 1950, *Ministre de l'Agriculture c. Dame Lamotte, Rec. Lebon* 110.
618. CC Decision No 96-373 DC of 9 Apr. 1996, *Loi organique portant statut d'autonomie de la Polynésie française, Rec.* 43, pt 83*.
619. *See* ECtHR, *Etienne v. France*, app. No 11396/08, 15 Sep. 2009.
620. The Council of State is exceptionally competent in the first instance as regards, for example, the review of regulatory acts of national scope such as the decrees of the President of the Republic or the decrees of the Prime Minister.

d'appel). The appeal decision may itself form the object of an appeal before the Council of State on points of law only. The administrative judge reviews the legality of the challenged administrative act by examining its 'external legality' (i.e., its formal validity in terms of its compliance with the enactment procedure, the competence of the authority which adopted the act, and the reasons on which the act is based), as well as its 'internal legality' (i.e., its substantial compliance with the law).

2. Annulment of an Administrative Act

541. The right of review is also, when the challenged administrative act is illegal, a right to obtain its annulment that is its retroactive repeal from the legal order. The 1925 *Rodière* case of the Council of State[621] ruled that the annulment of an administrative act meant its retroactive abrogation in order to ensure the effectiveness of the hierarchy norms since, indeed, an illegal act cannot have produced legal effects. However, if this principle remains in positive law, the Council of State also found that, as an exception (actually, less and less exceptional), the effective date of the annulment could be modulated in time by either giving it effect at the date of judgment or by postponing the effect at a later date in time.[622] This derogation from the principle of retroactivity must be justified by the excessively negative consequences for the public interest that such retroactivity would carry. In this case, the successful litigant obtains only partial satisfaction, since some effects of the illegal act will remain in force for a while.

3. Injunction and Penalty

542. Since the Law of 8 February 1995 on the organization of the courts and on civil, criminal, and administrative procedure,[623] the administrative judge has the power to order the administration to adopt an act to implement the decision made, if appropriate, under a penalty. It may entail an order requiring the administration to make a decision or, for example, to organize a new procedure such as a new examination or a new call for public tenders. The power conferred on the administrative judge ensures that the judgment s/he has taken will be acted upon, thereby addressing the concern of the effectiveness of the remedy.

621. CE, 26 Dec. 1925, *Rodière*, *Rec. Lebon* 1065.
622. CE, Ass., 11 May 2004, *Association AC! et autres*, *Rec. Lebon* 197.
623. Law No 95-125 of 8 Feb. 1995 on the organization of courts and on civil, criminal and administrative procedure.

II. Interlocutory Proceedings

543. The Law of 30 June 2000[624] established interlocutory proceedings before the administrative courts. These proceedings can be described as emergency or summary proceedings that litigants may use pending, where appropriate, a judgment on the merits. Three such proceedings exist in domestic law, namely 'a petition for an interim suspension (of the allegedly illegal act)' (*référé-suspension*), 'a petition for safeguard of fundamental liberties' (*référé-liberté*), and 'a petition for appropriate interlocutory measures' (*référé-mesures utiles*). The petition for an interim suspension[625] allows litigants to obtain, along with an application on grounds of excessive use of power, the suspension of the implementation of an administrative act pending the judgment on the merits. For such a remedy to be successful, two main conditions must be met: first, there must be an urgency justifying, without waiting for the trial court to decide on the case, the suspension of the application of the challenged administrative act; second, there must also be, in the eyes of the administrative judge, a serious doubt as to the legality of the challenged administrative act. The petition for safeguard of fundamental liberties[626] is of exceptional character and aims at protecting the litigant whose fundamental freedoms could be seriously infringed by the challenged administrative act. Three conditions must be met in this regard: first, a particularly characterized urgency requiring the judge to decide within forty-eight hours; second, that the contested administrative act is likely to seriously encroach onto the litigant's fundamental freedoms – these do not necessarily have to be constitutionally guaranteed and the administrative judge has a discretion to assess the character of the fundamental liberty at stake within the meaning of the law;[627] third, that the contested act is manifestly unlawful – this last condition being strictly assessed by the administrative judge since, unlike the petition for interim suspension, a simple doubt about the legality of the administrative act is not enough and it is necessary that its illegality is manifest in the eyes of the judge. Finally, as regards the petition for appropriate interlocutory measures, the law[628] provides that '[i]n case of urgency, and upon a simple application which would be deemed admissible even in the absence of a prior administrative act, the interlocutory judge may order any other appropriate measures without impeding the execution of any administrative decision'.

III. Administrative Responsibility

544. The appeal for excessive use of power is regarded as plainly effective if the illegality of the contested administrative act can, under certain conditions, engage the responsibility of the administration vis-à-vis the individual who suffered direct, certain, and personal harm from that illegal act. Since the 1973 *Sieur Driancourt*

624. Law No 2000-597 of 30 Jun. 2000 on interlocutory proceedings before administrative courts.
625. Article L. 521-1 Code of Administrative Justice.
626. Article L. 521-2 Code of Administrative Justice.
627. Article L. 521-2 Code of Administrative Justice.
628. Article L. 521-3 Code of Administrative Justice.

case,[629] the Council of State has regarded that an illegality of the administration is constitutive of a wrongdoing which may, where appropriate, incur liability. Several standard conditions of tort law must be met in this regard: besides the existence of the wrongful act, there must be a direct and certain causal link between the wrong and the damage caused by the administration; the damage must also constitute a compensable injury; and, last, the wrongdoing must be attributable to the public authority whose liability is sought.

629. CE, Sect., 26 Jan. 1973, *Ville de Paris c. Sieur Driancourt*, *Rec. Lebon* 77.

Chapter 5. Rights and Status of Foreigners

545. After some general considerations about domestic legislation regarding the principles and rules governing the status of foreigners, specific developments will examine the entry to the French territory, and the stay on the French territory, as well as the provisions on asylum, deportation and expulsion.

§1. Introduction

546. Domestic legislation regarding the principles and rules governing the status of foreigners was codified in 2004 in the Code on the Entry and Stay of Foreigners and Asylum Law (*Code de l'Entrée et du Séjour des Etrangers et du Droit d'Asile* or CESEDA).[630] Under the provisions of Article L. 111-1 of the CESEDA, 'individuals, who do not have French nationality, whether they have a foreign nationality or no nationality at all, are regarded as foreigners in the sense of this Code'. The status of foreigners in French law mainly results from ECHR law and EU law, including the Schengen Agreement originally signed on 14 June 1985, the 2003 'Dublin II' regulation as amended by the 'Dublin III' regulation,[631] plus from a number of bilateral agreements signed by France with other countries. A number of conventions of universal application also contribute to the development of the status of foreigners such as, for example, the Covenant on Civil and Political Rights of 16 December 1966, and the International Convention on Children's Rights of 20 November 1989. The importance of norms of international law should not, however, suggest an absence of constitutional norms relating to the rights of foreigners. Whether in relation to asylum law or to the principle of equality, constitutional principles govern many aspects of the status of foreigners, with regard to their entry into, or stay in, the French territory, as well as the conditions under which they might leave the territory.

§2. Entry into French Territory

547. As held by the Constitutional Council, 'no principle or rule of constitutional law guarantees to foreign nationals the enjoyment of general and absolute rights to enter into and stay in the national territory'.[632] The right to enter the French territory is variable depending on the circumstances of the case and on the individual concerned. The entry into the French territory is made freely or, as the case may be, requires government approval. According to the Schengen Agreement, all

630. This acronym will be used in the following paragraphs.
631. Regulation (EU) 604/2013 of the European Parliament and of the Council of 26 Jun. 2013 establishing the criteria and mechanisms for determining the Member State responsible for examining an application for international protection lodged in one of the Member States by a third-country national or a stateless person, OJ L 180/31-180/59, 29.6.2013.
632. CC Decision No 2006-539 DC of 20 Jul. 2006, *Loi relative à l'immigration et à l'intégration*, *Rec.* 79, pt 6.

nationals of an EU Member State can freely cross the border.[633] The same is true for nationals of the Member States of the EEA. However, outside of a number of bilateral agreements between France and a third State, entering the French territory requires a visa (i.e., an administrative authorization).

548. Under the general provisions for the entry into the French territory, Article L. 211-1 of the CESEDA provides that

> 'to enter France, a foreigner must present:
>
> 1. Any documents and visas required under international conventions and regulations;
> 2. Subject to international conventions, a proof of accommodation provided for in Article L. 211-3 of the CESEDA, if required, and any other documents provided for by decree in the Council of State relating, firstly, to the purpose and conditions of his/her stay and, secondly, where appropriate, to the covering of his/her livelihood, the covering by a licensed insurance provider of his/her medical and hospital expenses, including welfare for care expenses which may incur in France, as well as regards the guarantee of his/her repatriation;
> 3. Any documents required for the exercise of a professional activity if s/he intends to exercise one.'

549. There are several types of visas which depend on the type of stay intended by the foreign national:

(1) The 'airport visa' merely allows transit onto the French territory for a maximum duration of five days – which may be necessary, for example, to catch a connection in an airport.
(2) The short-stay visa called 'Schengen visa', which apply within the territories of all Member States of the Schengen area, is issued for a maximum period of ninety days. It may be granted for several reasons such as tourism, business, or visiting family, and allows travel throughout the Schengen area.
(3) The long-stay visa, under Article L. 211-2-1 of the CESEDA, allows access to the French territory for a period exceeding three months. It may be issued for various reasons such as plans to pursue further education, starting employment, or joining a French spouse. When such visa is issued to a student, it is tantamount to a residence permit covering the period of study. In other cases, it may require obtaining a residence permit on arrival in France.

550. Apart from the exceptions enumerated under Article L. 211-2 of the CESEDA, the administrative authorities do not have to give reasons for refusing to issue a visa. The circumstance of not holding a visa, or the circumstance of, even when

633. This is sought to be changed in light of the past events, notably the November 2015 Paris attacks and the refugee crisis.

in possession of a valid visa, constituting a threat to public order will result in a refusal to enter into the French territory or in the risk of being placed in a holding area.

§3. Stay in French Territory

551. Staying in the French territory is authorized by a residence permit (*titre de séjour*) which is evidenced by a residence card (*carte de séjour* or *carte de résident*). In addition to the conferred right to remain in the territory, such permit allows, under the application of the principle of equality between French nationals and foreigners, access to public services in particular – but not to the civil service.

I. The Residence Permit

552. After obtaining a long-stay visa, a temporary residence card may be issued to the foreign national. Before the reform initiated in 1993 and continued in 2003 and 2006, the ordinary residence permit for foreigners having personal and family ties in France was the residence permit valid for a ten-year period. Under current legislation, the ordinary residence permit is issued for a renewable period of one year, with special provisions to be applied in the case of family reunification.

A. The Temporary Residence Permit

553. According to Articles L. 313-1 et seq. of the CESEDA, the temporary residence permit (*carte de séjour temporaire* or *carte de résident temporaire*) is, in principle, for one year. It may be longer on request, particularly for students or foreigners with a 'scientific-researcher' temporary residence permit. The reason for the residence permit depends on the situation of the foreign national. First, such permit may be a 'visitor' temporary residence permit which, under Article L. 313-6 of the CESEDA, is issued to the 'foreigner who proves that s/he can live from his/her own resources and who undertakes to not engage in any occupation in France'.

554. Second, such permit may be marked 'student' which, under Article L. 313-7 of the CESEDA, is granted to 'a foreigner who establishes that s/he is following a programme of studies in France, or that s/he has been studying therein, and who proves that s/he has sufficient means of subsistence'. Such permit may also be granted by the administrative authority to a foreign national who regularly entered the French territory, in case of need related to his/her studies, or when the foreigner has been schooled uninterruptedly in France since the age of sixteen and pursues higher education, without the need to produce a visa of more than three months.[634]

634. Before 2016, Art. L. 311-7 CESEDA imposed a further condition, namely that [s]ubject to France's international commitments and the exceptions provided by the legislative provisions of this Code,

555. Third, Article L. 313-7-1 of the CESEDA provides for the issuance of specific residence permits marked '*stagiaire*' to foreigners who carry out a professional internship in France (i.e., an internship under a training contract approved by the competent administrative authority) and that, same as above, they have sufficient means of subsistence. In case of need related to the conduct of the course and subject to regular entry into France, the administrative authority may grant the residence permit.[635]

556. Fourth, the residence permit may be marked 'scientific researcher' for the foreign national conducting, as provided for under Article L. 313-8 of the CESEDA, 'research or providing university-level education in the context of a hosting agreement signed with a public or private organization with a research mission or higher education previously approved under the conditions defined by decree in the Council of State'.

557. The fifth possible residence permit is that marked 'artistic and cultural profession' which, under Article L. 313-9 of the CESEDA is issued to a 'performer' or to an author of an artistic or literary work.

558. Sixthly, under Article L. 313-10 of the CESEDA, a residence permit may be issued in a professional capacity for, but not limited to, a foreign national who has a contract of employment in France. The CESEDA provision indicates that it is '[f]or the exercise of paid employment in a trade and a geographic area characterized by recruitment difficulties and appearing on a list established nationally by the administrative authority (...); [for the exercise of] a commercial, industrial or craft profession, provided in particular that the foreign national proves an activity which is economically viable and consistent with safety, health, and public tranquillity, and that s/he meets the obligations imposed on nationals for the exercise of the occupation provided for'; for 'seasonal workers' or for highly skilled employees (i.e., such permit is referred to under the name 'EU Blue Card').

559. Seventh, and finally, a residence permit may be issued automatically, under Article L. 313-11 of the CESEDA, to those who justify personal or family ties in France, when they meet conditions, including age, integration and the reality of family ties – such permit is therefore marked 'private and family life'.

B. The Residence Permit

560. As provided for in Article L. 314-1 of the CESEDA, the residence permit is issued for a ten-year period and may be issued to individuals such as those who have been residing in France for more than five years and who have special ties

---

the granting of the temporary residence permit [and the residence permit "skills and talents"] [were] subject the to production by foreigners a visa for a stay longer than three months.' This provision was abrogated in 2016.

635. Same remark as above regarding the abrogation of Art. L. 311-7 CESEDA.

there, particularly family ties. Furthermore, these individuals must, as provided by law, meet integration conditions under Article L. 314-2 of the CESEDA.[636] The residence permit is automatically issued, to name just the first few cases provided for under Article L. 314-11 of CESEDA, to '(…) 2. A foreign child of a French national citizen if that child is eighteen to twenty-one years old or in accordance with Article L. 311-3 or if s/he is supported by his/her parents as well as to relatives in ascending line of such a national and his/her spouse who is dependent on him/her, provided they produce a visa for a stay of more than three months; 3. To a foreigner who is entitled to a work accident or occupational disease annuity paid by a French organization where the degree of permanent disability is equal to or greater than 20% as well as to dependents of a foreigner, beneficiaries of a death pension related to a work accident or illness paid by a French organization; 4. To a foreigner who served in a combat unit of the French army (…).' The permit is also issued, as of right, to the foreign person who meets the conditions in order to acquire French nationality as provided for under Article L. 314-12 of CESEDA.

561. Alongside this residence permit, the CESEDA also provides for the possibility of a long-term residence permit for recipients of a retirement pension paid by a French organization ('retirement card' or *carte retraité*), or for a 'skills and talents' residence permit (*carte de séjour compétences et talents*) for the person 'likely to contribute significantly and in a lasting way, because of his/her skills and talents, to the economic development [of France] or to the development in the intellectual, scientific, cultural, humanitarian or sports spheres of influence of France and the country of which s/he is a national'.

II. The Protection of Private and Family Life

562. The private and family life of the foreign national is constitutionally protected. Under the tenth paragraph of the Preamble to the 1946 Constitution, 'the Nation shall provide the individual and their family with the conditions necessary for their development'. In that respect, the Constitutional Council has identified the right to lead a normal family life as a constitutional principle which it does not base on Article 8 paragraph one of the ECHR – according to which '[e]veryone has the right to respect for his private and family life, his home and his correspondence' – but rather grounds such right on the basis of this one autonomous constitutional

636. These conditions are 'the Republican integration of the foreigner in French society, appreciated in particular with regard to his/her personal commitment to respect the principles governing the French Republic, the effective respect of these principles and his/her knowledge of the French language [except for foreigners over the age of sixty-five who are not subject to the condition relating to knowledge of the French language], which must be at least equal to a level defined by decree in the Council of State'. As for the assessment of the condition of integration, 'the administrative authority refers to the mayor of the municipality in which s/he resides for opinion.' As regards the assessment of the level of knowledge of the French language, this condition shall apply by March 2018.

principle (contrary to the Council of State).[637] In its 1993 Decision on Immigration,[638] the Constitutional Council held that 'while the legislature may take specific provisions in respect of foreigners, the legislature is bound to respect the constitutionally protected fundamental rights and freedoms granted to all those who reside in the territory of the Republic; that if these rights and freedoms have to be reconciled with the protection of public order which is a constitutional objective, among those are the right to liberty and security, including in particular the freedom of movement, freedom of marriage, and the right to lead a normal family life'.[639] With regard to respect for private life of the foreign national, the Constitutional Council considers that 'the freedom proclaimed by Article 2 of the [1789 Declaration] implies the right to respect for private life'.[640] Therefore, foreign nationals, including undocumented immigrants, are entitled in particular to freedom of marriage according to the case law of the Constitutional Council: '[R]espect for the freedom to marry, as a component of personal freedom protected under Articles 2 and 4 of the [1789 Declaration], precludes the irregular nature of the stay of a foreigner's stay from being an obstacle, by itself, to the marriage of the individual concerned.'[641] In addition, under certain conditions laid down in Article L. 411-1 et seq. of the CESEDA, foreign nationals are entitled to the right to so-called family reunification that is the right to claim that family members, particularly spouse and children, be allowed to join them and be reunited with them on the French territory.

III. The Application of the Principle of Equality

563. On the basis of constitutionally protected rights, foreign nationals are also entitled to the enjoyment of the principle of equality which application is, however, limited to the exercise of non-political rights and excluded in the case of holding certain offices. In the above-mentioned 1993 decision, the Constitutional Council held that 'while the legislature may take specific provisions in respect of foreigners, the legislature is bound to respect the constitutionally protected fundamental rights and freedoms granted *to all those who reside in the territory of the Republic*' (emphasis added).[642] In recognizing the equal application of fundamental rights and freedoms to foreigners and nationals, the Council based its reasoning on a factual criterion – that of the presence on the French territory. Despite acknowledging the application of the equality principle, the Constitutional Council has not, however, recognized a perfect equality of rights in that context. The Council considered that,

637. CE, Ass., 8 Dec. 1978, *GISTI*, *Rec. Lebon* 493.
638. CC Decision No 93-325 DC of 13 Aug. 1993, *Loi relative à la maîtrise de l'immigration et aux conditions d'entrée, d'accueil et de séjour des étrangers en France*, *Rec.* 224*.
639. *Ibid* pt 3.
640. CC Decision No 2007-557 DC of 15 Nov. 2007, *Loi relative à la maîtrise de l'immigration, à l'intégration et à l'asile*, *Rec.* 360, pt 11*.
641. CC Decision No 2003-484 DC of 20 Nov. 2003, *Loi relative à la maîtrise de l'immigration, au séjour des étrangers en France et à la nationalité*, *Rec.* 438, pt 94.
642. CC Decision No 93-325 DC of 13 Aug. 1993, *Loi relative à la maîtrise de l'immigration et aux conditions d'entrée, d'accueil et de séjour des étrangers en France*, *Rec.* 224, pt 63*.

since foreigners were in an objectively different situation to that of French nationals, some restrictions could be imposed on their rights by the legislature while still respecting their fundamental rights and freedoms. Accordingly, political rights, such as the right to vote, are not granted to foreign nationals. Similarly, access to certain professions, especially in the public service, is not permitted without that constituting an infringement of the principle of equality. However, in application of the same equality principle, the Constitutional Council has ruled against the exclusion of foreign nationals from the benefit of a social allowance in the following terms: 'the exclusion of foreigners legally residing in France from the benefit of the supplementary allowance, since they cannot avail themselves of the provisions of international agreements or of regulations enacted on the basis thereof, violates the constitutional principle of equality'.[643]

564. In application of the principle of equality and on the basis of EU law, the Council of State decided that the same rules should apply to objectively comparable situations: 'by restricting, under the first set of measures, to individuals aged between eighteen and twenty-five only who are nationals of a Member State of the [EU] or of a State party to the [EEA], free access to the monuments under their charge and thereby excluding long-term residents who are legally in these same States, the decision of 11 March 2009 of the National Monuments Centre [*Centre des Monuments Nationaux*] and the deliberation of 27 March 2009 of the Public Establishment of the Louvre did not comply with the provisions of Council Directive 2003/109/EC of 25 November 2003.'[644]

§4. Asylum

565. Asylum may be granted to a foreign national on either two grounds: it may be granted on a constitutional basis (*asile constitutionnel*), on the one hand, or it may be granted on a legal basis (*protection subsidiaire*), on the other.

I. Constitutional Protection

566. Under the fourth paragraph of the Preamble to the 1946 Constitution, '[e]very man persecuted for his action in favour of freedom has the right to asylum in the territories of the Republic'. The Constitution incorporates the right to asylum while defining its scope: 'The Republic may enter into agreements with European States which are bound by similar international obligations with regard to asylum and human rights and fundamental freedoms protection, with a view to determining their respective competences in the examination of asylum applications submitted to them (paragraph one). However, should such application not fall within their

643. CC Decision No 89-269 DC of 22 Jan. 1990, *Loi portant diverses dispositions relatives à la sécurité sociale et à la santé, Rec.* 33, pt 35. For a decision of the Council of State with a similar conclusion, *see* CE, 3/5 SSR, 30 Jun. 1989, *Ville de Paris c. Lévy*, app. No 78113.
644. CE, Sect., 18 Jan. 2013, *SOS Racisme*, app. No 328230, pt 11.

jurisdiction under the agreements thereof, the authorities of the Republic shall still have the right to grant asylum to any foreign individual who is persecuted by virtue of his [/her] action in favour of liberty or who seeks the protection of France for another reason (paragraph two)'. (Article 53-1 Constitution).

567. The 'right to constitutional asylum' seeks to balance the application of EU law rules, on the one hand, with the application of French constitutional principles, on the other. According to the Schengen Agreement, asylum applications should be treated by only one European State. This principle of 'non-duplication' aims at avoiding multiple asylum applications in various countries of the Schengen area. Yet, the Preamble to the 1946 Constitution provided at the time that the individual persecuted for his/her action in favour of freedom was always entitled to a right to asylum in France. In that respect, the Constitutional Council held that the Schengen Agreement could only be consistent with the Constitution provided it respected the constitutional right to asylum thereof, despite the EU principle of non-duplication of asylum applications.[645] In that respect, the Council ruled that 'the fourth paragraph of the Preamble to the 1946 Constitution obliges French administrative and judicial authorities to conduct a review of the situation of asylum seekers falling under this paragraph, that is those who are persecuted for their action in favour of freedom'.[646] Following the above-mentioned 1993 Decision of the Constitutional Council,[647] the constitutional revision of 25 November 1993 aimed at preventing France from conflicting with the Schengen Agreement. The resulting Article 53-1 of the Constitution thus makes the examination of an asylum application only optional – the State no longer has an obligation to treat asylum applications filed by individuals who claim to be persecuted because of their action in favour of freedom, but only has the 'right' to process such requests. Article 711-1 of the CESEDA, as amended, provides that '[r]efugee status is afforded to anyone persecuted for his/her action in favour of freedom and to anyone over whom the Office of the UN High Commissioner for Refugees exercises its mandate under Articles 6 and 7 of its statute as adopted by the UN General Assembly on 14 December 1950, or who meets the definition in Article 1 of the Geneva Convention of 28 July 1951 relating to the Status of Refugees. These individuals are governed by the provisions applicable to refugees under the aforementioned Geneva Convention'.

II. Subsidiary Protection

568. Besides constitutional asylum, the CESEDA provides that France, as part of the Schengen Agreement, has competence to grant a 'subsidiary protection' to

645. CC Decision No 91-294 DC of 25 Jul. 1991, *Loi autorisant l'approbation de la convention d'application de l'accord de Schengen du 14 juin 1985 entre les gouvernements des Etats de l'Union économique Benelux, de la République fédérale d'Allemagne et de la République française relatif à la suppression graduelle des contrôles aux frontières communes, Rec.* 91, pt 31.
646. CC Decision No 93-325 DC of 13 Aug. 1993, *Loi relative à la maîtrise de l'immigration et aux conditions d'entrée, d'accueil et de séjour des étrangers en France, Rec.* 224, pt 88*.
647. *Ibid.*

certain individuals. Under Article L. 712-1 of the CESEDA, '[s]ubject to the provisions of Article L. 712-2, the benefit of subsidiary protection is granted to anyone who does not meet the requirements for recognition of refugee status mentioned in Article L. 711-1 and who proves that s/he is exposed in his/her country to one of the following threats: a) The death penalty; b) Torture or inhuman or degrading treatment; c) As a civilian, a serious, direct and individual threat against his/her life or person due to great widespread violence resulting from a situation of international or internal armed conflict'. Pursuant to Article L. 712-2 of the CESEDA, 'subsidiary protection is not granted to an individual if there are serious reasons for considering: a) that s/he has committed a crime against peace, a war crime or a crime against humanity; b) that s/he has committed a serious non-political crime; c) that s/he has been guilty of acts contrary to the purposes and principles of the United Nations; d) that his/her activity on the territory constitutes a serious threat to public order, public safety or national security'.

569. Asylum applications are processed by the French Office for the Protection of Refugees and Stateless Persons (*Office Français de Protection des Réfugiés et Apatrides* or OFPRA), established by the Law of 25 July 1952 on the right to asylum,[648] whose decisions are subject to review before the National Asylum Court (*Cour Nationale du Droit d'Asile* or CNDA) with a right of judicial review by the Council of State.

§5. Deportation and Expulsion

570. The constitutional principle of the free movement of persons[649] is limited by the possibility of compelling a foreign national to leave the French territory. In addition to extradition – which can always be refused by France, especially when the country requesting extradition does not respect fundamental rights and freedoms of the person[650] – the deportation of a foreign national may occur when s/he has illegally entered into the French territory, or has been staying illegally in the French territory, which may result from an invalid residence permit or its absence from the outset. Deportation may also occur when the foreign national constitutes a threat to public order under Article L. 521-1 of the CESEDA. The deportation may be ordered by a decision called an 'obligation to leave French territory' – usually referred to by its acronym '*OQTF*' as in French, '*Obligation de Quitter le Territoire Français*'. Under Article L. 511-1 of the CESEDA, this decision may specify a deadline to leave the country as well as a particular country of destination, or leave the decision to the foreign national as to voluntarily leave the country. Besides, the authority pronouncing an *OQTF* does not have to give reasons for its decision. Such a decision may also be taken by a judge in a criminal trial for illegal residence in

648. Law No 52-893 of 25 Jul. 1952 on the right to asylum.
649. CC Decision No 2005-532 DC of 19 Jan. 2006, *Loi relative à la lutte contre le terrorisme et portant dispositions diverses à la sécurité et aux contrôles frontaliers*, *Rec*. 31, pt 16*.
650. CE, Ass., 26 Sep. 1984, *Lujambio Galdeano*, *Rec. Lebon* 307.

the French territory.[651] In certain circumstances, the individual who is the subject to an obligation to leave the French territory can be placed in an immigration detention centre pending his/her deportation under Article L. 551-1 et seq. of the CESEDA. Where the foreign national represents a serious threat to public order, s/he may be expelled which is, however, prohibited in the case of certain categories of foreigners, such as minors, except in the case of 'urgent need for national security or public safety' under Articles L. 521-2 et seq. of the CESEDA. Finally, a foreign national who is guilty of an offence or a crime may be subject to a ban from the French territory, which can be temporary or permanent.

Selected Further Reading

On French Citizenship and Nationality

Paul Lagarde, *La nationalité française* (4th ed., Dalloz 2011).
Christian Le Bart, *Citoyenneté et démocratie* (La Documentation française 2016).
Jean-Philippe Thiellay, *Le droit de la nationalité française* (Berger Levrault 2011).
Patrick Weil, *Etre français. Les quatre piliers de la nationalité* (L'aube 2014).
Patrick Weil, *How to be French. Nationality in the Making since 1789* (Duke University Press 2008).

On Fundamental Rights and Liberties

Xavier Dupré de Boulois, *Droit des libertés fondamentales* (PUF 2018).
Xavier Dupré de Boulois (ed.), *Les grands arrêts du droit des libertés fondamentales* (Dalloz 2017).
Katarzyna Blay-Grabarczyk and Laure Milano (eds), *Le nouveau cadre législatif de la lutte contre le terrorisme à l'épreuve des droits fondamentaux* (Fondation Varenne 2017).
Henri Oberdorff, *Droits de l'homme et libertés fondamentales* (LGDJ 2017).

On Constitutional Problems of Minorities

Gilles Guglielmi and Geneviève Koubi (eds), *L'égalité des chances* (La Découverte 2000).
Gilles Pélissier, *Le principe d'égalité en droit public* (LGDJ 1996).
Patrick Weil, *La République et sa diversité. Immigration, intégration, discrimination* (Seuil 2005).

651. For an application of the constitutional principle of proportionality of penalties in this area, *see*, e.g., CC Decision No 2011-217 QPC of 3 Feb. 2012, *M. Mohammed Alki B. [Délit d'entrée ou de séjour irrégulier en France]*, *Rec.* 104*.

ON JUDICIAL CONTROL OF ADMINISTRATIVE ACTION

Gilles Dumont, Martine Lombard and Jean Sirinelli, *Droit administratif* (12th ed., Dalloz 2017).
Pierre-Laurent Frier and Jacques Petit, *Droit administratif* (11th ed., LGDJ 2017).
Patrick Gérard, *La juridiction administrative* (La Documentation française 2017).
Marceau Long et alii, *Les grands arrêts de la jurisprudence administrative* (21st ed., Dalloz 2017).
Bruno Odent and Didier Truchet, *La justice administrative* (PUF 2008).
Didier Truchet, *Droit administratif* (7th ed., PUF 2017).

ON RIGHTS AND STATUS OF FOREIGNERS

Emmanuel Aubin, *Droit des étrangers* (3rd ed., Gualino 2014).
Xavier Vandendriessche, *Le droit des étrangers* (6th ed., Dalloz 2018).
Patrick Weil, *La France et ses étrangers, l'aventure d'une politique de l'immigration de 1938 deja nos jours* (Gallimard 2005).

Part V. Specific Issues

571. This Part is concerned with a diversity of specific issues related to French constitutional law, namely constitutional provisions on war, treaty and foreign affairs powers, taxing and spending powers, emergency powers, as well as constitutional provisions on the relationship between the Church and State.

Chapter 1. War, Treaty and Foreign Affairs Powers

572. The Constitution is ambiguous on the subject of the distribution of powers between the President of the Republic, on the one hand, and the government and the Prime Minister, on the other. The reading of Article 5 of the Constitution together with Articles 20 and 21 reflects this ambiguity. Article 5 proclaims in particular that the President of the Republic is 'the guarantor of national independence, of the integrity of the territory, and of due respect for treaties'. The prominence of the role of the President of the Republic in the field of national defence, treaty and foreign affairs is all the more affirmed in the normal functioning of the regime when the parliamentary majority is of the same political side as that of the President. Even though war and foreign affairs traditionally fall under the competence of the Executive, this does not prejudice the functions of control of the other branches of government.

§1. War and National Defence

573. The general ambiguity concerning Articles 5, 20 and 21 of the Constitution also applies to the specific issue of war and national defence. According to Article 15 of the Constitution, the President of the Republic is the Commander-in-Chief of the Armed Forces and makes decisions in this capacity. Nonetheless, by virtue of Article 19 of the Constitution, acts done by the President of the Republic on the basis of Article 15 are subject to the requirement of countersignature. Under the same Article 15, the President of the Republic 'shall preside over the higher National Defence councils and committees'. The most important of these councils is the Defence and National Security Council, formerly known, before 2010, as the Council of Internal Security. The Council is composed, in plenary session, apart from the President of the Republic, of the Prime Minister, the Minister for Defence, the Minister for Home Affairs, the Minister for Foreign Affairs, the Minister for the Economy, the Minister for Finance and any minister who may be concerned by the agenda. The composition of the restricted Defence and National Security Council is determined by the President of the Republic.[652]

574. In contrast, and under the power of the government 'to determine and conduct the policy of the Nation', Article 20 of the Constitution specifies that the government has 'power over the administration and the armed forces'. Similarly, as regards the Head of Government, Article 21 mentions that the Prime Minister 'shall be responsible for National Defence'. However, constitutional practice has established, especially in the normal functioning of the regime, the primary role of the President of the Republic in relation to war and national defence matters. As a result, despite the constitutional provisions and the requirement of countersignature in particular, the decisions in relation to war and national defence are primarily

652. Article R. 1122-1 et seq. of the Code of Defence.

those of the President of the Republic. It is explicitly the case as regards the potential recourse to nuclear weapons that is entrusted with the President alone.[653]

575. In relation to war, Parliament enjoys control powers. Initially, the intervention of Parliament was limited to the authorization of declarations of war (Article 35 Constitution). However, since contemporary conflicts have involved the intervention of armed forces without such declarations of war, this power of authorization has become somehow obsolete. The 2008 constitutional amendment modified the mechanism governing the role of Parliament in case of armed conflicts. The revised version of Article 35 obliges the government to inform Parliament of the intervention of armed forces abroad, and of its objectives, no later than three days after the beginning of the intervention. A debate is possible but it cannot be followed by a vote. If the intervention lasts for more than fourth months, it has to be authorized by Parliament. Article 35 also specifies that the government can ask the National Assembly to make the final decision.

§2. Treaties and Foreign Affairs

576. As in the case of war and national defence, the President of the Republic plays a prominent role in relation to treaties and foreign affairs. The significance of this role is expressly provided for in the Constitution, even though this is a power which is shared with the Prime Minister. The role of Parliament is primarily one of control.

I. Diplomatic Representation and Representation in Supranational Organizations

577. The powers of the President of the Republic in foreign affairs derive from Articles 5 and 52 of the Constitution. The President represents France abroad. However, this competence is shared with the government and the Prime Minister on the basis of Articles 20 and 21 of the Constitution. This situation leads to a double of representation of France on the international stage in periods of cohabitation whereby both the Head of State (President of the Republic) and Head of Government (Prime Minister) are represented. More particularly, the President of the Republic has competence to accredit ambassadors and envoys extraordinary to foreign powers, and reciprocally, foreign ambassadors and envoys extraordinary are accredited to him (Article 14 Constitution). Ambassadors and envoys extraordinary are recommended by the Minister for Foreign Affairs and appointed, according to the procedure under Article 13 of the Constitution, by decree in the Council of Ministers.

653. Article R. 1411-5 of the Code of Defence.

II. The Treaty-Making Power

578. The regime of treaties and international agreements is governed by Articles 52 to 55 of the Constitution. In addition, the Constitution provides for specific provisions in relation to the participation of Parliament in the development of EU secondary law.

A. *The Negotiation of Treaties*

579. The central position of the President of the Republic in relation to the negotiation of international agreements, even in periods of cohabitation, is provided for by Article 52 of the Constitution. According to its first and second paragraphs respectively, the President 'shall negotiate and ratify treaties' and 'shall be informed of any negotiation leading to the conclusion of an international agreement not subject to ratification'. In contrast, the government is competent for what the Constitution qualifies as international agreements and for simplified agreements which require neither ratification nor approval and which are binding upon signature. The negotiation and signature of treaties are not carried out personally by the President of the Republic but under his authority. The negotiation is notably entrusted with the Minister for Foreign Affairs while the signature of treaties can be made by plenipotentiaries on behalf of the President.

B. *The Ratification of Treaties*

580. Treaties are ratified by the President of the Republic in the form of a decree that is submitted to the requirement of countersignature (Article 52 Constitution). Ratification remains a discretionary power. The President of the Republic is not bound to ratify a treaty, even if he has negotiated and signed it and if Parliament has authorized ratification. In contrast, international agreements not subject to ratification require approval by the government. From the perspective of international law, the difference between ratification and approval is irrelevant. Ratified treaties and approved agreements are then published in the *JO* and enjoy an authority superior to domestic laws from publication (Article 55 Constitution). Article 53 of the Constitution adds a further condition as regards the ratification or approval of certain treaties and international agreements. These include peace treaties, trade agreements, agreements related to international organizations, to the finances of the State, to the modification of provisions of a legislative nature, to the status of persons and to those which involve the transfer, exchange or acquisition of territory. In this case, their ratification or approval has to be authorized by law. The authorizing law can be passed by Parliament or by referendum (Article 11 Constitution). In addition, the transfer, exchange or acquisition of territory requires the consent of the population concerned (Article 53 in fine Constitution).

581. Article 54 of the Constitution provides for a priori constitutional review of international agreements by the Constitutional Council. If the Council, on a referral from the President of the Republic, from the Prime Minister, from the President of either of House of Parliament or from sixty members of the National Assembly or sixty members of the Senate, regards an international instrument as being incompatible with the Constitution, its ratification or approval cannot take place unless the Constitution has been amended.

C. Parliamentary Powers in Relation to EU Law

582. The process of European integration and the transfer of competences it has involved have justified the concomitant increase of the powers of the French Parliament as regards the development of EU law. These powers are provided for under Title XV of the Constitution entitled 'Of the European Union'. Introduced on the occasion of the ratification of the Treaty of Maastricht in 1992, Article 88-4 of the Constitution imposed a duty on the government to inform Parliament of any drafts of EU acts of a legislative nature. This duty of information has now been extended to any drafts or proposals for acts of the EU. Each House of Parliament can, independently, adopt resolutions with a view to express their opinion on these drafts or proposals. However, such resolutions are not binding. Since the 2008 constitutional amendment, Article 88-4 also provides for the creation of a committee in charge of European affairs in each House of Parliament.

583. Article 88-5 of the Constitution provides for the empowerment of Parliament in case of the accession of a new State to the EU. Accordingly, a treaty pertaining to a new membership requires ratification through referendum. By exception, the same procedure as that concerning amendments to the Constitution by Parliament convened as Congress, in application of the third paragraph of Article 89 of the Constitution, can alternatively be followed if a motion to that purpose is adopted by both Houses of Parliament in identical terms by a three-fifths majority of the votes cast.

584. Article 88-6 of the Constitution relates to the powers granted to national parliaments by Protocol No 2 to the Treaty of Lisbon on the application of the principles of subsidiarity and proportionality. The first paragraph affirms that either the National Assembly or the Senate can, independently, address to the Presidents of the European Parliament, the Council of Ministers and the European Commission 'a reasoned opinion as to the conformity of a draft European legislative act with the principle of subsidiarity'. The second paragraph of Article 88-6 relates to the possibility of instituting proceedings before the CJEU in order to enforce the principle of subsidiarity. This power is granted respectively to either House of Parliament, and the government merely refers the proceedings to the CJEU. Under the third paragraph of Article 88-6, these proceedings are of right when they are required by sixty members of the National Assembly or sixty members of the Senate.

585. The Treaty of Lisbon introduced simplified revision procedures known as the 'passerelle clauses'. According to Article 48 of the TEU, the European Council can decide, unanimously and with the consent of the European Parliament (EP), to change the decision-making process in the Council from unanimity to qualified majority, or from a special legislative procedure to the ordinary procedure. Similarly, on the basis of Article 81 of the TFEU, the Council can decide, unanimously, on a proposal from the Commission, and after consulting the EP, to change the procedure as regards some measures concerning family law with cross-border implications from the special legislative procedure to the ordinary legislative procedure. In both instances, the proposal of simplified revision has to be transmitted to national parliaments and the opposition of one national parliament makes it impossible to adopt the simplified revision. Article 88-7 of the Constitution provides for this parliamentary opposition in the French legal order. To that purpose, a motion has to be passed in identical terms by the National Assembly and the Senate.

Chapter 2. Taxing and Spending Powers

586. Numerous provisions of constitutional value relate to taxing and spending powers. Articles 13 and 14 of the 1789 Declaration affirm the principle of equality, necessity and consent to taxation. Article 34 of the Constitution establishes the competence of the legislative power in matters relating to taxing and spending powers. Article 72-2 of the Constitution proclaims in particular the free disposition of their resources by local authorities. Overall, these constitutional provisions relate either to the procedures that are specific to the exercise of taxing and spending powers or to the principles governing finance and taxation.

§1. The Constitutional Specificities of Financial Legislation

587. The singularity of French financial legislation lies in the fact that the Prime Minister may condition the passing of a bill to a vote of confidence (Article 49 third paragraph Constitution). If the procedure of no confidence fails, the bill is considered as passed. Since the 2008 constitutional amendment, the Prime Minister can have recourse to this procedure only once per session. However, this restriction does not apply to finance bills or Social Security financing bills which, due to their importance, are governed by derogatory procedures that set strict time limits as regards their passing.

I. Finance Laws

588. The specific procedure as regards finance laws is set by Article 47 of the Constitution and by an Organic Law of 1 August 2001 that defines, in its Article 1, finance laws as those determining 'the nature, amount and allocation of the resources and expenditure of the State, as well as the resulting budgetary and financial balance'.[654] The legislative procedure as regards finance laws is necessarily initiated by a government bill. Moreover, finance bills must be tabled first before the National Assembly (Article 39 Constitution). Then, the National Assembly has to reach a decision on first reading within forty days (Article 47 second paragraph Constitution). Beyond this period, the government must refer the bill to the Senate which has to reach its decision within fifteen days. In addition, in order to ensure a timely passing of the finance law, the government can implement the procedure provided for by Article 45 of the Constitution, which also applies to ordinary legislation, and put an end to the exchange between the two Houses of Parliament by giving the last word to the National Assembly. Article 40 of the Constitution is also of particular importance as regards the passing of finance laws since it affirms that '[p]rivate members' bills and amendments to bills thereof [introduced by Members

654. Organic Law No 2001-692 of 1 Aug. 2001 on finance laws.

of Parliament] shall not be deemed admissible where their enactment may result in either a decrease in public revenue or the creation or increase in public expenditure'.

589. A finance law has to be passed within seventy days after it has been tabled. Otherwise, the provisions of the bill can be implemented by ordinance (Article 47 third paragraph Constitution), a situation that has never happened so far. In contrast, when the failure to pass the finance legislation before the beginning of the year falls on the government due to a late tabling, 'the government shall as a matter of urgency seek Parliament's authorization to collect taxes and shall make available by decree the funds needed to meet commitments already voted for'. (Article 47 fourth paragraph Constitution). According to Article 45 of the 2001 Organic Law, 'commitments already voted for' are 'the minimum appropriations that the government considers as being indispensable to continue executing public services in the conditions that have been approved the previous year by Parliament'. A finance settlement law is associated to each finance law in order to control the execution of the budget. The procedure is initiated by a government bill which it has to be certified by the domestic Court of Auditors and the law has to be passed according to the same conditions that govern finance laws. Article 46 of the 2001 Organic Law states that the bill has to be tabled no later than 1 June of the year following the year of the execution of the budget to which it pertains. Therefore, the enactment of the finance settlement bill precedes the discussion of the new finance bill. Finance settlement laws play an essential role in the mission of evaluation of public policies entrusted with Parliament (Articles 24, 47-2, 48 and 51-2 Constitution). Due to the particularities of the enactment procedure of finance laws, it may be tempting to include in them provisions other than financial. Such provisions are known as 'financial riders' or 'budgetary riders'. Article 1 of the 2001 Organic Law states that 'finance laws determine … the nature, cost and allocation of resources and charges of the State'. On this basis, the Constitutional Council has declared such budgetary riders as being unconstitutional since these do not fall within the scope of finance laws.[655]

II. Social Security Financing Laws

590. A special procedure governing social security financing laws was introduced in 1996. It is now governed by Article 47-1 of the Constitution and by Organic Law of 2 August 2005.[656] This procedure mirrors that on finance laws. Similarly, the procedure can only be initiated by a government bill that must be tabled first before the National Assembly. The National Assembly has to reach a decision on first reading within a time limit of twenty days, rather than the forty days applying to finance bills. Upon expiry of this period, the government must

655. CC Decision No 81-136 DC of 31 Dec. 1981, *Troisième loi de finances rectificative pour 1981*, *Rec.* 48, pt 3.

656. Organic Law No 2005-881 of 2 Aug. 2005 on social security financing laws.

refer the bill to the Senate which has to reach its decision within fifteen days. For the rest, the procedure defined in Article 45 of the Constitution applies.

591. A social security financing law has to be passed within fifty days after it has been tabled (Article 47-1 Constitution). Otherwise, the provisions of the bill can be implemented by ordinance. In contrast with Article 47 of the Constitution, no provision provides for the situation where a failure to pass a social security financing law before the beginning of the year falls upon the government. Provisions included in these laws which pertain to other purposes than the financing of social security are known as 'social riders'. Similarly to budgetary riders, they are repugnant to the Constitution.[657]

§2. Constitutional Principles relating to Budget and Taxation

I. Constitutional Principles Relating to Budget

592. Finance laws are governed by five main budgetary principles, namely the principles of annuality, specialty, unity, universality and sincerity.

A. The Principle of Annuality

593. The principle of annuality is mentioned in Article 1 of the above-mentioned 2001 Organic Law. It means that the authorization as regards resources and expenditure is only valid for a year. In France, the budgetary year runs from 1 January to 31 December. A number of exceptions apply to this principle. Some finance provisions apply for a period shorter than a year. That is most notably the case of amending finance laws that allow modifications of a finance law during the year of its application. The exceptions to the principle of annuality also concern finance provisions that exceed one year. For instance, by virtue of Articles 8 and 15 of the above-mentioned 2001 Organic Law, authorization of commitment allows budgetary allocations of funds that exceed one year. Under limited conditions, notably with the authorization of the Minister for Finance, carry-overs of payment appropriations can also be allowed when allocations are not used by the end of the year.

B. The Principle of Specialty

594. According to the principle of specialty, finance laws associate specific resources with specific expenditure. Accordingly, in finance laws, credits used to be distributed by titles and chapters corresponding to specific expenditures and such distribution constrained the government. The 2001 Organic Law has modified this

---

657. For instance, CC Decision No 2005-528 DC of 15 Dec. 2005, *Loi de financement de la sécurité sociale pour 2006*, *Rec.* 157.

traditional presentation of finance laws and opted for logic of results rather than means. Under its Article 7, finance laws are now divided into missions of the State. These missions are subdivided into programmes, the number of which is lesser than the number of former chapters. Accordingly, a greater liberty is left to the administration as regards the use of credits in order to fulfil these objectives and the control of the execution of the budget is made easier. As a result, the 2001 Organic Law has also restricted the former exceptions to the principle of specialty (i.e., transfer of appropriations, special funds).

C. The Principle of Unity

595. Article 6 of the 2001 Organic Law applies the principle of unity by requiring all resources and expenditure to be listed in a single document. However, some exceptions to this principle exist. A first exception is the use of supplementary budgets. Under Article 18 of the 2001 Organic Law, supplementary budgets are restricted to 'the operations of the State services not having the status of legal persons resulting from the activity of production of goods or of provision of services giving rise to the payment of fees'. Official publications and administrative information as well as air control and operation are the only remaining supplementary budgets. Special accounts constitute another exception to the principle of unity. These were created to record temporary movements of funds. Under the 2001 Organic Law, only four special accounts remain.[658] Supplementary budgets and special accounts, even though based on finance laws, are not included in the general budget of the State. They constitute techniques of 'de-budgeting' (*débudgétisation*) whereby the budget of the State is lowered, even though parliamentary control is still enforced. De-budgeting can also prevent parliamentary control when it consists of autonomous budgets whereby an expenditure of the State is delegated to other legal persons governed by either public or private law and entrusted with a mission of public service. Such transfers are reviewed by the Constitutional Council.[659]

D. The Principle of Universality

596. The principle of universality consists of two rules that are mentioned in Article 6 of the 2001 Organic Law. First, the rule of non-compensation, or of non-contraction, involves that revenues and expenditure must be mentioned in full in the budget. They cannot be compensated so that the budget would only reflect their balance. Second, the rule of non-affectation prohibits the attribution of specific revenues to specific expenditure. In contrast, revenues as a whole cover expenditure as a whole. There are some exceptions to the principle of universality. The rule of non-compensation, for instance, does not apply to special accounts (except for the account of financial aid). Similarly, numerous exceptions concern the rule of non-affectation. Supplementary budgets and special accounts are exempted from the rule

658. These are listed in Art. 19 and governed by Arts 21–24 of the 2001 Organic Law.
659. CC Decision No 94-351 DC of 29 Dec. 1994, *Loi de finances pour 1995*, *Rec.* 140.

of non-affectation. Moreover, certain taxes are dedicated to specific expenditures. For instance, the audiovisual licence fee participates in financing public television and radio.

E. The Principle of Sincerity

597. The principle of sincerity ensures that Parliament is presented with accurate, complete and coherent information as regards the budget of the State. This principle emerged from the case law of the Constitutional Council and is now included in Article 32 of the 2001 Organic Law. The Constitutional Council recognized the constitutional value of this principle on the basis of Articles 14 and 15 of the 1789 Declaration.[660]

II. Constitutional Principles of Taxation

598. Taxes have to be differentiated from charges. The former correspond to a financial contribution to meet public expenditure and are disconnected from any specific service. In contrast, charges are the financial compensation related to a service. Legality, equality, annuality and necessity are the constitutional principles governing taxation.

A. The Principle of Legality

599. Article 14 of the 1789 Declaration declares that citizens have to consent to taxation. Also, the law shall determine '[t]he rate, basis and modalities concerning the collection of all types of taxes'. (Article 34 Constitution). Although the Constitution grants some powers to local authorities in relation to taxation (Article 72-2 Constitution), the conditions of exercise of these powers are determined by law. This is the case, for instance, for the determination of the tax base and rate of the taxation by local authorities. Moreover, the legislature retains a monopoly in levying new taxes.

B. The Principle of Equality

600. Equality before taxation is an application of the general principle of equality but is also mentioned specifically in Article 13 of the 1789 Declaration whereby taxation 'must be equally distributed among all citizens, in proportion to their ability to pay'. Therefore, equality before taxation is not absolute. The Constitutional Council has declared as being in conformity with the principle of equality the fact

660. CC Decision No 2006-538 DC of 13 Jul. 2006, *Loi portant règlement définitif du budget de 2005*, *Rec.* 73.

that the legislator treats different situations differently, notably on the basis of differences in contributory capacity.[661] Considerations of general interest can also justify adaptation of the principle of equality in taxation. For instance, the Constitutional Council has decided that tax advantages to support certain economic activities complied with the Constitution.[662]

C. The Principle of Annuality

601. The principle of annuality of finance laws involves that levying taxes has to be authorized annually by Parliament. As a result, even though it does not question the existence of taxes itself, the government's power to collect taxes has to be renewed each year.

D. The Principle of Necessity

602. The principle of necessity of taxation, as recognized by the Constitutional Council, is derived from Article 13 of the 1789 Declaration that declares that '[f]or the maintenance of the public force, and for the expenditure of the administration, a general tax is indispensable', as well as from Article 14 where is it stated that '[e]ach citizen has the right to ascertain (…) the need for a public tax'.[663] While the principle of necessity founds the legitimacy of taxation, it has little legal consequences. Nonetheless, the Constitutional Council has, for instance, justified on this basis fiscal provisions purporting to fight against tax avoidance[664] or to prevent unjustified medical expenditure.[665]

661. CC Decision No 81-133 DC of 30 Dec. 1981, *Loi de finances pour 1982*, *Rec.* 41.
662. CC Decision No 93-320 DC of 21 Jun. 1993, *Loi de finances rectificative pour 1993*, *Rec.* 146.
663. CC Decision No 93-330 DC of 29 Dec. 1993, *Loi de finances pour 1994*, *Rec.* 572; CC Decision No 2001-453 DC of 18 Dec. 2001, *Loi de financement de la sécurité sociale pour 2002*, *Rec.* 164.
664. CC Decision No 83-164 of 29 Dec. 1983, *Loi de finances pour 1984*, *Rec.* 67.
665. CC Decision No 2001-453 DC of 18 Dec. 2001, *Loi de financement de la sécurité sociale pour 2002*, *Rec.* 164.

Chapter 3. Emergency Powers

603. The general regime of emergency powers originates from case law. Under the theory of 'exceptional circumstances', notably in times of war, administrative courts regard certain administrative acts as valid, even though they would be repugnant to the principle of legality in normal circumstances.[666] Aside from this regime, emergency powers primarily consist of the extraordinary powers enjoyed by the President of the Republic under Article 16 of the Constitution, the regime of the state of siege and the regime of the state of emergency.

§1. Presidential Extraordinary Powers under Article 16 of the Constitution

I. The Enforcement of Article 16 of the Constitution

604. Article 16 of the Constitution defines in broad terms the conditions of its implementation. Even though the decision to have recourse to this constitutional provision depends in fine on a decision of the President of the Republic, a limited scrutiny is provided for under the Constitution.[667]

A. The Conditions of Enforcement of Article 16

605. Article 16 of the Constitution lays down two cumulative criteria as to the conditions under which it can be resorted to. These concern exceptional circumstances entailing specific consequences. First, Article 16 is designed for situations where 'the institutions of the Republic, the independence of the Nation, the integrity of its territory or the fulfilment of its international obligations [are] under grave and immediate threat'. Second, the consequences of these circumstances must be that 'the proper functioning of the constitutional public powers [is] interrupted'. Article 16 has only been applied once, from April to September 1961, following the putsch of the generals in Algeria.

B. Scrutiny of the Enforcement of Article 16

606. The enforcement of Article 16 of the Constitution depends on a decision of the President of the Republic. Such decision constitutes one of the President's discretionary powers and, as such, is exempt from the requirement of countersignature (Article 19 Constitution). The decision to have recourse to Article 16 is considered

666. CE, 28 Jun. 1918, *Heyriès*, *Rec. Lebon* 651; CE, 28 Feb. 1919, *Dames Dol et Laurent*, *Rec. Lebon* 651.

667. *See also* above Part II. Form of Government, Chapter 4. The Executive, §3. Powers, I. Division of Powers between the President of the Republic and the Government, A. Discretionary Powers of the President of the Republic.

as an act of State by the Council of State and, as such, is not subject to its review.[668] Yet, the Constitution provides for a limited form of control in the form of non-binding opinions by other constitutional organs. Before having recourse to Article 16, the President must consult the Prime Minister, the Presidents of each House of Parliament and the Constitutional Council. The opinion of the Constitutional Council is published.[669] Furthermore, the President of the Republic must inform the Nation of his use of Article 16. During the implementation of Article 16, Parliament sits as of right. Nonetheless, the extent of the powers it can exercise is not defined. Since the 2008 constitutional amendment, the Constitution also provides that the Constitutional Council can deliver an opinion, albeit non-binding, on the implementation of Article 16. After thirty days of the exercise of presidential extraordinary powers, on referral from the president of either House of Parliament, sixty members of the National Assembly or sixty members of the Senate, the Constitutional Council publicly examines whether the conditions required to avail such powers are still fulfilled (Article 16 in fine Constitution). The same examination by the Constitutional Council takes place, as of right, after sixty days and at any moment thereafter.

II. The Nature of the Presidential Powers under Article 16 of the Constitution

607. Article 16 of the Constitution mentions that the President of the Republic can take any 'acts required by such circumstances'. The nature of these acts depends on their content. They are of a regulatory nature if they fall within the regulatory field and could therefore be reviewed by administrative courts. They are of a legislative nature if they pertain to the matters listed in Article 34 of the Constitution, with the consequence that they cannot be reviewed by the Council of State.[670] Therefore, exceeding also the competence of the Constitutional Council, these acts are not subject to any judicial review. Despite the extremely broad scope of the powers that the President of the Republic can exercise under Article 16 of the Constitution, three limits exist. First, the National Assembly cannot be dissolved. Second, '[t]he (…) acts shall be designed to ensure that the constitutional public powers are promptly in a position to carry out their mission'. Even though its opinion is not binding, the Constitutional Council has to be consulted on these acts. Third, the Constitutional Council has ruled that the Constitution cannot be amended while Article 16 is being implemented.[671]

668. CE, 2 Mar. 1962, *Rubin de Servens*, *Rec. Lebon* 143.
669. Article 53 of Ordinance No 58-1067 of 7 Nov. 1958 on the Organic Law on the Constitutional Council.
670. CE, 2 Mar. 1962, *Rubin de Servens*, *Rec. Lebon* 143.
671. CC Decision No 92-312 DC of 2 Sep. 1992, *Traité sur l'Union européenne*, *Rec.* 76, pt 19*.

§2. The State of Siege

608. The state of siege applies in case of armed conflict. Having legislative origins,[672] it is now governed by Article 36 of the Constitution. The state of siege is put into force through a decree in the Council of Ministers and its extension beyond twelve days must be authorized by Parliament. The state of siege can only be applied 'in case of imminent danger resulting from a foreign war or an armed insurrection'. The decree designates the territory to which it applies and determines its duration of application. Police powers and the powers vested in the civil authority for the maintenance of order are transferred to military authorities and extended. Notwithstanding the state of siege, all the rights guaranteed by the Constitution continue to be exercised when their enjoyment is not suspended under the provisions relating to the state of siege under the Code of Defence.[673]

§3. The State of Emergency

609. The state of emergency is governed by Law of 3 April 1955.[674] According to its Article 1, the state of emergency can be declared 'on the whole metropolitan territory, or part of it, in overseas departments, in overseas territories governed by Article 74 of the Constitution and in New Caledonia, either in case of imminent danger resulting from serious breaches of public order, or in case of events having, by their nature and their gravity, the character of a public calamity'. Under the regime of the state of emergency, police powers remain exercised by civil authorities but they are extended. Notably, this regime allows restrictions on fundamental rights and liberties of individuals suspected of being a threat to public security. For example, the state of emergency allows the prefect or the Minister for Home Affairs to limit or prohibit traffic in certain places, to prohibit certain public meetings or temporarily close certain public places, to authorize administrative searches, or to pronounce house arrests.

610. Following the attacks perpetrated in Paris and Saint-Denis on 13 November 2015, the state of emergency was declared at a Council of Ministers meeting on the night of Friday 13 November to Saturday 14 November.[675] Prolonged six times

672. Law of 9 Aug. 1849 on the state of siege and Law of 3 Apr. 1878 on the state of siege. *See also* above Part IV. Citizenship and the Administration of Justice, Chapter 2. Fundamental Rights and Liberties, §1. General, II. Implementation of Fundamental Rights and Liberties, C. Limitations to Fundamental Rights and Liberties.

673. Articles L. 2121-1 to L. 2121-8 of the Code of Defence.

674. Law No 55-385 of 3 Apr. 1955 on the state of emergency (as lastly amended in July 2017). *See also* above Part IV. Citizenship and the Administration of Justice, Chapter 2. Fundamental Rights and Liberties, §1. General, II. Implementation of Fundamental Rights and Liberties, C. Limitations to Fundamental Rights and Liberties.

675. Before November 2015, the state of emergency was declared five times: three times in relation to the Algerian troubles – in 1955 in the departments which formed the French Algeria, in 1958 and 1961 in the metropolitan territory; one time in 1984 in relation to overseas troubles in New Caledonia; and one time in 2005 to put an end to riots in a number of French suburbs which concerned twenty-five departments, including the entire Ile-de-France (suburban areas outside Paris).

by the French Parliament, the state of emergency ended on 1 November 2017, when the Law of 31 October 2017 came into effect, strengthening domestic security and the fight against terrorism.[676]

676. Law No 2017-1510 of 30 Oct. 2017 strengthening domestic security and the fight against terrorism. Some of the several laws which prolonged the state of emergency from November 2015 till November 2017 also amended some aspects of the regime (*See* Laws of 20 Nov. 2015, of 21 Jul. 2016, and of 19 Dec. 2016).

Chapter 4. The Constitutional Relationship Between Church and State

611. Since the promulgation of the Law of 9 December 1905 (the 1905 Law) on the Separation of the Churches and State, France is a secular State.[677] Under its Article 2, '[t]he Republic does not recognize, pay or subsidize any religion'. Secularism has become a principle with constitutional value under the 1946 Constitution[678] and then under the current Constitution which recognizes in its First Article that 'France is an indivisible, *secular*, democratic and social Republic' which 'shall ensure equality of all citizens under the law without discrimination based on origin, race or *religion*', and '*respects all beliefs*' (emphases added)'.

612. The separation regime established by the 1905 Law organizes cults in religious associations and modifies the management of places of worship and the status of ministers of religion. The pre-1905 regime was that of the Concordat set up in 1802. Under this regime, the State recognized four religions, namely the Catholic, Reformed, Lutheran and Jewish religions, which were organized and financed under public law. The recognized cults were organized in a public service of worship in that the State was responsible for the treatment of the ministers of religion and participated in their appointment and in the determination of the religious constituencies. Other cults were not recognized and were often considered sects. The 1905 Law put an end to this regime of recognized cults or established religions: from then on, there would be no more religion receiving legal consecration and all cults should be on an equal footing. In laying down the principle of non-recognition, the law does not establish a legal 'indifference' of the religious fact, but it simply puts an end to the opposition between recognized and unrecognized cults. From then on, the State may no longer ignore any cult. Cults, ceasing to be public institutions, are now subject to the regime of private law since, under Article 2 of the 1905 Law, public establishments of worship, previously responsible for the management of places of worship, must be replaced by cultural associations that fall under the 1901 Law on Associations. The same article inscribed in the law the suppression of public funding for the exercise of worship.

Selected Further Reading

On War, Treaty and Foreign Affairs Powers

Christian Lequesne, *Ethnographie du Quai d'Orsay. Les pratiques des diplomates français* (CNRS Editions 2017).

677. Law of 9 Dec. 1905 on the separation of the Churches and State (as amended). *See also* above Part IV. Citizenship and the Administration of Justice, Chapter 2. Fundamental Rights and Liberties, §2. Civil and Political Rights, II. Intellectual Freedoms, B. Freedom of Religion and Freedom of Education, 1. Freedom of Religion.
678. *See* Art. 1 of the 1946 Constitution: 'France is a secular Republic.'

Pierre Servent, *Les présidents et la guerre 1958–2017* (Perrin 2017).
See also Selected Further Reading under Part II. Form of Government.

On Taxing and Spending Powers

François Adam, Olivier Ferrand and Rémy Rioux, *Finances publiques* (4th ed., Dalloz 2018).
Charles Waline, Pascal Desrousseaux and Stanislas Godefroy, *Le budget de l'Etat* (La Documentation française 2012).
Franck Waserman, *Les finances publiques* (9th ed., La Documentation française 2018).

On Emergency Powers

Olivier Beaud and Cécile Guérin-Bargues, *L'état d'urgence. Etude constitutionnelle, historique et critique* (LGDJ 2016).
William Bourdon, *Les dérives de l'état d'urgence* (Plon 2017).
Paul Cassia, *Contre l'état d'urgence* (Dalloz 2016).
Pascal Mbongo (ed.), *L'état d'urgence. La prérogative et l'Etat de droit* (Fondation Varenne 2017).

On the Constitutional Relationship Between Church and State

Jean Baubérot, *Histoire de la laïcité en France* (PUF 2013).
Eoin Daly, 'Ostentation and republican civility: Notes from the French face-veiling debates' 14 (3) European Journal of Political Theory 298 (2015).
Eoin Daly, 'Public Funding of Religions in French Law: The Role of the Council of State in the Politics of Constitutional Secularism', 3 Oxford Journal of Law and Religion 103 (2014).
Guy Haarscher, *La laïcité* (PUF 2008).
Myriam Hunter-Hénin, 'Why the French Don't Like the Burqa: Laïcité, National Identity and Religious Freedom', 61 ICLQ 1 (2012).
Liberté religieuse et régimes des cultes en droit français, (Cerf 2005).
Mathilde Philip-Gay, *Droit de la laïcité* (Ellipses 2016).
See also Société, droit et religion (CNRS Editions).

Selected Bibliography

Publications in English

John Bell, *French Constitutional Law* (Oxford University Press 1995).
Sophie Boyron, *The Constitution of France: A Contextual Analysis* (Hart 2013).

Publications in French

Philippe Ardant and Bertrand Mathieu, *Droit constitutionnel et institutions politiques* (29th ed., LGDJ 2017).
Pierre Avril and Jean Gicquel, *Lexique de droit constitutionnel* (5th ed., PUF 2016).
Guy Carcassonne and Marc Guillaume, *La Constitution* (14th ed., Points 2017).
Vlad Constantinesco and Stéphane Pierré-Caps, *Droit constitutionnel* (7th ed., PUF 2016).
Olivier Duhamel and Guillaume Tusseau, *Droit constitutionnel et institutions politiques* (4th ed., Le Seuil 2016).
Louis Favoreu et alii, *Droit constitutionnel* (20th ed., Dalloz 2018).
Hugues Fulchiron and Laurent Eck, *Introduction au droit français* (LexisNexis 2016).
Jean Gicquel and Jean-Eric Gicquel, *Droit constitutionnel et institutions politiques* (31st ed., LGDJ 2017).
Olivier Gohin, *Droit constitutionnel* (3rd ed., LexisNexis 2016).
Francis Hamon and Michel Troper, *Droit constitutionnel* (38th ed., LGDJ 2017).
Anne-Marie Le Pourhiet, *Droit constitutionnel* (8th ed., Economica 2017).
Ferdinand Mélin-Soucramanien, *Constitution de la République française* (15th ed., Dalloz 2017)
Ferdinand Mélin-Soucramanien and Pierre Pactet, *Droit constitutionnel* (35th ed., Dalloz 2017)
Frédéric Rouvillois, *Droit constitutionnel, 2. La Ve République* (4th ed., Flammarion 2014)
Jean-François Sirinelli, *La Ve République* (PUF 2013).
Michel Verpeaux, *La Constitution* (2nd ed., Dalloz 2016).
Michel Verpeaux, *Droit constitutionnel français* (2nd ed., PUF 2015).

Selected Bibliography

Older Classics

Below is a selected list of landmark works by famous French constitutionalists.

Joseph Barthélemy and Paul Duez, *Traité de droit constitutionnel* (Dalloz 1933, reed. Economica 1985).
Raymond Carré de Malberg, *Contribution à la théorie générale de l'Etat* (Sirey 1922, 2 Volumes, reed. Dalloz 2003).
Léon Duguit, *Traité de droit constitutionnel* (3rd ed., De Boccard 1927–1930, 3 Volumes, reed. 1972).
Maurice Duverger, *La Ve République* (PUF 1959).
Adhémar Esmein, *Eléments de droit constitutionnel français et comparé* (1896, 4th ed., Sirey 1906, reed. LGDJ 2001).
Maurice Hauriou, *Précis de droit constitutionnel* (2nd ed., Sirey 1929).
Georges Vedel, *Cours de droit constitutionnel et d'institutions politiques* (Cours de droit 1958–1959, 1959–1960, 1960–1961).

Periodicals

Below is a selected list of journals specialized in French constitutional law.

Constitutions (Est. 2010).
Droits (Est. 1985).
Jus Publicum (online only, est. 2008).
Les nouveaux Cahiers du Conseil constitutionnel (Est. 1997).
Pouvoirs (Est. 1977).
Revue française de droit constitutionnel (Est. 1990).
Revue du droit public (Est. 1894).

Websites

Below is a selected list of official websites relating to the institutional, political and constitutional organization of France.

Constitutional Council [www.conseil-constitutionnel.fr].
Council of State [www.conseil-etat.fr].
Court of Cassation [www.courdecassation.fr].
'La Documentation française, la marque reconnue d'un éditeur public' [www.la-documentationfrancaise.fr] is a public publisher which specializes in publications in the area of law and public administration.
'Legifrance, le service publique de la diffusion du droit' [www.legifrance.gouv.fr] offers comprehensive access to French legislation and case law.
National Assembly [www.assemblee-nationale.fr].
President of the Republic [www.elysee.fr].
Senate [www.senat.fr].
'Vie publique, au cœur du debat public' [www.vie-publique.fr] gives access to many official publications and offers the possibility to track legislation in progress.

Table of Legislation

Listed below are constitutional laws, organic laws, ordinary laws, and other domestic and European acts referred to in the text and discussed at various degree of analysis

Constitutional Laws

Constitutional Law No 2008-724 on the modernization of the institutions of the Fifth Republic
Constitutional Law No 2007-238 of 23 February 2007 amending Title IX of the Constitution
Constitutional Law No 2005-205 of 1 March 2005 on the Charter for the Environment
Constitutional Law No 2003-276 of 28 March 2003 on the decentralized organization of the Republic
Constitutional Law No 2000-964 of 2 October 2000 on the term of office of the President of the Republic
Constitutional Law No 98-610 of 20 July 1998 on New Caledonia
Constitutional Law No 93-952 of 27 July 1993 revising the Constitution of 4 October 1958 and amending its Titles VIII, IX, X and XVIII

Organic Laws

Organic Law No 2016-1690 of 9 December 2016 on the competence of The Defender of Rights for the guidance and protection of whistleblowers
Organic Law No 2016-506 of 25 April 2016 on the modernization of the rules applicable to the presidential election
Organic Law No 2014-125 of 14 February 2014 prohibiting the cumulation of local executive functions with the mandate of deputy or senator
Organic Law No 2013-1114 of 6 December 2013 implementing Article 11 of the Constitution
Organic Law No 2013-906 of 11 October 2013 on transparency of public life
Organic Law No 2012-272 of 28 February 2012 on the reimbursement of campaign expenses of the presidential election

Organic Law No 2011-410 of 14 April 2011 on the election of deputies and senators
Organic Law No 2011-333 of 29 March 2011 on The Defender of Rights
Organic Law No 2010-704 of 28 June 2010 on The Economic, Social and Environmental Council
Organic Law No 2009-403 of 15 April 2009 concerning the application of Articles 34-1, 39 and 44 of the Constitution
Organic Law No 2009-38 of 13 January 2009 implementing Article 25 of the Constitution
Organic Law No 2005-881 of 2 August 2005 on social security financing laws
Organic Law No 2004-758 of 29 July 2004 on the financial autonomy of local authorities
Organic Law No 2004-193 of 27 February 2004 completing the autonomous status of French Polynesia
Organic Law No 2001-692 of 1 August 2001 on finance laws
Organic Law No 2000-294 of 5 April 2000 on incompatibilities between electoral mandates
Organic Law No 99-209 of 19 March 1999 on New Caledonia

Laws

Law No 2017-1510 of 30 October 2017 strengthening domestic security and the fight against terrorism
Law No 2017-1339 of 15 September 2017 for trust in political life
Law No 2017-286 of 6 March 2017 aimed at reinforcing the accounting obligations of the political parties and the candidates
Law No 2016-1691 of 9 December 2016 on transparency, the fight against corruption and the modernization of economic life
Law No 2016-1547 of 18 November 2016 on the modernization of justice in the twenty-first century
Law No 2016-1321 of 7 October 2016 for a Digital Republic
Law No 2016-731 of 3 June 2016 reinforcing the fight against organized crime, terrorism and their financing, and improving the efficiency and the guarantees of criminal procedure
Law No 2016-508 of 25 April 2016 on the modernization of various provisions applicable to the elections
Law No 2016-87 of 2 February 2016 creating new rights for sick people and people at the end of life
Law No 2015-991 of 7 August 2015 on the new territorial organization of the Republic
Law No 2015-925 of 29 July 2015 on the reform of the right to asylum
Law No 2015-912 of 24 July 2015 on intelligence (secret services)
Law No 2015-177 of 16 February 2015 on the modernization and simplification of law and procedures in the areas of justice and home affairs
Law No 2015-29 of 16 January 2015 on the delimitation of the regions, on regional and departmental elections, and on modifying the electoral calendar

Law No 2014-896 of 15 August 2014 on the individualization of sentences and reinforcing the effectiveness of criminal sanctions
Law No 2014-873 of 4 August 2014 for the substantive equality between women and men
Law No 2014-773 of 7 July 2014 of orientation and programming relating to the policy of development and international solidarity
Law No 2014-126 of 14 February 2014 prohibiting the cumulation of local executive functions with the mandate of representative in the European Parliament
Law No 2014-58 of 27 January 2014 of modernization of the territorial public action and affirmation of the metropolises
Law No 2013-907 of 11 October 2013 on transparency of public life
Law No 2013-715 of 6 August 2013 amending Law No 2011-814 of 7 July 2011 relating to bioethics by authorizing under certain conditions the research on embryos and embryonic stem cells
Law No 2013-404 of 17 May 2013 opening marriage to couples of persons of the same sex
Law No 2013-403 of 17 May 2013 on the election of departmental councillors, municipal councillors and community councillors, and modifying the electoral calendar
Law No 2012-347 of 12 March 2012 on the access to tenured employment and the improvement of the employment conditions of contractual agents in the public service, to the fight against discrimination and containing miscellaneous provisions pertaining to public service
Law No 2011-1977 of 28 December 2011 on finances for 2012
Law No 2011-803 of 5 July 2011 on the rights and the protection of persons in psychiatric care and the modalities of their treatment
Law No 2011-672 of 16 June 2011 on immigration, integration and nationality
Law No 2011-392 of 14 April 2011 on police custody
Law No 2011-334 of 29 March 2011 on The Defender of Rights
Law No 2011-267 of 14 March 2011 on the policy for the achievement of homeland security
Law No 2011-140 of 3 February 2011 to strengthen Parliament's means of controlling the government's action and evaluating public policies
Law No 2011-103 of 27 January 2011 on the balanced representation of women and men in administration and supervisory boards and on professional equality
Law No 2010-1563 of 16 December 2010 of the reform of the local authorities
Law No 2010-1192 of 11 October 2010 prohibiting the concealment of the face in the public space
Law No 2010-1 of 4 January 2010 on the protection of journalists' sources
Law No 2009-323 of 25 March 2009 of mobilization for housing and fight against exclusion
Law No 2009-39 of 13 January 2009 on the commission provided for under Article 25 of the Constitution and the election of deputies
Law No 2008-352 of 16 April 2008 aiming to reinforce the cross-border, transnational and interregional cooperation by the bringing into conformity of the General Code of the Local Authorities with the European regulation on a European grouping of territorial cooperation

Table of Legislation

Law No 2008-174 of 25 February 2008 on security detention and the declaration of criminal irresponsibility on account of mental disorder

Law No 2007-290 of 5 March 2007 instituting the enforceable right to housing and concerning miscellaneous measures in favour of social cohesion

Law No 2006-340 of 23 March 2006 on the equal pay between women and men

Law No 2006-64 of 23 January 2006 on the fight against terrorism and containing various provisions relating to security and border controls

Law No 2005-370 of 22 April 2005 on the rights of the patients and the end of life

Law No 2005-102 of 11 February 2005 for the equality of rights and opportunities, the participation and the civic rights of disabled people

Law No 2004-186 of 30 December 2004 creating the high authority of fight against discriminations and for equality

Law No 2004-228 of 15 March 2004 regulating, in accordance with the principle of secularism, the wearing of symbols of clothing displaying a religious affiliation in public primary and secondary schools

Law No 2004-204 of 9 March 2004 adapting justice to the evolution of criminality

Law No 2003-1176 of 10 December 2003 modifying Law No 52-893 of 25 July 1952 on the right to asylum

Law No 2002-304 of 4 March 2002 on the surname

Law No 2002-92 of 22 January 2002 on Corsica

Law No 2001-504 of 12 June 2001 reinforcing the prevention and repression of sectarian movements violating human rights and fundamental liberties

Law No 2000-1354 of 30 December 2000 to facilitate the compensation of convicts recognized as innocent and relating to diverse coordination provisions in criminal procedure

Law No 2000-597 of 30 June 2000 on interlocutory proceedings before administrative courts

Law No 2000-516 of 15 June 2000 reinforcing the protection of the presumption of innocence and the rights of the victims

Law No 2000-493 of 6 June 2000 promoting equal access of women and men to electoral mandates and elective offices

Law No 2000-295 of 5 April 2000 on the limitation of multiple electoral mandates and functions and their conditions of exercise

Law No 99-1071 of 16 December 1999 enabling the Government to proceed, by way of ordinances, with the enactment of the legislative part in respect of certain codes

Law No 99-944 of 15 November 1999 on the Solidarity Civil Pact

Law No 98-349 of 11 May 1998 on the entry and residence of foreigners in France and the right to asylum

Law No 98-170 of 16 March 1998 on nationality

Law No 97-1159 of 19 December 1997 devoting electronic surveillance as a means of enforcing custodial sentences

Law No 96-142 of 21 February 1996 on the legislative part of the General Code of Local Authorities

Law No 95-125 of 8 February 1995 on the organization of courts and on civil, criminal and administrative procedure

Law No 95-73 of 21 January 1995 on the policy pertaining to security

Law No 93-933 of 22 July 1993 reforming the law of nationality
Law No 93-122 of 29 January 1993 on the prevention of corruption and the transparency of economic life and public procedures
Law No 91-646 of 10 July 1991 on the secrecy of correspondence transmitted by means of telecommunications
Law No 91-428 of 13 May 1991 on the status of the local authority of Corsica
Law No 90-55 of 15 January 1990 on the limitation of election expenses and the clarification of the financing of political activities
Law No 88-227 of 11 March 1988 on the financial transparency of political life
Law No 87-1127 of 31 December 1987 on reforming administrative litigation
Law No 86-1067 of 30 September 1986 on freedom of communication
Law No 86-897 of 1 August 1986 on the reform of the legal regime of the press
Law No 86-14 of 6 January 1986 laying down the rules guaranteeing the independence of the members of the Administrative Courts and Administrative Courts of Appeals
Law No 85-1372 of 23 December 1985 on the equality of spouses in matrimonial regimes and of parents in the management of the goods of minor children
Law No 84-53 of 26 January 1984 on statutory provisions relating to the territorial civil service
Law No 83-663 of 22 July 1983 supplementing Law No 83-8 of 7 January 1983 on the distribution of powers between the municipalities, the departments, the regions and the State
Law No 83-635 of 13 July 1983 modifying the Labour Code and the Criminal Code as regards the professional equality between women and men
Law No 83-634 of 13 July 1983 on the rights and obligations of civil servants
Law No 83-8 of 7 January 1983 on the distribution of powers between the municipalities, the departments, the regions and the State
Law No 82-659 of 30 July 1982 on the special status of the region of Corsica: competences
Law No 82-652 of 29 July 1982 on audiovisual communication
Law No 82-526 of 22 June 1982 on the rights and obligations of tenants and landlords
Law No 82-214 of 2 March 1982 on the special status of the region of Corsica: administrative organization
Law No 82-213 of 2 March 1982 on the rights and freedoms of municipalities, departments and regions
Law No 81-994 of 9 November 1981 derogating from the State monopoly on radiodiffusion
Law No 81-908 of 9 October 1981 abolishing the death penalty
Law No 78-17 of 6 January 1978 on informatics, computerized data and freedoms
Law No 75-356 of 15 May 1975 reorganizing Corsica
Law No 75-17 of 17 January 1975 on the voluntary termination of pregnancy
Law No 74-904 of 29 October 1974 on the revision of Article 61 of the Constitution
Law No 72-626 of 5 July 1972 establishing a judge of the execution and relating to the reform of the civil procedure

Law No 70-643 of 17 July 1970 to strengthen the guarantee of the individual rights of citizens
Law No 70-459 of 4 June 1970 on parental authority
Law No 65-570 of 13 July 1965 reforming matrimonial regimes
Law No 64-707 of 10 July 1964 reorganizing the Paris area
Law No 62-1292 of 6 November 1962 on the election of the President of the Republic by universal suffrage
Law No 59-1157 of 31 December 1959 on the relationships between the State and private educational institutions
Law No 55-1052 of 6 August 1955 on the status of French Southern and Antarctic Lands and Clipperton Island
Law No 55-385 of 3 April 1955 on the state of emergency
Law No 53-611 of 11 July 1953 relating to economic and financial recovery
Law No 52-893 of 25 July 1952 on the right to asylum
Law No 49-956 of 16 July 1949 on publications intended for the youth
Law No 46-451 of 19 March 1946 tending to classification as French departments of Guadeloupe, Martinique, Réunion and French Guiana
Law of 9 December 1905 on the separation of the Churches and State
Law of 1 July 1901 on the contract of association
Law of 15 November 1887 on the freedom of funerals
Law of 29 July 1881 on the freedom of the press
Law of 30 June 1881 on freedom of assembly
Law of 3 April 1878 on the state of siege
Law of 9 August 1849 on the state of siege

Others Acts

Domestic

Decrees

Decree No 2016-1118 of 11 August 2016 on the terms of expression of the refusal of organ removal after death
Decree No 2015-233 of 27 February 2015 concerning the Disputes Court and the preliminary rulings
Decree No 2012-875 of 16 July 2012 on the creation of a commission for the renovation and deontology of public life
Decree No 2009-14 of 7 January 2009 on the public rapporteur before administrative courts and the proceedings thereof
Decree No 2004-617 of 29 June 2004 on the modalities and effects of the electronic publication of certain administrative acts in the *JO*
Decree No 2001-213 of 8 March 2001 implementing Law No 62-1292 of 6 November 1962 on the election of the President of the Republic by universal suffrage
Decree No 2000-318 of 7 April 2000 on the regulatory part of the General Code of Local Authorities

Decree No 93-1362 of 30 December 1993 relating to declarations of nationality, decisions of naturalization, reinstatement, loss, revocation and withdrawal of French nationality

Decree No 53-934 of 30 September 1953 on reforming administrative litigation

Ordinances

Ordinance No 2011-1540 of 16 November 2011 transposing Directive 2008/52/EC of the European Parliament and of the Council of 21 May 2008 on certain aspects of mediation in civil and commercial matters

Ordinance No 2004-164 of 20 February 2004 on the modalities and effects of the publication of laws and certain administrative acts

Ordinance No 58-1360 of 29 December 1958 on the Organic Law concerning The Economic and Social Council

Ordinance No 58-1270 of 22 December 1958 on the Organic Law on the status of the judiciary

Ordinance No 58-1210 of 13 December 1958 on the Organic Law on the allowance of MPs

Ordinance No 58-1100 of 17 November 1958 on the functioning of parliamentary assemblies

Ordinance No 58-1067 of 7 November 1958 on the Organic Law on the Constitutional Council

Ordinance No 45-2441 of 19 October 1945 on the French Nationality Code

Recommendations

Recommendation No 2011-1 of 4 January 2011 on the principle of political pluralism in radio and television services during an election period, as amended

European

Regulation (EU) 604/2013 of the European Parliament and of the Council of 26 June 2013 establishing the criteria and mechanisms for determining the Member State responsible for examining an application for international protection lodged in one of the Member States by a third-country national or a stateless person, OJ L 180/31-180/59, 29.6.2013

Table of Case Law

*Listed below are decisions of the Constitutional Council, the Council of State, the Court of Cassation, and the Disputes Court referred to in the text. Also listed are the decisions of the CJEU and the ECtHR referred to in the text. Decisions of the Constitutional Council which are marked with * are those which are available in English on the website of the Constitutional Council. For domestic judicial decisions, it was decided to keep the name in French.*

Constitutional Council

CC Decision No 2017-648 QPC of 4 August 2017, *La Quadrature du Net et autres [Accès administratif en temps réel aux données de connexion]**

CC Decision No 2014-439 QPC of 23 January 2015, *M. Ahmed S. [Déchéance de nationalité], Rec.* 26*

CC Decision No 2013-669 DC of 17 May 2013, *Loi ouvrant le mariage aux couples de personnes de même sexe, Rec.* 721*

CC Decision No 2012-297 QPC of 21 February 2013, *Association pour la promotion et l'expansion de la laïcité [Traitement des pasteurs des églises consistoriales dans les départements du Bas-Rhin, du Haut-Rhin et de la Moselle], Rec.* 293*

CC Decision No 2012-261 QPC of 22 June 2012, *M. Thierry B. [Consentement au mariage et opposition à mariage], Rec.* 312

CC Decision No 2012-647 DC of 28 February 2012, *Loi visant à réprimer la contestation de l'existence des génocides reconnus par la loi, Rec.* 139*

CC Decision No 2011-217 QPC of 3 February 2012, *M. Mohammed Alki B. [Délit d'entrée ou de séjour irrégulier en France], Rec.* 104*

CC Decision No 2011-157 QPC of 5 August 2011, *Société SOMODIA [Interdiction du travail le dimanche en Alsace-Moselle], Rec.* 430

CC Decision No 2011-125 QPC of 6 May 2011, *Mr Abderrahmane L. [Transfer into the custody of the Public Prosecutor], Rec.* 218*

CC Decision No 2011-625 DC of 10 March 2011, *Loi d'orientation et de programmation pour la performance de la sécurité intérieure, Rec.* 122*

CC Decision No 2010-60 QPC of 12 November 2010, *M. Pierre B. [Mur mitoyen], Rec.* 321

CC Decision No 2010-20/21 QPC of 6 August 2010, *M. Jean C. et autres [Loi Université], Rec.* 203

CC Decision No 2010-14/22 QPC of 30 July 2010, *M. Daniel W. et autres [Garde à vue]*, *Rec.* 179*
CC Decision No 2010-605 DC of 12 May 2010, *Loi relative à la concurrence et à la régulation du secteur des jeux d'argent et de hasard en ligne*, *Rec.* 78*
CC Decision No 2009-595 DC of 3 December 2009, *Loi organique relative à l'application de l'article 61-1 de la Constitution*, *Rec.* 206*
CC Decision No 2009-580 DC of 10 June 2009, *Loi favorisant la diffusion et la protection de la création sur Internet*, *Rec.* 107*
CC Decision No 2007-560 DC of 20 December 2007, *Traité de Lisbonne modifiant le traité sur l'Union européenne et le traité instituant la Communauté européenne*, *Rec.* 459*
CC Decision No 2007-557 DC of 15 November 2007, *Loi relative à la maîtrise de l'immigration, à l'intégration et à l'asile*, *Rec.* 360*
CC Decision No 2007-556 DC of 16 August 2007, *Loi sur le dialogue social et la continuité du service public dans les transports terrestres réguliers de voyageurs*, *Rec.* 319
CC Decision No 2006-544 DC of 14 December 2006, *Loi de financement de la sécurité sociale pour 2007*, *Rec.* 129
CC Decision No 2006-543 DC of 30 November 2006, *Loi relative au secteur de l'énergie*, *Rec.* 120*
CC Decision No 2006-540 DC of 27 July 2006, *Loi relative au droit d'auteur et aux droits voisins dans la société de l'information*, *Rec.* 88*
CC Decision No 2006-539 DC of 20 July 2006, *Loi relative à l'immigration et à l'intégration*, *Rec.* 79
CC Decision No 2006-538 DC of 13 July 2006, *Loi portant règlement définitif du budget de 2005*, *Rec.* 73
CC Decision No 2006-535 DC of 30 March 2006, *Loi pour l'égalité des chances*, *Rec.* 50
CC Decision No 2005-532 DC of 19 January 2006, *Loi relative à la lutte contre le terrorisme et portant dispositions diverses à la sécurité et aux contrôles frontaliers*, *Rec.* 31*
CC Decision No 2005-528 DC of 15 December 2005, *Loi de financement de la sécurité sociale pour 2006*, *Rec.* 157
CC Decision No 2005-512 DC of 21 April 2005, *Loi d'orientation et de programme pour l'avenir de l'école*, *Rec.* 72
CC Decision No 2004-509 DC of 13 January 2005, *Loi de programmation pour la cohésion sociale*, *Rec.* 33
CC Decision No 2004-505 DC of 19 November 2004, *Traité établissant une Constitution pour l'Europe*, *Rec.* 173*
CC Decision No 2004-497 DC of 1 July 2004, *Loi relative aux communications électroniques et aux services de communication audiovisuelle*, *Rec.* 107
CC Decision No 2004-496 DC of 10 June 2004, *Loi pour la confiance dans l'économie numérique*, *Rec.* 101
CC Decision No 2003-485 DC of 4 December 2003, *Loi modifiant la loi n° 52-893 du 25 juillet 1952 relative au droit d'asile*, *Rec.* 455
CC Decision No 2003-484 DC of 20 November 2003, *Loi relative à la maîtrise de l'immigration, au séjour des étrangers en France et à la nationalité*, *Rec.* 438

CC Decision No 2003-468 DC of 3 April 2003, *Loi relative à l'élection des conseillers régionaux et des représentants au Parlement européen ainsi qu'à l'aide publique aux partis politiques*, *Rec.* 325

CC Decision No 2003-469 DC of 26 March 2003, *Révision constitutionnelle relative à l'organisation décentralisée de la République*, *Rec.* 293

CC Decision No 2002-463 DC of 12 December 2002, *Loi de financement de la sécurité sociale pour 2003*, *Rec.* 540

CC Decision No 2001-454 of 17 January 2002, *Loi relative à la Corse*, *Rec.* 70

CC Decision No 2001-453 DC of 18 December 2001, *Loi de financement de la sécurité sociale pour 2002*, *Rec.* 164

CC Decision No 2001-448 DC of 25 July 2001, *Loi organique relative aux lois de finances*, *Rec.* 99

CC Decision No 2000-442 DC of 28 December 2000, *Loi de finances pour 2001*, *Rec.* 56

CC Decision No 2000-23 REF of 23 August 2000, *Larrouturou*, *Rec.* 137

CC Decision No 2000-24 REF of 23 August 2000, *Hauchemaille*, *Rec.* 134

CC Decision No 99-421 DC of 16 December 1999, *Loi portant habilitation du Gouvernement à procéder par ordonnances, à l'adoption de la partie législative de certains codes*, *Rec.* 49

CC Decision No 99-419 DC of 9 November 1999, *Loi relative au pacte civil de solidarité*, *Rec.* 116

CC Decision No 99-412 DC of 15 June 1999, *Charte européenne des langues régionales ou minoritaires*, *Rec.* 71*

CC Decision No 98-407 DC of 14 January 1999, *Loi relative au mode d'élection des conseillers régionaux et des conseillers à l'Assemblée de Corse et au fonctionnement des Conseils régionaux*, *Rec.* 21

CC Decision No 98-405 DC of 29 December 1998, *Loi de finances pour 1999*, *Rec.* 326

CC Decision No 98-401 DC of 10 June 1998, *Loi d'orientation et d'incitation relative à la réduction du temps de travail*, *Rec.* 258

CC Decision No 98-400 DC of 20 May 1998, *Loi organique déterminant les conditions d'application de l'article 88-3 de la Constitution relatif à l'exercice par les citoyens de l'Union européenne résidant en France, autres que les ressortissants français, du droit de vote et d'éligibilité aux élections municipales, et portant transposition de la directive 94/80/CE du 19 décembre 1994*, *Rec.* 251*

CC Decision No 97-389 DC of 22 April 1997, *Loi portant diverses dispositions relatives à l'immigration*, *Rec.* 45

CC Decision No 96-383 DC of 6 November 1996, *Loi relative à l'information et à la consultation des salariés dans les entreprises et les groupes d'entreprises de dimension communautaire, ainsi qu'au développement de la négociation collective*, *Rec.* 128

CC Decision No 96-378 DC of 23 July 1996, *Loi de réglementation des télécommunications*, *Rec.* 99

CC Decision No 96-377 DC of 16 July 1996, *Loi tendant à renforcer la répression du terrorisme et des atteintes aux personnes dépositaires de l'autorité publique ou chargées d'une mission de service public et comportant des dispositions relatives à la police judiciaire*, *Rec.* 66*

CC Decision No 96-373 DC of 9 April 1996, *Loi organique portant statut d'autonomie de la Polynésie française, Rec.* 43*
CC Decision No 95-360 DC of 2 February 1995, *Loi relative à l'organisation des juridictions et à la procedure civile, pénale et administrative, Rec.* 195
CC Decision No 94-359 DC of 19 January 1995, *Loi relative à la diversité de l'habitat, Rec.* 176
CC Decision No 94-352 DC of 18 January 1995, *Loi d'orientation et de programmation relative à la sécurité, Rec.* 170
CC Decision No 94-351 DC of 29 December 1994, *Loi de finances pour 1995, Rec.* 140
CC Decision No 94-345 DC of 29 July 1994, *Loi relative à l'emploi de la langue française, Rec.* 106
CC Decision No 94-343/344 DC of 27 July 1994, *Loi relative au respect du corps humain et loi relative au don et à l'utilisation des éléments et produits du corps humain, à l'assistance médicale à la procréation et au diagnostic prénatal, Rec.* 100*
CC Decision No 94-346 DC of 21 July 1994, *Loi complétant le code du domaine de l'état et relative à la constitution de droits réels sur le domaine public, Rec.* 96
CC Decision No 93-330 DC of 29 December 1993, *Loi de finances pour 1994, Rec.* 572
CC Decision No 93-325 DC of 13 August 1993, *Loi relative à la maîtrise de l'immigration et aux conditions d'entrée, d'accueil et de séjour des étrangers en France, Rec.* 224*
CC Decision No 93-323 DC of 5 August 1993, *Loi relative aux contrôles et vérifications d'identité, Rec.* 213
CC Decision No 93-320 DC of 21 June 1993, *Loi de finances rectificative pour 1993, Rec.* 146
CC Decision No 92-316 DC of 20 January 1993, *Loi relative à la prévention de la corruption et à la transparence de la vie économique et des procédures publiques, Rec.* 38
CC Decision No 92-313 DC of 23 September 1992, *Loi autorisant la ratification du traité sur l'Union européenne, Rec.* 94
CC Decision No 92-312 of 2 September 1992, *Traité sur l'Union européenne, Rec.* 76*
CC Decision No 92-308 DC of 9 April 1992, *Traité sur l'Union européenne, Rec.* 55*
CC Decision No 91-294 DC of 25 July 1991, *Loi autorisant l'approbation de la convention d'application de l'accord de Schengen du 14 juin 1985 entre les gouvernements des Etats de l'Union économique Benelux, de la République fédérale d'Allemagne et de la République française relatif à la suppression graduelle des contrôles aux frontières communes, Rec.* 91
CC Decision No 91-290 DC of 9 May 1991, *Loi portant statut de la collectivité territoriale de Corse, Rec.* 50*
CC Decision No 90-283 DC of 8 January 1991, *Loi relative à la lutte contre le tabagisme et l'alcoolisme, Rec.* 11

CC Decision No 90-277 DC of 25 July 1990, *Loi relative à la révision générale des évaluations des immeubles retenus pour la détermination des bases des impôts directs locaux, Rec.* 70
CC Decision No 90-274 DC of 29 May 1990, *Loi visant à la mise en œuvre du droit au logement, Rec.* 61
CC Decision No 89-269 DC of 22 January 1990, *Loi portant diverses dispositions relatives à la sécurité sociale et à la santé, Rec.* 33
CC Decision No 89-271 DC of 11 January 1990, *Loi relative à la limitation des dépenses électorales et à la clarification du financement des activités politiques, Rec.* 21
CC Decision No 89-257 DC of 25 July 1989, *Loi modifiant le code du travail et relative à la prévention du licenciement économique et au droit à la conversion, Rec.* 59
CC Decision No 88-244 DC of 20 July 1988, *Loi portant amnistie, Rec.* 119
CC Decision No 87-232 DC of 7 January 1988, *Loi relative à la mutualisation de la Caisse nationale de crédit agricole, Rec.* 17
CC Decision No 86-224 DC of 23 January 1987, *Loi transférant à la juridiction judiciaire le contentieux des décisions du Conseil de la concurrence, Rec.* 8
CC Decision No 86-217 DC of 18 September 1986, Loi relative à la liberté *de communication, Rec.* 141
CC Decision No 86-210 DC of 29 July 1986, *Loi portant réforme du régime juridique de la presse, Rec.* 110
CC Decision No 85-197 DC of 23 August 1985, *Loi sur l'évolution de la Nouvelle-Calédonie, Rec.* 70
CC Decision No 84-181 DC of 11 October 1984, *Loi visant à limiter la concentration et à assurer la transparence financière et le pluralisme des entreprises de presse, Rec.* 73
CC Decision No 83-168 DC of 20 January 1984, *Loi portant dispositions statutaires relatives à la fonction publique territoriale, Rec.* 38
CC Decision No 83-165 DC of 20 January 1984, *Loi relative à l'enseignement supérieur, Rec.* 30
CC Decision No 83-164 of 29 December 1983, *Loi de finances pour 1984, Rec.* 67
CC Decision No 82-153 DC of 14 January 1983, *Loi relative au statut général des fonctionnaires, Rec.* 35
CC Decision No 82-146 DC of 18 November 1982, *Loi modifiant le code électoral et le code des communes et relative à l'élection des conseillers municipaux et aux conditions d'inscription des Français établis hors de France sur les listes électorales (Quotas par sexe), Rec.* 22*
CC Decision No 82-143 DC of 30 July 1982, *Lois sur les prix et les revenus, notamment ses articles 1, 3 et 4, Rec.* 57
CC Decision No 82-141 DC of 27 July 1982, *Loi sur la communication audiovisuelle, Rec.* 48
CC Decision No 82-137 DC of 25 February 1982, n°82-137, *Loi relative aux droits et libertés des communes, des départements et des régions, Rec.* 38
CC Decision No 81-132 DC of 16 January 1982, *Loi de nationalisation, Rec.* 18
CC Decision No 81-136 DC of 31 December 1981, *Troisième loi de finances rectificative pour 1981, Rec.* 48

CC Decision No 81-133 DC of 30 December 1981, *Loi de finances pour 1982*, *Rec.* 41

CC Decision No 80-127 DC of 20 January 1981, *Loi renforçant la sécurité et protégeant la liberté des personnes*, *Rec.* 65

CC Decision No 80-119 DC of 22 July 1980, *Loi portant validation d'actes administratifs*, *Rec.* 46

CC Decision No 80-117 DC of 22 July 1980, *Loi sur la protection et le contrôle des matières nucléaires*, *Rec.* 42

CC Decision No 79-109 DC of 9 January 1980, *Loi relative à la prévention de l'immigration clandestine et portant modification de l'ordonnance n° 45-2658 du 2 novembre 1945 relative aux conditions d'entrée et de séjour en France des étrangers et portant création de l'office national d'immigration*, *Rec.* 29

CC Decision No 79-105 DC of 25 July 1979, *Loi modifiant les dispositions de la loi n° 74-696 du 7 août 1974 relatives à la continuité du service public de la radio et de la télévision en cas de cessation concertée du travail*, *Rec.* 33

CC Decision No 78-95 DC of 27 July 1978, *Loi complétant les dispositions de l'article 7 de la loi n° 60-791 du 2 août 1960 relative à l'enseignement et à la formation professionnelle agricole*, *Rec.* 26

CC Decision No 77-87 DC of 23 November 1977, *Loi complémentaire à la loi n° 59-1557 du 31 décembre 1959 modifiée par la loi n° 71-400 du 1er juin 1971 et relative à la liberté de l'enseignement*, *Rec.* 42

CC Decision No 76-72 DC of 12 January 1977, *Loi autorisant le Gouvernement à modifier par ordonnances les circonscriptions pour l'élection des membres de la chambre des députés du territoire Français des Afars et des Issas*, *Rec.* 31

CC Decision No 75-59 DC of 30 December 1975, *Loi relative aux conséquences de l'autodétermination des îles des Comores*, *Rec.* 26

CC Decision No 74-54 DC of 15 January 1975, *Loi relative à l'interruption volontaire de grossesse*, *Rec.* 19*

CC Decision No 73-51 DC of 27 December 1973, *Loi de finances pour 1974*, *Rec.* 25.

CC Decision No 71-44 DC of 16 July 1971, *Loi complétant les dispositions des articles 5 et 7 de la loi du 1er juillet 1901 relative au contrat d'association*, *Rec.* 25*

CC Decision No 70-39 DC of 19 June 1970, *Traité des Communautés européennes*, *Rec.* 15

CC Decision No 62-20 DC of 6 November 1962, *Loi relative à l'élection du Président de la République au suffrage universel direct, adoptée par le référendum du 28 octobre 1962*, *Rec.* 27

CC Decision No 6-18 L of 16 January 1962, *Nature juridique des dispositions de l'article 31 (alinéa 2) de la loi n°60-808 du 5 août 1960 d'orientation agricole*, *Rec.* 31

CC Decision No 61-1 AUTR of 14 September 1961, *Demande d'avis présentée par le Président de l'Assemblée nationale (Recevabilité de la motion de censure)*, *Rec.* 55

CC Decision No 59-5 DC of 15 January 1960, *Résolution modifiant les articles 95 et 96 du règlement de l'Assemblée nationale*, *Rec.* 15

CC Decision No 59-1 FNR of 27 November 1959, *Proposition de loi déposée par MM. Bajeux et Boulanger, sénateurs, tendant à la stabilisation des fermages (et à abroger le décret n° 59-175 du 7 janvier 1959 relatif au prix des baux à ferme), Rec.* 71

Council of State

CE, 3/8 SSR, 15 February 2013, *Association Grande Confrérie de Saint-Martial et autres*, apps No 347049/347050
CE, Sect., 18 January 2013, *SOS Racisme*, app. No 328230
CE, Ass., 19 July 2011, *Commune de Montpellier*, app No 313518
CE, Ass., 19 July 2011, *Communauté urbaine du Mans-Le Mans Métropole*, app No 309131
CE, Sect., 9 June 2010, *Association CAP SUR L'AVENIR 13*, No 327423
CE, 4/5 SSR, 2 September 2009, *Association Réseau d'alerte et d'intervention pour les droits de l'Homme*, apps No 318584/321715
CE, Ass., 8 February 2007, *Société Arcelor Atlantique et Lorraine et autres, Rec. Lebon* 56
CE, Sect., 26 April 2006, *M. A., Rec. Lebon* 255
CE, Ass., 11 May 2004, *Association AC! et autres, Rec. Lebon* 197
CE, Sect., 18 December 2002, *Mme Duvignères, Rec. Lebon* 463
CE, Ass., 28 June 2002, *Ministre de la Justice c/Magiera*, app No 239575
CE, 3 December 2001, *SNIP (Syndicat national de l'industrie pharmaceutique), Rec. Lebon* 624
CE, Ass., 26 October 2001, *Mme Catherine Senanayake, Rec. Lebon* 514
CE, Ass., 1 September 2000, *Larrouturou, Meyet et autres, Rec. Lebon* 365
CE, 28 July 2000, *Association France Nature Environnement, Rec. Lebon* 322
CE, 4/6 SSR, 3 May 2000, *Mademoiselle Marteaux*, app No 217017
CE, Ass., 30 October 1998, *Sarran, Levacher et autres, Rec. Lebon* 368
CE, Ass., 6 June 1997, *Aquarone, Rec. Lebon* 206
CE, Ass., 3 July 1996, *Koné, Rec. Lebon* 255
CE, Ass., 27 October 1995, *Commune de Morsang-sur-Orge, Rec. Lebon* 372
CE, Ass., 10 September 1992, *Meyet, Rec. Lebon* 327
CE, Ass., 26 September 1984, *Lujambio Galdeano, Rec. Lebon* 307
CE, Ass., 20 October 1989, *Nicolo, Rec. Lebon* 190
CE, 3/5 SSR, 30 June 1989, *Ville de Paris c. Lévy*, app. No 78113
CE, Ass., 12 October 1979, *Rassemblements des nouveaux avocats de France, Rec. Lebon* 371
CE, Ass., 8 December 1978, *GISTI, Rec. Lebon* 493
CE, Ass., 8 June 1973, *Dame Peynet, Rec. Lebon* 406
CE, Sect., 26 January 1973, *Ville de Paris c. Sieur Driancourt, Rec. Lebon* 77
CE, Ass., 2 March 1962, *Rubin de Servens, Rec. Lebon* 143
CE., Sect., 18 December 1959, *Société 'Les Films Lutétia', Rec. Lebon* 693
CE, Sect., 26 June 1959, *Syndicat général des Ingénieurs-Conseils, Rec. Lebon* 394
CE, Ass., 28 May 1954, *Barel, Rec. Lebon* 305
CE, Ass., 29 January 1954, *Institution Notre Dame du Kreisker, Rec. Lebon* 64.

CE, Sect., 9 March 1951, *Sociétés des concerts du Conservatoire*, *Rec. Lebon* 151
CE, Sect., 3 March 1950, *Demoiselle Jamet*, *Rec. Lebon* 247
CE, Ass., 17 February 1950, *Ministre de l'Agriculture c. Dame Lamotte*, *Rec. Lebon* 110
CE, 8 December 1948, *Demoiselle Pasteau*, *Rec. Lebon*, 464
CE., Ass., 26 October 1945, *Aramu*, *Rec. Lebon* 213
CE, 28 April 1938, *Demoiselle Weiss*, *Rec. Lebon* 379
CE, Ass., 3 July 1936, *Damoiselle Bobard et autres*, *Rec. Lebon* 721
CE, Sect., 7 February 1936, *Jamart*, *Rec. Lebon* 172
CE, 19 May 1933, *Benjamin*, *Rec. Lebon* 541
CE, 26 December 1925, *Rodière*, *Rec. Lebon* 1065
CE, 8 August 1919, *Labonne*, *Rec. Lebon* 737
CE, 28 February 1919, *Dames Dol et Laurent*, *Rec. Lebon* 651
CE, 13 December 1889, *Cadot*, Rec. *Lebon*. 1148
CE, 28 June 1918, *Heyriès*, *Rec. Lebon* 651

Court of Cassation

C. cass., Ass. plén., 11 April 2011, *Bull. crim.* 2011, No 1–4
C. cass., Crim., 15 December 2010, *Bull. crim.* I, 2010, No 207
C. cass., Civ. 1re, 13 March 2007, *Bull. civ.* I, 2007, No 13
C. cass, Ass. plén., 29 June 2001, *Bull. Ass. plén.* 2001, No 8
C. cass, Ass. plén, 23 February 2001, *Bull. Ass. plén.* 2001, No 5
C. cass., Ass. plén., 2 June 2000, *Fraisse*, *Bull. Ass. plén.* 2000, No 4
C. cass., Ass. plén., 11 December 1992, *Bull. Ass. plén.* 1992, No 13
C. cass., Req., 15 June 1982, *Patureau-Miran*, DP 1892 1, 596.
C. cass., Ch. mixte, 24 May 1975, *Administration des Douanes c. Sociétés 'Cafés Jacques Vabre'*, *Bull. Ch. mixte* 1975, No 4

Disputes Court

TC, 9 December 2013, *M et Mme P. c. Commune de Saint-Palais-sur-Mer*, app. No 3931
TC, 17 June 2013, *MB c. Société ERDF Annecy*, app. No 3911
TC, 8 February 1873, *Blanco*, *Rec. Lebon* 61

Court of Justice of the European Union

ECJ, C-131/12 *Google Spain SL, Google Inc. v Agencia Española de Protección de Datos (AEPD), Mario Costeja González* (13 May 2014) (unreported)
ECJ, C-127/07 *Société Arcelor Atlantique et Lorraine and others v. Premier ministre and others* (16 December 2008), [2008] ECR I-9895
ECJ, 4/73 *Nold KG v. Commission* (14 May 1974), [1974] ECR 491

European Court of Human Rights

ECtHR, *S.A.S.v. France*, app. No 43835/11, 1 July 2014
ECtHR, *Moulin v. France*, app. No 37104/06, 23 February 2011
ECtHR, *Brusco v. France*, app. No 1466/07, 14 October 2010
ECtHR, *Etienne v. France*, app. No 11396/08, 15 September 2009
ECtHR, *Pretty v. United Kingdom*, app. No 2346/02, 29 April 2002
ECtHR, *Selmouni v. France*, app. No 25803/94, 28 July 1999
ECtHR, *Tomasi v. France*, Series A 241-A, app. No 12850/87, 27 August 1992
ECtHR, *B. v. France*, Series A 232-C, app. No 13343/87, 25 March 1992

Index

The numbers here refer to paragraph numbers.

Abortion, 464
Administrative action, 112, 120, 401, 457, 528–544
Administrative courts, 39, 250, 263–268
See also Judiciary
Administrative judge,
See Administrative courts
Administrative law,
See Council of State, State liability
Administrative regulations and orders, 115–118
Affirmative action, 523–526
Amendment,
See Amendment procedure, 74–80
See also Supra-constitutionality
Arrêts de règlement, 103
Asylum, 70, 266, 511, 545–546

Constitutional protection, 566–567

Subsidiary protection, 568–569

Bicameralism, 6, 14, 184
Bills, government's bill, private member's bill,
See Legislation
Block of Constitutionality, 28, 66, 68–73, 110, 112, 293, 441, 485, 501, 506
Budget
and Taxation, 592–602

Case Law, 103–104
Constitutional Relationship between Church and State, 611–612
Church,
See Constitutional Relationship between Church and State
Citizenship, 36, 41, 402–435
Civil Courts, 251–257
commercial courts, 255
labour courts, 256
courts of appeal, 250, 257
See also Judiciary
Codification, 104, 122–123
Constituencies (electoral), 162, 165, 612
Constitution, 65–82
See also Amendment
See also Legislation
Constitutional Council, 297–307
a priori review, 302
a posteriori review, 303
composition, 305
jurisdiction, 298
organization and operation, 306
QPC, 303
Constitutional history, 2–29
Corsica, 349
Council of Ministers, 241
Council of State, 267–268
annulment (administrative acts), 541
review of legislation, 43, 59, 67, 71
See also Judiciary
Courts,
See Judiciary
Court of Auditors, 270–273
See also Judiciary
Court of Cassation, 261–262
See also Judiciary
Court of Justice of the Republic, 218, 249, 275–276
See also Judiciary
Criminal Courts, 93, 258–260
See also Judiciary
Customary law, 59, 106–108

Death penalty, 462, 568

Index

Decentralization, 32–33, 51, 302, 322–341
  See also Indivisibility of the Republic
Decree, 114–118
  See also Administrative regulations and orders
Defence,
  See War
Defender of Rights,
Delegation of powers, 116
Deputies,
  See Legislature, MPs

Economic, Social and Environmental Council, 180. 187, 241, 312–316
Elections,
  local authorities, 367–380
  President of the Republic, 144–149
Emergency powers, 222, 571, 603
  See also Extraordinary powers
  See also State of emergency
  See also State of siege
Equality, 41, 70, 111, 133, 135, 147, 318–319, 324, 334, 350, 390, 395
  budget and taxation, 600
  foreigners, 563–564
  minorities, 514–527
  nationality, 421
Extraordinary powers, 77, 101, 197, 205, 227, 244, 449, 604–607
EU law,
  parliamentary powers in relation to, 582–585
  special constitutional position of, 63–64
Executive,
  legal status, 215–218
  organ of the State, 209–214
  powers, 219–240
  supervision and control over, 188–193
  See also Government
  See also Head of State
  See also President of the Republic

Fifth Republic, 3, 24–29
Finance laws,
  See Taxing and Spending Powers
Financial legislation,
  See Taxing and Spending Powers
Fiscal,
  See Taxing and Spending Powers
Foreigners,
  asylum, 565–569
  deportation and expulsion, 570
  rights and status, 545–564
Foreign Relations,
  See Executive
  See War and Foreign Defence
Fourth Republic, 3, 18–23
French Citizenship, 402–435
  See also Citizenship
French State,
  characteristics, 30–48
Fundamental Principles recognized by the Laws of the Republic, 70, 110, 280, 293, 441, 499, 533
Fundamental rights and liberties,
  civil and political rights, 459–504
  economic, social and cultural rights, 505–512
  general protection, 436–458

Gender equality, 135, 369, 373, 377, 524–525
General Principles of Law, 70, 109–112, 120, 442
Giscard D'Estaing, 139, 158
Government,
  accountability, 189–191
  composition and organization, 212–214
  criminal liability, 218
  division of powers with the President of the Republic, 220–221
  forming, 210–211
  obligations and incompatibilities, 216–217

Head of State, 29, 43, 48, 141–158, 160, 185, 234, 282, 530, 577
Hollande, 140, 158, 169, 341
Houses of Parliament, 8, 14, 17, 71, 78, 86, 92, 98, 137
  See also Legislature

Immigration and Entry,
  See Nationality
Indivisibility of the Republic, 31–33
  See also Decentralization
International law, 57–61, 70–71, 82–83, 102, 247, 296, 329, 538, 546, 580
International treaties, 55–62, 106, 120, 458
Interpretation, 124–125

Judicial review, 5, 39, 59, 67, 101, 130, 149, 238, 245, 265, 267, 289
  administrative acts, 537–544

acts of local authorities, 400
in French constitutional law, 290–296
See also Constitutional Council
Judiciary, 245
independence, 277–283
judicial proceedings, 284–287
organization, 246–276
state liability, 288–289
See also Judicial review
Jury, 258

Language,
official language, 37
regional languages, 37, 51, 378, 489, 527
Law,
law-making process, 178–187
See Legislature
See Legislation
Legislation, 83–102
Legislature, 159–160
organ of the State, 161–165
legal status, 166–172
powers, 173–194
workings of Parliament, 195–207
Local authorities, 32–33, 43, 49–51, 91, 117, 126, 159, 176, 263, 318
decentralized, 362–400
different, 342–361
powers, 51
Lobbies and interest groups, 131–138

Macron, 134, 139, 140, 158, 276
Ministers,
appointment, 14, 213, 216
ministerial responsibility, 218, 275
regulatory powers, 233
Minorities,
See Fundamental rights and liberties
Mitterrand, 27, 29, 130, 139, 140, 158, 161, 224, 229, 332
Monarchy, 4–9, 11, 70, 81
MPs, 166–172
incompatibilities, immunities and privileges, 168–172
mandate, 167

National Assembly, 161–164
Nationality,
obtaining, 406–419
effects attached to, 420–423,
loss of, 424–435

Naturalization, 403, 410, 415–419, 428–429, 432–433
New Caledonia, 36, 314, 327, 348, 350, 359–361, 451, 527, 609

Ordinance,

Art 38, 96–97

Enabling legislation, 96

Ordinary laws, 87–94
Organic laws, 85–86

Parliament,
See Legislature
Political parties, 36, 43, 131–140
President of the Republic,
election, 144–149
mandate, 150–151
pre-eminence, 45–46
powers, 219–229
political unaccountability, 153
presidential function and office, 155–157
Presidents of the Fifth Republic, 158
temporary inviolability, 154
See also Head of State
Prime Minister,
appointment, 46, 130, 144
Principles of Law Particularly Necessary to our Time, 70, 72, 293
Publication, 126

Referendum laws, 98–100
Regulatory power, 26, 43, 51, 91–93, 96, 112, 114, 230–233
general, 116
specialized, 117
Republic,
democratic and social republic, 35–41
parliamentary republic, 43
See also Fifth Republic
See also Fourth Republic
See also Indivisibility of the Republic
See also Third Republic
Reservations of interpretation, 64
Residence permit, 552–561
Responsibility
administrative, 544
Revirements de jurisprudence, 104
Revolution,
of 1789, 4

Index

Rule of law, 36–40, 218, 247, 537

Secularism, 34, 492, 494
Semi-presidential, 44–48
Social Security financing laws, 590–591
State,
  characteristics of, 30–48
  population and demographics, 52–53
  territory, 49–51
  See also Constitutional Relationship between Church and State
State of Emergency, 244, 451, 609–610
State of Siege, 244, 450, 608
Superior Council of the Judiciary, *See* Judiciary
Supra-Constitutionality, 81

Taxing and Spending Powers, 586–602
  financial legislation, 587–591
  finance laws, 588–589
  social security financing laws, 590–591
Third Republic, 10–17
Treaty-Making Power, 576–81
Treaties, 55–64
  and Foreign Affairs, 576–581
  negotiation of, 579
  ratification of, 580
  See also Treaty-Making Power

Unity of the Republic, 323–328
Unwritten law, 106–108

War
  and National Defence, 573–575

Made in the USA
Monee, IL
13 September 2026

62974270R00190